CHRISTOPHER CULPIN

Making History

REVISED NEW EDITION

World History from 1914 to the present

Collins Educational

An Imprint of HarperCollins*Publishers*

Contents

Introduction

This book tells you about the history of the 20th century. The things you are going to read about happened in the lifetimes of your grandparents and your parents. They may even have taken part in some of the events described here. You have probably seen films or heard people talk about these things too. We study history to find out, as best we can, exactly what happened and why.

How can we know exactly what happened? To answer this question historians start with historical 'sources'. By questioning the sources a historian finds 'evidence' – information, ideas or opinions – to piece together the story. Each chapter of this book contains several 'sources; for you to consider. The 20th century has produced a great amount and variety of source material. Not all of it is in the form of written documents. The many photographs taken in this century provide us with some very helpful sources of evidence. We have no photographs of chariot-racing in ancient Rome, or the execution of King Charles I in 1649, but the picture opposite gives a more powerful impression of the changes in South Africa in the 1990s than we could gain in a thousand words.

History is not only about what happened; it is about why it happened. Again, we look to the sources for evidence. On 15 February 1942, the British base at Singapore surrendered to the Japanese. Why did this happen? Winston Churchill wrote:

> So there were no permanent forts covering the landward side of the naval base and the city! None of the officers on the spot, and none of my professional advisers at home seem to have realised this awful need.

However, another source provides evidence of a different reason. An Australian officer, in Singapore at the time, later wrote:

> I still have very vivid memories of our arrival in Singapore. We were being sent to a war station. Yet the first sight that met our eyes on the first evening was officers in mess dress and fashionable women in evening dress. It was not only unsuitable. It was wrong.

Clearly, different sources provide different evidence. A historian has to question the sources very carefully, judge their reliability and build up a picture of the event. Only then would a historian give an opinion about the real reasons for the fall of Singapore and different historians might give different predictions.

Many of you will be using this book to study for the GCSE examination. There are questions in the 'Assessment' section at the end of each chapter which give you examples of the kinds of things you may be asked to do for coursework or in the examination.

The first group of questions asks you to 'Describe, explain and analyse'. That is, to say what was happening, or what people felt, at a particular time, and why. Alongside most sources in the text, and at the end of some chapters, under the heading 'Evidence and interpretations', you will find questions about the sources. Some just help you to understand the sources a little better, others help you understand how historians deal with sources. Often the end of chapter questions go on to ask you to think about how different people reach different conclusions about the past. Usually they end by asking you what you think.

History is a subject where your own opinions are important. You do not have to agree with what I have written in this book. Under 'Topics for discussion' you have a chance to look back over the chapter, or compare chapters, and come to your own conclusions about what really happened. I hope you have some interesting discussions. In fact all the questions in the 'Assessment' section are better discussed before putting pen to paper.

There is a Glossary at the end of the book which explains unfamiliar words or phrases you may come across.

Finally, we must forget that history is about people. Most of the chapters have one or two brief biographies of someone who lived through the period described in the chapter. You can see how they lived their lives and how they made their decisions. I hope that by studying their lives and times, you can live your own life with a better understanding of what is going on in the world.

Christopher Culpin

1: The causes of the First World War

In 1900 world events were dominated by the continent of Europe. There was more industry and wealth in Europe than anywhere else in the world. Most of the ships trading across the oceans of the world were owned by Europeans, and large parts of Asia, Africa and South America had been colonised by European countries.

Tremendous political and social changes have taken place since then, making the world of the 1990s a very different place. One of the most important causes of change was the First World War. This chapter describes how and why the war broke out.

THE ASSASSINATION AT SARAJEVO

On 28 June 1914, Archduke Franz Ferdinand and his wife visited the town of Sarajevo. The Archduke was the heir to the throne of the empire of Austria-Hungary. Sarajevo is the capital of Bosnia which, at that time was part of this empire (see Map 1-1). As the car passed along the street, someone threw a bomb at it. The bomb bounced off the back of the car and exploded, injuring an officer in the car behind. The Archduke and his wife were unhurt.

Later that day the Archduke said that he wanted to change his plans and visit the injured officer in hospital. He set off again by car, but the driver was not told the route had changed.

◢ SOURCE 1B
The four cars moved out into the dense crowds in the original order, but at a faster pace. At the entrance to Franz Josef Street, the crowd made a lane and, by a fatal error, the cars turned back to the original route. The Governor, who sat facing the royal

◢ SOURCE 1A The Archduke and his wife, about to enter the royal car

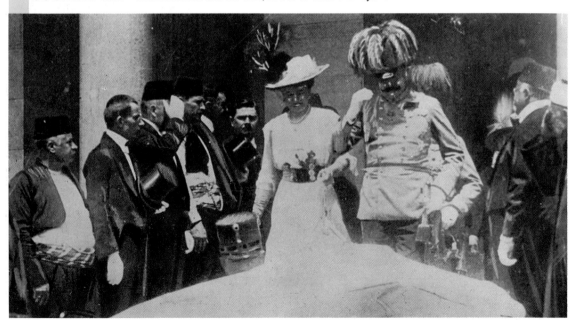

visitors, told the chauffeur he had taken the wrong turning. The car slowed down and came close to the right-hand pavement. A young man fired two shots at three yards range. The Archduke continued to sit upright, his wife sank upon his breast. For a few moments no one realised they had been shot. But the Archduke had been pierced through the artery of his neck and the Duchess through the abdomen.

Winston Churchill, *World Crisis*, 1923

The assassin was Gavrilo Princip, a 19-year-old Serb. Below are the words he spoke at his trial.

▶ SOURCE 1C

I fired twice at Ferdinand from a distance of four or five paces. I raised my hand to commit suicide, but some policemen and officers seized me and struck me. They took me away, covered with blood, to the police station. I am not a criminal, for I destroyed a bad man. I thought it was right.

Gavrilo Princip

❓ Questions

a Source 1C is a primary source. The words were spoken at the time by one of the people involved in the incident. Source 1B is a secondary source. It was written by Winston Churchill several years after the event. What sorts of primary evidence would Churchill have studied in order to write his book?

b Is the photograph, Source 1A, a primary or a secondary source for the assassination?

c In what ways could primary sources be misleading or biased?

d In what ways could secondary sources be misleading or biased?

e In what way do Sources 1B and 1C agree or disagree with each other?

f What evidence is there from these sources that the police at Sarajevo were not very efficient?

g Why do you think Princip tried to commit suicide?

h Look at the last three lines of Source 1C. What do they tell us about Princip? About the Archduke?

Six weeks after this assassination, the First World War started. Why should this assassination in a remote part of Europe have dragged the whole world into war?

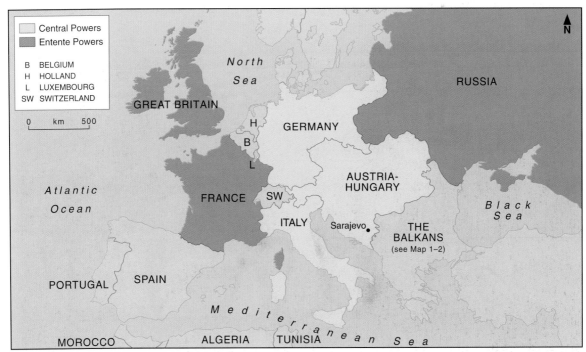

Map 1-1 Europe at the start of the First World War

THE GREAT POWERS IN 1914

If you look at Map 1-1 on page 3, you will see that the six most important and powerful countries in Europe were split into two armed groups. One group was made up of the Central Powers: Germany, Austria-Hungary and Italy. These three countries had joined together in the Triple Alliance. The other group was made up of the Entente Powers: Britain, France and Russia. Both groups were hostile to each other, and both were increasing their stocks of weapons. How did this situation begin?

The Central Powers

GERMANY

Germany was made up of many small states that had united and become one country only as recently as 1871. Led by Prussia, which was then the most powerful of these small German states, they had managed to do this by fighting a series of successful wars against Denmark, Austria and France.

Otto von Bismarck, who was Chancellor of the newly united Germany, firmly believed that all questions of the day could be solved by military strength: in his own words, by 'blood and iron'. The many successes of the German army had made it popular and respected with the German people.

Germany could afford to support a large and well-equipped army because of the success of its industry. By 1900 Germany's industrial output had overtaken Britain's, and was second only to that of the USA. The strong national feeling in Germany and its wealth from industry made the Germans keen to play a leading part in world affairs. Kaiser Wilhelm II was impatient to make Germany the leading country in Europe. In 1890 he dismissed Bismarck for being too cautious. The Kaiser was determined to build up the navy and win an empire for Germany which would rival that of Britain.

? Questions

a Look at Source 2A. These two men were cousins. How might that affect relations between Germany and Britain?

b How do you think King George would feel about the Kaiser's plan for a navy and an empire?

AUSTRIA-HUNGARY

The empire of Austria-Hungary was Germany's oldest ally. The Emperor Franz Josef ruled over this large and ancient empire, made up of many different peoples: Germans, Austrians, Hungarians, Czechs, Slovaks, Italians, Serbs, Croats, Poles

▼ SOURCE 2A
Kaiser Wilhelm II of Germany (left); King George V of Great Britain (right)

and others. German was the language of government, but each group spoke its own language and had its own customs. This made the empire very difficult to rule. Many of these people were demanding their independence. At the same time Franz Josef and his government were keen to take over even more land in the Balkans. (See Map 1-2 on page 7.)

In Germany, the Kaiser had ambitions to build a railway all the way from Berlin to Baghdad. He supported the Austrians in their Balkan plans. The two countries had been joined together in the Dual Alliance since 1879. Later Italy joined in, and in 1882 all three countries became members of the Triple Alliance.

ITALY

Italy was the weakest of all the Central Powers. It had become a united country only in 1870, just one year before Germany. Italy too was looking for new areas of land to colonise. Unlike Germany, however, Italy had very little industry. Most of its factories were situated in the north of the country. Southern Italy was very backward.

Lined up in opposition to the Central Powers were the three countries which made up the Triple Entente: France, Russia and Britain.

The Entente Powers

FRANCE

One of France's main aims ever since 1870 had been to take revenge on Germany for the terrible defeat it had suffered in the Franco–Prussian war of that year. France was building up its industrial strength, although it was not making such rapid progress as Germany. However, France knew that it would need allies as well as resources if it were to defeat Germany. The German Chancellor Bismarck had made a system of alliances with Austria-Hungary, Italy and Russia. This meant that France had few friends in Europe. When Kaiser Wilhelm dismissed Bismarck in 1890 he took charge of foreign policy himself. He did not keep up the Russian alliance. France was quick to make a treaty of friendship with Russia in 1892.

RUSSIA

Russia was by far the largest of the Great Powers in area and in population. Its lands and people stretched from Eastern Europe into Asia. By 1900, however, this vast country had made little progress

compared to Germany, Britain and France. After the alliance of 1892, French money helped to pay for some new industry. Most Russians still lived as peasants in thousands of Russian villages. The ruler of Russia, the Tsar, was in complete personal control of the country. Russia, at that time, was in some ways like Britain had been in the Middle Ages.

BRITAIN

In the 19th century Britain was the 'workshop of the world'. Its industrial goods were traded all over the world. By the turn of the century, the British lead was being challenged by Germany, France and the USA, but Britain was still a great trading nation. It still had the largest merchant fleet in the world. Its main concern was the British Empire, which stretched over nearly a quarter of the world's surface (usually coloured red on maps – see Source 2B). Britain held this vast empire together with its navy, the strongest in the world. The British attitude to Europe had long been one of 'splendid isolation', steering clear of European alliances, secure in the strength of its empire, its industry and its navy.

▶ **SOURCE 2B**

For of pluck he's brimming full, is
  young John Bull
And he's happy when we let him have
  his head;
It's a feather in his cap
When he's helped to paint the map
With another little patch of red.

Music-hall song

? Questions

a How do you think a source such as a music hall song is of use to a historian?

b What does this song tell us about British attitudes to the Empire?

When the British government began to look for allies in Europe it seemed sensible, at first, to join the Central Powers against France and Russia. Germany's royal family was very closely linked with Britain's. France was an old enemy and a rival in Africa. Russia was Britain's rival in the East, especially over Afghanistan. But an alliance with the Central Powers involved Austria-Hungary, with whom Britain had nothing in common.

Gradually, it became clear to the British government that the Kaiser's naval and colonial plans for Germany were a far greater threat to Britain's position than were Russia or France. The differences with France were settled, and in 1904 the 'Entente Cordiale' was signed between Britain and France. The next year, a war which was being fought between Japan and Russia ended in a Russian defeat. Britain believed it no longer had anything to fear from Russia in the East.

In 1907 therefore a Triple Entente was signed between Britain, France and Russia. This Triple Entente was not a very firm alliance, not as firm as the Dual Alliance of Germany and Austria-Hungary. This may have led the Kaiser to think that it might not hold together if war came.

With the countries of Europe divided into two power blocs, war could have come at any time in the early years of this century. Tension and rivalry increased. Armies were drilled and war plans prepared. Any small incident between the rival countries was likely to drag the whole of Europe into war. Many people thought that going to war would be a glamorous, heroic adventure. It was seen as an opportunity to win glory for oneself and one's country. By 1914 many young men on both sides welcomed it.

FOUR STEPS TO WAR

1 Naval rivalry – Dreadnoughts

Germany and Britain began a race to expand their navies as fast as possible. In 1906 Britain launched HMS *Dreadnought*. This battleship had heavier guns and thicker armour-plating and was faster than any other battleship in the world. It made all other warships out-of-date. Immediately, the Kaiser ordered his shipyards to produce a German version.

In 1908 Germany announced that it would build four Dreadnought-type warships each year. Feelings ran high in both countries as the arms

Table 1-1 The armies of Europe in 1914

The Central Powers	The Entente Powers
Germany: 2,300,000 well-disciplined, well-equipped troops	*France*: 2,000,000 well-trained troops
Austria-Hungary: 1,200,000 some nationality and language problems	*Russia*: 3,000,000 the largest army but poorly trained and poorly equipped troops
Italy: unprepared for war	*Britain*: 600,000 well-trained troops

▟ **SOURCE 2C**   HMS *Dreadnought*

race went on. In 1909 British music-hall audiences sang: 'We want eight and we won't wait.' Did all these preparations for war make war more likely?

2 Morocco

The Kaiser was jealous of the empires built up by Britain and France. He took every chance to embarrass Britain and France about their colonial possessions. For example, he supported the Boers in their war against Britain in South Africa, from 1899 to 1902. The Entente Cordiale of 1904 between Britain and France also worried him. He tested out the alliance to see how strong it was in two incidents involving Morocco on the North African coast (see Map 1-1 on page 3).

Britain and France had agreed that they must control the Mediterranean between them. Britain was powerful in the eastern Mediterranean and France in the western Mediterranean. This meant

that the French controlled parts of North Africa, such as Morocco. In 1905, the Kaiser visited Morocco and offered to help the Sultan of Morocco to throw the French out. A conference which included the French, the Germans and the Moroccans was held at Algeciras in 1906 to settle the point. Britain and France stuck together, and the Kaiser had to back down.

In 1911, the Kaiser sent a gunboat, the *Panther*, to Agadir in Morocco. He hoped to force France and Britain to allow him to expand his German territories in Central Africa. Again he was forced to withdraw.

These incidents did not bring war, but raised the level of tension and expectancy that something would happen.

3 The Balkans

The Ottoman, or Turkish, empire had once covered

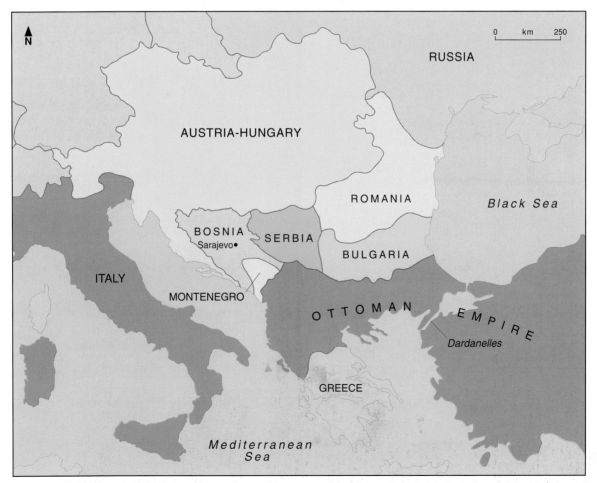

Map 1-2 The Balkans in 1900

all the Balkans. By 1900, several countries (Greece, Romania, Bulgaria and Serbia) had won their freedom from Ottoman rule (see Map 1-2 on page 7). The Ottoman empire in Europe was now small, but the Turks could not really hold on even to that. Two rivals came to fill the gap: Austria-Hungary (backed by Germany) and Russia.

Many of the peoples of the Balkans had links with Russia. The Serbs and Bulgars are Slavs, like the Russians. They are Orthodox Christians too, like the Russians, whereas the Austrians are Roman Catholic. Therefore they looked to Russia for help. Russia, for its part, wanted to be sure that the Dardanelles, the channel which gave it a sea route to the Mediterranean, did not fall into enemy hands. Russia supported independence and expansion for the Balkan states. In that way, there would always be independent Slav countries friendly to Russia in the area.

Independent Slav countries were just what

Austria-Hungary feared. If the Slavs in the Balkans became independent, the Slavs and others peoples inside Austria-Hungary would want independence. If that happened, Austria-Hungary would collapse. Most annoying of all to Austria-Hungary was little Serbia. Although small, Serbia had plans to create a 'Yugoslavia'– a country of the 'Southern Slavs' which would contain all the Slavs south of Austria.

In order to stop Serbian expansion to the west, Austria-Hungary took over Bosnia in 1908. Since many of the people in Bosnia were Slavs, this action greatly annoyed the Serbs. Several secret societies were formed in Serbia whose members were dedicated to throwing the Austrians out of the Balkans. One of these societies was called the 'Black Hand'.

In 1912, Greece, Serbia, Romania and Bulgaria attacked the Ottomans and drove them out of most of the Balkans. The area was divided up again in 1913, enlarging Serbia, making it even more

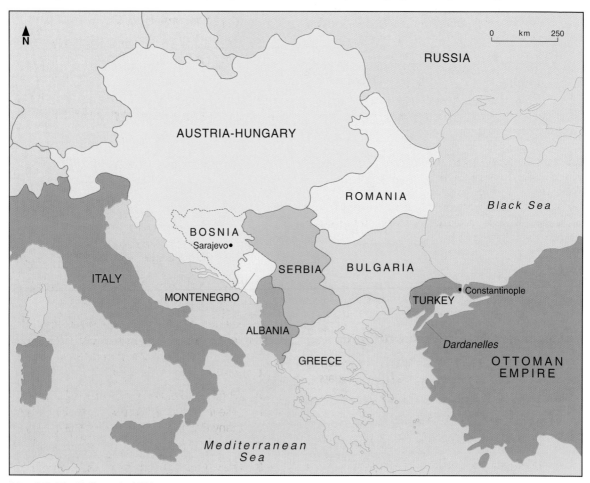

Map 1-3 The Balkans in 1914

determined to be leader of the Slav people in both the Balkans and Austria-Hungary (see Map 1-3). Naturally, Austria-Hungary was annoyed by this and wanted to teach Serbia a lesson. Russia, of course, backed Serbia.

4 Assassination at Sarajevo

Amidst all the tension created by this situation, the Archduke Franz Ferdinand visited Sarajevo, the capital of Bosnia. He was assassinated by Gavrilo Princip, a member of the Black Hand organisation.

From then on, the countries of Europe, one by one, slid into war. Germany offered to support Austria-Hungary if it came to war. This encouraged Austria-Hungary to give Serbia a tough ultimatum. It demanded that Serbia should accept Austrian control in running Serbia or else Austria would declare war. Serbia agreed to all but one of the demands. Russia offered to help Serbia and began to mobilise – that is, get ready for war. This was intended to be a bluff, but Austria went ahead and declared war on Serbia on 28 July 1914.

Germany was worried by Russian mobilisation: German war plans relied on Russia being slow to get ready for war. The Germans dared not let their time advantage over Russia slip away. All their plans were based on attacking France, through Belgium, first.

On 1 August, Germany declared war on Russia and on 3 August, on France. German troops entered Belgium. With Britain's allies at war and German troops across the Channel, Britain stood by its 1839 agreement to protect Belgium if it were attacked. Britain declared war on the Central Powers on 4 August 1914.

ASSESSMENT

Describe, explain and analyse

1 **a)** Explain the reasons for hostility between the following pairs of countries in the years up to 1914:

   i) France and Germany.

   ii) Britain and Germany.

   iii) Russia and Austria-Hungary.

b) Describe why these five countries, and Italy, joined together in the Triple Alliance and the Triple Entente.

c) Do you agree that the hostility between Britain and Germany was the most important cause of the war?

2 **a)** Put the following events from 1914 into chronological order:

   i) German troops enter Belgium.

   ii) Austria-Hungary issues ultimatum to Serbia.

   iii) Britain declares war on the Central Powers.

   iv) Austria-Hungary declares war on Serbia.

   v) Archduke Ferdinand assassinated at Sarajevo.

   vi) Russian army mobilises.

b) Explain why these events must have happened in the order you have put them in.

Evidence and interpretations

1 **A** 'The war was Germany's fault.'

   B 'The nations of Europe stumbled into war.'

   C 'Some nations were more to blame than others.'

   a) Write three short paragraphs, one in support of *each* of statements **A**, **B** and **C**, showing how the statement could be correct.

   b) Write a last paragraph explaining which statement you think is most correct.

2 Some interpretations separate out blame for the tension in the 10 years before 1914 from blame for the events which happened after the assassination at Sarajevo:

   A 'All governments were to blame for the increase in tension in Europe up to 1914, but Germany was most to blame for the events after Sarajevo.'

   B 'The German government was far more

responsible for the war because of the decisions it took between 1904 and 1913 than for anything it did after Sarajevo.'

Which of these two interpretations, **A** or **B**, do the facts in this chapter support most? Explain your answer.

3   **A** After the war the German government made enormous efforts to prove that Germany was not to blame.

B In the 1960s, a German historian, Fritz Fischer, blamed Germany for *both* the tension of the pre-war years *and* the events of 1914.

C Fischer was heavily criticised by other German historians.

Explain the motives of the people involved in **A**, **B** and **C**.

Topics for discussion

1   Was the war inevitable?

Do you think Europe was set on a course for war from the beginning of the century?

Do you think the slide to war could have been stopped at any point, and if so, how?

2   Assassinations.

Do you think assassination is ever justified?

Did Gavrilo Princip achieve what he wanted by assassinating the Archduke?

Compare the other important assassinations described in this book: J. F. Kennedy (Chapter 18), Martin Luther King (Chapter 18), Gandhi (Chapter 21), Anwar Sadat (Chapter 19).

2: The First World War 1914–1918

If there is a war memorial in your town, go and study it carefully. There may be names on it you can recognise. Count how many men from your town were killed in the First World War, then try to find out the number of people living in your town in 1914. (You should be able to get this information from your local library.) Remember that about half of this number would have been female and about a quarter of the rest were young boys or old men and not eligible for military service. Compare the number you have left over with the number of names on the war memorial. You will probably find that a very high proportion of the men from your town who were of military age were killed during the War. In all about 10 million soldiers lost their lives. What was this war like?

THE SCHLIEFFEN PLAN

The German commanders realised that if war came they faced the danger of fighting two enemies at once: France to the west and Russia to the east. This would mean splitting their forces in two. They had therefore worked out a plan, in 1895, to deal with this problem. It was called the Schlieffen Plan, and it was a calculated gamble. The Germans took two risks. The first was that the Russians would be slow to get ready for war. They hoped that they would have three clear weeks before Russia could mobilise its troops and have to be faced on the Eastern Front. The second risk they took was that Britain would not join in the war when Germany invaded Belgium. Britain had a treaty with Belgium which went back to 1839. In this treaty Britain had promised to support Belgium's neutral position in war and go to its help if attacked.

If they were right, and these two gambles worked, the Germans believed they would be able to defeat France rapidly. According to the Schlieffen Plan, the left wing of the German army would attack France along the frontier from Metz to Switzerland (see Map 2-1). Their only task was to keep the French army pinned down along this line where their attack was expected. Meanwhile, the right wing would sweep round through Belgium, taking France by surprise, cross northern France, capture Paris and trap the French army from behind. Their advance would be like a huge swinging door, with Metz as the hinge. Then, with France defeated, the German army could concentrate on attacking Russia. The whole plan was carefully worked out in detail to a strict timetable.

The German advance

The war began on 3 August 1914, when German troops invaded Belgium. Map 2-1 shows that the great German advance nearly succeeded. Their right wing swung through Belgium and France, until they were only 20 miles from Paris. However, several important things went wrong. First, the Belgians put up more resistance than expected, especially at Liège. This slowed down the German advance. The British kept to their treaty with Belgium and sent over the British Expeditionary Force.

The Kaiser was amazed and angry at Britain for going to war, and keeping to their treaty with Belgium which he called 'a scrap of paper'. He also called the BEF 'a contemptibly little army'. However, the BEF did attack the flank of the German right wing, forcing their line of advance to the east of Paris, not the west as planned. The Russians, for their part, mobilised more quickly than the Germans had expected and invaded Germany. The Germans had to send two divisions to try to stop them on the Eastern Front. Lastly, the German advance was too rapid for their own supply transport to keep up. By late August, the Germans had reached the River Marne, but were weakened, tired and hungry.

At this point, the Allies (France and Britain) counter-attacked. The battle front was so close to Paris that the French used taxis from the city to drive soldiers to the front line.

Source 1 tells us how one of the German generals described the actions of the French soldiers.

▼ SOURCE 1

That men will let themselves be killed where they stand, that is a well-known thing. But that men who have retreated for ten days, sleeping on the ground and half-dead with fatigue, should be able to take up their rifles and attack when the bugle sounds is a thing upon which we never counted. It was a possibility not studied in our War Academy.

General von Kluck

? Questions

a What do we learn from this about the German study of war?

b What do these words tell us about the French army in 1914?

c If the Schlieffen Plan failed, what severe problems do you think Germany would face?

The German advance was stopped at the Battle of the Marne and then pushed back. For five days the German army retreated until they managed to dig themselves into trenches and the allies found they could not advance any further. They too dug themselves in facing the German positions. If you look at Map 2-1 you will see that these trenches eventually stretched from the Channel coast to the Swiss border. There was little change in these positions until mid-1918. Both sides were held in a deadlock.

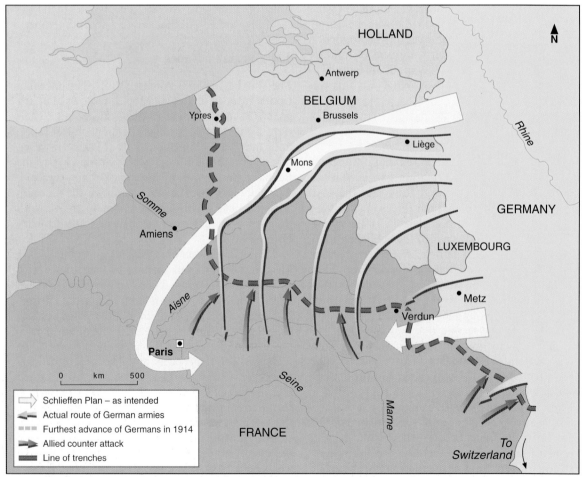

Map 2-1 The Western Front 1914. The Schlieffen Plan

WHY WERE SO MANY KILLED?

Casualties among the soldiers on all sides were enormous – an average of over 5,000 a day. There were several reasons for these figures:

1 Mass recruitment

The armies were huge, see Table 1-1 on page 6.

2 Mass transport

Huge armies could be transported about quickly and easily by train.

3 Industry

In the 50 years before the war, most European countries had developed heavy industries. The factories making iron, steel and chemicals now provided the materials for new deadly weapons to equip each army.

4 Defensive weapons

The most effective weapons were those used by soldiers in defensive positions: the rifle, the mortar, the heavy guns of the artillery and, above all, the machine-gun. The machine-gun, which was usually fired from a trench or dug-out, could kill with great efficiency.

▶ SOURCE 2

As dawn broke on 16th September the order 'Fix bayonets' was passed down the trench and in the wan light we grimly took stock of one another . . . . When the moment came I leapt among the first over the parapet.

For some minutes we ran onwards without a shot being fired, but gradually a machine-gun or two got to work, making some gaps in the line of running men. By the time our breath grew short the signal came to lie down. Then, at the end of a brief pause we raced on, drawing a blizzard of bullets from numbers of fresh machine-guns. Now the fire began to increase in volume, tearing more and more gaps in our line. Our rushes became shorter and faster. We literally dived head downwards to finish each run forward, and, once down, remained motionless, offering as small a target as possible.

Ernest Parker, *Into Battle 1915–1918*

❓ Questions

a   Why was the machine-gun such a successful weapon in situations like the one described in Source 2 and shown in Source 3A?
b   Do you think the attack was likely to succeed?
c   Which side, the attackers, or the attacked, would suffer most casualties?
d   How else could the attackers capture the enemy position?

▶ SOURCE 3A

British working party moving up to the trenches 1917

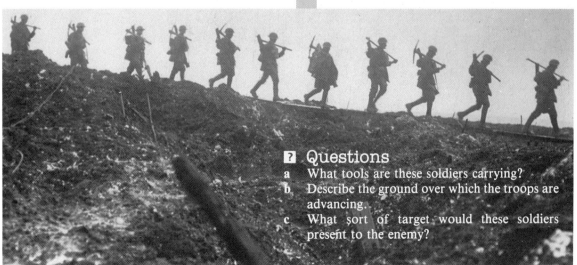

❓ Questions

a   What tools are these soldiers carrying?
b   Describe the ground over which the troops are advancing.
c   What sort of target would these soldiers present to the enemy?

▼ SOURCE 3B   Dug-out at Ypres, 1917

? Questions

a What materials have been used to make the trenches in Source 3B?

b What evidence is there in Source 3C that the area has been heavily shelled?

c These sources include a soldier's memoirs (Source 2), photographs (Sources 3A, 3B and 3C) and a painting (Source 3D). Which do you find most useful for finding out about life in the trenches?

d Write a paragraph about life in the trenches on the basis of these sources.

e Why do you think the soldiers tolerated such appalling conditions?

▼ SOURCE 3C
Fought-over ground on the Menin Road, 1917

SOURCE 3D

'Repelling a German counter-attack', a painting by Frank Dadd

SOURCE 4

Major-General (addressing the men before practising an attack behind the lines). 'I want you to understand that there is a difference between a rehearsal and the real thing. There are three essential differences: first, the absence of the enemy. Now (*turning to the Regimental Sergeant-Major*) what is the second difference?' *Sergeant-Major*. 'The absence of the General, Sir.'

Cartoon in *Punch*, February 1917

TRENCH WARFARE

The only place which was safe from the deadly fire of the machine-guns was in a trench dug into the ground. Every soldier carried tools to dig such as part of his equipment.

Along the north-west of the line of trenches, the ground was flat and wet. British soldiers held much of this section. The two lines of trenches faced each other, a few hundred metres apart. In front of the trenches were coils of barbed wire, to stop attacking soldiers. The stretch of land between the two lines of trenches was called 'No Man's Land'.

5 Tactics

The generals on both sides did not know how to break the deadlock. Their only method of attack was to pound the enemy trenches with artillery, then send the soldiers 'over the top' of the trenches, on foot, towards the enemy lines. They hoped that they could break through the enemy lines by sheer weight of numbers.

These wasteful attacks cost thousands of lives. The only thing that was gained was a few hundred metres of mud. The soldiers who were forced to live and die in these conditions did not always have a high opinion of the generals.

? Question

a What does this cartoon tell us about criticism of generals in Britain by 1917?

6 New ideas

GAS

Some new ideas were tried to drive the enemy out of their trenches. One of these was poison gas. This was first used by the Germans in the Second Battle of Ypres, in 1915, but was soon used by both sides. Its effect was horrible.

▼ SOURCE 5

Gas! Gas! Quick, boys – an ecstasy of fumbling,
Fitting the clumsy helmets just in time.
But someone still was yelling out and stumbling.
And floundring like a man in fire or lime . . .
Dim, through the misty panes and thick green light,
As under a green sea, I saw him drowning.
In all my dreams, before my helpless sight
He plunges at me guttering, choking, drowning

Wilfred Owen, 'Dulce et Decorum Est'

? Questions

a Explain 'misty panes and thick green light'.
b What effect did the gas have?
c How did this incident affect Owen?
d Do you think a poem is a good way of finding out about the war?

TANKS

One new invention which could end the deadlock of trench warfare was the tank. A few were used by the Allies at the Battle of the Somme in 1916, but they were not used in great numbers until the Battle of Cambrai in 1917. They were still very primitive in design.

▼ SOURCE 6A

The tanks, looking like giant toads, became visible against the skyline as they approached the top of the slope. Some of the leading tanks carried huge bundles of tightly-bound brushwood. We went forward into the enemy country in a manner never possible without tanks. It was broad daylight as we crossed No Man's Land and the German front line. The tanks appeared to have busted through any resistance. The enemy wire had been dragged about like old curtains.

G. Coppard, *With a Machine-Gun to Cambrai*

? Questions

a What were the tightly bound bundles of brushwood for?
b Why could the tanks 'bust through' so successfully?
c From the picture below, what is the difference in (1) the position of the guns and (2) the position of the tracks, from those in more modern tanks, such as the ones shown on page 142?

▼ SOURCE 6B

An early tank on the Western Front

MAIN EVENTS OF THE FIRST WORLD WAR ON THE WESTERN FRONT

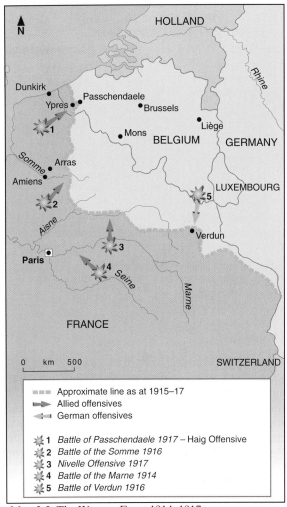

Map 2-2 The Western Front 1914–1917

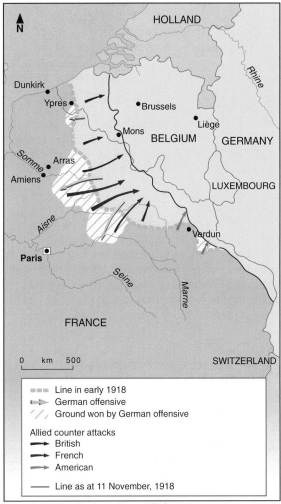

Map 2-3 The Western Front 1918

1914 – Battle of the Marne (see page 12) Both sides take up trench positions by end of year. British and French armies operate separately – no united command.

1915 – Germans attack at *Ypres*: gas first used.

1916 – Tremendous German attack on French at *Verdun*; French hold on, led by General Pétain, despite huge losses.

New British general, Sir Douglas Haig, attacks at Battle of the *Somme*; 20,000 killed on first day; a few kilometres gained.

1917 – USA enters on side of Allies.

British attack at *Arras*; Canadian soldiers capture *Vimy Ridge*.

New French general, Nivelle, attacks. Germans know the attack is coming, so their general, Hindenburg, has prepared defences: the Hindenburg Line. Terrible French losses. Some French soldiers mutiny.

To help French, Haig attacks again at *Passchendaele*, near Ypres. 300,000 killed in mud and rain.

1918 – Russia drops out of the war. Germany brings thousands of soldiers by train over to the Western Front. General Ludendorff prepares a final effort. British and French at last combine under one Supreme Commander, Marshal Foch. American troops and supplies arrive. German advance just held and turned back. Germans retreat. Ceasefire 11 November 1918 (see page 25).

THE HOME FRONT IN BRITAIN

The First World War was fought on many fronts, on land, sea and in the air, and it affected everybody, including civilians at home.

Most directly, many civilians in Britain were killed by enemy action: 121 were killed when the town of Hartlepool was shelled by a German battleship in 1914; Whitby and Scarborough were also shelled. There were bombing raids by Zeppelin airships in which 564 civilians lost their lives. Later in the war German bomber aircraft bombed British cities, causing even more loss of life. No longer were the British people safe in their island.

Conscription

Conscription was not started until 1916. Until then the British army was made up of volunteers.

Different kinds of pressure were put on young men to join up. Some women began giving white feathers to young men in the street who were not in uniform. Posters were issued and music-hall songs were composed which carried the same message.

▶ SOURCE 7D

Oh we don't want to lose you
But we think you ought to go,
For your King and your Country
Both need you so.

▶ SOURCES 7A/B/C

British recruiting posters

We shall want you, and miss you
But with all our might and main,
We shall cheer you, thank you, kiss
    you,
When you come back again.

Music-hall song

❓ Questions

a Explain how Source 7A caught people's attention.

b What feelings does Source 7B stir up?

c Why would Source 7C make men ashamed if they were not in the army?

d How do you think a man would feel on hearing the song in Source 7D sung by a glamorous singer at a music-hall?

e These posters were designed to stir up the emotions of young men so that they would join the armed forces. How do the feelings they stir up compare with the reality of life in the trenches?

Propaganda

A wave of patriotism swept the country in the first years of the war. Government propaganda encouraged this patriotism. There were posters like the ones on page 18. Everything was done to make the soldiers seem like heroes. News of victories filled the newspapers. Films were made of mock-up trenches and staged attacks 'over the top' to be

shown in the new cinemas which had rapidly become popular. The Defence of the Realm Act, 1915, gave the government sweeping powers to stop any criticism of the war.

As you know, the reality of the war was that soldiers were fighting in conditions which were far from heroic. The dreadful loss of life in the battles was hidden from the public by releasing the names of the dead only slowly, over several weeks. Most soldiers didn't particularly hate the Germans who they realised were stuck in an awful situation, just like they were. Soldiers at home on leave found a huge gap between how people at home saw the war and how they felt about it.

Conscientious objectors

In theory, British citizens had the right to refuse to serve in the armed forces if they were 'conscientious objectors'; that is, if they objected, because of their conscience or religious belief, to fighting. Pacifists, like Quakers and Jehovah's Witnesses, could explain their beliefs to a tribunal. They could then do other, non-military jobs, like driving ambulances.

In fact, in the warlike and patriotic atmosphere of Britain at that time, these tribunals could take a very harsh line. Some conscientious objectors – COs, or 'conchies' – had their objections refused. They had to join the army, and if they refused to

fight could be shot for disobeying orders. Some were sent to prison with hard labour. So strong was the feeling against COs that they lost the right to vote for five years after the war.

Women at work

At first women supported the war by encouraging recruitment. They provided 'comforts' for the troops: 232 million cigarettes, 16 million books and four million pairs of socks. People in 1914 had expected the war to be short and be 'over by Christmas'. Once it became clear this would not happen, women began to demand 'the right to serve' in more serious ways.

In peacetime Britain women were not treated equally at work. Many jobs were closed to them completely. But by 1915 there was an acute shortage of workers as so many men had gone off to fight. In this situation employers and Trade Unions relaxed their rules and took on women workers. Women worked in factories, particularly those making armaments and munitions, see Source 9. They also became bus conductors, bank clerks, ambulance drivers and nurses. Over 260,000 women worked on the land, growing essential food. Figures for the increasing numbers of women at work can be seen in Table 2-1. In total, 1,345,000 more women were working in 1918 than in 1914.

Women showed that they could do many jobs

► SOURCE 8
Conscientious objectors on a working party from Dartmoor Prison, 1917

SOURCE 9

Poster to persuade women to work in munitions factories making bombs, guns and filling shells with high explosive.

THESE WOMEN ARE
DOING THEIR BIT

LEARN TO
MAKE
MUNITIONS

for which they had previously been thought incapable. The national crisis of the war overcame male prejudices as nothing else could. Men were obliged to revise their opinions about whether women should work and what work they could do.

Although many women lost their jobs after the war when the soldiers came home, their contribution to the war effort meant that many men had to change their views about women's equality. In 1918 a restricted number of women (women over 30 who were local government electors or married to local government electors, about 60% of all women) gained the right to vote for the first time.

Although they were paid less than men for the same work, women war workers also enjoyed the freedom which a job and a wage gave them. Even when they lost their jobs after the war, their self-respect and confidence was not lost. Women in the 1920s demanded, and received, more freedom than

they had ever had before the war. Relations between the sexes in Britain were never the same again.

Table 2-1 Women in work in Britain in 1914 and 1918

Job	1914	1918
Munitions	212,000	947,000
Transport	18,200	117,200
Commerce	505,200	934,500
Agriculture	190,000	228,000
Government and teaching	262,000	460,200
Hotels and catering	181,000	220,000
Industry	2,178,600	2,970,600
Domestic service	1,658,000	1,250,000
Self-employed	430,000	470,000
Nursing* and secretarial	542,000	652,000

*This excludes members of the Voluntary Aid Detachments

❓ Questions

a How does Source 9 show why women were needed in the munitions factory?

b Why would the woman in this poster be unlikely to be able to vote in 1918?

c Use Table 2-1 to say which two areas of work saw the greatest increase in women workers in the war.

d Explain the reasons for your answer to question **c**.

e Why did the numbers in domestic service decline?

Food

All European countries had to import some of their food to feed their population. As food supplies from overseas were disrupted by the U-boat war, people began to suffer. There were shortages of meat, sugar, and butter. Basic foods, like bread and potatoes, were in short supply. A system of voluntary rationing, introduced in 1915, did not work very well. Compulsory rationing, and ration books, were not introduced until 1918.

However, some people did quite well out of the war: workers in certain key jobs were not allowed to join up and earned good money. The owners of firms supplying the armies did well and prospered.

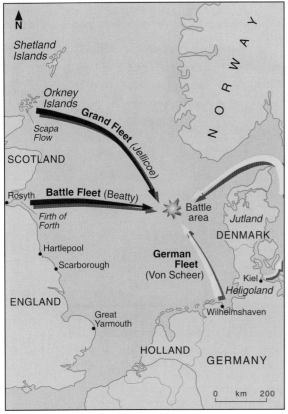

Map 2-4   The Battle of Jutland 1916

THE WAR AT SEA

The Kaiser had built up the German navy before the war, but the British navy was still much stronger. As soon as the war started the British navy blockaded all German ports. This cut off supplies of raw materials, machine tools and food to Germany. This gradual stranglehold on Germany was an important cause of its defeat. No country can fight a war for very long if it has no raw materials for its industries. Germany was soon very short of food as well. The winter of 1916–1917 was called the 'Turnip Winter' in Germany because turnips were almost all that the people had to eat.

If this blockade was important it was not what the public expected. They expected spectacular naval battles between the two carefully prepared fleets. In fact this never really happened. When war broke out, several German surface raiders were on the high seas. But they were soon caught and put out of action.

The admirals on both sides were very cautious. They both realised that if they lost a major sea battle they could 'lose the war in an afternoon'. The British tried to tempt the Germans into leaving their bases at Kiel and Wilhelmshaven, while the Germans tried to lure the British out of Scapa Flow and Rosyth. Early in the war, before the blockade was fully enforced, there were minor battles between cruisers at Heligoland in 1914 and at the Dogger Bank in the following year. Several German cruisers slipped out of port and shelled Yarmouth, Scarborough and Hartlepool before being driven off. By late 1915, however, both fleets were firmly anchored in port, behind a forest of mines and submarine nets. The German fleet in the Pacific was destroyed at the Battle of the Falkland Islands. By early 1915 the only German battleships left were penned up in German ports by the Allied blockade.

From 1915 onwards the Germans tried to tip the balance of the naval war their way by using submarines (U-boats) to sink ships bringing supplies to Britain. Any ship heading for Britain was declared a target. In May 1915 the passenger liner *Lusitania* sailing between the USA and Britain was sunk by a German U-boat. Over 1,000 passengers were killed. Many passengers were Americans, and the killing of American civilians produced a wave of strong anti-German feeling in the USA. U-boat warfare was cut down on the Kaiser's orders.

The Battle of Jutland

The main German High Seas Fleet had to act. The Germans knew they could not take on the entire British Grand Fleet but hoped to lure them into a surprise trap of submarines. On 30 May 1916 the German fleet left port with the cruisers leading the way as a bait to lure out the British fleet. On the same day Admiral Jellicoe, leading the British fleet, put to sea. The two fleets, 259 ships in all, met off the coast of Denmark in the Battle of Jutland (see Map 2-4). Smoke, mist and nightfall prevented a really decisive outcome. Both fleets returned home, the British having lost 14 ships and 6,000 men. German losses were 11 ships and 2,500 men. The battle highlighted weaknesses in British gunnery, armour and signalling.

However, the British fleet was still in control of the North Sea. As a New York newspaper put it, 'the German fleet has assaulted its jailer but remains in jail'. The great German fleet now rested at anchor until the war ended, by which time the sailors were ready to mutiny.

The convoy system

The Germans now had to return to unrestricted U-boat warfare – sinking everything on the high seas – as their only hope of winning the war. They nearly succeeded; British merchant ships were sunk in large numbers. In March and April 1917, 600 ships were sunk, amounting to nearly 1,000,000 tons of shipping in April. At one point London was reduced to only two days' supply of food.

Then a change of Prime Minister brought a change of tactics. David Lloyd George took over from Herbert Asquith and introduced a convoy system. In this system, merchant ships sailed in large groups escorted by fast destroyers. Although convoy escorts sank relatively few U-boats, they did make it much more difficult for U-boats to attack. Sea defences were also strengthened, and thousands of mines were laid in the English Channel and the North Sea. Gradually the situation improved and the emergency passed. Britain never suffered the severe shortages of food and other imported goods that Germany did.

Although there were no large, decisive sea battles, the war at sea was an important element in deciding the result of the First World War.

THE WAR IN THE AIR

Aeroplanes were still new inventions in 1914, and the part they could play in war had not really been thought out. At first they were used for reconnaissance – to find out what the enemy was doing. The light open planes could easily fly over enemy lines to take photographs. Soon, however, new developments took place. Fighter planes were designed and built. Planes were developed to carry bombs, although these were small and did little damage.

▶ **SOURCE 10A**   A Sopwith F1 Camel

▶ **SOURCE 10B**
British pilots ready for take-off on a bombing raid

? Questions

a   Notice the guns fixed on the plane in Source 10A. In which direction did they fire?

b   What do you think the flying conditions might be like for the pilots of these planes?

This aspect of the war, unlike the trench war, did produce individual heroes: Albert Ball (British), Billy Bishop (Canadian) and Baron von Richthofen (German) became famous for the number of planes they shot down. People began to realise the potential of air warfare. The Royal Flying Corps, which had been founded in April 1912, became the basis of the Royal Air Force in 1918.

Both sides also used airships during the war. At that time they could fly faster and carry more arms than aeroplanes. German Zeppelins bombed London and other British cities. Towards the end of the war large Gotha bombers also raided London.

During the war the size, efficiency and speed of aircraft improved. Both sides learned a great deal about aircraft design, and huge numbers of aircraft were produced. Although the number of people killed in air raids was not large, it became obvious that in any future war civilians would suffer even if they were many miles away from the fighting itself.

THE WAR ON OTHER FRONTS

The Eastern Front

Russia soon fell back on the Eastern Front. The brave attacks it launched into Germany in 1914 could not be kept up. The Germans stopped the Russian advance at Tannenberg and the Masurian Lakes (see Map 2-5).

Map 2-5   The Eastern Front

▶ SOURCE 11

The sight of thousands of Russians driven into two huge lakes to drown was ghastly and the shrieks and cries of dying men and horses I will never forget. So fearful was the sight of these thousands of men . . . struggling in the water that, to shorten their agony they (the Germans) turned their machine guns on them . . . The mowing-down of the cavalry brigade at the same time, five hundred men on white horses, all killed and packed so closely together that they remained standing . . . was the ghastliest sight of the whole war.

German officer at Tannenberg

? Question

a   What can you tell from this source about Russian equipment and tactics?

In 1915, German and Austrian troops advanced steadily. The huge Russian army could not stop them. The Russian soldiers fought bravely, but they were short of guns, ammunition, supplies and food. Their road and railway systems were not able to take the strain of war. Russian military commanders, led personally by the Tsar, were often incompetent. General Brusilov led a successful Russian counter-attack in 1916, but this put an even greater strain on the Russian economy. There were strikes and riots at home.

In March 1917, there was a revolution (see Chapter 4) and in January 1918, the new Communist rulers of Russia made peace with Germany. Germany gained hundreds of square kilometres of Russia, and could now throw all its strength into the Western Front.

Italy

Italy was allied to Germany and Austria-Hungary in 1914. The Italians, however, stayed neutral at first, then in 1915 declared war on Austria-Hungary. They hoped to gain some land on the Austrian border and a share in the German colonies if the Central Powers were defeated. A most unusual and difficult war was fought for two years, high up in the mountains and valleys of the Alps. In 1917 Germany had to send help to the Austrians and brought about a major Italian defeat at Caporetto. This left the Italians angry and ashamed, with important results for Italy after the war.

The Middle East

In the Middle East, British forces attacked the Turkish empire (see Map 2-6). Their efforts were greatly helped by a British officer, Colonel T. E. Lawrence, 'Lawrence of Arabia'. He encouraged the Arabs to fight a guerrilla war against the Turks (see Chapter 19). By the end of the war the British had captured Syria, Palestine and Mesopotamia from the Turks.

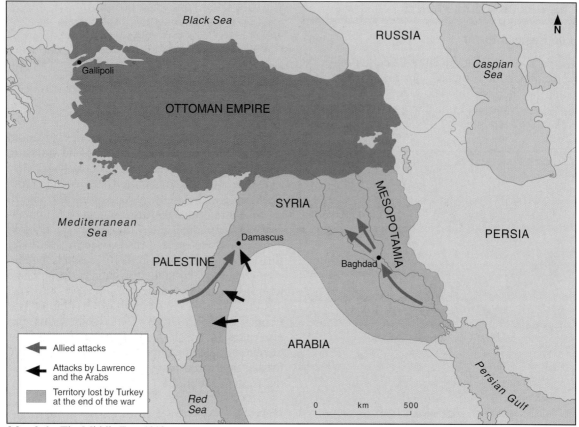

Map 2-6   The Middle East 1918

Gallipoli

In 1915–1916 Turkey itself was attacked. The attack was the idea of the British First Lord of the Admiralty, Winston Churchill. His plan was to break the deadlock on the Western Front by attacking the Central Powers from a completely new direction. The attack could also open up a route by which supplies could be sent to the Russians. Troops were landed at Gallipoli in a combined army and navy operation. The Turkish soldiers, however, fought bravely and well. The Allied forces were unable to move more than a few kilometres inland. The bravery of the Anzacs – the Australian and New Zealand troops – became a legend, but the Gallipoli campaign failed. After eight months of tough fighting the Allied troops withdrew.

THE END OF THE WAR

In 1917, the USA entered the war on the Allied side. Americans had been angered by the sinking of the *Lusitania* in 1915 and furious when the Germans announced early in 1917 that their U-boats would attack any ship trading with Britain. This was the main reason they decided to declare war on Germany. The old links between the United States and Britain and a shared belief in democracy also played a part. President Woodrow Wilson said that he wanted to make 'a world safe for democracy'.

That America had entered the war was good news for the Allies, even though it would take time for the American soldiers to arrive. It came just as Russia seemed to be dropping out of the war. The Russian Revolution and the delay before the Americans arrived gave Germany one last chance. General Ludendorff pulled together all his forces, including many which he could withdraw from the Eastern Front. All through the summer of 1918, German forces attacked the Allied trenches. They broke through in many places, seeing open country in front of them for the first time for four years. However, the Allies retreated, regrouped and stopped the German advances, see Map 2-3.

British and French food supplies were good, unlike those of the Germans. The first American troops began to arrive, and the Allies appointed one supreme commander, Marshal Foch, to unite their efforts. Having blocked the German attack, the Allies counter-attacked. Tanks were used in large numbers. The French had more than three hundred and the British more than five hundred. The Germans were pushed back all along the Western Front. The German commanders asked for an armistice before the fighting reached Germany itself. At the same time, there were riots and revolution among the starving German people. With chaos at home in Germany, fighting stopped on 11 November 1918.

Why did Germany lose the war?

The main reasons why Germany lost the war are:

a *The effects that the long war had on the Germany economy.* Once the Schlieffen Plan had failed, Germany had to fight on two fronts at once. It was unlikely ever to win a long drawn-out war on two fronts.

b *The arrival of the Americans.* This tipped the scales of economic and industrial strength decisively against Germany.

c *The naval blockade.* The shortages of raw materials weakened German industry, and lack of food broke the morale of the German people.

d *On the battlefield, the development of the tank made trench warfare out-of-date.* The Germans were not successful in developing a tank of their own. Allied tanks were very important indeed in 1918.

WILFRED OWEN 1893–1918

Wilfred Owen was born in Cheshire and lived in Liverpool. He was not a strong child, but enjoyed reading. At seventeen, he showed talent as a poet and a musician and started to study at London University. The war ended these plans, and he joined up in 1915. By 1917, he was an officer with the Manchester Regiment on the Western Front. He was injured, recovered in Scotland, then returned to the war in 1918. He won the Military Cross for bravery in October 1918 and was killed on 4 November 1918.

He was a quiet, thoughtful man and popular as an officer. He shared the dangers and

discomforts of trench life with his men and saw the worst side of the fighting. His time of recovery back home showed him the difference in attitude to the war between the soldiers and the public in Britain. Many of his poems show his disgust and horror at what the war did to people. He also learned to respect and understand the attitude of the ordinary soldier, as this poem shows:

> I mind as 'ow the night afore that show
> Us five got talking, – we was in the know –
> 'Over the top to-morrer; boys, we're for it.
> First wave we were, first ruddy wave; that's tore it.'
> 'Ah well', says Jimmy, - an' e's seen some scrapping' –
> 'There ain't more nor five things as can 'appen;–
> Ye get knocked out; else wounded – bad or crushy;
> Scuppered; or nowt except yer feeling mushy'.

ASSESSMENT

Describe, explain and analyse

1 **a)** Explain how each of the following factors led to the failure of the Schlieffen Plan in 1914:

   i) Belgian resistance at Liège.

   ii) British intervention.

   iii) Russian attacks in the east.

   iv) German supply problems.

   v) The Battle of the Marne.

   b) Was it likely that Germany would lose the war once the Schlieffen Plan had failed? Explain your answer.

2 **a)** Choose three of the following and show how they affected the nature of the fighting in the First World War:

   i) Machine-guns.

   ii) Trenches.

   iii) Tanks.

   iv) Gas.

   v) U-Boats.

   vi) Zeppelins.

   b) Which caused the most casualties?

   c) Do you agree that the machine-gun was the most important weapon of the war?

3 **a)** Describe conditions in the trenches on the Western Front in the First World War.

   b) Explain how industrialised warfare led to stalemate on the Western Front.

   c) What attempts were made to break the stalemate? How successful were they?

d) How was the stalemate eventually broken?

4 **a)** What were the main reasons for the defeat of the Central Powers in the First World War?

   b) Do you agree that the naval blockade was the most important reason?

Evidence and interpretations

There have been different opinions of the First World War generals. Some say they were: 'Butchers and Bunglers' who were responsible for the huge loss of life:

• They sacrificed their soldiers' lives;

• They gained little ground;

• They lived well back from the Front and were out of touch with their men.

Others say they were:

• Facing problems which no other generals have ever had to deal with, before or since;

• They had to fight the battles in that way;

• The Allies did win a great victory.

After reading this chapter, what can you say:

   a) To criticise the generals?

   b) To defend the generals?

Topics for discussion

Compare the living conditions and the fighting endured by ordinary soldiers on all sides in the First World War with those in any other war you have studied. Was the First World War the worst?

3: The Treaty of Versailles

The fighting in the First World War came to an end on 11 November 1918. The news meant different things to different people.

▼ SOURCE 1A

[In London] I could distinguish the hooting of motors, the ringing of handbells, the banging of tea-trays, the shrilling of police whistles, the screaming of toy trumpets. Among the many ludicrous incidents to be observed was a parson marching at the head of a group of parishioners, singing lustily, with a Union Jack stuck in the top of his silk hat.

World Crisis, Winston Churchil, pub. 1923

▼ SOURCE 1B

[On the Western Front] Thank God! The end of a frightful four years: the awful winters in waterlogged trenches . . . the terrible trench assaults and shellfire, loss of friends, exhaustion and wounds.

General Jack's Diary, pub. 1964

? Questions

a Put in you own words the different moods described by the writers in Sources 1A and 1B.

b Give reasons for the differences.

Now that the fighting had stopped, it was up to the politicians to work out a lasting peace. The representatives of the victors met at Versailles, near Paris. They worked out terms which would be presented to the defeated powers to sign. This took them well into 1919. The representatives in Versailles had many points to consider. If you had been in their place, what would you have done? After your study of Chapters 1 and 2, how would you answer these questions:

1 Who caused the war?
2 How should a defeated country be treated?
3 How could the peacemakers make sure there would never be such a war again?

You can compare your answers with the final terms of the treaty which are set out on page 30. You have the advantage of looking back on what happened after many years have passed. The men of 1919 were very close to the events and had to act quickly.

▼ SOURCE 2

(From left to right) Lloyd George (Britain), Orlando (Italy), Clemenceau (France), Wilson (USA)

? Questions

a Which of the four countries represented here was most affected by the war?

b How might that affect the attitude of its representative to the discussions?

c Which was the weakest country represented here?

d Which country represented here was least affected by the war?

e How do you think that might affect the attitude of its representative?

f All four of the countries represented here were

democracies. How might this fact influence the treaty?

g Which countries are not represented here although they were deeply involved in the war?

h Why do you think this is?

i Who were the main peacemakers, and what were their aims and motives?

THE VERSAILLES PEACEMAKERS

Wilson, USA

Woodrow Wilson, the American President, was an idealist who wanted to build a better, safer world out of the war. When he led the USA into war in 1917, he did so on the basis of his 'Fourteen Points'. He had put these forward in the hope that, if they were accepted, they would prevent another war from ever taking place.

THE FOURTEEN POINTS

1. There should be no secret treaties; all international agreements should be open.
2. The seas were to be free to all countries at all times.
3. Customs barriers between countries should be removed.
4. Armaments should be reduced.
5. The wishes of the people in colonies should be taken into account when settling colonial claims.
6. German forces must leave Russia.
7. Belgium should be independent.
8. Alsace-Lorraine should be returned to France.
9. Italy's frontier should be adjusted to avoid quarrels with Austria.
10. There should be self-determination for the peoples of Eastern Europe. This meant that the different nationalities should be allowed to govern themselves in independent countries.
11. Serbia should be given a coastline.
12. There should be self-determination for the peoples of the Turkish empire.
13. Poland should become independent from Russia and be given a coastline.
14. An international organisation to settle all disputes between countries should be set up, to be called the League of Nations.

Woodrow Wilson now hoped that these Fourteen Points would be the basis of the treaty. Notice that there is no mention of punishing Germany in them. All fourteen of the points were meant to remove any possible disagreement which might lead to war in the way that the Sarajevo incident had done in 1914.

Clemenceau, France

Clemenceau was an old man who had seen his country invaded by Germany in 1870 and again in 1914. Since then he had seen his country shattered by four years of war. Clemenceau was now determined on revenge. His main aim was to weaken Germany so that it could never attack France again and to gain compensation for all the damage suffered by France. Wilson's ideals had no appeal for him.

Lloyd George, Britain

Lloyd George saw the danger in punishing Germany too severely. However, he had just won an election in Britain in which he had gained votes by promising to 'make Germany pay', to 'squeeze Germany till the pips squeak' and even to 'hang the Kaiser'. He also disagreed with point 2 of Wilson's Fourteen Points. He thought that Britain's safety depended on controlling the seas.

Making peace

Clearly, there was going to be some disagreement among the four countries concerned. None of them got everything they wanted. The German Army had surrendered on the basis of fair treatment under the 14 Points. But Wilson had to give way to the others in order to keep their support for the idea which was most important to him: point 14, the setting up of the League of Nations. This point was written into the treaty. Several other points from the fourteen were accepted but only when it suited Clemenceau, Lloyd George and Orlando.

The peacemakers did not have much time to consider the problem. They had to act quickly, for Europe was in chaos:

1. A terrible flu epidemic was killing more people, already weak from food shortages, than the whole war had done.
2. In Germany the Kaiser had abdicated and fled to Holland. A new, democratically elected republic was set up. The new German republic

hoped for reasonable terms from the treaty.

3. Following the example of the Russian Revolution in 1917 Communists tried to seize power in parts of Germany and Hungary.

4. In Eastern Europe some people had taken the law into their own hands and set up their own-states before the treaty gave them the right.

Lastly, the conference met near Paris, in the heart of a country badly hit by four years of war. The peacemakers could not get away from feelings of revenge: they might have done so more easily if they had met on neutral ground.

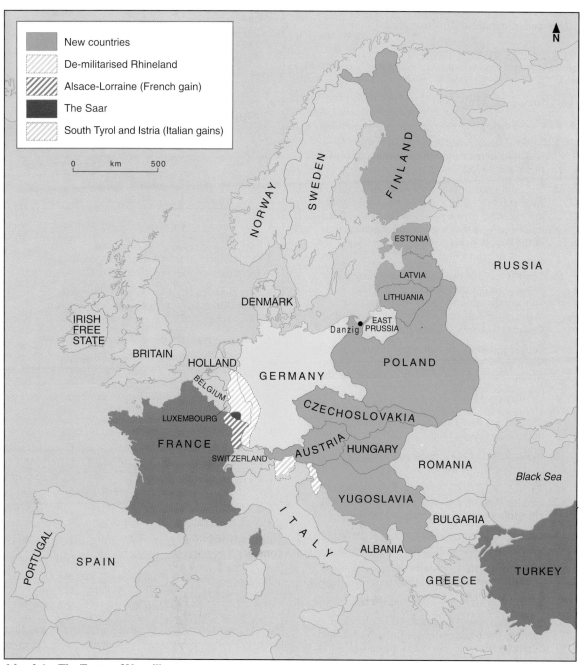

Map 3-1   The Treaty of Versailles

A DICTATED PEACE

Note that there was no representative from Russia, the former ally of Britain and France. There was no one present from the defeated countries: Germany, Austria-Hungary, Turkey and Bulgaria. It was not a negotiated peace.

In the light of these facts and knowing the aims of the main peacemakers, judge for yourself the terms of the Treaty of Versailles.

THE TERMS OF THE TREATY

Territory (see Map 3-1)

1. Alsace-Lorraine was returned to France. (It had been seized from France by Germany after the war of 1870.)

2. The Saar (part of Germany, with an important coalfield) was taken from Germany and given to France for fifteen years. At the end of this time, a vote was to be taken among the people of the Saar to decide which country they wanted to belong.

3. The left bank of the Rhine in Germany was to be occupied by the Allies. A strip 50 km wide on the right bank was to be demilitarized – that is, no forts, army bases, weapons or soldiers were to be allowed inside it.

4. Poland was made an independent country. It was given a 'corridor' to the Baltic Sea. This 'Polish Corridor' cut off East Prussia from the rest of Germany.

5. Danzig, a city with both Polish and German citizens, was made a 'free city' and placed under international rule.

6. Finland, Lithuania, Latvia and Estonia, formerly parts of Russia, were made independent countries.

7. Czechoslovakia, formerly part of Austria-Hungary, was made an independent state.

8. Austria and Hungary became two separate countries.

9. A new independent country, Yugoslavia, was created out of a much enlarged Serbia.

10. Italy was given South Tyrol and Istria.

11. Romania, Greece, Belgium and Denmark all received small pieces of land from the defeated countries.

Colonies

Germany and Turkey had all their former colonies taken away from them. They were given to other countries as mandates. This meant that the countries receiving them had to agree to lead them, eventually, to independence. The League of Nations was to make sure that the territories under mandate were properly looked after.

a The German empire
Tanganyika was given to Britain, the Cameroons to France, South-West Africa to South Africa and the Pacific islands to Japan.

b The Turkish empire
Palestine, Jordan and Iraq were given to Britain; Syria and Lebanon to France.

Arms

1. The German army was to be cut down to 100,000 men.

2. All wartime guns and weapons were to be melted down as scrap metal.

3. The German navy was to be cut down to 36 ships. Germany was not allowed to have any submarines in future.

4. Germany was not allowed to have an air force.

5. Germany was forbidden ever to make an alliance with Austria again.

Blame

By article 231 of the treaty, Germany had to accept total blame for the war.

Reparations

Because Germany was held to blame for the war, it was decided that it should pay reparations to the Allies to compensate them for their losses. This was alter fixed at £6,600 million.

HOW DID GERMANY REACT TO THE TREATY?

The German fleet had been handed over to the British, who anchored the battleships at their naval base at Scapa Flow in the Shetlands. When the terms of the treaty were announced, the German crews deliberately scuttled (destroyed) their ships.

? Questions

a Why do you think the Germans scuttled their fleet?

b What does this action tell us about the German feelings towards the treaty?

▼ SOURCE 3
The scuttling of the battleship *Bayern*

The German people and their government were angry and bitter about the terms of the treaty. In land, people and assets they lost the following: 13% of their land, 12% of their people, 10% of their coal, 48% of their iron, 15% of their agricultural production and 10% of their manufacturing industries. The loss of their armed forces deeply wounded their national pride. The victorious countries did not cut down their armed forces to anywhere near the same levels. The 'war guilt' clause hurt most of all. Even if the German government of 1914 had been solely to blame for the war (which is doubtful), why punish a new government trying to replace the Kaiser's rule with democratic government? A mood of bitter resentment grew in Germany which later made people eager to listen to Hitler's criticisms of the treaty. However, the German army could not fight any longer, the people were starving and the government knew they had no choice: they had to sign the treaty. Below is an eye-witness account of the signing, written by a member of the British delegation at Versailles.

▼ SOURCE 4

Through the doors at the end come four officers of France, Britain, America and Italy. Then, isolated and pitiable, come the two German delegates. They keep their eyes fixed upon the ceiling. They are deathly pale. They do not appear as representatives of brutal militarism. The one is pale and pink eye-lidded: second fiddle in a Brunswick orchestra. The other is moon-faced and suffering: an ordinary private.

Sir Harold Nicolson, *Peacemaking 1919*

? Questions

a   Can you tell what feelings the writer has about the signing of the treaty?

b   What clues does Harold Nicolson give about the kind of people who were now ruling Germany?

CRITICISMS OF THE TREATY

Apart from its effect on Germany, the treaty has been criticised for many reasons. Most of all, it failed to keep the peace, for only 20 years later world war broke out again. The treaty ignored some minority groups and set up small, weak countries from others. Both these actions made Europe less stable. The old Austria-Hungary was split up according, where possible, to the wishes of its many peoples. But it had been built up as a single economic unit. Now road, rail and river links were broken and industries cut off from their suppliers or their markets. This contributed to the economic weaknesses of the new countries. Some of these, like Czechoslovakia, had large minorities of other peoples inside their borders (see Map 3-2).

Wilson's aim of self-determination (point 10 of the Fourteen Points) was not applied to all national minority groups equally. German minorities in particular were ignored: in 1919, there were three

and a half million Germans in Czechoslovakia, one million Germans in Poland and half a million German-speaking Austrians in Yugoslavia and Italy. Self-determination did not seem to apply to the peoples who were on the wrong side at the end of the war. Some new countries had little experience of democracy and soon fell under the rule of dictators. Many were too small and weak to resist Hitler in 1940–1941 or to resist the USSR in 1945.

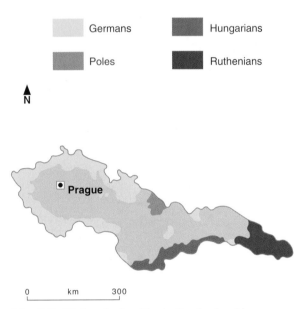

Map 3-2   National minorities in Czechoslovakia

On the other hand, the tangle of national minorities was really an impossible problem for the peacemakers to solve. Of the countries set up in 1919 only Finland has had uninterrupted independence since then. Austria was annexed by Hitler from 1938 to 1945.

National status, granted in 1919, was an important factor in the resistance of Poland, Hungary, Czechoslovakia, Lithuania, Latvia and Estonia to being absorbed into the Soviet Empire from 1945 to 1989.

In Yugoslavia, independence lasted right through from 1919 to 1990, but then hostility between national minorities burst out in a terrible civil war and the country fell apart. National differences also led to the split up of Czechoslovakia in 1990. (You can read more about these events in Chapters 13, 17 and 23 of this book).

ASSESSMENT

Describe, explain and analyse

1 **a**) How did the First World War affect the USA, Britain and France?

   b) How did the situation of their countries affect the aims of each of the three main peacemakers at the Treaty of Versailles: Woodrow Wilson, Lloyd George and Clemenceau?

   c) Which of the terms of the Treaty of Versailles would have pleased each of the three peacemakers?

2 Look at Source A and read Source B.

▼ ## SOURCE A

A British cartoon from 1919. It shows the peacemakers leaving Versailles; Clemenceau is saying 'Curious, I seem to hear a child crying'. The child is labelled 'Class of 1940', that is, those who would have to become soldiers in 1940.

PEACE AND FUTURE CANNON FODDER

The Tiger: "Curious! I seem to hear a child weeping!"

▼ ## SOURCE B

Harold Nicolson, a British representative at Versailles, wrote in his diary: "We arrived, determined that a peace of justice and wisdom should be made. We left, knowing that the treaties were neither just nor wise."

   a) What is the opinion of the authors of both these sources about the Treaty?

   b) Which of the two do you think is the more useful piece of evidence? Explain your answer.

   c) In what ways did the Treaty fail to be 'just and wise'?

3 Compare the map of Europe after the Treaties (page 29) with Europe in 1914 (page 3) and the Balkans in 1914 (page 8).

Austria was dealt with by the Treaty of St Germain; Hungary by the Treaty of Trianon; Bulgaria by the Treaty of Neuilly; Turkey by the Treaty of Sèvres.

   a) What did these treaties do to these four countries?

   b) Do you think these treaties were based on self-determination or a wish to punish the losers?

   c) What would be the reaction of the peoples of Austria, Hungary, Bulgaria and Turkey to these treaties?

Topics for discussion

1 Get into groups. Each person is a British, French or US representative at Versailles. You have to discuss two items:

   i) A piece of territory where the people are 75% Polish and 25% German.

   ii) A German colony.

   What do you say about each item?

2 **a**) In what ways might the Treaty of Versailles be called unfair?

   b) Why did these unfairnesses happen?

   c) What better solutions can you think of which would have made the Treaty fairer?

4: The Russian Revolution

Russia is a huge land of flat plains, pine forests and long, wide rivers. In 1917 after a series of revolutions, it became the first country in the world to form a Communist government. This was a key event in 20th-century world history. Why did it happen?

The revolutions of 1917 had many causes. Some were short term and had arisen quite recently, whereas others were long term and had been brewing up for many years.

THE LONG-TERM CAUSES OF THE RUSSIAN REVOLUTION

Peasants

Before the revolution, 75% of Russians lived in villages like the one below.

▶ SOURCE 1   Peasants, late 19th century

? Questions
a What are the houses made of?
b How can you tell that the people are very poor?
c What do you think conditions would be like in this village during the winter?

The people who lived in this village were poor peasants. Until 1861 they had belonged to their masters, who could buy and sell them like cattle.

NOTICE
In this house one can buy
A COACHMAN
and
A DUTCH COW ABOUT TO CALVE

The peasants were freed in 1861 and given small amounts of land for which they had to pay the government back. They therefore had small farms and heavy debts, with the result that they were very poor. Most of the peasants could not read or write, so they knew very little about how to improve the land. They still used the old farming methods, working on their plots by hand. They envied the rich with their huge estates.

In Russia, a small number of upper-class people held most of the wealth and power. They had large town houses and vast country estates. The Russian Orthodox Church was also rich and powerful.

Workers

During the 1890s, industry began to develop in Russia. Huge iron foundries, textile factories and engineering works were set up. Many were owned by the government or by foreigners. Most were in the big cities such as Moscow and St Petersburg. Peasants moved to the cities to get jobs in the factories. Some just came in the winter when it was impossible to work the land. Some came to stay. By 1900, 20% of the Russian people were workers living in cities.

Factories in Russia were very large, half of them employing more than 1,000 people. The factory workers had problems of their own.

SOURCE 2B

Wages are being reduced. Rent allowances and bonuses are being taken away. Hours of work are being extended. Workers who make trouble are being blacklisted. The system of fines and beating up is in full swing.

Report by Joseph Stalin, 1901

? Questions

a   What was happening to the working day?
b   What do you think 'blacklisting' means?
c   What is the main item in the room shown in Source 2A and why was it so important?
d   Compare living conditions in town and country.
e   If 75% of the Russians were peasants and 20% were workers what percentage was left? Who do you think they were?

The Tsar

The ruler of Russia was called the Tsar. He made all decisions himself. He could ask for advice, but did not have to take it. There was a secret police force which spied on everyone. Anyone who spoke

SOURCE 2A
Workers in the city of Putilov, 1900

out against the government could be shot, or sent to Siberia. Books and newspapers were censored. Sometimes the Tsar's secret police stirred people up to blame all their troubles on Jews, who were then attacked. The position of the Tsar was also supported by the Church. The priests in every town and village taught that he was the 'Little Father' of all the Russian people and must be obeyed.

Nicholas II became Tsar of Russia in 1894. The picture below shows him with his wife Alexandra, their daughters, and their only son, Alexis.

▼ SOURCE 3
Tsar Nicholas II and his family

Is it possible, do you think, to tell what people's characters are like from looking at their faces? Nicholas, in fact, was weak-willed and hated making decisions. He was, however, devoted to his wife and family. His son and heir had a terrible disease called haemophilia, which means that his blood would not clot. Any bump caused agonising internal bleeding, and a bruise or cut could cause death. Alexandra was naturally always worried about her son, and Nicholas tried to comfort her. In this situation, how difficult do you think it would be for Nicholas to be a successful tsar?

The long-term causes of the Revolution were therefore:

1. An undemocratic government which was neither fair nor very good.
2. The bad working and living conditions for the workers in towns.
3. The extreme poverty of the peasants and their need for more land.

The opposition

Some people, of course, were against this system. They were split between the reformers and a smaller group of revolutionaries. The reformers, or Liberals, wanted to modernise Russia gradually. They admired the parliamentary systems of Britain, France and the USA. They wanted free elections, more education for the people and no censorship.

The revolutionaries, on the other hand, wanted to throw out the whole tsarist system and build a different one. One group of revolutionaries were Marxists – that is, they believed in the ideas of Karl Marx, a nineteenth-century German writer who had once lived in London. Marx said:

1. All history is about struggles between different classes: for example, the middle class against the nobles, or the workers against the bosses.
2. The system in Europe is unfair because the factory owner (capitalist) makes a profit out of the workers (proletariat) who actually do the work.
3. In the end, there will be a violent revolution when the workers throw out the bosses and take over the country. The workers will then run the country for the benefit of all.

BOLSHEVIKS
The Marxist revolutionaries could not say these things in Russia, of course. The Tsar's secret police would arrest them and send them to Siberia. Therefore the revolutionaries lived in exile in Western Europe. They quarrelled among themselves, but the most dedicated of the Marxist revolutionaries were the Bolsheviks, led by Vladimir Lenin. Although there were not many of them, Lenin made the Bolsheviks into a well-organised group. Their newspaper *Iskra* ('The Spark') was smuggled into Russia. Lenin planned for the day when his chance would come to spark off a real revolution.

THE DUMA
No one took much notice of a few hundred Bolsheviks, however. The Liberals were much more popular, especially among educated Russians. They had even made a tiny gain: there was, from 1906, a Russian parliament called the Duma. This had been granted by the Tsar in the following way. From 1904 to 1905, Russia had fought a war

against Japan. The Russians expected to win easily but in fact lost heavily. This defeat caused strikes and demonstrations in the Russian cities. For a few days in 1905, the Tsar nearly lost control of his country. He offered to call a Duma with free elections. Some of his opponents accepted this, and the protests died down. The Tsar then used his soldiers to crush the rest of his opponents.

When the Duma met, it began to criticise the Tsar and demand more changes. Nicholas was not used to being criticised and did not like it. The Duma was dismissed, and elections for the next one were controlled by the Tsar. Soon the Duma faded into the background: if it tried to do anything against the wishes of the Tsar, he dismissed it.

Two facts became clear: first, no revolution would take place as long as the army stayed loyal to the Tsar; and second, the Tsar could not be trusted. As for the Duma, it hardly counted for anything: it was a gun without bullets.

THE SHORT-TERM CAUSES OF THE RUSSIAN REVOLUTION

The First World War brought revolution nearer. The Tsar's rule was bad enough in peacetime, but a large-scale war showed just how inefficient it was.

The war went badly. An early advance into Germany in 1914 had been halted by two major defeats at the battles of Tannenberg and the Masurian Lakes (see page 23).

◤ SOURCE 4A
Russian soldiers attacking, Spring 1916

◤ SOURCE 4B
In recent battles, a third of the men had no rifles. The poor devils had to wait until their comrades fell before their eyes and they could pick up weapons.

Russian General, 1914

❓ Questions
a What is wrong with attacking as shown in Source 4A against Austrian machine-guns?
b What effect would the situation in Source 4B have on the morale of Russian soldiers?
c Putting Sources 4A and 4B together, what can you say about the bravery of the ordinary Russian soldier?
d Putting Sources 4A and 4B together, what can you say about the way the Russian commanders ran the war?

Rasputin

In 1915, the Tsar took over personal command of the Russian army. This meant that he took the blame for losing the war. Meanwhile Russia was left in the hands of his wife, Alexandra. She had put her trust in Gregori Rasputin, a drunken peasant who said he was a holy man. He had strange hypnotic powers and seemed to be able to help her son's illness. The war produced more and more problems for Russia, but both Alexandra and Rasputin, who had great influence over her, were against any changes.

SOURCE 5

A cartoon of 1915 showing Rasputin with Nicholas and Alexandra.

? Questions

a   What is the cartoonist trying to say about Rasputin's power?

b   What effect would Rasputin's power have on people's feelings about Nicholas?

c   Nicholas and Alexandra were not really puppets on the knees of a giant Rasputin. What does this cartoon actually tell us about what was going on in Russia?

d   Why is it unlikely that the cartoon would be seen in Russia?

Several nobles were so worried about the results of Rasputin's influence over Nicholas and Alexandra that he was murdered in 1916.

Inflation and unrest

All over Russia, things were going badly wrong by 1917. The peasants were angry because the army took away the young men and the best horses, making farmwork difficult. Prices, especially food prices, rose, and hunger was widespread. Workers in the cities could not afford high food prices, for wages had not risen nearly so fast. If they tried to strike for better wages, they were accused of being disloyal. For this they could be sent to Siberia for as long as twenty-five years. Soldiers coming home from the war told of defeat, bad generals, no guns, no boots and no medical supplies.

In the cities, soldiers were ordered to stop strikes and demonstrations. This was bitterly resented. Many soldiers had been peasants and workers themselves before the war started. Why should they fire at fellow-Russians when they had joined up to fight Germany?

THE REVOLUTIONS OF 1917

In March 1917 a revolution took place in Russia which put an end to the Tsar's rule in Russia for good. It was the first of the two revolutions in Russia that year. Demonstrations and bread riots broke out in Petrograd (formerly called St Petersburg) and other cities and reached a peak in March.

The following incident in Petrograd is typical of the sort of things happening at this time:

SOURCE 6A

A tired old man, carrying a dinner-basin tied up in a red handkerchief, tried to push his way through the crowd. A soldier stopped him . . . . The old man explained that if he could reach the other side of the river, his daughter might let him have a little food . . . . The soldier refused and turned away. The old man trailed wearily after him . . . . This annoyed the officer: he ordered the soldier to take the old man away. The soldier did not move . . . . The officer rode up to the old man and slashed him furiously across the face with his whip. The old man dropped his basin and began to cry. Without a word, the soldier drew his sabre and killed the officer.

Pandemonium broke loose. Soldiers killed all their officers. The crowd went mad and tried to rush the bridge.

N. Poliakoff, *Coco the Clown*

▶ SOURCE 6B

A soldier distributing revolutionary newspapers in Moscow, February 1917

? Questions

a Which of the three people in Source 6A did most to cause the riot – the old man, the soldier or the officer?

b Source 6A just describes one incident. How helpful is it in helping us understand the March 1917 Revolution?

c How does Source 6B change your understanding of the incident in Source 6A?

In Petrograd, the rioters were joined by factory workers on strike. When the soldiers were asked to fire on the rioters, they refused, and joined in the strike.

It was now clear that the Tsar could no longer rely on the obedience of his troops. He saw that he had lost control and abdicated on 17 March. This left Russia without an effective ruler. The Duma formed a Provisional Government led by Alexander Kerensky.

The Provisional Government promised to hold elections soon and also promised to divide up the land among the peasants more fairly. But Kerensky felt he had to stick by the alliances Russia had made with France and Britain and stay in the war against Germany. At the same time, soldiers and workers were electing their own councils in the big cities. These councils were called 'soviets', and at first they supported Kerensky.

Lenin

Lenin was in Switzerland at this time. The Germans made a deal with him: they would give him a train to take him to Russia. They hoped that in return he would cause a revolution which would take Russia out of the war.

As soon as he arrived in Russia in April, Lenin declared his opposition to Kerensky. He said that the war was a war of capitalists and should be stopped. He said the real enemies of the Russian people were not the Germans, but the landowners and capitalists.

▶ SOURCE 7

We call you to a revolution. We call on you not to die for others but to destroy others, to destroy your class enemies at home.

‘Peace, Land and Bread’

Lenin

? Questions

a Why would these words be popular among soldiers?

b Who were the 'class enemies' of the soldiers?

c The three words of the slogan, 'Peace, Land and Bread', each applied to three separate groups of people. Who were they?

Kerensky tried hard to keep up the spirits of the Russian army but failed. The German army was better equipped. Soon there were more defeats.

Food prices at home continued to rise. All Kerensky's promises seemed to be for the future. Lenin offered what the people wanted there and then. The Bolsheviks began to gain support among the workers' and soldiers' soviets. In July, the Bolsheviks tried to get control of the government but were defeated. Lenin had to leave the country wearing a wig to change his looks.

Then the Russian General Kornilov, who still supported the Tsar, turned his army against Kerensky. He wanted to remove Kerensky and bring the Tsar back to power. Kerensky was saved by the Bolsheviks: Bolshevik railway workers stopped Kornilov's advance, while Bolshevik soldiers and civilians formed armed Red Guard units. Kerensky's weakness became all too clear.

? Questions

a What is the mood of the men in Source 8A?
b What reasons might they give for deserting?
c What would they want to do next?
d Look carefully at the men in Source 8B. How many are in uniform?
e Who do you think the rest are?
f Where do you think their guns have come from?

By October, Lenin was ready to act. Law and order in Russia had almost collapsed. In the countryside, peasants were seizing landowners' estates. In the army, Bolshevik ideas were spreading. Thousands of soldiers deserted and went home. In the cities, the armed Red Guard units were prepared to fight. Kerensky had lost the support of the people.

On the night of 24–25 October 1917, Red Guards stormed the Winter Palace where the members of the government were meeting. Kerensky was sent into exile and Lenin became ruler of Russia. This Bolshevik seizure of power was called the October Revolution.

◤ SOURCE 8A   Russian soldiers deserting

◤ SOURCE 8B
Red Guard unit in Petrograd

ASSESSMENT

Describe, explain and analyse

1 Look at Sources 4A, 4B, 8A and 8B.

   a) Explain why the soldiers fought so bravely at the beginning of the war.

   b) What might be the motives of the soldiers in Source 8A for deserting?

   c) Why might soldiers join the Red Guard unit, Source 8B?

2 **a**) Describe how the First World War affected the peasants, industrial workers, the Tsar's government.

   b) Why did the war make revolution in Russia more likely?

   c) Why did the March Revolution succeed?

3 The Bolshevik takeover of power in Petrograd in October, 1917 succeeded for several reasons.

   a) What had Kerensky done which lost him support?

   b) What did Lenin do which made the takeover succeed?

   c) What else happened in Russia in 1917 which made it possible for the Bolsheviks to seize power?

Evidence and interpretations

a Photographs such as those in Sources 1 and 2A only show one particular place at one moment in time, but there were thousands of Russian villages and towns. What is the value of these sources as evidence?

b Sources 1, 3B and 8B are posed pictures. Are they: useless because the people are posing? Useful despite being posed? Explain your answer.

c Sources 4A and 6B are not posed. Does that make them more useful as evidence?

d Look at the picture below and read Source 6A again. What are the strengths and weaknesses of each as sources of evidence of the March 1917 revolution?

5: Lenin and Russia 1917–1928

Lenin and the Bolsheviks had forced themselves into power in October 1917, yet there were only about 250,000 Bolsheviks in the whole of Russia. The First World War was still raging, and starvation threatened the country. The Bolsheviks controlled Petrograd, but in other places their takeover was not so easy. The Moscow Soviet only won control of the city after several days of fighting. It seemed impossible that Lenin could hold on to power. However, he did hold on with ruthless determination. He was sure that the Bolsheviks must win and that history and the Russian people would prove that his ideas were right.

THE BOLSHEVIK REVOLUTION

As soon as the new Bolshevik government was formed, Lenin made many new laws.

▶ SOURCE 1A
* All classes and class divisions, all class privileges and ranks are abolished. There is established the general title of Citizen of the Russian Republic.
* All ranks and grades in the army, beginning with the rank of corporal and ending with the rank of general, are abolished. The army of the Russian Republic now consists of free and equal citizens.
* Private property in land is hereby abolished. All land is declared to be the property of the whole toiling people. All citizens who are willing to till the land, either by themselves or in groups, are entitled to its use.
* The Soviet laws on workers' control are confirmed as a first step to transforming the factories, workshops, mines, railways and other means of production and transport into the property of the Workers' and Peasants' State.
* The passing of all banks into the possession of the Workers' and Peasants' State is confirmed as one of the conditions for freeing the toiling masses from the burden of capitalism.
* The Workers' and Peasants' Government calls upon all peoples and governments to start immediate negotiations for peace. We appeal to the workers of England, France and Germany.
* The Soviet of People's Commissars decrees that . . . those newspapers and magazines will be closed which (a) call for open opposition to the Workers' and Peasants' Government, (b) encourage treason by frankly slanderous distortion of the facts.
* The Cheka (Secret Police) ask all local soviets to seek out, arrest and shoot immediately all (a) agents of enemy spies, (b) speculators (c) organisers of revolts, and (d) buyers and sellers of arms.

Decrees and Declarations Issued
November 1917–February 1918

? Questions
a Which of these decrees would be popular with peasants?
b Which would be popular with soldiers?
c Which would be popular with workers?
d Which of these made Russia a freer, more democratic country?
e Which of these restricted freedom in Russia?
f What did Lenin intend to do to Russian industry and banking?

g In what ways does Lenin's policy for industry and banking differ from his policy for the land?

h Why do you think the workers abroad did not respond to Lenin's appeal for peace?

i What power, a very dangerous one, does the last decree give to the Cheka?

Other decrees gave women equal rights. Divorce was made easy, free education for all was planned, and some of the minority peoples in Russia – for example, the Ukrainians and Georgians – were offered more independence.

Lenin tried to deal with the shortage of food in towns by sending soldiers out into the countryside to seize grain. This often left the peasants without enough to live on and without seed-corn to plant. He defended this ruthless action and the harshness of some of the decrees in Source 1A by the Marxist theory of the 'Dictatorship of the Proletariat'. The Bolsheviks claimed to represent the proletariat, the working people. Until this was accepted by everyone, it would be necessary, Lenin said, for the Bolshevik Party to act as a dictator.

Most of the Bolshevik supporters in Russia were in the army, the navy and among the workers of Moscow and Petrograd. They therefore controlled the important centres of power. The Bolsheviks used the telegraph to spread revolution. They telegraphed the revolutionary decrees out to the cities, towns and villages of Russia, hoping that local groups would act on them. Some of the decrees did not really follow strict Marxist theory. Lenin passed them in order to win the support of the peasants, as the Bolsheviks had few supporters in rural areas.

Assembly elections

This lack of support was seen very clearly in the elections for the Assembly held in January 1918. Many Russians had wanted free elections for what would be their first real parliament. Since Lenin had blamed Kerensky for not calling elections quickly enough after the March Revolution, he could hardly put them off now that he was in power. In the elections, the Bolsheviks only won 175 seats out of 707. Most seats went to the Social Revolutionary Party (SR), which had support among the peasants. This clearly showed how little support the Bolsheviks had outside the cities.

When the Assembly met for its first session, Lenin ordered armed Bolshevik Red Guards to surround the building. After this session, the first freely elected assembly in Russia's history was closed. It was never allowed to meet again. Trotsky's words show the Bolsheviks' attitude to the Assembly: 'You are a mere handful, miserable and bankrupt. You may go where you belong, to the rubbish-heap of history!'

Lenin's policy of the dictatorship of the proletariat thus made many enemies. Not only those who wanted the Tsar back, but many who had supported the March Revolution of 1917 only ten months earlier now turned against the Bolsheviks.

▼ SOURCE 1B

This painting, made by an official artist many years later, shows some Russian people reading some of the decrees given in Source 1A

? Questions

a Make a list of all the different types of people in this picture.

b How are they reacting to what they read?

c Use your answers to questions **a** and **b** to explain that this is a propaganda picture.

Treaty of Brest-Litovsk, 1918

Lenin had hoped that the Russian Revolution would spark off revolutions all over Europe. He thought that this would bring an end to the First World War, as the soldiers of all the armies would refuse to fight. This did not happen. The Russians had opened peace talks with the Germans soon after the revolution. They deliberately kept the talks going on for as long as they could, hoping for the expected revolution. In the end, the Germans lost patience and forced Trotsky, Lenin's representative, to sign the Treaty of Brest-Litovsk. This treaty was very harsh on Russia, but Lenin had no choice but to accept it. The Russian army was crumbling, and he had promised peace to the soldiers.

The Treaty of Brest-Litovsk (see Map 5-1) took away 25% of Russia's population, 25% of the railway system, 35% of the grain-producing area and 70% of the industry. As you can see from the map, some of this land was to be returned to Russia by the Treaty of Versailles.

Britain and France were angry with Russia for leaving the war. They considered that Russia had broken the treaties it had made with them before 1914. The Treaty of Brest-Litovsk gave Germany a sudden advantage: thousands of German troops would be taken from the Russian Front and sent by train to strengthen the German army on the Western Front. Grain from Russian corn lands helped ease the growing hunger in Germany caused by the naval blockade. Britain and France began to look for ways of opening up the Eastern Front again. They made contact with the Bolsheviks' enemies within Russia.

The Civil War

From 1918 to 1921, Russia suffered a terrible civil war. The Bolsheviks in 1918 controlled only the areas round Moscow and Petrograd. They were now attacked by their many enemies. The Bolsheviks were called 'Reds', since red is the colour of the Communist flag. Their opponents were called 'Whites'. This name was about all the Whites had in common: there were Tsarists and Liberals, Social Revolutionaries and Anarchists (those who believed all types of government were wrong). At the same time, local groups took advantage of the chaos to set up their own governments. All they wanted was to be free of control from Moscow. At one time, there were 30 separate governments controlling various parts of Russia.

The Whites were also helped by several countries: Britain, France, the USA and Japan. At first, these countries hoped to open up the Eastern Front with Germany again. Later, they wanted to crush the new Communist state to prevent its ideas from spreading. Russia was also invaded by Finland and Poland during the civil war. To the dismay of the Bolsheviks a large number of Czech prisoners of war, held in Central Siberia, took the law into their own hands: they demanded to be sent home but refused to hand over the weapons they had seized. For a while, they controlled large sections of the Trans-Siberian railway (see Map 5-2).

A Red Army had to be put together if the Bolshevik State was to survive. Leon Trotsky, the

Map 5-1 Treaty of Brest-Litovsk 1918

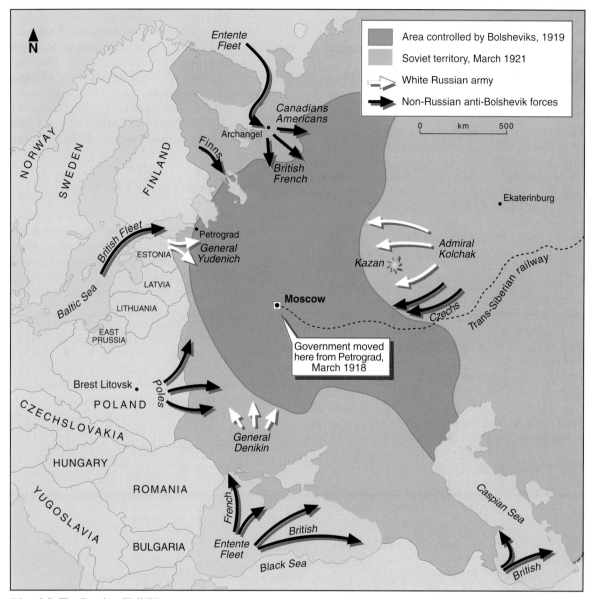

Map 5-2 The Russian Civil War

brilliant organiser of the October Revolution, took on the task. Nearly all the officers of the Russian army of 1914–1918 were Tsarists and had either fled or stayed to fight for the Whites, so he had to start almost from scratch.

▶ SOURCE 2

We were constructing an army all over again and under fire at that. Out of bands of irregulars, refugees escaping from the Whites, peasants and workers, we formed companies, battalions, regiments and even divisions. Even after retreats and defeats, the flabby, panicky mob would be transformed in two or three weeks into an efficient fighting force. What was needed for this? It needed good commanders – a few dozen experienced fighters, a dozen or so Communists ready to make any sacrifice; boots for the bare-footed, a bath-house, propaganda, food, underwear, tobacco, matches . . .

Leon Trotsky

? Questions
a Where did Trotsky get his soldiers?
b How does he describe them before training?
c What does he say the troops need?
d What impression of Trotsky do you get from this source?

Trotsky himself spent the years of the civil war rushing from front to front in a special train. The train had an office, sleeping accommodation and a printing press to turn out propaganda leaflets. He made speeches, encouraged the soldiers and made sure that supplies were available. Later, he took on ex-Tsarist officers, but attached a Communist Party Commissar to each one to ensure that they stayed loyal. Fortunately for Trotsky, the Whites did not act together. The Czech forces were defeated at Kazan late in 1918. In 1919 and 1920, the Red Army dealt one by one with the forces of General Denikin in the south, General Yudenich in the west and Admiral Kolchak in the east.

In 1918, a nervous Bolshevik commander at Ekaterinburg, keen to weaken the Tsarist cause, ordered the Tsar and all his family shot. Cruelty towards prisoners and civilians was soon common on both sides. The foreign powers were sickened by this and by the divisions among the Whites. By 1920, they had withdrawn their support, and the White forces crumbled away.

War Communism

Meanwhile, Lenin's government was prepared to go to any lengths to win the war. His ruthless policy in these years was called 'War Communism'. This stated that everyone between 16 and 60 had to work, except the ill, and pregnant women. Workers could be sent to work anywhere in the country. Strikes were illegal. Food Detachments of 75 men with two machine-guns were sent into the country-side to seize food. The Red Army was allowed to take any supplies it needed. Anyone suspected of opposition, or hoarding food or failing to co-operate, could be arrested and shot by the Cheka.

Why did the Reds win the Civil War?

The main reasons for the Reds' successes were that the White forces did not act together, whereas the Reds were united under Trotsky's command. The White armies were hundreds of kilometres apart, and they found it difficult to get supplies. The Reds held the heartland of Russia, which included most of the railway system, so their supply system was better. The Whites seized anything they wanted in the way of food or horses from the local people. The Reds did very much the same, but the Whites seem to have been hated more. This was probably because the Whites were mainly upper-class Russians and because they had foreign help.

The average Russian was very patriotic, and, in this situation, the Reds seemed the more patriotic side. Young men joined the Red Army to fight for Russia and for Communism against the foreigners and the Tsarists. The ruthless efficiency of 'War Communism' ensured that Trotsky had the supplies he needed.

▼ **SOURCE 3A** Starving children, October 1921

Famine, 1921

By 1921, Russia was in a state of total collapse after seven hard years of war. The First World War and then the civil war had disrupted life to such an extent that land was not being farmed. War Communism had brought passive resistance from the peasants. They could not fight the Food Detachments, but they could refuse to farm the land. They saw little point in growing crops only to have the harvest taken away from them. In some areas, the seed-corn had been taken anyway so crops could not be sown. Towns were deserted as people went into the countryside to look for food. Those who remained were sometimes too weak to work. Workers' control brought chaos to factories and railways. Agricultural production was down by 50%, and industrial production down by 90% compared to the 1913 figure. In addition to all this, there was a drought in 1921. No one knows how many Russian people died, but figures vary from five million to twenty-five million.

▶ **SOURCE 3B**

Train after train, abandoned by the Whites, stood idle, stopped by the defeat of Kolchak, by running out of fuel, by snowdrifts. Some of them served as fortresses for armed bands of robbers or hide-outs for escaping criminals. But most of them were communal mortuaries, mass graves of the victims of the cold and of the typhus.

In the abandoned fields, the rye grain spilled and trickled on the ground. Never in his life had he seen rye so ominously rusty brown.

Boris Pasternak, *Dr Zhivago*, published in 1958

? Questions
a What do you think has happened to the parents of the children in Source 3A?
b Boris Pasternak, the author of Source 3B, lived in Russia at this time. How useful is this source to us?
c Write a paragraph about life in Russia at this time based on these two sources.

In early, 1921, there was a mutiny among the sailors at the naval base at Kronstadt, near Petro-grad. They called for a third revolution, more free elections, free speech and free trade unions. These were not Whites, but men who had supported the Bolsheviks from the beginning. Now they were disgusted with the rules of War Communism and the state of Russia. Trotsky ordered his Red Army to crush the mutiny. It was a bloody battle and was followed by more executions.

New Economic Policy (NEP)

The Kronstadt mutiny and the sorry state of the country led Lenin to introduce changes. He backed down from pure Communist or Marxist doctrine and let aspects of capitalism return.

▶ **SOURCE 4**

We were forced to resort to War Communism by war and ruin . . . it was a temporary measure. Our poverty and ruin are so great that we cannot hope to restore large-scale factory state socialist production at one stroke. Hence it is necessary to help to restore small industry. The effect will be the revival of capitalism on the basis of a certain amount of free trade.

Lenin, 1921

? Questions
a Does it sound as if the NEP was likely to be permanent?
b In which aspect of life in Russia was there most need for some free trade?

Was NEP a success?

Peasants were allowed to farm their own land and sell their own produce. The government took a percentage of their produce as tax. The more they produced, the more they could keep. Peasants were allowed to hire labourers to work for them. Gradually, a class of better-off peasants, the kulaks, began to appear. This practice was against all the principles of Communism, but farming soon recovered, production passed the 1913 figure and there was food on sale again in the towns.

As you can see from Source 4, people were also allowed to run small businesses again. Shops, small factories and trades began to flourish. Lenin kept what he called 'the commanding heights of the economy' in the hands of the state. These were the vital heavy industries – coal, iron and steel – together with railways, shipping and banking. Yet even here some of the principles of Communism were broken. High salaries were paid to experts to run the factories, and bonuses were paid to those who met high production targets.

DEATH OF LENIN

In 1918, a Social Revolutionary called Dora Kaplan had fired several shots at Lenin. Unfortunately, the doctors were forced to leave two bullets in his body. In 1922, he suffered a stroke and never fully recovered. He died in January 1924.

Lenin's incredible energy and determination had changed the history of the world. He had organised the Bolshevik Party until it was ready for revolution. He had called for a second revolution in 1917, and he had led the Bolshevik state through the difficulties of its first seven years. He was obviously a ruthless man, and he cannot be excused the brutalities of those years. He was responsible for setting up the Cheka and the labour camps (see page 42). However, it must be said that he did not want personal power and glory: he did not carry out personal attacks on private enemies. The worst deeds of the secret police and the full horror of the labour camps were to come under his successor, Joseph Stalin. Before he died, Lenin wrote:

▼ SOURCE 5
Comrade Stalin, having become General Secretary, has concentrated enormous power in his hands. I am not sure that he always knows how to use that power wisely. On the other hand, Comrade Trotsky . . . is probably the most able man in the Central Committee, but too self-confident, too much attracted by administration.

From Lenin's 'Political Testament', 1922

Stalin is too crude and this fault is very bad . . . in a General Secretary. Therefore I propose to comrades to find a way to remove Stalin and appoint a man more patient, more loyal, more polite, more attentive to comrades.'

Added by Lenin in January, 1923

? Questions
a   What does Lenin consider is dangerous about Stalin?
b   Which of the two, Stalin or Trotsky, do you think he prefers?

Stalin or Trotsky?

Lenin was only 53 when he died. His death left the Party with the problem of who was to follow him. Trotsky was clearly the most able of the Communist leaders: he had organised the October Revolution and the Red Army brilliantly. However, the other Communist leaders were afraid of him. They thought he might become another Napoleon, turning the principles of the revolution to his own glory. So they ignored Lenin's warning about Stalin. A struggle for power between Stalin and Trotsky lasted for four years.

Gradually, Stalin emerged as the leading figure. Stalin did not seem important at first – one of the other Communists called him a 'grey blur'. However, he had taken on the dull and hard work of General Secretary of the Russian Communist Party. From there, he put his supporters into key posts all over the country. Trotsky did not think it necessary to make allies among the other Communists. The struggle was carried on over policies: Trotsky wanted to press on with 'World Revolution', Stalin joined the group wanting to establish 'Socialism in one country' (that is, Russia) first. Trotsky found himself isolated. He was dismissed from all his posts in 1927. The next year, he was sent to Siberia and finally exiled from Russia completely in 1929. Stalin was then able to remove all other leaders from key positions so that he was in complete control.

ASSESSMENT

Describe, explain and analyse

1   a) Russian soldiers deserted from the army in 1916 and 1917 yet many fought for the Communists from 1918–1921. Why did they do both these things?

b) The sailors at Kronstadt had been among the Bolsheviks greatest supporters, yet they mutinied in 1921. Why did they do this?

c) Why did Trotsky crush the mutiny?

2 a) Describe *two* features of War Communism and explain why it was introduced.

b) Describe two features of the New Economic Policy (NEP) and explain why it was introduced.

3 a) The Reds won the Civil War for several reasons. Some reasons were to do with the weaknesses of the Whites. Describe some of these weaknesses and explain how they helped the Reds to win.

b) Describe some of the advantages the Reds had and show how they helped them to win.

c) How important was Trotsky to the victory of the Reds?

Evidence and interpretations

▼ SOURCE A
A photograph of Lenin in about 1900

▼ SOURCE B
Painting of Lenin returning to Russia in April 1917

▼ SOURCE C
On 10 October Lenin showed that the moment was ripe for the seizure of power. Kamenev and Zinoviev alone acted as cowards and opposed the resolution. The uprising was carried out with military precision and in full accord with Lenin's instructions. Lenin's genius as a leader of the masses, a wise and fearless strategist, was strikingly revealed.

From a biography of Lenin published in the USSR in 1976

▼ SOURCE D
For many years evidence of Lenin's violent arguments with his colleagues over the uprising was concealed. Even today the facts are not all known. An important section of the party, centred round Kamenev and Zinoviev, felt the uprising would be a disaster. Bolshevik plans for the uprising went forward lazily. So far as the record goes, Lenin did little or nothing for the three days before the attack.

From a description of the revolution by an American author, published in 1978

SOURCE E

Lenin was one of the most sinister figures that ever darkened the human stage. This evil man was the founder and mainstay of Bolshevism. He was a revolutionary whose thirst for blood could never be quenched.

From Lenin's obituary in the the *Morning Post*, a British newspaper, January 1924

a   Lenin travelled to Russia by train in April, 1917, but he didn't drive it. In what other ways has the artist of Source B made him look a hero?

b   In what ways does the author of Source C also make Lenin out to be a hero?

c   Find as many ways as you can in which Source D contradicts Source C.

d   The author of Source D says that evidence of the disagreements in the Communist Party about the uprising have been concealed. Why do you think it was concealed?

e   What facts would you select from Chapters 4 and 5 to support the judgement of Lenin given in Source E?

f   Sources B, C and E are clearly biased, either for or against Lenin. What use are they to us in finding out about Lenin and his part in history?

g   'A genius' (Source C); 'an evil man' (Source E). Use these sources and your own knowledge to explain which of these opinions of Lenin you agree with most.

Topics for discussion

1   Russia was invaded in 1914 and again in 1920. What effect would this have on:

Russian people's attitudes to foreigners?

Russian people's concern for their own defence?

2   Look at Lenin's decrees, Source 1A. He had complete power to change what he wanted. What four decrees would you make for Britain today if you were in a similar position?

6: The rise of Hitler

During the First World War Adolf Hitler was a corporal in the German army. When the fighting ended he was lying in hospital recovering from a gas attack. By 1933 Hitler was Chancellor (Prime Minister) of Germany. Winston Churchill described the Germans in 1934 as 'that wonderful, scientific, intelligent, docile, valiant people'! How could it happen that a man like Hitler came to be their ruler?

GERMANY 1919–1923

Germany was in turmoil in the years after the war. There were four reasons for this. They are the the background factors which Hitler was able to play on in his rise to power.

1 Resentment over the war and the Treaty of Versailles

By 1918 the Allied naval blockade was working well. The German people were very short of food. Their morale was low, but they still did not know how bad the situation really was. The fighting had not reached Germany when the war ended, so the Kaiser was able to keep the news of all German defeats from the people. Only German victories were announced. As a result, it was a terrible shock to the Germans when General Ludendorff asked for peace and the Kaiser abdicated and fled to Holland.

This is how Hitler and many other Germans felt at the time.

▸ **SOURCE 1A**
So it had all been in vain. In vain all the sacrifices. In vain the hours in which, with mortal fear clutching at our hearts we did our duty. In vain the death of two millions. Had they died for this, so that a gang of wretched criminals could lay hands on the fatherland?

Adolf Hitler, *Mein Kampf*, 1925

The terms of the Treaty of Versailles were another bitter blow for the German people. Source 1B below shows how one newspaper announced the news of the treaty.

▸ **SOURCE 1B**
VENGEANCE, GERMAN NATION!
Today, in the Hall of Mirrors, the disgraceful treaty is being signed. Do not forget it. The German people will reconquer the place among the nations to which they are entitled. Then will come vengeance for the shame of 1919.

Deutsche Zeitung, 28 June 1919

? Questions
a How does Hitler describe the deaths of German soldiers in the First World War in Source 1A?
b What other sacrifices had the German people made?
c How does Hitler describe the new rulers of Germany?
d What word does he use for his country?
e In Source 1B, what does the newspaper call on the German people to do?
f Use these two sources to describe the impact of the war and the Treaty of Versailles on the German people.

The Germans had been very proud indeed of their army and navy before the war. They could not believe that they had been defeated. They hated the Treaty of Versailles for cutting their armed forces right down. Most Germans believed that Germany must be great again. Hitler was able to make good use of their resentment.

2 The threat from Communism

After the Russian Revolutions of 1917, many Communists believed that world revolutions would follow. Karl Marx had always expected Germany to be the first country to have a Communist revolution. In the chaos in Germany from 1918 to 1919 the Communists did seem to be about to take over. There were Communist revolutions in the naval base at Kiel; in the capital, Berlin; in Munich, where Hitler was living; and in other cities too.

The German government which took over control of Germany when the Kaiser abdicated made a deal with the army. With some volunteer regiments called *Freikorps*, they crushed the Communists. The Communists in Berlin were defeated and their two leaders clubbed to death. Nearly 600 people were killed in Munich.

The Communist revolution in Germany failed, but the Communists were still strong, right up until 1933. Many people feared them. Hitler was able to take advantage of this fear to win support for himself, especially from businessmen and from the middle classes.

3 Suspicion of parliamentary government

With Berlin in chaos, the new democratic government met in the town of Weimar in 1919. For this reason the government of Germany, until 1933, was called the Weimar Republic. Friedrich Ebert was its first president. His government had to agree to the armistice of 1918 and sign the Treaty of Versailles in 1919. Many German patriots blamed the Weimar Republic for what they thought to be these disasters. They began to believe that it was the politicians of the new republic who had asked for peace rather than Ludendorff. The story grew that the politicians had 'stabbed the army in the back'. Hitler called them a 'gang of wretched criminals' (Source 1A). On the other hand, the Communists also hated them for crushing their revolution.

Before the war most important political decisions had been left to the Kaiser. The German people had never had any real experience of democracy. Many still felt that the army and the upper classes were really the rightful rulers of Germany. Therefore the Weimar Republic always seemed shaky.

There were several political parties in the Reichstag, which was the name given to the Weimar parliament. A party could form an overall majority only by making a coalition with another party. These coalitions usually did not last long and were very easily upset.

SOURCE 2
Seats held by the political parties in 1919

Nationalists	44
People's Party	19
Centre Party	91
Democratic Party	75
Social Democrats	165
Independent Social Democrats	22
TOTAL	416

? Questions
a Does any one party have an overall majority?
b What is the smallest number of parties which could gain an overall majority?
c Why do you think coalition governments tend to be weak?

Many Germans mistrusted parliamentary democracy, especially when things went wrong. By 1933, they were ready to try a dictatorship.

4 Economic crisis

The German economy was in great difficulties after the war. First of all, the war itself had cost Germany a great deal of money. Now unemployment was high and there were few jobs for the soldiers returning from the war. The Treaty of Versailles took away from Germany some important industrial areas, such as the Saar with its rich coalfields. The Versailles Treaty also said that the Germans had to pay reparations to the Allies for the damage and cost of the war. In 1921 the amount of reparations was fixed at £6,600 million.

The British and French had borrowed huge sums of money from the USA during the war. The USA wanted the loans repaid. Britain and France were therefore anxious for Germany to pay up, but the German economy could not stand this. Inflation soon reached incredibly high levels. Paper notes were printed for huge sums, but were worth almost nothing.

The French were angry because Germany could not pay reparations, and in 1923 sent troops into the industrial area of the Ruhr in Germany. They hoped to take goods from the area's factories and mines. The workers there went on strike in protest. As a result, the value of the mark (the German currency) went down until it became worthless.

▼ SOURCE 3A
Laundry baskets being taken to the bank to collect the week's wages, Berlin, 1923

▼ SOURCE 3B
The exchange rate of the German Mark and US Dollar

One US dollar was worth:

1914	4 marks
1919	9 marks
1921	70 marks
1922 (Jan.)	192 marks
1922 (Aug.)	1,000 marks
1923 (Jan.)	18,000 marks
1923 (July)	160,000 marks
1923 (Aug.)	1,000,000 marks
1923 (Nov.)	4,200,000 marks

? Questions

a In what ways would ordinary day-to-day matters such as shopping and travelling be difficult under the conditions shown in Source 3A?

b What would happen to people's savings?

c What would happen to people on fixed wages?

d What would happen to people who had borrowed money?

Once again, many people – rather unfairly – blamed the Weimar government. Middle-class people on fixed wages with some hard-earned savings suffered more from this inflation. Later, many in this class supported Hitler.

The Nazi Party in the early years

After the war Hitler decided to go into politics. Many new parties were springing up at that time, and in 1919 he went to a meeting in Munich of the German Workers' Party. It had very few members and almost no money. Hitler was surprised to be made Committee Member Number Seven of this small party, without even being asked. He had intended to set up his own party but decided to join them instead. Soon he was in control of the little group. He changed its name to the *National Socialist German Workers' Party* (NSDAP) or Nazi for short. In 1920, he helped to launch the Nazi Party's twenty-five point programme. It contained a great mixture of ideas. Some of the points were nationalistic – aimed at making Germany great again; some were socialist – to help working people; some were anti-Semitic – against Jews. Most of the points were borrowed from other parties' programmes anyway, but the mixture was Hitler's own.

▼ SOURCE 4A

1. We demand the union of all Germans to form a great Germany.
2. We demand the abolition of the Treaty of Versailles.
3. We demand land for settling our surplus population.
4. None but those of German blood may be a member of Germany; no Jew, therefore, may be a German.
8. We demand that all non-German immigration be stopped.
11. We demand the abolition of incomes unless earned by work.
14. We demand profit sharing in great industries.
15. We demand generous provision for old age.
19. We demand education of gifted children at state expense.
23. We demand that all newspaper owners, editors and journalists should be members of the German nation.

From the Nazi Party's 25-point programme, 1920

Hitler's own beliefs were much simpler:

1. Race. He believed that the German people belonged to a superior race called the Aryans, and that they were the master-race, the *herrenvolk*.
2. Anti-Versailles. He was against the terms of the Treaty of Versailles. Germany must be a great country again, re-taking all that it had lost, by war if necessary.
3. Anti-Communist. He was bitterly anti-communist, because Communism made class conflict more important than national conflict.
4. Anti-Weimar, anti-democratic. He believed in dictatorship, and despised democracy. 'A hundred blockheads do not equal one man of wisdom', he said.

▼ SOURCE 4B

Should the Jew, with the aid of his Marxist creed, triumph over the people of this world, his crown will be the funeral wreath of mankind, and this planet will orbit through space without any human life on its surface as it did millions of years ago.

Adolf Hitler, *Mein Kampf*, 1925

▼ SOURCE 4C

'Power!', said Adolf, 'We must have power!'
'Before we gain it', I replied firmly, 'let us decide what to do with it.'
Hitler, who could hardly bear contradiction, thumped the table and barked: 'Power first! Afterwards we can act as circumstances dictate.'

From the memoirs of Otto Strasser, an early Nazi

❓ Questions

a   Read Source 4A. Which demands are:
(i) nationalist? (ii) Socialist?
(iii) Anti-Semitic?
b   In what ways does Source 4B combine two of Hitler's own beliefs?
c   What does Source 4C tell us about Hitler's own principles?
d   How far do Hitler's own beliefs coincide with those of the early Nazi Party and how far are they different?

The new Nazi Party soon began to attract attention. This was partly because the programme

SOURCE 5A The SA about to round up opponents

offered something for everyone, but it was also because of the violence of his supporters. Hitler had set up an armed, uniformed and disciplined force within the Party: the Storm-troopers or SA. They were also called Brownshirts because of the uniforms they wore. They were directed to keep order at Party meetings. Later they broke up the meetings of opponents and stopped them from speaking.

Hitler explains how the SA dealt with hecklers at one of his meetings in his book, *Mein Kampf*.

SOURCE 5B

The trouble had not begun when my storm-troopers attacked. Like wolves, they flung themselves in packs of eight or ten upon the enemy. After only five minutes, I hardly saw one of them who was not covered in blood. The hall looked almost as if a shell had struck it. Many of my supporters were being bandaged, others had to be driven away, but we had remained masters of the situation.

Adolf Hitler, *Mein Kampf*, 1925

SOURCE 6

Hitler knew how to whip up those crowds jammed closely in a dense cloud of cigarette smoke – not by argument, but by his manner: the roaring and

screeching and especially the power of his repetitions delivered in a certain infectious rhythm. This was a technique he had developed himself and it had a frightening primitive force.

He would draw up a list of existing evils and imaginary abuses, and after listing them, in higher and higher crescendo, he screamed: 'And whose fault is it? It's all . . . the fault . . .of the Jews!'

The beer-mugs would swiftly take up the beat, crashing down on the wooden tables and hundreds of voices, shrill and female or male beer-bellied, repeated the imbecile line for a quarter of an hour.

C. Zuckmayer, *A Portrait of Myself*

? Questions

a What does Source 5A tell us about the SA?
b What does Source 5B tell us about Hitler's attitude to violence?
c Why do you think many Germans were impressed by the uniformed, marching storm-troopers?
d What does the writer of Source 6 think about the scene he describes? How can you tell?
e Use these sources to describe what happened at an early Nazi Party meeting in a beer hall in Munich.

During these years, many men who later became notorious Nazis joined the party. As well as Goebbels, there was Roehm, Goering, Hess, Himmler, Streicher and Rosenberg.

In 1923, Hitler felt he had enough support to try to seize power. At a meeting in a beer hall in Munich, he announced that he was taking over the government. The next morning, together with the war hero General Ludendorff and Nazi supporters, he marched into Munich. However, the police did not join him and he failed to gain enough support. He was arrested, tried and sentenced to five years in Lansberg prison. In fact, he served only nine months. He used the time to write his book *Mein Kampf* (My Struggle) describing his life, his beliefs and what he set out to do. One lesson he had learned from the Beer Hall Putsch, as it was called, was that he should win power legally next time.

THE STRESEMANN YEARS 1923–1930

While Hitler was in prison, the German government managed to improve the situation in the country. This led to a short period of almost normal life in Germany. As most of Germany's problems were concerned with relations with other countries, the job of Foreign Minister was obviously important. For most of this period, this post was held by Gustav Stresemann, a very able diplomat.

At first, Stresemann was Chancellor, and in 1923 introduced a new currency, the *rentenmark*. This brought inflation under control. French troops left the Ruhr. German industry began to pick up, and unemployment declined.

In 1924 the USA agreed to lend money to Germany so that reparations could be paid again. This was called the Dawes Plan (see Table 6-1).

In 1925, Stresemann signed the Locarno Pact. Part of the agreement was that France, Belgium

and Germany should keep to the borders established in the Versailles Treaty. France agreed never to send troops into Germany again. The effect of the pact was to remove tension between countries. The next year, Germany joined the League of Nations. This was another sign that Germany was no longer an outcast. How did this recovery affect the Nazis?

There was a decline in the bitterness and anger which Hitler appealed to in his speeches. Table 6-2 shows the 1928 election results. You can see the Nazis had little support. The only sign of the deep-rooted German desire for military power was the election of the old First World War Field Marshal, Paul von Hindenburg, as President. Stresemann died in 1929.

Table 6-2 The German elections, 1928
Seats in the Reichstag

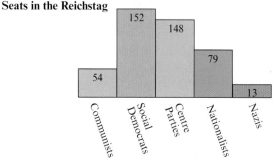

HITLER COMES TO POWER 1930–1933

From his low position in 1928, Hitler became Chancellor in 1933. Why was he able to do this? What were the short-term reasons?

In October 1929, the USA was plunged into Depression in what became known as the Wall Street Crash (see Chapter 10, pages 94–96). American loans to Germany under the Dawes Plan stopped, and soon the German economy was in trouble again. Wages fell and unemployment increased until, by 1933, one in three Germans was unemployed. Not only factory workers but clerks, teachers and other middle-class Germans lost their jobs. Food prices fell, and small farmers found it difficult to make a living.

In the middle of all this despair and confusion, the Nazis promised full employment and a great Germany again. They also put forward scapegoats for all Germany's problems. They said the Jews and Communists were to blame. This last point particularly appealed to some rich businessmen,

Table 6-1 The Dawes Plan, 1924

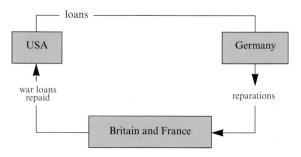

who made large gifts to Nazi party funds. The Nazi rallies at election times now made a big show.

▶ SOURCE 7

I'm beginning to comprehend, I think, some of the reasons for Hitler's astounding success . . . he is restoring pageantry and colour and mysticism to the drab lives of twentieth century Germans . . .

The hall was a sea of brightly coloured flags. Even Hitler's arrival was made dramatic. The band stopped playing. There was a hush over 30,000 people packed in the hall. Then the band struck up the Badenweiler march, a very catchy tune and used only, I'm told, when Hitler makes his big entries. Hitler appeared at the back of the auditorium, and followed by his aides Goering, Goebbels, Hess, Himmler and the others, he strode slowly down the long centre aisle while 30,000 hands were raised in salute . . . .

In such an atmosphere no wonder, then, that every word dropped by Hitler seemed like an inspired word from on high. Man's – or at least the German's – critical faculty is swept away at such moments and every lie pronounced is accepted as high truth itself.

William Shirer's Berlin Diary,
published in 1941

❓ Questions

a Describe how the atmosphere at a Nazi rally was built up.

b What effect did this atmosphere have on the audience?

c What does William Shirer think of the meeting? How can you tell?

d If his evidence is biased, does that mean it is no use to a historian? Explain your answer.

Many Germans were now tired of the Weimar government. They blamed it for their defeat in 1918 and the terms of the Treaty of Versailles in 1919. They remembered the terrible inflation after the war and the humiliating French occupation of the

Ruhr in 1923. Now the Weimar government seemed unable to deal with unemployment. Like the other democratic countries in Europe, Britain and France, it seemed to be powerless to help the people in this crisis.

Even the Weimar politicians began to show their lack of faith in democracy. The President, Hindenburg, did not believe that the Reichstag could solve the problems which faced Germany. He began to use his power to bypass the Reichstag and rule by presidential decree – a form of dictatorship. The German Chancellors worked with him in this. They often had little support in the Reichstag and were more interested in personal power than in the national interest.

In these circumstances, the 1930 elections showed remarkable results: the leading Weimar parties – the Social Democrats and Centre Parties lost many seats. The Communists went from 64 seats to 77. Even more astonishing, the Nazis, down to 12 seats before the election, went up to 107 seats (see Table 6-3 below). In other words, there was a shift to the extremist parties – the Communists and Nazis – both of whom openly planned to overthrow the Weimar democracy.

Table 6-3 The German Elections, 1930
Seats in the Reichstag

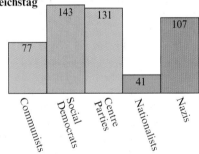

In 1932, Hitler gained more publicity by standing in the presidential elections. He came a good second to Hindenburg. In the Reichstag elections of that year, the Nazis increased their vote to 37% of the votes cast. They obtained 230 seats, and became the biggest single party in the Reichstag.

Hitler could, perhaps, have been stopped if the other parties had been united against him. However, some of the right-wing parties hoped to get into power by joining with the Nazis. The left-wing parties, Socialists and Communists, would not work together. The Socialists were still a large party, and the Communists were gaining support

SOURCE 8

The Marshal and the Lance Corporal: 'Fight with us for peace and equal rights', 1933 election poster

among the workers in the cities, but they would not co-operate. The Communists thought that the Nazis would cause a revolution which would make the people see the Nazis for what they were and then sweep the Communists into power.

Hitler, however, was not yet ruler of Germany, as he did not have an overall majority in the Reichstag, and by autumn it looked as though support for the Nazis was declining. But the Weimar politicians feared that Hitler might try to seize power. So early in 1933, Chancellor Franz von Papen, the leader of a group of right-wing politicians, made an alliance with Hitler. They persuaded Hindenburg to appoint Hitler as Chancellor and von Papen as Vice-Chancellor. Von Papen believed that he could use the Nazis' popular support to increase his own power. He believed that it would be easy for him to rule through Hitler and tell him what to do. Hitler, however, wanted to try to win an overall majority

for the Nazis. In February 1933 he called for new elections.

❓ Questions

a Look at Source 8. Why would it help Hitler to be seen alongside Marshal Hindenburg?
b In what way does this poster once again refer to the old issue of Germany as military power?
c Did Hitler bring Germany 'peace and equal rights'?

Hitler gains power

The Nazis usually gained votes among the middle classes, small farmers and the young unemployed. They regularly used violence at elections. Now, however, they were in the government, so they could control the police and newspapers. Goering was in charge of two-thirds of the police forces in Germany. In addition, he recruited 50,000 'extras' from the SA. Opponents were beaten up and their meetings wrecked. Nazi meetings received full protection. Then, just before the election, the Reichstag caught fire. A young Communist was arrested and blamed, although it is possible that the Nazis set fire to the building themselves in order to throw suspicion on to the Communists. Amid violence and bullying, the election took place. The results are shown in Table 6-4 below.

Table 6-4 The German Elections, 1933
Seats in the Reichstag

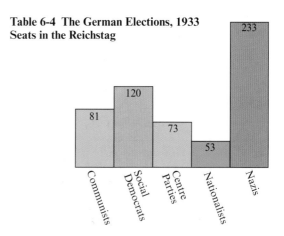

Look at the figures carefully. The Nazis still did not have an overall majority. Hitler never did win an overall majority at an election. However, the Nazis expelled the Communists and joined with the Nationalists. This gave them 286 out of 560 seats. Hitler had gained control of Germany at last.

ASSESSMENT

Describe, explain and analyse

1 The Beer-hall Putsch of 1923 failed; Hitler's bid for power in 1933 succeeded.

a) Describe the differences in each case in:

i) the position of the Nazi Party,

ii) the condition of Germany, and

iii) Hitler's aims.

b) Use these differences to explain why Hitler failed in 1923 and succeeded in 1933.

2 From the list below choose three long-term and three short-term reasons why Hitler was able to seize power in 1933:

i) The terms of the Treaty of Versailles.

ii) Germany's defeat in 1918.

iii) The effects of the Wall Street Crash.

iv) The lessons of the Beer-hall Putsch.

v) Criticisms of the Weimar Republic.

vi) Hitler's powers as a speaker.

vii) The Storm-troopers.

viii) The Reichstag Fire.

a) Describe the items you have chosen.

b) Explain how they helped to bring the Nazis to power in 1933.

c) Explain why they are long-term or short-term causes.

3 a) What effect did the terms of the Treaty of Versailles have on the German people?

b) Do you think these terms weakened support for democracy in Germany?

c) Do you think the peacemakers can therefore be blamed for the rise of Adolf Hitler?

Evidence and interpretations

Look at Sources 5A, 5B, 6, 7 and 8.

1 Which of Sources 5A and 5B is more useful to us as evidence of the SA?

2 What do Sources 6 and 7 tell us about Hitler as a speaker?

3 The authors of both these sources were hostile to the events they were describing. How does that affect the evidence from these sources?

4 Two Nazis describe the effect Hitler had on them at one of these meetings: 'His blue eyes met my glance like a flame. This was a command. Now I know which road to take.' (Goebbels)

'I felt sure that no one who heard Hitler that night could doubt he was the man of destiny. I had given him my heart.' (Kurt Ludecke)

What effect do these statements have on our understanding of Hitler as a speaker?

5 Use these sources and the information in this chapter to explain how Hitler managed to win the support of large numbers of German people.

Topics for discussion

From what you have read so far do you think Hitler was a madman, or a clever politician, or very lucky?

7: Hitler's Germany

Hitler was determined to set up the 'Thousand-Year Reich' based on the ideas he had written about in *Mein Kampf*. His first step was to put an end to democracy in Germany and make himself dictator. He did this rapidly, ruthlessly, but legally.

DICTATORSHIP

Hitler's dictatorship was based on two acts.

1. THE ENABLING ACT

Hitler forced the Reichstag to pass the Enabling Act. This was done by arresting or banning many members of opposition parties. By passing the Enabling Act, Hitler was dictator of Germany. The Act gave him the legal power to make laws without consulting the Reichstag.

2. ONE PARTY RULE

The Nazi party became the only legal political party. Other parties were banned. Trade unions were abolished. Local government was put in the hands of Nazi party officials, and local elections were no longer held.

❓ Questions

a The meeting in Source 1 does not look like a parliament as we know it. In what ways does the layout of the hall make discussion difficult?

b In what ways are the members of the Reichstag not acting like members of a parliament?

c How does the decoration of the hall support Hitler's dictatorship?

▼ SOURCE 1
Hitler speaking to the Reichstag, 1939

'The Night of the Long Knives'

Hitler, however, still did not control the German army. It considered him to be an upstart and was suspicious of what he planned to do. The army was also worried about the Storm-troopers, the SA. The SA leader, Ernst Roehm, wanted to make the SA more powerful so that it would become a kind of second German army. The SA was now a force of four million men all trained in street fighting. Roehm's power rivalled that of Hitler himself. Hitler clearly had to make a choice between the army and the SA. By this time, however, the SA were an embarrassment to him. Now he was safely in power he did not need these violent bullies. He was moving in the highest circles in German society and did not want to be reminded of his street fighting gangs. On the night of 29 June 1934, Hitler ordered his SS killers to act.

Hundreds of SA leaders, including Roehm and many other possible rivals, were swiftly murdered during the night. This was called 'The Night of the Long Knives'.

SOURCE 2

'They salute with both hands now', cartoon by Low in a British newspaper, 1934

THEY SALUTE WITH BOTH HANDS NOW.

❓ Questions

a What does the cartoonist Low call the swastika?

b Explain why he uses this term.

c What is Low's attitude to Hitler in this cartoon?

The SS

The SA was finished. The job had been done by the SS, the *Schutz Staffel*. These black-shirted units had been formed in 1926 as Hitler's personal body-guard. Now they increased in number and importance. Usually they were more middle class than the SA had been. Heinrich Himmler was their leader, but all SS men swore a personal oath of loyalty to Hitler. They could never be a threat to him like the SA.

Soon after the Night of the Long Knives, President Hindenburg died. Hitler took over the position of President as well as remaining as Chancellor. The army swore an oath of loyalty to him as head of the German Reich. He took the simple title of *Der Führer* – the Leader.

LIFE IN NAZI GERMANY

The Nazis sought to control totally every aspect of the lives of every man, woman and child in Germany. This is called 'totalitarianism'.

PROPAGANDA

All aspects of life in Germany were now under Nazi control. Books, plays, films and art were strictly censored. The German people read and heard only what the Nazis wanted them to read and hear. Dr Joseph Goebbels, the Minister of Propaganda, controlled the newspapers and the radio. Books by Jews or anti-Nazis were taken from schools and libraries. Huge bonfires were made of them in every town (see Source 3A). The Nazis made sure cheap radios were available. The

SOURCE 3A
Nazis salute next to a pile of smouldering books, 1933

number of radios in Germany quadrupled between 1933 and 1939. They told the German people only of Hitler's successes, who Germany's enemies were and how Hitler was dealing with them.

Hitler despised the mass of people; he said their understanding of issues was so feeble that they need only be fed simple slogans. The one most often used by the Nazis was '*Ein Reich, ein Volk, ein Führer*' (One state, one people, one leader). This impression of unity was reinforced by huge party rallies. Here, with enormous flags, loud brass bands and thousands of supporters, individuals were lost in the crowd, all adoring their leader.

Pictures of Hitler showed him as a strong man, the saviour of Germany, a knight in shining armour. He also liked to be seen as a kind, protective figure, looking after little children.

Women and children

The Nazis said that women's equality was one of the bad influences of the Weimar Republic. They discouraged married women from working by giving money to those who gave up their jobs on getting married. Women were really only expected to stay at home, have children and look after their husbands. There were medals for having lots of children: bronze for four, silver for six and gold for eight.

The Nazis concentrated especially hard on propaganda for children. They saw them as the future citizens of the 'Thousand-year Reich'. They expected them to be physically tough but totally obedient.

SOURCE 3B   A Nazi rally at Nuremberg

In school the curriculum was carefully controlled. All lessons had a Nazi angle and teachers had to join the Nazi Teachers' Association. If they did not teach Nazi ideas pupils would report them to their parents and they would be sacked. Pupils all had to read *Mein Kampf* and were taught Nazi racist theories such as the superiority of the German people and the inferiority of non-Aryan races like the Jews.

Even outside school propaganda did not stop. At the age of six children could join the 'Pimpfen'. Then there were separate organisations for boys and girls from 10 onwards. At 14 boys joined the Hitler Youth and girls the League of German Maidens. They marched, sang Nazi songs and went on work camps. There, they had to listen to more hours of Nazi propaganda lectures. In 1933 the Hitler Youth had 2.3 million members, or 30% of young people; by 1939 there were 7.9 million members or 82% of young people.

SOURCE 4A
The German nation in its greatness is the subject of the teaching of History, educating young people to respect the great German past, the basic racial forces of the German nation. Only important events should be portrayed:
the powerless and insignificant have no history.

From the German Institute of Education guidelines for the teaching of History, 1938

SOURCE 4B
The People's State ought to allow much more time for physical training in the school. Not a day should pass in which the young pupil does not have one hour of physical training in the morning and one in the evening. Every kind of sport should be included, especially boxing.
In the education of a girl, the final goal always to be kept in mind is that she is one day to be a mother.

Adolf Hitler, *Mein Kampf*, 1925

❓ Questions

a Look at Sources 3A and 4B. How important were books and learning to the Nazis?

b What kind of future does Hitler plan for boys?

c What kind of future does he plan for girls?

d What is meant by: 'The powerless and insignificant have no History.' (Source 4A)? Do you agree?

e Use Sources 4A, 4B and 4C to explain how Hitler intended to control the minds of children and young people.

SOURCE 4C
A swearing-in ceremony for members of the Hitler Youth

Opposition

Those who dared to speak out against the Nazis put their lives at risk. Any kind of opposition to the Nazi state was considered to be treason. The *Gestapo* (the state secret police) had the right to arrest people merely on suspicion. They could imprison their suspects or execute them without trial. Neighbours, even families, spied on each other and reported private conversations.

Not all Germans accepted Hitler's dictatorship without question. Thousands of Germans fled, many to Britain and the USA. Among them were famous writers, artists, musicians, scientists and doctors. They simply did not want to live where there was so little freedom. A few brave men stayed in Germany to oppose Hitler. Some were Christians, like Pastor Niemoeller; some were Socialists or Communists, like Willy Brandt; some were in the army, like General Beck. The most spectacular of the army's efforts to oppose Hitler was the Bomb Plot of 1944, in which Hitler was injured but not killed (see Chapter 13, page 146).

Economic life

However, by 1937, after four years of Nazi rule, most ordinary Germans were satisfied with Hitler. In 1933, the economy had been in a poor state, with six million people unemployed. By 1937, unemployment was under one million. Hitler had reduced the figures partly by conscripting people into the Labour Corps, which worked on a number of Public Work Schemes all over Germany. Wages were low and hours were long. Workers protested, but with trade unions abolished there was little they could do about it. Employers prospered in these conditions.

Mainly, however, unemployment was reduced by expanding the German army, navy and air force and supplying them with equipment. From 1935, Hitler was preparing for war. Directly against the terms of the Treaty of Versailles, he ordered tanks, aeroplanes and ships to be built. This, of course, meant huge contracts for the iron and steel industries. German industry prospered and provided jobs. Inventors tried to find substitutes for imports. Imports were expensive and could be even harder to get in wartime. To avoid importing rubber and cotton, Hitler encouraged the growth of the plastic and nylon industries. His aim, which was never fully achieved, was 'autarky' – self-sufficiency, especially in time of war.

He also ordered work to start on a cheap 'people's car', the Volkswagen, although very few were built by 1939. With such an economic recovery, it is not surprising that many Germans were ready to go along with Hitler.

▼ SOURCE 5
Members of the German Labour Corps

❓ Question

a What propaganda slogan could Goebbels add to this photograph?

PERSECUTION OF THE JEWS

Germans who did 'go along' with Hitler had to close their eyes to one particular aspect of Nazism. Hitler had always insisted that all non-Aryan races were inferior. He could now put his insane racial ideas into practice. Blacks and gypsies in Germany were attacked. At the Olympic Games held in Berlin in 1936, Hitler stormed out in a rage after the black American athlete, Jesse Owens, won a gold medal.

But the main victims of his attention were the Jews. His policy was to make life more and more difficult for the Jews. At first, Jewish shops were boycotted and Jews forbidden to inherit land. Then civil servants and doctors who were 'non-Aryan' were dismissed. In 1935, he passed the Nuremberg Laws.

▶ SOURCE 7A

1. 'Only a national of German or similar blood is a citizen of the Reich. A Jew is not a citizen of the Reich. He has no vote. He may not fill public office.
2. Marriage between Jews and nationals of German blood is forbidden.'

An extract from the Nuremberg Laws

❓ Question

a What effect do you think these laws would have on the lives of ordinary Jewish people?

▶ SOURCE 7B

Jews in the concentration camp at Buchenwald

In 1938 a Jew murdered a German diplomat in Paris. The Nazis ordered an attack on Jews and their property. During *Kristallnacht* (the Night of Glass) over 7,000 Jewish shops were destroyed, 119 synagogues burned down and Jewish homes destroyed all over Germany. Many Jews were arrested. The Nazi government also decided that the German Jews must pay a fine of one and a quarter billion marks for their so-called 'abominable crimes'.

Many thousands of German Jews left Germany during these years, but thousands still remained. By 1939, they were forbidden to go to school or university. Soon the Gestapo began to round up Jews and send them to concentration camps such as Auschwitz, Dachau, Belsen, Buchenwald and Treblinka. These camps were run by special 'Death's Head' units of the SS. Some people from the camps were used as slave labour, some were used as human 'guinea pigs' in horrifying scientific experiments. It is unbelievable that the German people did not know what was going on, but by this time, Germans were too terrified to speak out.

In 1941, Hitler began the policy called the 'Final Solution'. This was an attempt to kill all the Jews in Europe. From Germany, Poland, France, Holland, Czechoslovakia, Russia and all the countries conquered by Hitler, Jews were transported to the concentration camps where they were to be killed. At first, the plan was to shoot them. Later, 20th-century industrialised methods were applied to extermination. Victims were gassed in hundreds, then in thousands in specially-built gas chambers, and their bodies burned. It is estimated that six million Jews had been killed by 1945.

▶ SOURCE 7C

I was ordered to establish extermination facilities at Auschwitz in June 1941. I visited Treblinka to find out how they carried out their exterminations. The camp commandant told me he had liquidated eighty thousand in one half year. He used carbon monoxide gas and I didn't think his methods were very efficient. So at Auschwitz, I used Cyclon B. It took from three to fifteen minutes to kill the people in the chamber. We knew when the people were dead because their screaming stopped. After the bodies were removed, our special commandos took off the rings and extracted the gold from the teeth of the corpses. Another improvement we made over Treblinka was that we built our gas-chambers to take two thousand people at one time.

Auschwitz Commandant at his trial
at Nuremberg, 1945

? Questions

a Does the Auschwitz commandant in Source 7C seem to regret his actions?

b What seems to be his main concern?

JOSEPH GOEBBELS 1897–1945

You, have read about Nazi rallies and Nazi propaganda. The success of the Nazis in winning power in Germany was mainly due to the impression they made on the people. The mastermind of this side of Nazism was Joseph Goebbels. Goebbels was born in the Rhineland area of Germany, the son of a clerk. He was a clever boy, and his parents saved hard to send him to university. After university he tried to make a career as a journalist.

Then, in 1924, he became friendly with some Nazis and joined the party. He was soon a leading figure: he was a good organiser and a brilliant speaker. In 1926 Hitler made him organiser for Berlin. The Nazis were not well-known in this city and Goebbels had to build up

the party from nothing. He made his name there, and in 1928 was made editor of the Nazi newspaper *Der Angriff* ('The Assault').

Goebbels was a German patriot, but not, in many ways, a typical Nazi. He did not hate Jews, until Hitler taught him to. He admired his Jewish teachers and was engaged at one time to a half-Jewish girl. He was also a supporter of the more socialist side of National Socialism: he wanted change and some help for poorer Germans. However, he clearly saw that Hitler could become ruler of Germany and linked his career to helping Hitler achieve that aim.

The parades, processions, demonstrations, ceremonies and rallies by which Nazis impressed the German people were nearly all his idea. A small, crippled man himself, he clearly enjoyed these demonstrations of power. He shared Hitler's belief that if you tell a lie often enough it will be believed. When the Nazis came to power he was given the specially created post of Minister of Public Enlightenment and Propaganda. He was responsible for all newspapers, radio, films, books, music, painting and all the arts, as well as propaganda. Within a year all non-Nazi information had been crushed. The Germans heard only what Goebbels wanted them to hear.

Goebbels did not get on well with other Nazis. His lower middle-class origins did not make him popular with the fashionable aristocrats and army generals who joined Hitler. In 1937–1938 he even thought of leaving the party during a love affair with a Czech film-star. He opposed the war when it came. By 1943, with Hitler running the war, Goebbels was running the country. He was a hard worker and came into his own in this task. He stayed with Hitler to the end. When Hitler committed suicide, Goebbels was declared Chancellor. It lasted one day, then Goebbels, his wife and six children all committed suicide.

DIETRICH BONHOEFFER 1906–1945

Dietrich Bonhoeffer had a happy childhood in a large, well-off and loving family. His father was a professor at Berlin University. Bonhoeffer himself went to Berlin University from 1923 to

1927. He trained as a Protestant minister in the German Lutheran Church.

However, his thoughts about religion in the modern world led him to form his own point of view quite early. In the past, he said, people needed religion to explain all the uncertain and unpleasant things in life. In the 20th century, with human beings in control of their world, what is the need for religion? He answered his own question by showing his own opposition, based on his religion, to Hitler and Nazism.

He was against Nazism from the beginning, as it was against individuals thinking for themselves. The right to have one's own beliefs, make one's own decisions, is what is important, he said. From 1933 to 1935 he worked in London, pointing out the dangers of Nazism. Back in Germany he led the Protestant protest movement against Hitler; in 1938 he met other members of the anti-Hitler resistance. He had many opportunities to escape, and went to the USA in 1939. Friends begged him to stay, but he said he had to face the fight in Germany.

In 1942 he flew to Sweden on a secret mission to meet some British friends. He wanted to know what terms the British would offer for a peace if Germany were taken over by anti-Hitler forces. Churchill, however, was only interested in a German surrender.

He was arrested in 1943 and kept in prison in Berlin. His *Letters and Papers from Prison*, written at this time and smuggled out, have made him famous. When the 'Bomb Plot' of 1944 was discovered, hundreds of known anti-Nazis were arrested. Letters showed that Bonhoeffer and his brother were linked to the plotters. He was moved to a Gestapo prison, then to the labour camp at Buchenwald. There he continued to help and comfort other prisoners. He was hanged in April 1945, when the war was nearly over.

Bonhoeffer's ideas have lived on. His view that governments should be judged, and condemned if they are wrong, has encouraged others since his time. His life showed that not all German people were Nazis. Some had the courage to oppose Hitler.

ASSESSMENT

Describe, explain and analyse

1 **a)** Describe how the Nazi government controlled the lives of: women; children; workers.

b) What were their aims in each case?

c) Use your description to explain the meaning of the word 'totalitarian'.

2 **a)** The Nazis liked to claim that they were popular. What things did they do in the 1930s which many Germans would approve of?

b) Which people would not approve of the Nazi government at this time?

c) Why is it difficult to find out if they really were popular?

3 **a)** How did Hitler deal with:

i) opposition in the Reichstag?

ii) opposition in the country?

iii) opposition inside the Nazi Party?

b) In which cases did he act legally and when did he use violence?

Evidence and interpretations

How did the Nazis use propaganda?

SOURCE A

The memory of the masses is very restricted and their understanding is feeble. So all effective propaganda must be confined to few bare essentials expressed in simple terms. These slogans must be persistently repeated.

Propaganda must not investigate the truth unless it is favourable to its own side.

Men are won over less by the written word than by the spoken word. Every great movement owes its strength to great orators not writers.

Adolf Hitler, *Mein Kampf*, 1925

SOURCE B

Nazi propaganda poster. The woman represents Germany. The flag reads: 'Loyalty, Honour and Order.'

SOURCE C

Illustration from a German children's book

Mein Führer!

SOURCE D

German youth must no longer be confronted with choice. It must be consciously shaped according to the principles of Nazism.

Spoken by an official of the Nazi Teacher's League, 1937

a   What did Hitler say in Source A about: slogans? truth? speeches?

b   Give an example of each of these aspects of Nazi propaganda from Chapters 6 and 7 of this book.

c   Use Sources B and C to describe the impression of Hitler given by his propaganda.

d   Why does the official in Source D say that choice is to be avoided?

e   What evidence is there in these sources and from Chapters 6 and 7 that the Nazis took propaganda very seriously?

f   Write a paragraph on the aims of Nazi propaganda.

g   Write a paragraph on the methods used by Nazi propaganda.

8: Stalin and Russia 1928-1939

By 1928 Joseph Stalin had gained complete control of Russia as General Secretary of the Communist Party (see page 48).

Under the last of the Tsars, Nicholas II, some industry had grown up. However, the First World War and then the civil war had disrupted the country so much that industry had been set back. Most Russians were peasants in 1928. They had been given the land in 1917 by the Communists in the October Revolution. Some were doing well under the New Economic Policy (NEP). Farms were small and their methods old-fashioned. Many harvests were still cut by hand with a sickle and threshed by hand with a flail.

THE FIVE-YEAR PLANS

Stalin wanted to modernise Russia, to make it an advanced industrial country. Modern industry also means modern agriculture. It needs a guaranteed supply of food to feed the factory workers. In the 1920s some peasants were holding back food in order to force prices up. Stalin could not let this happen and wanted to bring the peasants under state control. The Five-Year Plans therefore had to cover agriculture as well as industry. Stalin said the need for change was urgent.

▶ SOURCE 1
One feature of the history of old Russia was the continual beating she suffered because of her backwardness. She was beaten by the Mongols and the Turks, the British and the French. Such is the law of exploiters, to beat the backward and weak. It is the jungle law of capitalism.

We are fifty or a hundred years behind the advanced countries. We must make good this distance in ten years. Either we do it, or we shall be crushed.

Joseph Stalin, 1931

? Questions
a What does Stalin mean by 'jungle law'?
b What does he say will happen if Russia does not make the leap?
c How would this speech appeal to all Russians, not just Communists?

Stalin's method of modernising Russia was through a series of Five-Year Plans. The plan was made by a central planning office called Gosplan. Gosplan laid down production targets for each industry to meet by the end of the five years. This was then used as a basis on which to draw up targets for every factory within that industry. Factory managers then had to calculate targets for every workshop, every shift and every worker.

The figures for five major industries are shown below.

Table 8-1 The First Five-Year Plan

	1928 production	1932 target	1932 actual production
Electricity (milliard KWh)	5.05	17.0	13.4
Coal (million tons)	35.4	68.0	64.3
Oil (million tons)	11.7	19.0	21.4
Pig-iron (million tons)	3.3	8.0	6.2
Steel (million tons)	4.0	8.3	5.9

Note: It is five years from 1928 to 1932 (1932 is the fifth year of the Plan).

You can see for yourself that only the oil industry reached its target. However, the 1932 figures are an enormous advance on the 1928 figures in all cases. If you then look at the figures for 1937, when the Second Five-Year Plan ended, this growth is even more amazing.

Table 8-2 The Second Five-Year Plan

	1937 actual production
Electricity (milliard KWh)	36.2
Coal (million tons)	128.0
Oil (million tons)	28.5
Pig-iron (million tons)	14.5
Steel (million tons)	17.7

Agriculture

These huge changes in industry could not take place without changes in agriculture (see Table 8-3).

For the Five-Year Plans to work, there would have to be new cities, with more workers. The peasants would have to provide not only food, but also workers. The peasants would have to provide food for export as well. Russia would then get foreign currency to buy the machines which were not available there.

COLLECTIVISATION

The Communists had never been popular among the peasants. The old Bolshevik Party had been supported mainly by workers and soldiers before the revolution. Under the NEP, farming was run on capitalist lines: each peasant ran his own little holding for his own profits. Some better-off peasants, the *kulaks*, did quite well. Lenin had discussed applying Communism to agriculture by setting up collective farms. Stalin now began putting collectivisation into practice as part of the First Five-Year Plan.

A collective farm is one which combines all the small farms of all the peasants in a village into one large unit. In theory, this single large farm can be run more efficiently. Fields will be larger, so machines, fertilisers and modern farming methods can be used. Few peasants before collectivisation could afford to buy tractors. Under Stalin, MTS (Motor Tractor Stations) were set up. Tractors from a MTS could go out to work in a group of collectives.

The most common type of collective was the *kolkhoz*. Here, villagers pooled their land, animals, tools and machines. They worked the fields of the

Table 8-3 Changes in the Agricultural System

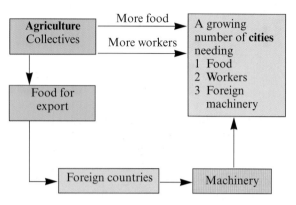

kolkhoz and in return they were paid a share of the profits. They were also allowed to keep small plots of land of their own to grow vegetables and fruit and keep a few animals.

Put like this, collectivisation sounds a good idea. However, two points are ignored. First, collectives were set up at great speed. Second, collectivisation meant a great extension of state control and Communist Party control over the life of every Russian peasant. A collective was run by a committee of which the chairman was always a Communist Party member. The deputy director of every MTS was a member of OGPU, the secret police. The Five-Year Plans required certain crops to be grown in certain quantities. Some of these were crops for industry: cotton, sugar-beet or flax. Some were crops to feed the workers in the new factories of the growing cities. Each collective had to supply a certain amount (not a percentage) of its crop to the state regardless of the harvest. Stalin called this the 'First Commandment'. To the Russian peasants, these tremendous changes, which had to be carried out almost overnight, seemed to destroy their whole way of life.

ATTACK ON THE KULAKS

The peasants disliked collectivisation, but the kulaks hated it. Stalin started an attack on the kulaks in 1928. He accused them of being 'enemies of the state' and of 'disrupting the economy'. He hoped to stir up jealousy among the poor peasants against the more prosperous kulaks so that they would accept collectivisation. However, the peasants objected to state control of agriculture, whatever their feelings about the kulaks. When the Communist Party officials reached a village, the kulaks were arrested and sent away at once, either to a remote area or to a labour camp. Any peasants who openly resisted the setting-up of the collective were shot. But resistance could take many forms.

SOURCE 2A

Men began slaughtering their cattle every night in Gremyachy. As soon as it grew dark, one could hear the muffled bleating of sheep, the death squeal of a pig. Both peasants who had joined the collective and individual farmers killed off their stock. 'Kill, it's not ours now', 'Kill, the State butchers will take it anyway'. 'Kill, they won't give you any meat on a collective', the rumours spread around.

From a novel by M. Sholokhov
Virgin Soil Upturned, 1935

SOURCE 2B

Government propaganda photograph showing tractors on a collective farm in the Ukraine, 1935

Questions

a What does Source 2A tell us about the attitudes of peasants towards collectivisation?

b What effect would this slaughter of animals have on meat production on the collective in the.next few years?

c What effect would tractors, like those in Source 2B, have on the work of the collective?

d Why were tractors so important to government plans for agriculture?

e What do you think would be the attitude of the peasants to the introduction of tractors?

f How useful is Source 2A, a novel, for finding out about Soviet agriculture in the 1930s?

g How useful is Source 2B, a government propaganda photograph, for finding out about Soviet agriculture?

Despite resistance, collectivisation went ahead ruthlessly. The kulaks disappeared. Those who resisted were put in labour camps. The rest were removed to Siberia or sent to work on the poorest land with large quotas of crops to hand over to the state. As far as we know, most of the four million kulaks died as a result of Stalin's policy. On the collectives, the rest of the peasants worked half-heartedly. Most had little experience with new crops and new methods. Sometimes, the experts sent in from Moscow made mistakes. Production of grain and meat fell between 1928 and 1932.

However, the First Commandment ordered a fixed quantity to be handed over by each collective to the state. If there was then not enough food left for the collective itself, then that was too bad for the peasants. Famine soon spread throughout the Russian countryside. Probably as many as three million people died. For Stalin, however, agriculture had been brought under the control of the state. It could now play its part in the modernisation of Russia.

Industry

Look back to the tables of figures for industrial production on pages 69 and 70. Targets were not always met, but production did increase enormously. How was this achieved? The factories which were already there in 1928 obviously had to expand their production a great deal, but this would not have been enough. New towns, cities and industrial areas had to be built, some of them in entirely new areas. In the south, the Donbass area, and in Siberia, the Kuzbass and Magnitogorsk areas became industrialised. New factories were built in the Caucasus, the East and Central Asia, out of reach of foreign invaders. New cities, also, grew at lightning speed.

A visiting worker from the USA described the building of the huge steel works at Magnitogorsk:

Stalin praised heroism of this sort in his speeches.

▼ SOURCE 3A

A quarter of a million souls, communists, kulaks, foreigners, convicts and a mass of blue-eyed Russian peasants building the largest steel works in Europe in the middle of the Russian steppe. Here men froze, hungered and suffered, but the construction went on with a disregard for individuals and a mass heroism unparalleled in history.

J. Scott, *Behind the Urals*, 1942

▼ SOURCE 3B

Greetings and congratulations on their victory to the workers of the great Red Banner Works, the first in the USSR. The fifty thousand tractors which you are to produce for your country every year will be fifty thousand projectiles shattering the old bourgeois world and clearing the way for the new socialist order in the countryside.

Joseph Stalin, 1930

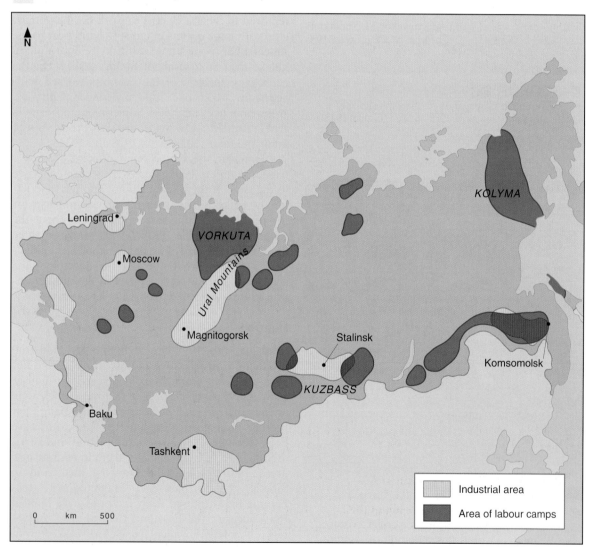

Map 8-1 Industry in Russia in the 1930s

◤ SOURCE 3C

'With the banner of Lenin, we triumphed in the battles for the October Revolution.
With the banner of Lenin, we won decisive successes in the struggle for the victory of
Socialist construction. So with this banner, we shall triumph in the proletarian
revolution throughout the world.' (*Quotation from Stalin*)

❓ Questions

a Look at the list of people working at Magnitogorsk in Source 3A. Who are they and why is each group there?

b What is Stalin's attitude to the workers in Source 3B?

c Why would the tractors in Source 3B help the collectivisation programme?

d Who are the enemies in Source 3C?

e How does Source 3C make Stalin seem to be a hero?

HOW WERE PEOPLE'S LIVES AFFECTED?

In order to reach their targets, the Russian people were called upon to make superhuman efforts. In most cases, they had very little choice: the targets were worked out and they had to be met. They worked long hours, and were fined if they were late. If workers complained about anything they were called saboteurs. Bad workmanship – even by a completely unskilled worker – was also punished as a crime. Women were expected to work in factories and nurseries were provided so that young mothers could return to work. Rates of pay were low and food prices high. The Five-Year Plans concentrated on heavy industry, so very few consumer goods were made. The shops were empty; clothes were dull and badly made and household items difficult to find. Housing, especially in the new towns, was cramped and poorly built.

A few workers did earn good money. Since skilled workers were in short supply, Stalin offered huge wages to foreign workers to come and work on the new schemes. The author of Source 3A quoted above could earn up to one hundred dollars a day. This was at a time when there was massive unemployment in Europe and the USA.

STAKHANOV

Occasionally a Russian worker was made a hero: coal-miner Alexei Stakhanov shovelled 102 tonnes of coal in one shift in 1935. He was made a hero: given extra holidays, better housing and other privileges. 'Stakhanovism', as it came to be called, occurred in other industries. The result for the other workers, however, was that targets were then set even higher and even greater efforts were expected of everybody. Stakhanovism was against the principles of Communism. Marx had written that people should be paid according to their needs. To Stalin, however, anything which increased production was allowed.

STALIN'S DICTATORSHIP

We have seen how the Cheka was set up by Lenin to deal with opposition. Its powers increased during the civil war and, although the name was changed over the years (OGPU, NKVD), the secret police remained. Stalin's policies were bound to bring opposition. Anyone who spoke out against the Plans, or against Stalin personally, could be arrested. To be a kulak, or the son of a kulak, was a crime. Sentences were usually ten or 25 years in a labour camp. These labour camps were set up in areas where special industrial projects were to be built, often in remote parts of the USSR. Here the prisoners worked on dams, canals, factories and hydro-electric power stations. No wages were paid, and there was not enough food. The poor food and the harshness of the climate meant that thousands died. The NKVD simply replaced the dead with others.

▼ SOURCE 4

At the end of the day, there were corpses left on the worksite. The snow powdered their faces. One was hunched over beneath an overturned wheelbarrow: he had hidden his hands in his sleeves and frozen in that position. Two were frozen back to back, leaning against each other. At night, the sledges went out and collected them. And in the summer, bones remained from corpses which had not been removed in time and together with the shingle, they got into the concrete mixer. And in that way, they got into the concrete of the last lock at the city of Belomorsk and will be preserved there for ever.

Alexander Solzhenitsyn, *The Gulag Archipelago,* 1973
(Note: the 'gulags' were the labour camps, hundreds of them, strung like islands – an archipelago – across the USSR)

Not all the work of *Zeks* (prisoners) was done in remote areas. Moscow's underground system was built by prisoners at great speed and with a huge loss of lives, as safety was ignored in order to get the work done quickly.

▼ SOURCE 5
Moscow underground station

? Questions

a Describe the walls, lighting and ceiling of this station.

b Why do you think Stalin made such an effort to build underground stations like palaces?

The millions of prisoners in the camps made a country within the country of the USSR. Eight and a half million people were arrested by the NKVD in the 1930s, of whom about a million were shot. Others simply disappeared. Being taken away by the NKVD was the same as a death sentence. Wives, for example, were regarded as widows from the moment their husbands were arrested. In 1939, there were seven million prisoners living in the camps. The actions of the secret police meant that the rest of the people were scared into doing as they were told by Stalin.

STALIN'S PURGES

Ordinary Russians who spoke their minds, or who were simply in the wrong class, made up most of the victims of the NKVD. However, Stalin also used the NKVD against leading Communists. He had reached the stage where he could not accept any criticism and he could not even bear anyone else to be popular. In December 1934, the popular Communist Party boss of Leningrad, Sergei Kirov, was killed in a car accident. The 'accident' was probably arranged by Stalin. Nevertheless, he put the blame on several other leading Communists. This was made the excuse for the first of his purges. One by one, the old Bolsheviks were arrested. Some were shot, but some confessed to ridiculous charges after torture, or in order to save themselves. At great show-trials in 1935 and 1936, leading Communists who had been Bolsheviks for 30 or more years 'confessed' to being American agents or Trotskyists.

After this, Stalin turned on the army and the Party. One-fifth of the officers in the army were arrested, tried and disappeared: half a million Party members went the same way: of the 139 members of the Central Committee of the Communist Party, 98 were arrested and shot.

❓ Questions

a What impression does this picture give of Stalin's relationship to Lenin in 1917?

b Was their relationship in fact like this?

c Why do you think the artist drew the picture in this way?

d Which period does this source tell us more about: 1917 or 1935? Explain your answer.

▼ SOURCE 6

Drawing made in 1935 showing Stalin's supposed meeting with Lenin in 1917

STALIN'S PERSONALITY CULT

Not only did Stalin want no rivals for control of the country, he wanted personal credit for the USSR's successes too.

Stalin's picture appeared everywhere: in every school, office, station, factory, town hall and street. Many towns were named after him, like Stalingrad, Stalinsk and Stalino. Stalin was supposed to be the cause of every success: 'The country is being led from victory to victory by the steersman of the Party, the great Stalin.' Slogans about Stalin, songs, pictures and stories filled newspapers, cinemas, radio and school books. Pictures like Source 6 even made him out to have been more important in the past than he really was. The names of rivals like Trotsky were removed from official histories of the Revolution. Children were taught to think of him as the 'father' of Russia – and to tell the secret police if their parents criticised him. With this hero-worship on the one hand, and the terror of the NKVD on the other, only people slavishly loyal to Stalin could survive. Although the USSR was a Communist state, the dictatorship of Stalin was just as complete, and in some ways even more bloody, than that of Hitler. Make this comparison yourself and see if you agree.

JOSEPH STALIN 1879–1953

Stalin's real name was Joseph Djugashvili; like other Communist leaders, he adopted another name while in prison. Stalin means 'man of steel'. He was from Tblisi, Georgia, in the south of Russia. His father was a factory worker who died when Stalin was eleven. His mother struggled to keep her son at school until the age of fifteen. At that age, he began training as a priest. The training was strict, the life was hard and Stalin rebelled. He began to read protest books, both Socialist and Georgian nationalist. He began to go to political lectures and in the end was expelled from the training college.

Stalin then began to work as a Socialist organiser. He encouraged strikes, wrote articles and made speeches. He was arrested in 1902, escaped in 1904 and returned to Georgia. By this time, he was a Bolshevik supporter, but in his remote Georgia, he played little part in Party matters. Here, he organised bank raids to supply the Bolsheviks with funds. When the revolutions of 1917 took place, he hurried to Moscow.

However, there were many more clever and exciting people among the Bolsheviks in Moscow at that time. Stalin was given unimportant jobs dealing with national minority groups, like the Georgians. He showed an ability to work hard at paperwork and was efficient at dull, routine jobs. Hardly noticed by others who were interested in ideas, policies, speeches and argument, he became General Secretary of the Communist Party. This became his power base. As the Communist Party was now ruling Russia, it increased in membership and importance. Stalin dealt with Party organisation and soon, all over Russia, there were people who owed their positions to him. He also dealt with purges – removing people who opposed the Party leaders. This was another way of making the Communist Party of Russia into a personal tool of Joseph Stalin.

Lenin had warned the Party about Stalin's power, but they ignored his warning. When Lenin died, the other leaders joined Stalin to oppose Trotsky. With Trotsky out of the way, Stalin then removed the others. His extraordinary ruthlessness in pushing through the Five-Year Plans, industrialisation and collectivisation is described in this chapter. He also seems to have become almost insanely suspicious and jealous. The purges of 1934–35 shocked many Russians. Stalin's own wife committed suicide in 1932 following a purge at Moscow University, where she was a student.

When Germany attacked the USSR in 1941, Stalin used the same ruthlessness to defend his country. Any policy was followed which would help the war effort: even the Russian Orthodox religion, suppressed since 1917, was encouraged. Stalin showed personal bravery in staying in Moscow, within earshot of the German guns. The victory in 1945 was, like everything else, put down to the personal leadership of Stalin by the Soviet propaganda machine.

In the years after the war, Stalin built up the USSR as a superpower, in opposition to the USA. Eastern Europe became the USSR's new empire of satellites. Fear and suspicion of the West brought the hostility of the Cold War.

Inside the USSR, the long, slow task of rebuilding the country after the war began. There were more Five-Year Plans and the same hard work and dull, unrewarding life of toil. Just before he died in 1953, Stalin seemed about to launch another purge, this time aimed especially at Jews.

Stalin ruled the USSR for 25 years. They were years of unbelievable change for the USSR; they were also years when the USSR was Stalin's own personal empire.

ASSESSMENT

Describe, explain and analyse

1 **a**) Describe the state of Russian agriculture in 1928. You should include a description of different kinds of peasants, farming methods and the effects of NEP.

b) Why did Stalin want to modernise Russian agriculture?

c) Why were his plans opposed by many peasants? Were their fears justified?

2 **a**) Why did Stalin introduce Five-Year Plans?

b) Describe how the Five-Year Plans were intended to work.

c) Do you agree that they were more successful for industry than for agriculture?

3 **a**) Explain how Stalin made himself dictator of the USSR. Your answer could include descriptions of some of the following:

- Control of the Communist Party.
- Labour camps.
- Purges.
- Propaganda.
- Personality cult.

b) Which aspect of his dictatorship would affect ordinary Russians the most?

Evidence and interpretations

Read these four interpretations of Stalin's Five-Year Plans:

1 Russians don't like factory discipline so Stalin's ruthless policies were necessary.

2 The purges and putting 8 million people in labour camps seriously weakened Russia's industrial effort.

3 'People began to believe in excessive centralisation.' 'The policy for the kulaks swept away a considerable part of the middle peasantry. All this had a dire effect on the country's development.' Mikhail Gorbachev, 1987.

4 Stalin was an evil and cruel tyrant.

a What were Stalin's 'ruthless policies' (no.1)?

b What were the purges and the labour camps (no.2)?

c Explain Gorbachev's comments about central control and the kulaks (no.3).

d What information from this chapter would you use to support no.4?

e Compare numbers 1 and 2. Use what you have found out in this chapter to decide which do you think is more correct.

f Compare numbers 1 and 3. Use what you have found out in this chapter to decide which you think is more correct.

g What is your final judgement on Stalin?

9: Britain between the wars

Most countries went through difficult times in the years between the First and Second World Wars. Many of these difficulties were caused by economic problems such as the Depression, unemployment and inflation. In some countries – Germany, Italy, Russia and the USA, for example – the crisis brought out new people with fresh ideas and adventurous policies. Britain too had economic problems, but the politicians in power during these years were mild, cautious men. There were no vicious dictators in Britain, but there was no New Deal, as in the USA, either (see Chapter 10). On the other hand, these were peaceful years in Britain. In contrast to Germany, for example, where hundreds died in street fights, the British generally accepted their problems. Although there were moments when soldiers appeared on British streets, the policies of extremists had little appeal to ordinary people.

POST-WAR ECONOMIC PROBLEMS

For a year or two after the First World War, there was a brief improvement in the economy. Soldiers left the army and found jobs. Industry supplied the luxury goods which people had not had during the war. However, this little boom soon ended. From 1920 until the Second World War, at least one million, and often more, were unemployed in Britain. Many people only had a few months' work in 19 years.

The main recession was felt in Britain's older industries – coal, steel, textiles, shipbuilding and also in farming. One of the problems was that these industries had been established in the 19th century. Now, factories and machines were beginning to get out of date. Countries with new factories and machines could make more goods more cheaply. Even before the war, Britain's older industries had begun to meet serious competition from other countries. To make matters worse, customers had had to look to other countries for supplies during the war. Not all of them turned back to Britain afterwards.

Return to the Gold Standard

In 1925 Britain 'returned to the Gold Standard'. This means that the pound was backed by gold as it had been before the war. This made the pound a very good, stable currency to buy. The rate of exchange went up against foreign currencies, but this made the price of exports very high. Many foreign customers could no longer afford to buy British products. They could buy cheaper coal from Eastern Europe, cheaper steel from Germany, Sweden or the USA, cheaper textiles from the Far East, cheaper ships from Norway or Japan and cheaper corn from Canada or the USA.

POST-WAR PRICES

Welfare and housing

The Liberal Party had made a start on setting up a welfare state before the First World War. Many people had hoped to continue these policies after the war. Promises were made to tackle the great problem of bad housing – the slums which blighted every British city. In 1918 Lloyd George promised returning soldiers 'a country fit for heroes to live in'. This became the slogan 'homes for heroes'. Addison's Act, 1919, made local government responsible for housing needs in their area. A right to decent housing was an important principle, but only 170,000 houses were built under this Act.

Other improvements in health, education and welfare did not come until after the Second World War. Economic crisis was one reason but over-cautious and unimaginative politicians were also to blame.

The decline of the Liberals

The Liberal Party had been the main ruling party for eight years before the First World War. However, in 1916 David Lloyd George, a leading Liberal, split from the rest of the party because he disagreed with the way the government was running the war. He formed a coalition with the Conservatives. He was Prime Minister, at the head of a small, vigorous War Cabinet. He wanted to continue this coalition after the war and won the 1918 election easily. Most of his supporters, however, were Conservatives. The opposition groups were the Irish (who refused to come to Westminster), the Labour Party and the rest of the Liberals. For the next few years, Labour gradually grew stronger. They became the main opposition party, replacing the Liberals. Labour, with its close links with the trade unions and its bases during these years in industrial cities, seemed the obvious voice for working people. However, while Labour was growing and Liberalism declining, the governments remained mainly Conservative, or Conservative-dominated coalitions.

In 1922, the Conservatives refused to back Lloyd George any longer. A purely Conservative government was formed, and in 1923 Stanley Baldwin became its leader. He was Prime Minister for the years 1923–1924, 1924–1929 and 1935–1937. Baldwin liked to give the impression of being a solid country farmer, but he was in fact a clever man, with business experience.

The first Labour government

After the 1924 election, the Conservatives were the biggest single Party, but held fewer seats than Labour and Liberals combined. The King asked Ramsay MacDonald, the Labour leader, to become Prime Minister of the first-ever Labour government. However, MacDonald had to rely on Liberal support to stay in power. Many people were worried at the idea of a Labour government, but Ramsay MacDonald was far from being a 'Red Revolutionary'. His cabinet included an engine-driver, a steelworker and a millworker, though its members wore top-hats for official occasions. They worked hard to make Labour appear a 'respectable' party.

MacDonald could only pass laws which the Liberals would agree to. The most important was Wheatley's Housing Act, 1924, which gave loans to local councils to build cheap, good houses to rent. Nearly a million council houses were built under this act by 1930. They were well-built 'cottage'-style houses, often with good-sized gardens, like those shown in Source 1B.

❓ Questions

a What important principle did Addison's Act, 1919, set up?

b List as many reasons as you can why the houses in Source 1B are an improvement on those shown in Source 1A.

▼ SOURCE 1A
Slum housing in Wigan

SOURCE 1B
New estate on Becontree, Essex, 1923

In the autumn of 1924, the Liberals refused to back MacDonald any longer. An election was then called, and Baldwin was returned as Conservative Prime Minister. His Minister of Health, Neville Chamberlain, improved pensions for widows and the old, and reorganised the system of unemployment benefit. During this time, however, the country was plunged into the events which became known as the General Strike.

THE GENERAL STRIKE 1926

Why was there a General Strike?

The coal industry was typical of Britain's older industries. In the nineteenth century, coal was the basis of Britain's industrial strength and was exported abroad on a large scale. During the First World War, the mines had been taken away from their private owners and run by the government. Wages were good, and the miners' unions wanted this government control to continue. In 1921, however, the mines were handed back to their private owners. Many pits were old and expensive to run and their machinery was out-dated. The depression in British industry reduced demand for coal at home. Coal prices fell dramatically. In the summer of 1920 coal was worth £5.75 per ton. By the spring of 1921 it was worth £1.20 per ton. Even so, because of the return to the Gold

Standard the price of coal was still too high for foreign buyers. Private owners wanted a profit from their mines. The only way they felt they could do this with prices falling and markets shrinking was to cut wages.

Both mine owners and miners were often hard, obstinate men. One owner, the Duke of Northumberland, had an income of £52,000 a year from mining. However, he did not think that the bad conditions of miners' cottages which he owned were his fault. The hard conditions in mining made the miners tough and unwilling to compromise.

SOURCE 2
Each man is shifting coal at a speed approaching two tons an hour . . . When I am digging in my garden, if I shift two tons of earth in an afternoon, I feel that I have earned my tea. But earth is tractable stuff compared with coal and I don't have to work kneeling down, a thousand feet underground, in suffocating heat and swallowing coal dust with every breath I take; nor do I have to walk a mile, bent double, before I begin.

From George Orwell, *The Road to Wigan Pier*, 1937

The Triple Alliance

A popular idea among socialist trade unionists at this time was syndicalism. They believed that several Trade Unions should go on strike together to bring the country to a halt and so take over the government for working people. In the years after the Russian Revolution of 1917 this did not seem so unlikely.

The miners' union planned to increase their strength by combining with the railwaymen and the transport workers unions in a 'triple alliance'. A strike in one of these industries usually stopped work in the other two, so it seemed sensible for them to join together to increase their strength.

▸ SOURCE 3   Cartoon from *Punch*

? Questions

a How does the cartoonist show the Triple Alliance?
b What is his attitude to the three unions?

When the owners proposed wage-cuts in 1921, the miners called a strike. They asked their two allies to support them, but the other two unions felt the miners were being obstinate and refused. Miners called this Black Friday, 1921. After a long, bitter strike, they had to go back to work at the lower wages.

In 1925 prices dropped again and the owners proposed an increase in hours worked per day from seven to eight, and a reduction in pay. The triple alliance held together this time. Faced with a big strike, Baldwin granted a subsidy to keep wages up and hours down for nine months. This was called Red Friday, 1925. The government however, felt that it could not subsidise the miners for ever and prepared for a show-down. It set up the OMS (Organisation for the Maintenance of Supplies). This was a system of volunteers who would keep the country going in a crisis. The miners' leaders also prepared. They asked for the support of the TUC (Trades Union Congress), the body representing all unions. The TUC was not keen, but agreed when the mine owners announced terms of longer hours and lower wages after the subsidy ended. However, the TUC made little preparation for a General Strike by all workers. They thought the government would pay up again to prevent it happening. Baldwin, on the contrary, was ready when the subsidy ended on 1 May and made no more offers. With many TUC leaders unhappy about it, a General Strike was called for 4 May 1926.

The strike itself

A General Strike is a strike of workers from all the major industries. In 1926, in addition to the miners, the railwaymen, transport workers, builders, chemical workers, printers, engineers, gas workers and shipbuilders came out. Industry and transport came to a halt. City streets were clogged as people tried to drive to work. There were no newspapers. Many children could not get to school. Office workers slept at their offices or in hotels. The TUC had deliberately not called out health, water, sanitation or food workers. Nevertheless, between three and four million out of five and a half million trade unionists stopped work.

The OMS set to work as planned. Middle-class men and women and students drove buses and trains, unloaded ships and tried to keep things going. Sometimes they made mistakes, and sometimes they were attacked by strikers.

▸ SOURCE 4A
The engine was throbbing and presently it gave a jerk which knocked the backs of our heads against the

carriage. It did this three times and then made a start on that journey to Manchester. We got nearly as far as Harrow . . . Suddenly, there was a grinding of brakes and the whole train ran off the rails and came to a standstill. We all jumped out. Our gentleman driver alighted and raised his hat with a cheery smile. 'That's torn it!' he said. 'So sorry! Some little thing went wrong.'

Sir Philip Gibbs, *The Pageant of the Years*

SOURCE 4B

London bus with volunteer driver

Since no newspapers were printed, news was difficult to get. The BBC had just started and took the government view of the Strike. On Baldwin's instructions, Ramsay MacDonald, the Labour leader, and the Archbishop of Canterbury, who wanted peace, were both forbidden to speak. Winston Churchill set up a newspaper called *The British Gazette*, to give the government point of view, while the TUC put their point of view in their paper, *The British Worker*.

SOURCE 5A

The General Strike is . . . a direct challenge to ordered government. An effort to force upon some forty-two million British citizens the will of less than four million others. The strike is intended as a direct hold-up of the nation to ransom.

The British Gazette

SOURCE 5B

The General Council [of the TUC] does not challenge the constitution. The sole aim of the Council is to secure for the miners a decent standard of life. The Council is engaged in an industrial dispute. There is no constitutional crisis.

The British Worker

SOURCE 6A

I learnt from one of the dockers' pickets that about one hundred and fifty tons of meat had been taken overnight from one of the ships and were now being moved by this unnecessary display of force.

The men, whose normal work is to handle thousands of tons of such cargo each day, lined the streets with arms folded, smiling and chatting, waving a greeting to the soldiers.

The British Worker

SOURCE 6B

[*Newspaper Headline*] How London is Fed. Raising the Siege at the Docks.

Twenty armoured cars and one hundred food lorries. A long line of motor lorries swinging into Hyde Park during the weekend bore witness to the fact that the strikers had suffered early defeat in their attempt to starve London.

The British Gazette

SOURCE 6C
Armoured cars escorting a food convoy from the docks

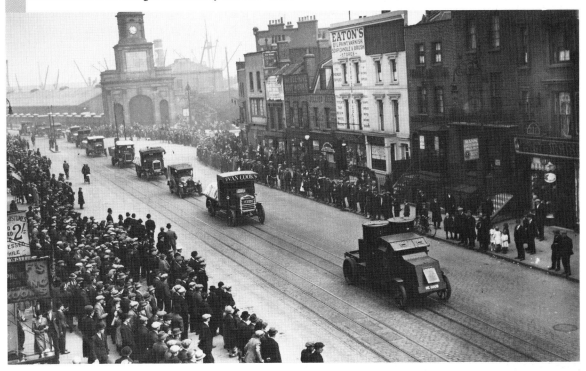

❓ Questions

a What impression of the OMS does Source 4A give?

b The volunteer driver in Source 4B has a police escort and barbed wire across the bonnet of the bus to prevent anyone getting at the engine. Does this evidence prove that the General Strike was violent?

c Explain in your own words what Sources 5A and 5B are saying about the Strike.

d Which of the two do you think gives a more accurate interpretation of what was going on in the General Strike?

e What differences are there in the descriptions of the same event given in Sources 6A and 6B?

f How far does Source 6C support either of the two accounts?

g How peaceful was the General Strike? Use only these sources to answer this question.

h What else would you want to know before you could present a reliable answer to question **g**?

i Use these sources and your own knowledge to describe the aims and methods of each side in the General Strike.

In fact, the Strike was very peaceful. No shots were fired in anger. There was some destruction: for example, the Flying Scotsman express train was derailed. One local strike committee took the following action, described in this cable: 'Found lorries labelled "FOOD" not carrying food. Put in canal. Hope correct.' As we have seen, armoured cars appeared in London. In Plymouth, strikers and police played each other at football.

The morale of the strikers was high. They felt they had solid backing for their strike, and although the country was not in chaos, they had shown their strength. The OMS could not keep things going for long. The volunteer workers and students would sooner or later have to return to their jobs and studies. The TUC leadership, however, was unhappy with the situation. They did not like being accused of attacking the constitution. After nine days, they called off the strike on the basis of some vague promises by Baldwin.

The miners fought on, alone. They stuck to their slogan of 'Not a minute on the day, not a penny off the pay'. In the end, they were driven back to work in November 1926, seven months after the General Strike. Their strike pay was not enough for their families to live on. In the face of hunger, they returned to work bitterly. Their strike had been a failure, but the defeat built up a mood of resentment which lasted through two generations.

LABOUR VICTORY

The government followed up its victory. The Trades Dispute Act 1927 made sympathetic strikes (one union striking in support of another) illegal. Many strikers returning to work were victimised by their employers. Union membership declined. Many working people turned instead to the Labour Party. In the 1929 election, Labour became the biggest single party for the first time ever. Ramsay Mac-Donald became Prime Minister, but could still be out-voted if Conservatives and Liberals combined against him.

THE GREAT DEPRESSION

Ramsay MacDonald soon had to face a major economic crisis. The Wall Street Crash, in October 1929, had brought ruin to the US economy. From 1924 onwards the USA had lent 5.7 billion dollars abroad, half of the sum to Europe. These loans were now drastically cut. The effect of this was to bring severe depression and unemployment to most industrial countries. The effect on Germany was described in Chapter 6. Britain was a trading nation and needed to sell to other countries. Its customers now had no money to spend. Exports fell from £729 million in 1929 to £389 million in 1931.

Ramsay MacDonald took Britain off the Gold Standard in 1931. This move lowered the value of the pound and made exports less expensive, but it was not enough. By 1932 there were nearly three million unemployed in Britain: one in five of the working population. Worst hit were those old industries which had been struggling for years: 34% of coal miners, 47% of steel workers and 62% of shipbuilders were unemployed.

Ramsay MacDonald's answer to this crisis was the same as a Conservative Prime Minister's: to cut public spending. He proposed cuts in the dole, in salaries of teachers, soldiers, policemen and civil servants. The Labour Party split over these proposals. Ramsay MacDonald decided to put the crisis in the country before his loyalty to the Labour Party and became Prime Minister of a National Government, a coalition with Conservatives and Liberals.

The National Government

The Labour Party felt he was putting the bankers before the people and expelled him from the Party. The National Government ruled Britain from 1931 to 1939, with opposition from a much reduced Labour Party and a few Liberals.

Under the insurance scheme at the time, an unemployed worker received fifteen weeks of unemployment pay automatically. After that, he received 'the dole'. After the 1931 cuts, this was hardly enough to live on.

◤ SOURCE 7A

I saw a man crouching over a stove in a dark room, the light of a fire touching his features as he coughed and coughed. One woman sank in a chair, her form wasted and death written more plainly on her face than I have ever seen it. Her unemployed husband stood by, trying with a tattered shawl to warm a baby three months old. He smiled proudly down at it. His teeth were rotten with decay.

Evening Standard, 1936

Living on the dole was a constant worry, and this had its effect on family life. The women had to cope with the problems of feeding and clothing their families. For men, there was a feeling of uselessness – their skills were not needed, their children were suffering, their lives were pointless.

◤ SOURCE 7B

If only he had work. Just imagine what it would be like. On the whole, my husband has worked about one year out of twelve and a half. His face was lovely when I married him, but now he's skin and bones. When I married, he was robust and he had a good job. He was earning eight to ten pounds a week. He's a left-handed ship's riveter, a craft which could be earning him a lot of money.

He fell out of work about four months after I was married, so I've hardly known what a week's wage was. Through all the struggling I've still not lost my respectability . . . We don't waste nothing. And there's no

enjoyment comes out of our money –
no pictures, no papers, no sport.
Everything's patched and mended in
our house.

Mrs Pallas, BBC Radio Interview, 1934

▼ SOURCE 7C

Unemployed man in Wigan, 1939

▼ SOURCE 7D

He was standing motionless as a
statue, cap pulled over his eyes, gaze
fixed on the pavement, hands in
pockets, shoulders hunched, the bitter
wind blowing the thin trousers tightly
against his legs.

George Orwell, *The Road to Wigan Pier*, 1937

? Questions

a What effect has living on the dole had on the men
in Sources 7A and 7B?

b What obvious signs of poverty are there in
Source 7C?

c Which is more useful for finding out about life
on the dole, Source 7C or Source 7D?

d Source 7A is from a newspaper, Source 7B is
oral evidence and Source 7D is from a writer
who visited areas with high unemployment.
What are the advantages and problems in
using each of these types of evidence?

e Use these sources and your own knowledge to
write about the effects of unemployment.

In another attempt to save money, the government
introduced a means test in 1931. This meant that
officials came round to investigate everybody who
claimed the dole to see if it should be cut. If you
had some savings, then you could not receive dole;
if your child had a part-time job, your dole was cut.
If you had some valuable item at home, it had to be
sold; if a widowed father moved in with one of his
married children, his dole would be cut.

The means test saved some money, but it was
hated because of its petty interference in people's
lives.

The Jarrow Crusade

By 1934, there was some recovery in economy
and by the mid-1930s some parts of Britain were
doing quite well. In fact unemployment remained
very patchy. In Scotland it was 18%, Northern
Ireland 23%, in Wales 28%, in the Midlands 10%
and in London 6½%.

However, in certain towns unemployment was
astronomical. Jarrow, a shipbuilding town on the
Tyne, had 80% unemployment. When the shipbuilding yards closed down, nearly all the workers
in the town lost their jobs. In 1936, 200 Jarrow
'crusaders' marched to London with a petition for
the Prime Minister.

There were many 'hunger marches' in the
1930s, but the Jarrow Crusade got the most publicity. The marchers arrived in London, and delivered
their petition asking for contracts for government
ships to be placed at the Jarrow yard. Then they
caught the train back, to find that their dole money
was cut while they were on the Crusade because
they had not been 'available for work'.

The kind of government spending the Jarrow
marchers wanted was suggested by the British
economist J. M. Keynes. Hitler and Roosevelt, in
very different ways, took up his ideas but British
politicians rejected them.

Agriculture continued to go through difficult
times. Corn prices were low, so farmers turned
to livestock instead. Unfortunately fewer workers

SOURCE 8
The Jarrow Crusade on its way to London

were needed for stock-rearing. Machines such as tractors replaced many labourers. Wages for farm workers remained low, and all these factors brought a 15% drop in the number of people employed in agriculture between the wars. This process was called 'the drift from the land'.

Economic recovery

New industries, in new areas, prospered. Electrical goods, household goods, aeroplanes, cars and chemicals all did well. In 1920, three million homes had electricity; by 1937 this had increased to nine million. Courtalds and British Celanese produced artificial fibres like rayon, celanese and tricel. Each year, at least half a million cheap cars like the Austin, Morris or Hillman were made on the assembly lines.

For workers in these factories and in the service industries (giving services to other industries or to the public, such as catering), mainly in southeast England and the Midlands, the 1930s were not too bad. Wages were steady and prices were falling. Fairly cheap houses were built – to buy, not to rent – usually semi-detached, strung out along the roads out of towns. New suburbs grew up. 2½ million private houses were built between the wars. For a small deposit and repayments of 60p a week you could own your own house.

Many people began to enjoy new pleasures. Families were smaller, and a cheap car gave a new freedom to go where one liked. Butlin's Holiday Camps opened up the idea of holidays for the family at a price many could afford. The radio was soon a necessary item in every home. Twenty

Assembly line at Cowley, 1938, for Morris cars

Mosley at a BUF rally held in the Albert Hall, 1934

million people per week went to the cinema. There were almost two Britains: the expanding, busy towns of the southeast and Midlands, with their rows of 'semis', shops full of goods and almost full employment; and the run-down towns and cities of the north, Scotland, Wales and Northern Ireland, with slums, no money for improvement and unemployment blighting the lives of a quarter, a third or even a half of the people.

Political life

In 1935, Ramsay MacDonald gave way to Baldwin, the Conservative Leader, as Prime Minister of the National Government (which was really a Conservative government in any case). When Baldwin retired in 1937, Neville Chamberlain took over as Prime Minister. A little was done for the unemployed: in 1935 the cuts made in 1931 were removed. In 1937, a system of special loans for hard-hit areas was set up. These measures were too little, too late, but after the Second World War these ideas developed further.

Through it all, the unemployed made little real protest and extremist political parties had little support. The Communist Party never had more than one Member of Parliament. Sir Oswald Mosley, a former Labour Cabinet Minister, set up a Fascist Party called the British Union of Fascists (BUF) in 1932.

? Questions
a From which country have Mosley's followers borrowed their salute?
b What is the uniform of the BUF?

The BUF gained some support, and there were battles between the Fascists and their opponents in the East End of London in 1936. Soon the wearing of uniforms was banned by the Public Order Act of 1937, and Mosley's 'private army' was disbanded. He was arrested when the war began and kept in prison until 1956. Whatever their problems, the British people rejected fascism as an option for them.

The abdication of Edward VIII

People seemed more stirred by the Abdication Crisis of 1936. In January of that year King George V died. The new King, Edward VIII, was relaxed, informal, fun-loving and unmarried. He had also shown some sympathy for the unemployed in South Wales, following a visit there. Later in 1936, he declared that he wanted to marry an American divorcee, Mrs Wallis Simpson. Baldwin and the Archbishop of Canterbury said that she would not be acceptable as Queen. Edward abdicated in order to marry her, and his brother became King George VI.

The Second World War

Chamberlain's policy of building up the armed forces from 1938 did gradually bring employment back to many areas. By 1940 the country was fighting for its life in the Second World War. Chamberlain had resigned, and in the crisis Britain turned to a man mistrusted, almost ignored, in the years of peace – Winston Churchill.

SIR WINSTON CHURCHILL 1874–1965

Sir Winston Churchill is most famous for his leadership of Britain in the Second World War. However, this period of his life came towards the end of a busy and varied career as a soldier, newspaper reporter and Member of Parliament.

Winston Spencer Churchill came from an aristocratic family. He was grandson of the 7th Duke of Marlborough and the son of Lord Randolph Churchill, a Victorian politician, and his American wife Jenny. He went to Harrow School, where he was not a clever pupil. From there, he became a soldier, training at Sandhurst and joining the 4th Hussars. As a young man, he restlessly looked for action and was bored by long, peaceful days with his regiment in India. He began to read a great deal at this time.

When Kitchener led an army into the Sudan, Churchill tried to join his forces. He was rejected, so he became a newspaper reporter attached to Kitchener's force. As a reporter, he took part in the last great cavalry charge in history, at the Battle of Omdurman in 1898. He also worked as a reporter in the Boer War. The Boers captured him, but he escaped.

After these adventures, he became Conservative MP for Oldham in 1900. He joined the Liberals in 1904 and was made President of the Board of Trade in 1908. He was Home Secretary when the first Labour Exchanges were set up in 1909. As First Lord of the Admiralty from 1911, he helped build up the British navy ready for the war.

When the First World War broke out, he tried to seek a way of breaking the deadlock of the trench warfare on the Western Front. His idea was the Gallipoli campaign (see Chapter 2). This was intended to knock the Turks out of the war, help Russia and defeat Austria-Hungary. Unfortunately it was a failure, with heavy loss of life. This disaster shadowed his reputation for years to come. He resigned and went to France to lead an infantry battalion. At the end of the war, he was made Minister of War. His efforts to help the Whites in the Russian Civil War (see Chapter 5) brought him the undying suspicion of Stalin and the Russians.

The years between the wars were not successful ones for Churchill. He lost his seat as a Liberal MP in 1922 but returned to Parliament as a Conservative in 1924. Stanley Baldwin made him Chancellor of the Exchequer from 1924 to 1929. Baldwin was clever enough to see that anything less than a big job would make Churchill difficult to handle. He had always criticised the Labour Party and was a leading opponent of the General Strike. During the strike, he used his skills as a newspaperman as editor of the government newssheet *The British Gazette*.

This opposition meant that there was no place for him in Ramsay MacDonald's National Government of 1931. As the 1930s wore on, he became a bitter critic of Hitler and of Chamberlain's appeasement policy. Again he was unpopular with the government, and he was almost on his own in these years. Most of the country was in favour of appeasement and saw Churchill and his few friends as 'war-mongers' looking for trouble.

Then came the war and Britain's early failures. In May 1940, Chamberlain resigned and King George VI asked Churchill to become Prime Minister. In a famous speech, he showed the tough, realistic determination to win, which made him famous: 'I have nothing to offer but blood, toil, tears and sweat.' He was ready to take on huge responsibilities and to take decisions. He dominated the government and the country. His brilliant speeches touched off the patriotism and courage of the British people. His sturdy figure, his cigar, his bulldog expression and his 'V' sign became the symbol of Britain's resistance to Nazism.

During the war, he met President Franklin Roosevelt and they became friends. Although he was nearly 70, he travelled to the USA, Africa and Russia. Then, in 1945, came peace and a general election. Churchill was loved, but the party he led, the Conservatives, were not, and they were defeated. He was Prime Minister again from 1951 to 1955 and retired as an MP in 1964. He died the following year, and was given a lavish state funeral.

ASSESSMENT

Describe, explain and analyse

1 **a)** Describe how Britain was affected by the General Strike.

b) Choose three reasons for the Strike from the list below and explain them:

i) Foreign coal prices.

ii) Triple Alliance.

iii) Coal-miners' attitudes.

iv) Coal-mine owners' attitudes.

v) The OMS.

c) What were the long-term reasons for the Strike?

2 Some industries did well and some did badly in Britain between the wars.

a) Which industries did well and where were they located?

b) Which industries did badly and where were they located?

c) Explain the reasons for the success of those in (**a**) and the failure of those in (**b**).

Evidence and interpretations

Britain between the wars has been called 'The Wasted Years'. They were years of terrible hardship which left a legacy of bitterness.

a Use the sources and information in this chapter to find support for these statements.

b These statements are not a complete interpretation of the inter-war years. Use the sources and information in this chapter to contradict the statements above.

Topics for discussion

1 Many countries, including Germany, Italy and Russia became dictatorships in these years. They were certainly crisis years for Britain. Why didn't Britain follow the same path?

2 People from depressed areas of Britain could have got jobs if they had moved to areas where industry was doing well. Do you think people should be expected to do this?

3 What feelings would these years leave in the minds of many British people about:

Housing; employment; the means test; coal-miners?

10: The USA between the wars

In the previous few chapters, we have seen how dictators, like Hitler and Stalin, tried to organise their countries. For many people, the years between the wars posed problems to which only dictators seemed to have the answers. One of these problems was unemployment. In 1932, one in four of the American workforce was unemployed. Could the world's largest democracy, the USA, solve this problem and still remain a democracy? Before looking at the answer, we need to study how the problem arose.

THE ROARING TWENTIES

Isolationism

The USA had been led into the First World War by President Woodrow Wilson. He had called it 'a war to end wars.' When he returned to the USA after his efforts at Versailles, he found that most Americans no longer wanted anything to do with the rest of the world. There were many reasons for this. One hundred thousand Americans had been killed, and the war itself had disrupted trade with other countries. In 1920, half the people in America had been born outside the USA, mostly in Europe. They had left their homes in Europe to start new lives in the USA. Many of these immigrants had unhappy memories of their early years. To them Europe meant poverty and harsh, sometimes cruel, government. Moreover, Communist ideas seemed to be sweeping Europe after the Russian Revolution. Many Americans were deeply opposed to Communism. They thus wanted to avoid any contact with Europe.

Woodrow Wilson hoped that the USA would play a big part in world affairs, through his League of Nations, but he found little support for it. The USA never signed the Treaty of Versailles and never joined the League of Nations. America's policy came to be called isolationism: the wish to stay out of any involvement with other countries. This policy remained unchanged until 1941.

SOURCE 1
It was like hearing the squeak of a timid fieldmouse after the thunder of battle had rolled away. Faced by the responsibilities of leadership in the world, such as had never come to any nation, America backed out of the room, frightened and stammering.

History of the American Presidential Elections,
A. Schlesinger and H. Israel

Questions
a What is the attitude of the writers to America's refusal to join the League?
b How can you tell?

Intolerance

IMMIGRATION

American hostility to foreigners did not end with isolationism. For many years America had kept an 'open door' to immigrants from all over the world. Now this policy began to change.

From 1921 the 'open door' began to close. The number of immigrants allowed into the USA was gradually cut until, by 1929, only 150,000 entry visas per year were granted – less than half the number allowed in 1921. There was also a quota system that made it easier for immigrants from western and northern Europe to enter, and discriminated against those wishing to come from southern or eastern Europe. Immigrants were allowed into the USA in proportion to the percentage of that nationality in the total population of the USA. However, in the 1920s most of the people wanting to come in were Jews from eastern Europe or Italians and Greeks from southern Europe. Americans who had come from north-western

SOURCE 2

Cartoon, 1891: Uncle Sam looks at new immigrants

Europe and had lived in the USA for several generations were known as WASPs (*W*hite, *A*nglo-*S*axon *P*rotestants). They had always held power and feared losing control to Jews and Roman Catholics.

? Questions

a   Can you tell, from the paper at Uncle Sam's feet, what sort of people were thought to be coming into the USA?

b   In what other ways does the cartoonist show hostility to immigrants?

Racism

This racist attitude was also felt against people already living in the USA. A group called the Ku Klux Klan gained strength in the 1920s. Most of its members were poor whites afraid of blacks and immigrant workers, who were willing to work for low wages. Although the Klan was started in the southern USA, its strength grew in the north and west. Covered in white sheets, with pointed hoods, Klan members attacked and terrified blacks, Jews and Roman Catholics.

Sometimes their victims were tarred and feathered, lynched or had their houses burned down. The Klan's leader was called 'The Imperial Wizard' and the group had five million members by 1925.

SOURCE 3   A Ku Klux Klan meeting

? Questions

a Suggest two reasons why the Klan members wore white hoods.

b Why do you think this ceremony was held at night?

Why was there an industrial boom?

Many Americans, however, forgot Woodrow Wilson's high ideals and got on with 'normal' life. 'Normal' life for most of them meant the business of working hard and making money. The 1920s was a boom time in the American economy. American industry, backed by huge reserves of coal, steel, and oil, and undamaged by the Great War, expanded enormously. Industrial goods such as steel, tin, glass, chemicals and machine-tools were produced on a huge scale.

Most noticeable, however, was the boom in consumer goods. Radios, telephones, gramophones, watches, cameras, washing machines, vacuum cleaners and hundreds of other items were produced in large numbers. Things which had been luxuries before the First World War were now made at a price that millions could afford.

There were slick, colourful advertisements encouraging people to 'keep up with the Joneses' and buy the latest novelty. Department stores sold these goods in every main street. Radio advertising brought the news of new products into every home.

Table 10-1   The increase in American production of consumer goods, 1920–1929

	1920	1929
Motor cars	9 million	26 million
Telephones	13 million	20 million
Radios	0.06 million	10 million

THE CAR INDUSTRY

The most striking example of these consumer industries was the car industry. In Detroit, Henry Ford set up a fully automated factory. Each worker did only one small job on the assembly line, and by 1925 Ford produced one car every ten seconds. The

▶ SOURCE 4   Street in a mid-western town: Parkville, Missouri. A painting by Gale Stockwell, 1933

average cost of a car dropped from $850 in 1908 to $290 in 1925. Most popular and famous was the Model T Ford.

The car industry took 20% of the US steel production, 80% of its rubber and 75% of its glass.

? Questions

a Describe the typical American small-town street shown in Source 4.

b What do you think this street would have looked like in 1900?

THE CINEMA INDUSTRY

People had money to spare for entertainment, and an industry grew up to provide for the newest, most popular form of entertainment: going to the cinema. During the 1920s, thousands of silent black and white films were produced. Hollywood became the base of this new industry, and soon stars such as Charlie Chaplin, Mary Pickford, Douglas Fairbanks and Rudolf Valentino became known all over the world. In the USA alone, one hundred million cinema tickets were sold every week.

GOVERNMENT POLICIES

Industry was also helped by the economic side of America's isolationist policy. Americans wanted to help their own industries and make trade difficult for foreigners. The government therefore set up high tariffs or import duties. This meant that any foreign-made item coming into the USA had an extra tax attached to it. Its price to the American public was therefore increased. In this way, American industry was protected, because their products were cheaper and sold better.

With work available for most people, trade unions declined. Some employers, like Henry Ford, would not allow a union in their factories. Union membership went down from five million in 1920 to three million in 1932.

The Presidents who were in power during the 1920s preferred to leave American business to look after itself. Woodrow Wilson was defeated in the 1920 election by Warren G. Harding. President Harding (1920–1923) was a pleasant enough man but too easy-going. He was taken advantage of by his corrupt poker-playing friends called the Ohio Gang. The scandal may have helped bring on his sudden death in 1923. He was succeeded by Calvin Coolidge (1923–1928). Coolidge had said 'the business of America is business'. He was an honest

man, but did little, and made no changes in the policies of high tariffs and government help for industry which had gone on under Harding's administration. When 'Silent Cal' as he was known, died, the American humourist, Dorothy Parker said, 'How could they tell?'

PROHIBITION

If ordinary American businesses bent the laws a little, one vast and very profitable business was completely outside the law: that of making and selling alcohol. In 1919, the US Congress passed the Eighteenth Amendment to the Constitution, declaring the manufacture and sale of alcoholic beverages illegal. This was called Prohibition.

Many Americans were very religious people and felt that alcohol was the root of social problems. Perhaps it was, but many other Americans still liked a drink. Their thirst was met by gangsters who took over the entire alcohol business. They ran illegal bars called speakeasies, imported alcohol drink ('bootleg'), or had it made secretly ('moonshine'). Gangsters like Dutch Schultz and Al Capone made millions of dollars by operating outside the law from the beginning. They settled their business rivalries in gunfights like the notorious 'St Valentine's Day Massacre' in Chicago. Prohibition not only provided opportunities for gangsters; it turned many ordinary Americans into criminals.

With plenty of money about, and plenty of new things to spend it on, many Americans enjoyed the carefree, live-for-the-moment atmosphere of the twenties. Women experienced new freedom in jobs and fashions. The music of the black bands in the speakeasies gave its name to this period: the Jazz Age.

Did everyone enjoy the boom?

When Herbert Hoover successfully stood for President in 1928, he declared: 'We in America are nearer the final triumph over poverty than ever before in the history of mankind.' Within a year, the boom was all over. America was heading into the depths of a Depression, all the worse for the contrast with the preceding years. How did this happen?

Even as Hoover spoke, the prosperity so obvious in every town and city was not enjoyed by everybody. Farmers, for example, had never shared in the 1920s boom. The use of new machinery like

SOURCE 5
Rural poverty in the USA between the wars: farmland eroded by dust storms

the combine harvester meant that they were producing food too cheaply. The prices they received at home for their farm produce were very low. Nor could farmers sell abroad: high tariffs prevented foreign countries from selling goods in the USA, so foreigners did not have dollars to buy American farm produce. Moreover, there was strong competition from other countries like Canada on the world market. Many farms did not have electricity, so it was impossible for farmers to use the new household gadgets even if they could have afforded them.

Black Americans did not share in the boom either. Many blacks from the south had moved to the cities to look for work. They joined poor whites in low-paid factory jobs, and poor people could not buy consumer goods on a large scale.

The fact was that the gap between rich and poor was very large: the top 5% of Americans earned one-third of all income. The 1920s boom was a boom in mass-produced goods, but there was a limit to how many fridges, watches, washing machines and so on families who could afford them wanted to buy. By the later 1920s, the boom was slackening off. Too many goods were being produced for the home market to absorb, and it was not possible to switch to selling abroad. Foreign countries could not buy American goods because

they lacked dollars. Also, many countries protected their own industries with high tariffs as the Americans did.

THE WALL STREET CRASH

The end eventually came in 1929 with the Wall Street Crash. Wall Street in New York City is the financial centre of the USA, where shares are bought and sold.

Imagine you want to start a company. You need capital (money). You may not have enough yourself, so you sell shares in your new company in order to provide money to set it up. For their shares, the investors get two benefits if you do well: first, you pay the shareholders interest – a dividend – from your profits; second, because other people might want shares in your company if it is doing well, they might offer those who have shares more money than they paid for their shares to begin with.

In the 1920s, dividends went up and share prices went up because so many people wanted to buy. If you had bought shares, at whatever price, you could still sell six months or a year later at a higher price. Soon people did not take much notice what company they were buying shares in. Some companies did not actually make anything.

They made their profits by simply buying and selling shares. Dividends in the 1920s went up, overall, by 65%. Wages, in contrast, rose by only 5%.

By 1929, it was clear that American industry was making goods faster than it could sell them and that profits were falling. Cautious people began to sell shares. The panic spread: more and more people realised that their shares were worth a lot only if someone was willing to pay for them. They began to turn their shares into cash. On 24 October 1929, thirteen million shares were sold on the Wall Street Stock Exchange, and prices of shares suddenly fell.

Once the rush to sell shares began the situation went from bad to worse. Many Americans had borrowed money to buy shares, hoping to pay back their loans when their shares rose in price. When shares fell, they could not pay back the loans: they were financially ruined. American banks are often small and independent. If enough customers could not pay back their loans, the bank itself could go bankrupt. If this happened, ordinary people who had savings in the bank lost their savings. In this way, the Wall Street Crash affected all sections of the population all over the country.

▼ SOURCE 6A
Unemployed workers in New York queuing for free bread, 1930

THE GREAT DEPRESSION

The Wall Street Crash soon affected industry. As production declined, unemployment rose and money became scarce.

Table 10-2 The Downward Trend in America

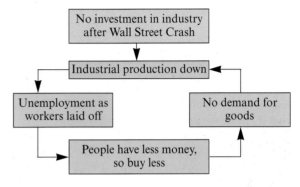

Table 10-3   The rise in unemployment in America, 1920 to 1932

Year	Unemployed (in millions)	Percentage of workforce
1920	1.6	3%
1930	4.3	9%
1931	8.0	16%
1932	12.0	24%

In some cities, the figures were much worse than this. In 1931 in Chicago, 40% of the workers were unemployed. Unemployment among black workers was as high as 70% in some areas.

By 1932, industrial output was down by 40%, wages were down by 60%, farm production was down by 70%. As factories closed, workers found themselves unable to pay rent or to repay mortgages, or even to buy food. In the 1920s, governments had done little to look after the poor and unemployed. Now their number had increased dramatically and there was no system to cope with the results of unemployment: no dole, no social security. The unemployed workers had to rely on charity from the churches and relief organisations.

▶ **SOURCE 6B**

He drove his old car into a town. He scoured the farms for work. Where can we sleep the night? Well, there's a Hooverville on the edge of the river.

He drove his old car to Hooverville. He never asked again for there was a Hooverville on the edge of every town.

The rag-town lay close to water. The houses were tents, weed-thatched enclosures, paper houses, a great junk pile. The man put up his own tent as near to water as he could get. Or if he had no tent he went to the city dump and brought back cartons and built a house of corrugated paper. When the rains came the house melted and washed away.

He scoured the countryside for work, and the little money he had went for petrol to look for work.

John Steinbeck, *The Grapes of Wrath*, 1939

? Questions

a What does Source 6A tell you about the number of people unemployed in New York?
b What was a Hooverville (Source 6B)?
c Whom do you think they were named after?
d How can you tell from Sources 6A and 6B that the USA had no welfare state?
e Compare the statistics (Table 10-3), the photograph (Source 6A) and the extract from a novel (Source 6B). Which is the most accurate? Which is the most useful?

Cities seemed to change overnight. The streets so recently full of life were now filled with aimless people, begging or selling small items. In parks, families who had been thrown out of their homes built shacks of cardboard, corrugated iron, packing cases and other junk. Many city people moved to the countryside.

Depression in agriculture

In the country, however, things were worse. With so many people unemployed, farmers could not get good prices for their produce. They had not benefited from the boom in the 1920s so they had very little savings. Banks still demanded mortgage payments, and many farmers, with falling incomes, could not pay them. They had to sell up and move on. In parts of the farmlands of the west a drought occurred. This, combined with bad farming methods, turned the land into what was called the 'Dust Bowl'. Millions of acres of dried-out topsoil simply blew away in dust storms. Hundreds of small farmers packed up and went to California to find work as farm labourers. Poor black farmers from the south moved north to hunt for what little work there was in the cities.

Opposition

Considering the numbers of people involved and the depth of their poverty, there was surprisingly little violence. In Detroit, car workers fought with Henry Ford's police because they were locked out of the factory when there was no work. In Washington, ex-servicemen marched to the White House to claim their ex-servicemen's 'bonus' – a lump sum payable in 1945. The 'Bonus army' camped in the city until President Hoover sent soldiers to remove them and fighting broke out.

Americans did not know whom to blame for their troubles. In the 1920s they had been led to believe that anyone who worked hard could do well. If anyone did not succeed it was their own fault, because of their own laziness. Unemployment benefit did not exist. Most people felt that no one deserved to be paid if they had done no work. Now that the dream had been shattered, Americans felt ashamed, not angry.

President Hoover believed that American business had produced this boom because it had been left alone by the government. He now believed that business would also produce the solution to the Depression if it were left alone.

▼ SOURCE 7A
Roosevelt at the Hollywood Bowl, 1932

During 1930 and 1931 Hoover did little to help as things grew worse and worse. In the 1932 Presidential election, he was opposed by a man with a very different solution to these problems.

FRANKLIN D. ROOSEVELT AND THE NEW DEAL

The Democratic candidate who stood against Hoover was Franklin D. Roosevelt. He was from the rich upper classes of America, but he and his wife, Eleanor, had a real sympathy for the poor of the USA.

In 1921, he had contracted polio. He fought his way back to health, but remained unable to walk or stand without help for the rest of his life. This is why photographs usually only show his head and shoulders. In his 1932 campaign, he promised action instead of words.

▼ SOURCE 7B
I pledge you, I pledge myself, to a New Deal for the American people. This is more than a political campaign; it is a call to arms. Give me your help, not to win votes alone, but to win in this crusade to restore America.

I am waging war against . . .
Destruction, Delay, Deceit and Despair .

. . With confidence we accept the promise of a New Deal.

Franklin D. Roosevelt, speaking in Chicago, July 1932

❓ Questions
a What does Roosevelt promise the American people?
b How does he describe Hoover's faults?
c Describe in your own words the mood of the speech quoted in Source 7B.

Roosevelt's phrase, 'a New Deal', caught the imagination of the American people. He won the election and was President until his death in 1945. The events of the New Deal were the most inspiring response to the 1930s Depression made by any democratic country.

The New Deal

FDR, as he was called, did not come to the White House with a fixed plan. He gathered around him men and women with fresh ideas and gave them encouragement. Sometimes the new ideas worked, sometimes they did not; sometimes, differing ideas clashed and cancelled one another out, but at least, after Hoover, there was now excitement and action. Through all the ups and downs of the New Deal, FDR kept to three ideas: to help those people hard hit by the Depression, to revive

American business and to build a better America. Try to see which of these three ideas is uppermost in each of his many acts as we look at FDR's whirlwind First Hundred Days.

In the first week, he closed all the banks and had them investigated. Those which were sound were allowed to re-open. This meant that people would have confidence in them. In this same week, he cut salaries of civil servants and ended Prohibition.

AGRICULTURAL ADJUSTMENT ACT

Agriculture was helped by the Agricultural Adjustment Act, the AAA. Farmers had been over-producing, with the result that prices fell and were too low for them to make a proper living. The AAA set up a quota system: each farmer was to produce only a certain amount. This limit on supply pushed up the price at which they could sell. Any loss was made up by a government subsidy. Government money was used to help farmers who were having difficulty making the mortgage payments on their farms. An effort was made to bring electricity to farms: only one in ten farms had electricity in 1932, but by 1940 the figure was four in ten.

NATIONAL INDUSTRIAL RECOVERY ACT

Industry was covered by the National Industrial Recovery Act, the NIRA. This Act had many sections, but one of the most important was the National Recovery Administration, the NRA, which encouraged workers and employers to get together to work out a code of fair conditions: minimum wages, maximum hours and standards were agreed. Goods made under the codes were sold with a 'Blue Eagle' tag: buyers could tell they had been made to a good standard under agreed conditions.

HOME OWNERS LOAN CORPORATION

Householders were helped by the Home Owners Loan Corporation, HOLC. The government took over people's mortgages, and lent money at specially low interest rates to help people over the crisis period, in order that they would not have to leave their homes.

One new idea which FDR was prepared to try was to increase government spending – to 'spend his way out of trouble', as it was said. The English economist J. M. Keynes had suggested this: the idea was that in times of Depression, government should spend money to get the economy going again. (Compare the table below with Table 10-2 on page 95.)

Table 10-4 The effects of government spending

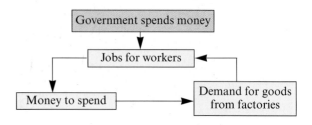

PUBLIC WORKS ADMINISTRATION

There were several examples of this policy of government spending in the New Deal. Another section of the NIRA set up the Public Works Administration, the PWA. By 1938 the PWA spent more than 1,000 million dollars on all sorts of projects: airports, hospitals, city halls, bridges, harbours and battleships. Another organisation, the Works Progress Administration, the WPA, organised schemes on a smaller scale. By 1938, it had spent 1,400 million dollars on schools, libraries and roads. It also gave work to writers, artists, photographers, actors and historians, and paid them to make improvements to life in local towns.

FEDERAL EMERGENCY RELIEF ADMINISTRATION

The Federal Emergency Relief Administration, the FERA, was founded to give quick relief where it was needed most. Millions of dollars were spent on providing soup kitchens, nursery schools for the children of the poor and schemes to provide employment.

CIVILIAN CONSERVATION CORPS

Roosevelt was especially worried by the problem of unemployment among young people. He set up the Civilian Conservation Corps, the CCC, in which young men could work for several months in the American countryside. They helped in the national parks, worked in forests, tidied up rivers and lakes. In the end, two and a half million young men took part in this scheme.

TENNESSEE VALLEY AUTHORITY

One area of the USA received special attention. The Tennessee River valley had a number of

SOURCE 8
A new dam being built in the Tennessee Valley

problems: erosion, flooding, lack of electric power and extreme poverty. The task of putting things right was too big for a single state to cope with. Roosevelt therefore set up the Tennessee Valley Authority, the TVA, and a number of dams were built on the Tennessee River. These had several effects: they could be used to prevent flooding; lakes formed allowed the river to be used for navigation for 630 miles; and the water could be used to provide hydroelectric power. In 1933, only 3% of farms in the TVA area had electricity. By 1953, 93% of them had it installed. New industries such as aluminium smelting, fertiliser production, paper and flour milling could be started up. The water could also be used to irrigate dry areas. Gradually, new farming methods were introduced to combat erosion. The lakes provided a new holiday area. In this way the TVA improved the lives of millions of people.

❓ Questions

a What different workers' skills would be needed on this site?

b Explain the long-term effects that this kind of building scheme could have.

SOCIAL SECURITY ACT

In 1935, the Social Security Act was passed. This set up pension schemes for old people, widows and disabled people. An unemployed insurance scheme was also set up, although not all workers were eligible at first. This Act turned out to be one of FDR's most lasting achievements.

The New Deal under attack

By 1935, however, both FDR and the New Deal were running into criticism. For some people, change did not come quickly enough. Huey Long, from Louisiana, wanted to attack the wealthy and to set up a national minimum wage. Father Charles E. Coughlin, a popular radio speaker at first supported the New Deal, then later proposed that America should adopt a form of fascism. He made speeches attacking Jews and trade unions.

Dr Francis Townsend put forward a plan for

retirement at 60 to give more job opportunities for young people. He was supported by many.

For other people, change had come too fast: government spending, higher taxes and increased trade union membership were attacked by conservatives. Attack from another direction came from the American Supreme Court. This Court, made up of nine judges, had the right to decide if any new law was in line with the Constitution of the USA or not. In 1935, they declared the NIRA unconstitutional, and all the work under the Act had to stop. This struck at the heart of the New Deal. Roosevelt knew that any more such decisions would wreck it.

None the less, FDR himself was popular. One of the reasons for this was his series of 'Fireside Chats', which he broadcast over the radio. He had the ability to talk to ordinary Americans as if they were alone together. He received more than five thousand letters a day. Here is one of them:

▼ SOURCE 9A

Dear Mr President,
This is just to tell you that everything is alright now. The man you sent found our house alright and we went down to the bank with him and the mortgage can go on for a while longer. You remember I wrote you about losing the furniture too. Well, your man got it back for us. I never heard of a President like you.

Letter to the White House

FDR continued the fight for the New Deal in the 1936 election.

▼ SOURCE 9B

Of course we will continue to improve working conditions for the workers of America . . . Of course we will continue to work for cheap electricity in our homes and on farms . . . Of course we will continue our efforts on behalf of the farmers of America . . . Of course we will continue our efforts for young men and women, for crippled, blind, unemployed, aged . . . Of course we will continue to protect the consumer.

F. D. Roosevelt, 1936

❓ Questions

a Which New Deal Act helped the person in Source 9A?
b Which New Deal Acts does FDR refer to in Source 9B?
c What is FDR's mood in the speech in Source 9B?

The later New Deal

FDR won the election of 1936 with a huge majority. As he said, 'Everyone is against the New Deal except the voters.' However, the next stage of the New Deal was more controversial. Roosevelt was annoyed by the decision of what he called the 'nine old men' of the Supreme Court in declaring the NIRA unconstitutional. He proposed to increase the size of the Supreme Court by putting in his own men to out-vote the nine. This produced an outcry, even from his supporters. He was forced to withdraw his proposal.

In 1937, despite all efforts of the New Deal, unemployment rose again, from under eight million in 1936 to over ten million. What more could he do? He could not spend even more: already 20% of Americans were working for the WPA. American businessmen were already annoyed enough. The Wagner Act of 1935 gave every worker the right to join a trade union. The AAA annoyed other people: to keep up prices, crops were ploughed into the ground and animals killed. Farmers from the Dust Bowl drifting to California found wages at poverty level. As the 1930s ended, the problems of the USA were far from solved. When FDR led his country into the war in 1941, there was still six million unemployed.

Was the New Deal a failure?

Roosevelt was a practical man, not a brilliant thinker. His answers to different problems could lead to conflicts. For example, higher food prices helped farmers but hit the poor. Cutting public spending to balance the budget led to more unemployment. Blue Eagle codes might protect the consumer, but they made business less profitable. For some people, he did not go far enough: unemployment remained high, poverty was still common, big businesses were still powerful. The TVA was like a democratic version of Stalin's plans, but it only covered one small part of the USA. No attempt was made to extend it to the whole country.

When Roosevelt opened a dam in the TVA in 1940, he said, 'These fine changes we have seen have not come by compulsion . . . No farmer was forced to join this conservation movement . . . No workman was compelled to labour here . . . This is a demonstration of what democracy can do.' The faults of the New Deal are the faults of democracy; its faults are certainly not as vicious as the faults of Hitler's or Stalin's policies. The New Deal showed that democracy was not powerless in the fact of great problems.

Roosevelt and the New Deal bought huge changes in the USA. The federal (central) government of the USA had been allowed to fall into disuse by the Presidents of the 1920s. Business could look after itself in a boom, but it did not look after the people in a Depression. FDR gave the federal government a job to do: to look after the weaker members of society – the old, the ill, the unemployed, the poor – and to build a better country. That was a vision of their country which many young Americans could accept, and after the war those who had been young New Dealers were to try again to make FDR's vision a reality. For all its faults, the USA is an idealistic country: the New Deal restored Americans' faith in their ideal of democracy.

FRANKLIN DELANO ROOSEVELT 1892–1945

F. D. Roosevelt was born into a rich New York family. The early part of his life was like that of any young man of his background. He went to Groton, a private school for the sons of wealthy families. After Harvard University, where he

studied history and government, he began to work as a lawyer. In 1905, he married Eleanor Roosevelt, a distant relative. She had strong opinions of her own and shared his concern for the lives of ordinary people.

In 1910, Roosevelt entered politics as a Senator in New York. He was a supporter of Woodrow Wilson and in 1913 was made Assistant Secretary for the Navy. In 1920, he was a Vice-Presidential candidate.

Success in politics had come very easily to him, but in 1921, disaster struck. He contracted polio and was told he would lose the use of his legs and probably his arms as well. For months he fought the illness and swam and exercised at Warm Springs, Georgia. By 1924, he could walk a little again and he had regained the use of his back and arms. Most noticeably, however, his outlook changed. Forced to lie still for hours on end, he began to read widely and develop his ideas. He kept his liveliness and humour, but became more understanding of those who had suffered.

In 1924 Roosevelt returned to politics, and in 1928 was persuaded to stand as Governor of New York. He was unsure if he should stand, but, as Al Smith, the retiring Governor, said: 'We don't elect a governor for his ability to do a double back flip.' Soon after his election came the Wall Street Crash. He insisted that governments ought to do something for those in need. A sum of $20 million was voted to be spent on schemes to provide work. At this time, President Hoover was doing nothing to deal with the effects of the Depression. The actions of the Governor of New York attracted a lot of interest. In 1932, he was chosen to stand for President against Hoover and won easily. It was in this campaign that he promised a 'New Deal'.

Roosevelt's confidence and his obvious belief that things could be improved inspired millions. He was hated by many Republicans, who called him a dictator and a madman. However, he had the support of ordinary American people. The successes of the New Deal are obvious. Despite its failures, he was re-elected President in 1936, 1940 and 1944.

By 1936 the actions of Hitler were worrying him. He hated all Hitler stood for. He was also worried by the Japanese, who were threatening the stability of the Pacific and the Far East.

As early as 1937 he warned his people that the USA would not be able to steer clear of a major war if it broke out. However, most Americans were still isolationists. Congress passed a series of Neutrality Acts. They forbade any trade, even in food, with a country at war. By this means they hoped to avoid getting dragged into war by the U-boat issue.

When war came and Hitler overran Europe, Roosevelt sent help to Britain. His victory in the 1940 Presidential election showed that most Americans agreed with this. The programme of Lend-Lease was started, by which Britain received guns, planes and ships to help fight the war. Roosevelt met Churchill in 1941, and they got on well. Together, they drew up the Atlantic Charter (see Chapter 20). This outlined their hopes for a better world after the war. The protests of the isolationists in the USA were silenced by Pearl Harbor (see Chapter 14), December 1941.

FDR was as inspiring a wartime leader as he had been in peace. He met Stalin in 1943 and 1945 and felt that he got on well with him. Perhaps if FDR had lived longer relations between the USSR and the USA would not have turned so sour after the war. However, in 1945, worn out after more than twelve years as President, he died just before the war came to an end.

ASSESSMENT

Describe, explain and analyse

1   **a**) What was the Wall Street Crash?

b) Explain why it affected the whole American economy.

c) Describe the effects of the Great Depression on: workers in cities; farmers; Black Americans.

2   This chapter says the New Deal had three aims:

i) To help people hit by Depression and unemployment.

ii) To revive American business.

iii) To improve the country.

a) Choose four of the New Deal 'alphabet agencies'. In each case, describe their work and explain how far it met each of the three aims.

b) How far did the New Deal succeed in each of its three aims?

Evidence and interpretations

▼ SOURCE A
Anyone willing to get up early enough can look out of the window and see thousands of workers' cars scooting down the roads to their factory or workplace. Even ten years ago this great mass of labour had to live just around the corner in a hovel next to the factory or hang on a bus at six o'clock in the morning.

from the *New York Herald Tribune* (newspaper), October, 1929

▼ SOURCE B
We in America today are nearer to the final triumph over poverty than ever before in the history of any land. The poorhouse is vanishing from among us.

Herbert Hoover, speaking in 1928

a   What does the *New York Herald Tribune* (Source A) use as a sign that all Americans were better off?

b   In what ways do these two sources agree with each other?

c   Was Hoover's interpretation of the 'Roaring Twenties' in Source B true at the time he was speaking? Explain your answer.

d   What signs of the real situation in the USA could the *New York Herald Tribune* have looked at?

e   What do these two sources tell us about the attitudes of many Americans at that time?

11: The League of Nations

While the heavy guns of the First World War were still booming many people were already thinking of ways to prevent war. They looked at the outbreak of war in 1914. It had started with a dispute between Serbia and Austria-Hungary which could not be settled except by war. How could they stop this happening again? The best idea seemed to be for all the countries in the world to join together in an organisation to keep the peace. Together, they would find a peaceful solution to all disputes. This organisation was to be called the League of Nations.

SETTING UP THE LEAGUE

The man who did most to get the League of Nations started was President Woodrow Wilson of the USA. Near the end of the First World War he presented his 'Fourteen Points' as a basis for a better world in the future. Point Fourteen was a plan to set up the League of Nations, to ensure peace forever (see page 28).

Wilson had to give way to Clemenceau and Lloyd George at Versailles on a number of points, but he never gave way on the idea of the League. The agreement to join the League was written into the Treaties of 1919. It was an optimistic and noble ideal.

The League was based at Geneva, in neutral Switzerland. It was made up of two main parts: an Assembly and a Council. The Assembly was like a parliament: each country had one vote. There were 42 member countries at the start. They met once a year, and any decision had to have their unanimous support. The Council met more often and could take decisions on a majority vote. The Great Powers (Britain, France, Italy, Japan) were permanent members of the Council. They were joined by a number of other countries in rotation (four at first, later nine).

Apart from the Assembly and Council, the Court of International Justice was set up at the Hague in the Netherlands. Its work was to settle legal disputes between countries.

Aims of the League

The aims of the League were:

1. to deal with disputes among nations;
2. to prevent war;
3. to protect the independence of countries and safeguard their borders;
4. to encourage each country to reduce its armaments.

Woodrow Wilson did not want the League to become, as he said, just a debating society. It would need to be able to apply some kind of sanctions or punishments to make its decisions work. One reason most people obey the law is because they are afraid of sanctions of one kind or another: fines, the disapproval of their neighbours, imprisonment and so on.

It is much more difficult to force a country to obey international law. Some countries, like some people, don't care.

Purpose of the League

Article 10 of the Covenant of the League of Nations set out the main purpose of the League. 'The members of the League undertake to preserve against external aggression the territory and existing independence of all members of the League. In case of threat of danger, the Council shall advise upon the means by which this obligation shall be fulfilled.'

Other articles went on to lay down three ways in which the League could try to make the decisions of the Assembly and Council effective. First, it could condemn a country and express disapproval of its actions. Second, it could impose economic sanctions upon a country: in other words, it could cut off supplies of raw materials and other goods. Third, if nothing else worked, it could use military force.

However, the League could work properly only when all the Great Powers wholeheartedly backed its actions.

Membership

Unfortunately, several of the Great Powers did not become members of the League in 1919. The most serious blow of all to those who supported the League was the refusal of the USA to become a member. By 1918, the USA was again wary of being involved in world affairs. One hundred thousand American soldiers had been killed in the war, and the idealistic feelings of 1917 had faded away. The Americans were determined to concentrate on problems at home and ignore what went on in the rest of the world. As the Senate refused to sign the Treaty of Versailles, the Americans never joined the League.

Russia was another country which did not become a member of the League in 1919. The Russian government, Communist since the Revolution of 1917, had set up an organisation called Comintern. Its purpose was to encourage Communist revolution all over the world. The Russians

would hardly therefore be allowed to join an organisation such as the League. They were not to become members until 1934. Finally, Germany was not allowed to join when the League was first set up, and did not become a member until 1926.

The USA, Russia and Germany were therefore out of the League. Only Britain and France were left to bear the burden of running the League with the help of two weaker powers, Italy and Japan. As we have seen, the main aim of the League was to keep the peace through collective security. If any member of the League was attacked, the whole League would come to their rescue and restrain the aggressor by economic or military sanctions. With the USA out of the League and Russia and Germany excluded, everything depended on whether Britain and France were ready to provide the muscle for the League to operate.

Table 11-1   Membership of the League of Nations

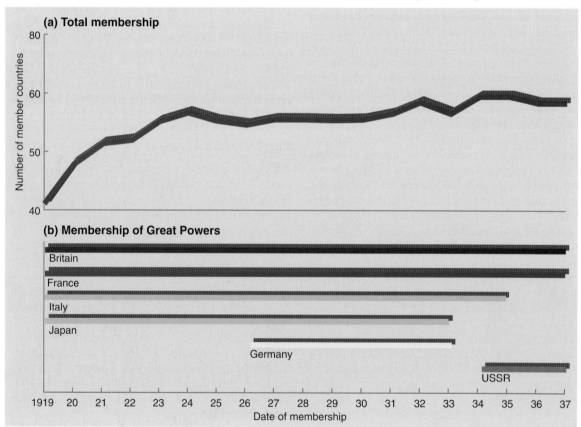

The attitudes of Britain and France

A great number of people in Britain supported the League, remembering the horrors of the 1914–1918 war. League of Nations Societies were founded in a number of towns. Rallies and League of Nations Days were held. However, the Conservative government and the military chiefs were less enthusiastic. The British had a vast empire to look after. Did they really want to step into every squabble in Europe and the rest of the world?

Moreover, the League was supposed to uphold all the terms of the Treaty of Versailles. But quite soon after 1919, Britain began to have second thoughts about one or two clauses in the treaty. Was it right to make Germany pay such heavy reparations? Could the 1919 borders never be changed? These doubts made some British politicians even cooler towards the League.

To the French, there was still only one enemy: Germany. If the League would help protect them against Germany, they were in favour of it. If it would not, they would have to make their own arrangements. Thus there were sometimes differences between what the League wanted and what Britain or France wanted.

SOURCE 1A
Belgian refugees fleeing from Brussels, 1914

The agencies

A wide range of agencies was set up by the League in order to deal with the many problems which beset both nations and individuals in the 20th century. Many could only be dealt with by international action.

The International Labour Organisation worked on suggestions for proper hours and conditions for workers all over the world. It collected a vast amount of information and tried hard to persuade countries to accept its suggestions. The Mandates Commission looked after the people in the mandated countries (see Chapter 3, page 30) set up by the Treaty of Versailles. It made sure that the power in charge of each Mandate, usually Britain or France, acted for the benefit of the people who lived in them.

Work was done by other agencies on famine relief, health, on the prevention of slavery and on stopping the international drugs trade. Efforts were made to make road, rail and shipping signals the same all over the world and to encourage countries to work together over their postal services, telegraph and radio communications.

The war had also left the League with the enormous problem of 400,000 prisoners of war and many thousands of homeless refugees. These had to be returned to their own countries if possible.

SOURCE 1B   German prisoners of war, France, 1916

? Questions

a   Why do you think the people in Source 1A were fleeing from Brussels?

b   Why would they and the prisoners in Source 1B be an international problem after the war?

The Norwegian explorer, Fridtjof Nansen, at the head of another agency, the Refugee Organisation, did wonderful work in helping prisoners of war and refugees all over Europe. By his efforts, and with League help, most were returned to their homes and families.

THE LEAGUE IN ACTION IN THE 1920S

Boundaries

Some of the League's first problems concerned boundary disputes, especially in eastern Europe. The confusion of different nationalities there had made the task of drawing fair boundaries for the new countries formed after the Treaty of Versailles almost impossible. Arguments over the decisions made at Versailles were referred to the League. The Council made minor changes in the boundary areas of Poland, Danzig, Memel and Silesia. Disputes over areas in Turkey, South Armenia and

the Baltic Sea were also settled by the League. The League failed to stop the war between Greece and Turkey in 1919–1922, but gave help to the refugees caused by the conflict.

The Corfu Incident, 1923

Then, in 1923 came a worrying event usually called the Corfu Incident. A conference of ambassadors from Britain, France, Italy and Japan was working on boundary problems between Greece and Albania. They sent an Italian general to investigate. He was shot in Greece. No one knows who shot him or why, but the new dictator of Italy, Mussolini, was furious. He sent forces to shell the Greek island of Corfu and demanded heavy compensation. A murder in south-east Europe, and an ultimatum! It reminded people of 1914 all over again.

The League discussed the matter and offered a solution. However, the ambassadors of the Great Powers stepped in. Under pressure from Mussolini they altered the terms of the agreement in favour of Italy. In this incident the League was ready to act, but the Great Powers acted on their own, ignoring the League. Unfortunately, bullying tactics, such as Mussolini had used, could pay off.

The 'Locarno Honeymoon'

In the 1920s both Britain and France signed agreements outside the League while trying to look after their own positions in Europe. These agreements both helped and undermined the League's own policies. In the early 1920s, for example, France made alliances with countries in eastern Europe to try to keep Germany isolated. Gradually, however, French, German and British ministers realised that a state of permanent hostility between Germany and Germany's old enemies was no good to any of them.

Germany had always rejected all the boundaries laid down at the Treaty of Versailles, but in 1925 it signed the Locarno Pact. In this treaty Germany promised to keep to the boundaries on its western borders laid down at Versailles. However, the Locarno Pact made no mention of Germany's eastern boundaries. By not including these, the countries who signed the Locarno Pact with Germany, like France and Britain, gave others the impression that if one day Germany wanted to alter its eastern boundaries with Poland and Czechoslovakia they would take no action. This certainly worried France's allies in eastern Europe. Thus the two great powers, France and Britain, were acting outside the terms of the League and were ignoring the idea of collective security.

For the time being, however, all was well among the nations. In 1926 Germany became a member of the League. In the same year, the Kellogg Pact was signed by 65 countries, including the USA and the USSR. All those who had signed promised never to go to war again. The five years from 1925 to 1929 have become known as the 'Locarno Honeymoon'. Even so, very little progress was made on disarmament. In the Treaty of Versailles each country had promised to reduce their armed forces. Only in Germany had this happened, but only because Germany had been forced to do so. The countries of Europe still did not trust one another.

THE LEAGUE OF NATIONS IN THE 1930s

The Wall Street Crash of 1929 and the Depression which followed all over the world put an end to this honeymoon. Distrust between Germany and France grew. France began to build the Maginot Line, a huge defence system along the German border which it believed would protect France from German attack. Its alliances with Germany's neighbours in eastern Europe were considered less important. Dictators came to power in several countries, riding on the back of the Depression. Most disturbing of these was, of course, Hitler in Germany. Before Hitler really started to alter the map of Europe, however, others had ruined the peace-keeping hopes of the League.

Manchuria, 1931

Map 11-1 The Japanese invasion of Manchuria, 1931

Another country badly hit by the Depression was Japan. The Japanese controlled Korea and operated the railway into the northern Chinese province of Manchuria (see Map 11-1). China was weak and split by civil war. Manchuria was a tempting prize. It had iron and coal deposits and could be a market for Japanese-made goods. In 1931, the Japanese army attacked and invaded Manchuria. There was no excuse for this, and

SOURCE 2   David Low cartoon, 1932

China appealed to the League. In fact, the Japanese generals were acting without orders from the government in Tokyo. The Japanese representative at the League promised to withdraw Japanese troops from Manchuria, but it was soon clear that the Japanese army was doing what it liked. The League investigated the matter, but, before it reported, the Japanese army had captured Manchuria and was attacking the rest of China. Even then, it was not clear what the League could do. The only countries with power in that part of the world were Russia and the USA, but neither was a member of the League. Finally, in 1933, the League condemned the Japanese invasion. Japan simply left the League, and carried on with its conquests in China and South-East Asia which led eventually into the Second World War. The League could take no further action to stop them.

? Questions

a   What is the cartoonist saying about the League and about Japan?

b   Explain how this cartoon is more effective than a lot of words.

German rearmament

As soon as Hitler came to power he was anxious to rearm Germany. To most Germans, and even to some British and French, this was not unreasonable. The League had failed to persuade other countries to cut down on their armaments. Germany, of course, had been told to disband most of its forces in 1919.

In 1932 another attempt to discuss disarmament was made at the World Disarmament Conference in Geneva. Again the members failed to agree, and the Conference broke up when Hitler walked out. The next year, in 1933, Hitler withdrew Germany from the League itself. This action, coming at the same time as the Manchuria fiasco, further weakened the League.

Moreover, in 1935 Britain made a naval agreement with Germany without consulting its allies. Hitler agreed to keep his navy to 35% of the strength of the British navy. The League was helpless to prevent this breaking of the terms of the Versailles Treaty, and Hitler continued to rearm regardless of other countries' attitudes.

Ethiopia

The death blow to the effectiveness of the League of Nations was the Italian invasion of Ethiopia in 1934–1935. Italy had always wanted to take over Ethiopia (known at that time as Abyssinia), one of the few uncolonised countries in Africa. In 1896 the Italians had invaded Ethiopia and been defeated. Mussolini also needed a successful war to distract the attention of the Italian people from his incompetent government. In 1934, Italian troops, using all the sophisticated weapons of modern warfare such as gas and flame-throwers, attacked the poorly armed Ethiopians. Ethiopia appealed to the League (see Map 11-2).

Italy was obviously in the wrong. The League condemned Mussolini's actions and imposed economic sanctions on Italy. Britain and France, however, were in a difficult position. They were the ones who would have to make the sanctions work, and they were nervous about upsetting Mussolini. France was particularly worried about Hitler's re-armament policy. Mussolini and Hitler were not yet allied in 1935, and France did not want to drive them together by opposing Mussolini too strongly. The result was that sanctions were never applied very firmly. Furthermore, oil, so essential for a modern war, had been left off the list of goods which could not be supplied to Italy. The British Foreign Secretary even worked out a deal with the French Premier for dividing-up Ethiopia – the Hoare–Laval pact – which gave nearly two-thirds of Ethiopia to Mussolini, leaving the remaining third for the Emperor Haile Selassie.

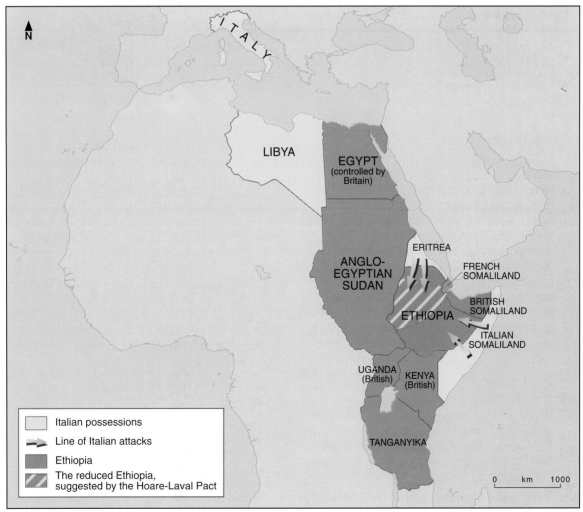

Map 11-2 Ethiopia 1934–1936

▼ **SOURCE 3A**

Haile Selassie addressing the League, 1936

▼ **SOURCE 3B**

I, Haile Selassie, Emperor of Abyssinia, am here today to claim that justice which is due to my people and the assistance promised to it eight months ago. I assert that the problem is a much wider one than the removal of sanctions. It is not merely a settlement of Italian aggression. It is the very existence of the League of Nations. It is the value of promises made to small states that their independence be respected and ensured. God and history will remember your judgements.

Haile Selassie's speech to the
League of Nations, 1936

? Questions

a Why does Haile Selassie think that the existence of the League is at stake?

b Why would other small states be concerned over the Ethiopian issue?

The League had been set up in order to deal with such an issue as the invasion of Ethiopia.

The aggressor was a powerful European country. Only collective action could have stopped Italy, and the League did not provide it. Mussolini left the League and completed the conquest of the whole of Ethiopia in 1937.

In the end, the British and French came off worst. Their efforts did not stop Mussolini from conquering Ethiopia, but the economic sanctions did push Mussolini closer to Hitler. Together they signed the Rome–Berlin Axis of 1936, a treaty of friendship and co-operation. The Hoare–Laval Pact showed Britain and France in a bad light. When the terms of the Pact were made public the two ministers were condemned inside and outside their own countries.

As a peace-keeping organisation the League of Nations was a failure. First Japan and then Italy had ignored the League and it was powerless to stop them. In the world of the late 1930s bullying and aggressive tactics seemed to be the route to success. In 1936, the Palace of Nations in Geneva was completed: it was intended to provide a permanent home for the League of Nations. It was ironic that it was completed just as the League appeared to be most ineffective.

THE REASONS FOR THE FAILURE OF THE LEAGUE OF NATIONS

1. *Membership.* Not all the great powers were members of the League. The USA never became a member. Germany did not join until 1926, and left the League in 1933. Russia was not invited to join at first, but in 1934 became a member in an attempt to join forces against Hitler. Japan left in 1933 and Italy in 1935. This fatally weakened the League.
2. *Organisation.* Meetings of the League were few and far between. Decisions were made very slowly. Sometimes they came too late for effective action.
3. *Sanctions.* The sanctions of the League were never successful in controlling aggression. The reasons for this were partly that some major powers were outside the League so no real collective security was possible, and partly the weakness of Britain and France. The final sanction of sending an army to oppose an aggressor was never used.
4. *The Treaty of Versailles.* The League was bound to uphold the terms of the treaty, to defend the peace settlement. It became clear as time went on that some of its terms were not satisfactory and would have to be changed.
5. *Britain and France.* The responsibility for making the League work fell on these two countries, yet enthusiasm for the League was never strong within the French and British governments. Often they preferred to sign treaties outside the League, and sometimes went behind the League's back, as over the Hoare–Laval Pact.
6. *The will to make it work.* In 1919 at Versailles there was a mood of idealism – people wanted to make a new and better world – but this idealism soon disappeared. The economic depression caused unemployment and a fall in the standard of living all over Europe. Dictators in Germany, Italy and Japan came into power as a result of the Depression who would not stop their aggressive policies at the request of the League. Their actions showed up the League's weakness.

However, despite all the failures, the good work of the League should not be forgotten. Nor should it be forgotten that in 1945 a new organisation was set up – the United Nations – with similar aims, and determined to learn from the lessons of the failure of the League of Nations.

WOODROW WILSON 1856–1924

Woodrow Wilson was born in Virginia in 1856. He received a good education and went on to University at Princeton. Later, he returned to Princeton, first as a professor, then as President of the University from 1902–1910. He married in 1885 and had three children.

Until 1910, Wilson had little to do with politics, so his rise to become President of the USA in two years was remarkable. In 1910, he was elected Governor of New Jersey. He soon made his name as an opponent of big business and protector of consumers. He was the Democratic Party candidate for the Presidency in 1912 and won easily. His idealism showed itself in some important new laws: the Farm Loans Act, which set up banks to give loans to farmers; the Child Labour Act, preventing employment of children; and the Pure Food Act.

In 1916, he was re-elected as President. He had said he would keep the USA out of the First World War, but by 1917 the German U-boat campaign was seriously damaging US shipping. He saw that, with Russia out of the war because of its Revolution, the Allies might be defeated.

He actually brought the USA into the war on the basis of great idealism: he said it was 'to make the world safe for democracy', and he issued the Fourteen Points. American industry geared itself for war. To the Allies, it was 'a race between Wilson and Hindenburg'. The first US troops arrived in Europe in June 1917 and contributed a great deal towards the Allied victory.

Woodrow Wilson was welcomed as a hero in Europe. Ordinary people saw his noble ideals leading to a better world than the politicians of Europe could offer. However, Clemenceau and Lloyd George were determined to have their way at Versailles and Wilson was able to rescue only some of his Fourteen Points, such as the League of Nations.

When he returned to the USA, he found many Americans against the treaty. Under the American Constitution, any treaty has to be agreed by a two-thirds majority in the Senate. Wilson was not good at compromising: his attitude was 'all or nothing'. He began a tiring rail tour of the western states, making many speeches to put his views across to the people. In November 1919, he had a stroke and remained an invalid until his death in 1924. The US Senate gave the treaty a majority, but not by two-thirds. The USA, therefore, never joined the League of Nations, the peace-keeping organisation for which Wilson had worked so hard.

ASSESSMENT

Describe, explain and analyse

1   Look at the six reasons given in this chapter (page 111) for the failure of the League of Nations. Choose the three which you think were the most important.

a) Describe how they helped the League to fail.

b) Explain why you think they are the most important reasons.

2   a) Write a paragraph explaining how each of the following three factors above brought about the failure of the League.

i) The organisation, membership and powers of the League.

ii) The attitudes and policies of Britain and France.

iii) The Depression, bringing dictators to power.

b) Which of the three do you think was the most important? Explain your answer fully.

3   'A success in the 1920s, a failure in the 1930s'

a) Is this statement true of the League in the 1920s?

b) Is it true of the League in the 1930s?

c) Why were the 1930s harder for the League to operate in than the 1920s?

Germany and the outbreak of the Second World War

WAS HITLER TO BLAME FOR THE SECOND WORLD WAR?

Hitler had made the aims of his foreign policy perfectly clear in his book *Mein Kampf*. As a first step, he intended to unite all German-speaking peoples. This went against the terms of the Treaty of Versailles, but one reason for Hitler's popularity in Germany was his determination to reject the treaty. The next step, having brought all Germans into one Reich (one state) would be to build an empire. Hitler wrote in *Mein Kampf*, 'When the territory of the Reich embraces all Germans, only then can the right arise, from the need of the people, to acquire foreign territory.' This foreign territory, which he called 'Lebensraum' – living space – would probably be in eastern Europe. It would be seized from people like the Poles and Russians, whom Hitler regarded as inferior.

This policy of expansion would be bound to lead, sooner or later, to war. Hitler's plan for the Nazi state was that it should be totally organised for war. Foreign observers and Germans close to Hitler were quite clear about this.

► SOURCE 1A

The whole teaching of Hitlerism is to justify war as an instrument of policy . . . and there is hardly a boy in Germany who does not view the preparation for ultimate war as the most important aspect of his life.

S. Roberts, *The Home that Hitler Built*, 1938

► SOURCE 1B

'Do you seriously intend to fight the West?' I asked. Hitler stopped and looked at me. 'What else do you think we're arming for?' he retorted. 'We must proceed step by step so that no one will impede our advance. How to do this I don't know yet. But that it will be done is guaranteed by Britain's lack of firmness and France's internal disunity.'

A. Rauschning, *No Retreat*, writing about 1934

? Questions

a The attitude to war in Britain in the 1930s was very different from that described in Source 1A. What was the British attitude? (Look back at Chapter 9 to remind you.)
b In Source 1B, did Hitler know when war would break out?
c In Source 1B, what weaknesses had Hitler seen in Britain and France?

Who else was to blame?

It would be wrong to think that Hitler had a detailed and clever 'master-plan'. As Source 1B shows, he had no idea when war would come. He showed great skill at creating opportunities and making the best of them. But other factors played their part: problems with the terms of the Treaty of Versailles; many countries were suspicious of the USSR; the French were always hostile to Germany; Britain was reluctant to stand up to Hitler. In the 'Steps to war' which follow, think about where blame lies at each point.

STEPS TO WAR, 1933–1937

1. LEAVING THE LEAGUE, 1933

One of Hitler's first actions was to leave the League of Nations. The League had been born out of the Versailles humiliation, and Hitler wanted no part in it. This action made it obvious that if Hitler was going to be stopped, it would not be through the League.

2.   *GERMANY'S NEIGHBOURS*

All Europe seemed united in opposing him. The weaker countries with German minorities like Poland and Czechoslovakia, which might have been among his first targets, were closely linked in alliance to France. Of course, Hitler's propaganda machine tried to show that these alliances 'hemmed Germany in'. Hitler also used them as an excuse for rearmament.

3. *AUSTRIA, 1934*

The invasion of Austria would be the most likely first step in Hitler's plan to unite all Germans into one state. Austria was not only German-speaking, it was also Hitler's own birth-place. In 1934, he arranged for Austrian Nazis to kill the Austrian Chancellor, Dollfuss. The Nazis then invited Hitler to become ruler of Austria. The attempt failed, however, when Mussolini sent Italian troops to the Austrian border to prevent a German take-over. Mussolini was suspicious of Hitler at that stage, and Germany was too weak to undertake a war with anyone, so Hitler backed down. This shows his ability to create opportunities, even up to the point of assassination, but also shows that he was not always successful. The Dollfuss affair taught Hitler that he would have to increase Germany's strength and make an ally of Mussolini.

4. *REARMAMENT*

The rearmament of Germany continued at speed through the 1930s. By 1935, for example, Goering had built up an air force, the *Luftwaffe*. Military service was introduced, and the German army provided itself with the latest weapons, especially tanks. Pocket battleships – that is, fast, heavily armed warships – and a number of submarines, were built. All this was, of course, contrary to the terms decided at Versailles. However, some countries, particularly Britain, now felt that the terms of the treaty were too harsh; why shouldn't Germany be allowed to have reasonable armed forces like every other country?

The disarmament of Germany in 1919 had not been followed by disarmament of the other powers. Several disarmament conferences had been held, but no real disarming had actually taken place. The old problems of mistrust remained. In 1935, Germany was still only building up its forces and did not yet represent a threat.

The Depression of the 1930s added strength to this view: several countries were solving their

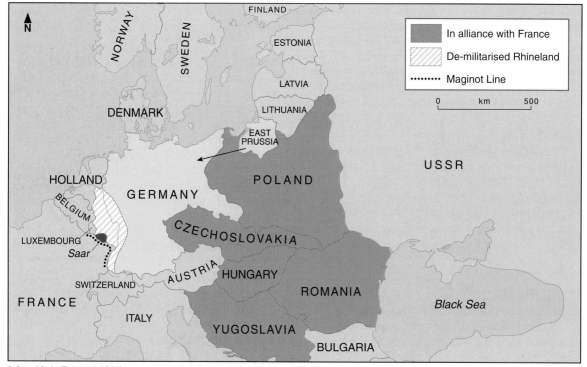

Map 12-1 Europe 1936

unemployment problems by strengthening their armed forces and giving government contracts to arms factories. If it solved Germany's unemployment problems, then could Hitler be blamed? France, for example, was building a huge defence system, called the Maginot Line, all along the Franco–German frontier (see Map 12-1). Hitler, of course, made a great deal of propaganda out of the 'unfairness' of Germany's position.

In 1935, Britain, France and Italy met at Stresa, and all three condemned German actions in Austria. However, in the same year, as we have seen, the Anglo–German naval agreement was signed, by which Britain agreed to allow the German navy to grow in size up to 35% of the strength of the British navy. Thus the unity shown at Stresa was soon broken. Mussolini's invasion of Ethiopia in the same year broke it still further. Britain and France opposed the invasion, then tried to make a deal with Mussolini (see Chapter 11, page 110). Even so, Mussolini looked around for another ally.

5. THE RHINELAND, 1936
The storm over Ethiopia provided a smoke-screen for Hitler's next action: the reoccupation of the Rhineland (see Map 12-1). The Rhineland had been demilitarised by the Treaty of Versailles: that is, no soldiers were allowed in the area.

In March 1936, German troops marched confidently into the Rhineland, but Hitler and his generals were far from confident.

SOURCE 2A
German troops march into Cologne following the reoccupation of the Rhineland, 1936

SOURCE 2B

The Reichstag, more tense than I have ever felt it, began promptly at noon. General Blomberg, the War Minister, was as white as a sheet and fumbled nervously with his fingers. Hitler began with a long harangue about the injustice of the Versailles treaty and the peacefulness of the German people. Then: 'In the interests of the primitive rights of its people to the security of their defence, the German government has re-established from today absolute and unrestricted sovereignty in the demilitarised zone'.

Now the six hundred deputies, all personal appointees of Hitler, little men with big bodies and bulging necks and cropped hair and pouched bellies and brown uniforms and heavy boots, little men of clay in his fine hands, leap to their feet, their right arms outstretched in the Nazi salute and scream 'Heil'. It was a long time before the cheering stopped. A few generals made their way out. Behind their smiles, you could not help detecting nervousness.

Next day: Hitler has got away with it. France is not marching . . . No wonder the faces of Goering and Blomberg were all smiles at noon . . . Oh, the stupidity (or is it the paralysis?) of the French. I learnt today that the German troops had strict orders to beat a hasty retreat if the French army opposed them in any way.

William Shirer, *Berlin Diary*, published 1941

Questions

a Why were the generals in Source 2B so nervous?

b Why do you think the Germans would have had to withdraw if the French had opposed them?

c What is the attitude of William Shirer, author of Source 2B, to the Reichstag deputies? How can you tell?

d If William Shirer is hostile to Hitler, how useful is this source to us?

William Shirer in Source 2B was quite correct: if the German troops had met any opposition in the reoccupation of the Rhineland, they would have been withdrawn. German rearmament had not yet made Germany strong enough to oppose France.

Why did the French do nothing? There were several reasons. France itself was split into several groups which were struggling for power. No united policy was possible. Britain would not help France. The French generals had decided to rely on a purely defensive policy and to put their trust in the Maginot Line. Several French generals were sympathetic to Fascism and not hostile to Hitler. All of these facts added up to a lack of will to take the initiative.

6. THE SPANISH CIVIL WAR

In the same year, 1936, the Spanish Civil War broke out. The right-wing General Franco led an armed rebellion against the Spanish Republican government. This gave a further twist to events which was very much to Hitler's advantage. Hitler and Mussolini regarded the rebellion of General Franco as part of the fight against Communism. Both sent men and supplies in large quantities to help Franco. The first cities to feel the horror of a German bombing raid were in Republican Spain.

The attitude of France and Britain was non-intervention – that is, not to help either side. Mussolini's disagreement with Britain and France over Ethiopia brought him closer to Hitler. In 1936 they signed an alliance: the Rome–Berlin Axis. Later the same year, Hitler signed an alliance with Japan called the Anti-Comintern Pact. This was aimed against Russia. Mussolini joined the Anti-Comintern pact in 1937, and the line-up of one of the sides in the Second World War was complete.

German rearmament continued. There was now no doubt about Germany catching up with Britain and France. Hitler was spending twice as much as Britain and France combined on his army, navy and air force. The German armed forces were soon much stronger than theirs. Dr Hjalmar Schacht, Hitler's Economics Minister, was putting the German economy on a war footing. Hitler was replacing generals who were not prepared to risk war to achieve his aims with those who were. Reluctantly, Britain and France began to rearm.

7. THE ANNEXATION OF AUSTRIA, 1938

In March 1938, Hitler ordered the Austrian Nazis to stir up trouble inside Austria. The Austrian Chancellor, Kurt von Schuschnigg, was forced to

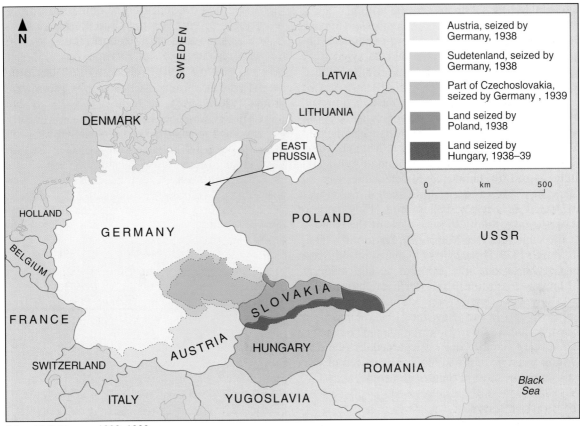

Map 12-2 Europe 1938–1939

make three Austrian Nazis ministers. Hitler's bullying of Schuschnigg shows how Germany was now using its strength: 'You, Herr Schuschnigg, have done everything to avoid a friendly policy. The German Reich is one of the Great Powers and no one will raise his voice if it settles its border problems. Italy? I see eye to eye with Mussolini. England? England will not move one finger for Austria. France? France could have stopped Germany in the Rhineland, but it is too late for France. Think it over, Herr Schuschnigg, think it over well. I can only wait until this afternoon.'

Schuschnigg ordered a plebiscite to be held in Austria: a national vote to see if Austrians wanted to be part of Germany. This could have made Hitler look foolish, so German troops occupied Austria before the plebiscite could be held. This act of annexation was known as the Anschluss. In this way, the first piece of foreign territory was added to Germany: the first of many. Schuschnigg was sent to a concentration camp, and an extermination camp was immediately set up at Mauthausen to deal with Austrian Jews.

8. CZECHOSLOVAKIA, 1938–1939

The next country on Hitler's list did not have to wait long. The German-speaking fringe of Czechoslovakia was called the Sudetenland (see Map 12-2). Hitler called on Henlein, leader of the Sudetenland Nazis, to stir up trouble there. The German papers began to publish anti-Czech propaganda, accusing the Czechs of persecuting Germans; for example: 'Bloody regime – new Czech murders of Germans'. However, Czechoslovakia was a democratic country with a determined President to lead it, Benes, a strong army and alliances with Britain, France and Russia. Hitler continued to threaten war. It seemed as if the whole continent would be dragged into war again.

9. APPEASEMENT

At this point, the British Prime Minister stepped into the situation. Neville Chamberlain flew to meet Hitler at Berchtesgaden to see if peace could be achieved by discussion. Hitler was willing to talk: if he could get what he wanted without fighting, so much the better. He demanded the

Sudetenland for Germany, on the grounds that it was a German-speaking area. Chamberlain agreed. His view was that Hitler did have certain reasonable demands and that war could be avoided by giving Hitler what he wanted. This attitude is called appeasement.

At a second meeting between the two, however, Hitler stepped up the bluff, pretending to be about to go to war. In desperation, Chamberlain and Mussolini called a third meeting, at Munich. Here, representatives of Germany, Britain, France and Italy agreed to hand the Sudetenland over to Germany. This was done, and Czechoslovakia was weakened as a result. Poland and Hungary also took the opportunity to seize parts of the country at the same time (see Map 12-2). Six months later, in March 1939, Hitler's army marched into the rest of Czechoslovakia: the promises he had made at Munich were obviously not worth anything at all.

Why did Chamberlain adopt this policy of appeasement? In the years since 1938, he has been heavily criticised for it. However, it must be remembered that Chamberlain was regarded as a hero in Britain when he returned home. His hatred of war was shared by most of the British people.

SOURCE 3A

Chamberlain in 1938, before meeting Hitler:
How horrible, fantastic, incredible it is that we should be digging trenches and trying on gas-masks here, because of a quarrel in a far-off country between people of whom we know nothing.

SOURCE 3B

Chamberlain again: I am myself a man of peace to the depths of my soul. Armed conflict between nations is a nightmare to me. But if I were convinced that any nation had made up its mind to dominate the world by fear of its force, I should feel that it must be resisted.

SOURCE 3C

Agreement signed at Munich, September 1938:
We, the German Führer and the British Prime Minister . . . regard the agreement signed last night as symbolic of the desire of our two peoples never to go to war with one another again.

We are determined to continue our efforts to remove possible sources of difference and thus to contribute to assure the peace of Europe.
    Adolf Hitler, Neville Chamberlain

SOURCE 3D

Chamberlain reading the Munich agreement at the airport on his return to Britain from Munich.

❓ Questions

a Use Sources 3A and 3B to describe Chamberlain's attitude to war.

b What does Source 3A tell us about his feelings about Czechoslovakia?

c How did Chamberlain treat Czechoslovakia in this crisis? (Look at this page to see which countries met at Munich.)

d Does Source 3C make any definite promise for peace?

e Why do you think Chamberlain failed to prevent Hitler from taking over the rest of Czechoslovakia?

SOURCE 4

Czechs, forced to give the Nazi salute, watch German forces march into Prague, March 1939

Chamberlain and the British people were anxious to avoid war if at all possible. British government statistics had estimated that German bombing would kill 1.8 million British people in the first 60 days of war. It is also true that Britain simply did not have the weapons, planes, guns or tanks for a large-scale war in 1938. Chamberlain felt that if war could not be avoided, at least it could be postponed for as long as possible until Britain was prepared. On the other hand, some British people sympathised with Hitler at this stage: they felt that Germany had been badly treated at Versailles. They also felt that Russia was a much greater menace than Hitler and admired Hitler's anti-Communist stand. Only a few Labour MPs and a few Conservatives, led by Winston Churchill and Anthony Eden, opposed appeasement. The worst aspect of appeasement, however, was that Chamberlain was prepared to allow the destruction of Czechoslovakia in order to preserve peace. Britain put its world empire before

'a far-off country' and 'people of whom we know nothing' – the unfortunate Czechs.

In the end, both Chamberlain and Hitler completely misunderstood each other: Chamberlain thought that Hitler was a trustworthy, honest gentleman like himself. Thus, when Hitler said, at Munich: 'I have no further territorial demands to make in Europe', Chamberlain believed him, and said it meant 'peace in our time'. Chamberlain felt that Hitler had a few reasonable requests to make which, if granted, would be the end of the matter. For his part, Hitler misunderstood Chamberlain too: he thought the British were completely spineless and would never go to war. He ignored the view expressed in Source 3B that in the end, Britain would act. When it became clear in March 1939 that appeasement had failed, Chamberlain joined France in alliance with Poland. Hitler, having outwitted Chamberlain at Munich, refused to believe that the British would go to war for the sake of Poland.

10. THE NAZI–SOVIET PACT, 1939

Poland was obviously to be Hitler's next victim. The only country which could effectively stop Hitler from seizing Poland was Russia. Stalin had, in fact, been frantically trying to join Britain and France in an alliance against Hitler. These two countries however, refused to have anything to do with Communist Russia. In desperation, therefore, Stalin signed a Non-Aggression Pact with Hitler: both sides agreed not to attack the other. The Nazi–Soviet Pact, as it was called, also contained secret clauses agreeing to carve up Poland between them.

The rest of the world could hardly believe this turn of events. Here were two dictators who were sworn enemies (as the cartoon, Source 5, suggests), making an alliance. The Nazi–Soviet Pact made the Second World War inevitable, because of Britain and France's alliance with Poland. The Pact only lasted two years and then Hitler attacked the USSR. The war between them broke Hitler's rule and propelled the USSR to superpower status for 50 years afterwards.

11. THE OUTBREAK OF WAR

In September 1939, Hitler launched his attack on Poland. Within a few weeks, Poland was defeated and divided up between the two dictators, as agreed. By then, however, to Hitler's surprise, Britain and France had declared war on Germany.

▼ **SOURCE 5** Cartoon in the *Evening Standard*

❓ Questions

a Why are Hitler and Stalin calling each other names in this way?

b What do you think the body lying between them represents?

c What do the clouds stand for?

ASSESSMENT

Describe, explain and analyse

1 **a**) Why did German forces marching into the Rhineland in 1936 cause a crisis?

 b) What were the attitudes of (i) Britain and (ii) France to Hitler's action?

2 **a**) Describe briefly what is meant by 'appeasement'.

 b) Why was appeasement popular in Britain in the 1930s?

 c) What were the views of those who opposed appeasement?

 d) What is your judgement of the policy of appeasement?

3 **a**) Describe how Hitler was able to expand the German Reich to include Austria, the Sudetenland and Bohemia (see Maps 12-1 and 12-2) without going to war.

 b) Explain why war broke out over his invasion of Poland.

4 Choose two long-term and two short-term causes of the Second World War from the list below. Describe them, explain how they caused the war and why they are long- or short-term.

   i) Treaty of Versailles.

   ii) Munich crisis.

   iii) German invasion of Poland.

   iv) Failure of League of Nations.

   v) Hitler's racist views.

   vi) Nazi–Soviet Pact.

5 **a**) Put the following events into chronological order: Munich crisis; outbreak of Second World War; re-occupation of the Rhineland; Germany leaves League of Nations; German occupation of Prague; Annexation of Austria (Anschluss); German invasion of Poland; Nazi–Soviet Pact.

 b) Explain why these events must have happened in the order you have put them in.

Evidence and interpretations

▼ **SOURCE A**

The general impression was that the majority of the [Conservative] Party are at heart anti-League and anti-Russian and that what they would really like would be a firm agreement with Hitler by which we could buy peace at the expense of the smaller states.

From Harold Nicolson's *Diary*, 16 July 1936

▼ **SOURCE B**

From the day Hitler came to power, I have felt that the democratic countries would have to face war. I believe he was taken too cheap...I cannot see any way of stopping Hitler except by force.

Ernest Bevin, Labour MP, speaking in March 1937

a What attitudes to Hitler are described in these two sources?

b Why were so many of the Conservative Party 'anti-League and anti-Russian'?

c What does Bevin mean by 'taken too cheap''?

d i) Appeasement was a shameful disaster.

 ii) Appeasement was a real attempt to avoid war.

 iii) Appeasement gained Britain time to prepare for war.

 Which of these three views would the people described in Source A and the author of Source B have agreed with at the time?

f From what you have found out in this chapter, which view do you agree with?

13: The Second World War in Europe

SOURCE 1A
Stuka dive bombers in action, 1940

WHAT WAS BLITZKRIEG?

In the First World War, the soldiers on the Western Front lived, fought and died in trenches which did not move more than a few kilometres in either direction all through the war. In the Second World War soldiers moved rapidly from place to place. Once an attack was launched, hundreds of kilometres could be covered in a day. The most important fighting machines of the Second World War were two which had been first used in the 1914–1918 war: tanks and aeroplanes. These two machines affected the way in which the Second World War was fought, just as the machine-gun and heavy artillery had affected the tactics of the First World War. Furthermore, the country which had a good supply of tanks and aeroplanes and knew how to make the best use of them would be bound to win.

At first this country was Germany. Hitler applied the experience of other nations regarding the best use of tanks and aeroplanes in a war. He therefore said that if ever he attacked another country he would 'hurl [himself] upon the enemy like a flash of lightning in the night.' A new word, Blitzkrieg, came into use. '*Blitzkrieg*' means 'lightning war', and Blitzkrieg tactics were used with devastating effect by the Germans from 1939 to 1941. What they did was to launch a surprise attack, move at very great speed and use overwhelming strength at certain key positions.

The first move of the Blitzkrieg came from the air. Dive bombers would destroy important positions: railway junctions, ammunition and petrol dumps, crossroads, bridges and airfields. If possible, enemy aircraft would be destroyed on the ground. The bomber pilots learned to strike with pinpoint accuracy. If there were any strategic key positions which might be useful to the invaders, parachute troops would be dropped. They could capture and hold an airfield or a bridge, for example, until the invading troops on the ground reached them. Ground troops would invade very soon after the first bombs exploded.

The invasion spearhead would be made up of fast-moving and well-armed columns of tanks. Behind them would come the motorised infantry – that is, soldiers transported by lorry or motorcycle. The invading forces would drive deep into enemy territory, not along a broad front, but in narrow columns. Each column would make for a target like a city, a port or an industrial area. With their communications in chaos, the defenders would find it almost impossible to organise defence in time. Within hours defeat would be unavoidable.

► SOURCE 1B

The scream of Stukas . . . like no sound ever heard in all the universe . . . Bomb after bomb exploded . . . the effect almost inconceivable . . . It was the perfectly appalling wind that was most terrifying. It drove like something solid through the house: every door that was latched simply burst off its hinges, every pane of glass flew into splinters, the curtains stood straight out into the room and fell back in ribbons. Everything that stood loose hit the opposite wall and was smashed. The ceilings fell with hardly a noticeable sound in the earth-shaking uproar.

Then, with a weird, smooth sound like the tearing of heavy silk the neighbouring houses began to collapse.

BELGRADE, 1941:
R. Mitchell, *The Serbs Choose War*

► SOURCE 1C

The tanks now rolled in a long column through the line of fortifications and on towards the first houses, which had been set alight by our fire. In the moonlight we could see men of the 7th Motor Cycle Battalion moving forward on foot beside us. Occasionally an enemy machine-gun or anti-tank gun fired, but none of their shot came anywhere near us. Our artillery was dropping heavy harassing fire on villages and the road far ahead of the regiment. Gradually the speed increased. Before long we were 500 yards, 1000, 2000, 3000 yards into the fortified zone. Engines roared, tank tracks clanked and clattered . . . We swung north to the main road which was soon reached.

The people in the houses were rudely awoken by the din of our tanks, the clatter and roar of tracks and engines. Troops lay bivouacked beside the road, military vehicles lay parked in farmyards and in some places on the road itself. Civilians and French troops, their faces distorted with terror, lay huddled in the ditches . . . On we went, at a steady speed, towards our objective. Every so often a quick glance at the map by a shaded light and a short wireless message to Divisional HQ to report the position, and thus the success of the 25th Panzer Regiment. Every so often I looked out of the hatch to re-assure myself that there was still no resistance and that contact was being maintained in the rear. The flat countryside lay spread out around us under the cold light of the moon. We were through the Maginot Line!

B. Liddell Hart, *The Rommel Papers*

▼ SOURCE 1D
Motorised German infantry in Poland, 1939

▼ SOURCE 1E
Wildly waving their legs, some already firing their Schmeisers, the parachutists came down, in the terraced vineyards, crashing through the peaceful olive boughs, in the yards of houses, on roofs, in the open fields where the short barley hid them.

D. M. Davin, *Crete*

? Questions

a In Source 1A you can see the sirens on the Stukas quite clearly. Read Source 1B. Why do you think the planes were fitted with sirens?

b What evidence is there in Source 1C to show that the advance of the tanks was a surprise?

c Why was the commander in Source 1C so careful to keep contact with the back of the column?

d What evidence is there in Sources 1C and 1D of the speed of the German advance?

e Look at the technology used in each of the five sources here. What was it?

f Was it being used in warfare for the first time?

g What was it like to use?

h What was it like to be on the receiving end of it?

THE PHONEY WAR, SEPTEMBER 1939 TO APRIL 1940

Hitler had begun the war by invading Poland. The German tank columns reached Warsaw, the Polish capital, in only nine days. The Russians invaded Poland from the east as they had agreed they would do in the Nazi–Soviet Pact. Poland was defeated in under a month. As you can see from Map 13-1, Polish territory was then divided between the USSR and Germany.

After this flurry of action little happened in the west for several months. The bombing raids which were expected to destroy British cities did not come. Mothers and children who had been sent to the country from the cities began to drift home. British planes dropped leaflets on Germany which explained to the German people that Hitler was bound to lose the war. There were naval engagements, such as the Battle of the River Plate in which the German battleship *Graf Spee* was sunk. German U-boats moved out into the Atlantic and began to sink British shipping.

The USSR became involved in a war with Finland, the 'Winter War' of 1939–1940, which took Russia a long time to win. The British called this period 'the Phoney War' because nothing seemed to be happening. The Germans called it the *Sitzkrieg*, the 'Sit-down War'.

In fact both sides were not really ready for war. Hitler was not yet fully equipped to take on a major war. The British were certainly not prepared, while the French were putting all their faith in their massive defence system, known as the Maginot Line.

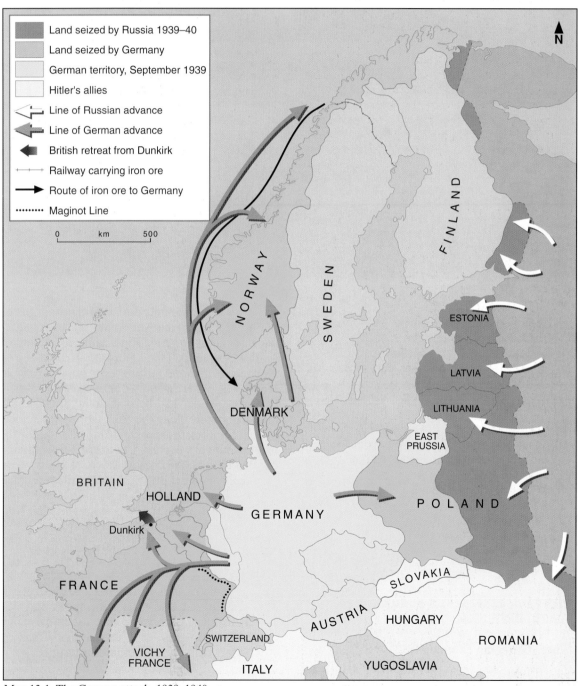

Map 13-1 The German attack, 1939–1940

◤ SOURCE 2A
French soldiers travelling by electric train inside the Maginot defences

◤ SOURCE 2B
We need tanks of course, but you cannot hope to achieve a real breakthrough with tanks. As to the air, it will not play the part you expect. It'll be a flash in the pan.

Maurice Gamelin, French general

❓ Questions

a What does Source 2A tell you about the amount of money the French had put into the Maginot Line?

b What does Source 2B tell you about French military attitudes at the beginning of the war?

c Compare Source 2B with Sources 1A, 1B and 1C. Is General Gamelin right?

d How do Sources 2A and 2B explain why Germany was not attacked at this time?

THE FALL OF WESTERN EUROPE, APRIL–JUNE 1940

The Norwegian campaign

The British Prime Minister, Neville Chamberlain, still hoped that the Germans would see reason. In April 1940 he announced that 'Hitler had missed the bus' and that the war would not continue. A few days later, however, Hitler launched an attack against Denmark and Norway. He set up a Norwegian named Quisling as a puppet ruler in Norway, a pattern soon to be repeated elsewhere in Europe. Hitler had been shipping Swedish iron ore to Germany along the coast of Norway, and he needed to protect this route. Iron was vital for the manufacture of weapons. The British knew this and decided to mine the coastal waters of Norway. On the same day as the British ships began laying their mines Hitler began to push northwards. An Anglo–French expedition was sent to help the Norwegians. It was a humiliating failure.

◤ SOURCE 3A
The troops lacked aircraft, anti-aircraft guns, anti-tank guns, transport and training. There were neither snow-shoes nor skis, still less skiers. Thus began this ramshackle campaign.

Winston Churchill, *History of the Second World War*, published 1948–1954

SOURCE 3B

They were dumped into Norway's deep snows and quagmires of April slush without a single anti-aircraft gun, without one squadron of supporting airplanes, without a single piece of field artillery . . . [British officers said], 'We have simply been massacred . . . It is the planes . . . We were completely at the mercy of the Jerries. Their bombers flew low over us at five hundred feet. They scattered us. We were up to our hips in snow'.

Leland Stowe, *Chicago Daily News*, April 1940

? Questions

a   Why would a campaign in the north of Norway need special equipment?
b   How far do the two sources 3A and 3B agree or disagree about British lack of equipment in the Norwegian campaign?
c   Which do you think is more reliable in its description of the campaign, the history book (Source 3A) or the newspaper (Source 3B)?

Winston Churchill becomes Prime Minister

In early May the British Parliament turned against Chamberlain and he resigned. Winston Churchill

SOURCE 4A

A painting by Charles Cundall of the evacuation at Dunkirk

became Prime Minister. Immediately a more war-like approach was clear. 'I have nothing to offer but blood, toil, tears, and sweat', he told the House of Commons on 10 May 1940. 'You ask what is our policy. It is to wage war by sea, land and air, with all our might and with all the strength God can give us.'

France attacked

On the same day that Churchill made this speech the Germans launched a Blitzkrieg attack against the Low Countries and France. It was a great success. German tanks rolled swiftly across Holland and Belgium. Other troops attacked France through the Ardennes region avoiding the Maginot defences. Holland surrendered within five days. By the tenth day the Germans had reached the Channel, and, eight days later, Belgium surrendered.

Dunkirk

The British Expeditionary Force had been sent across the Channel, but they and the French, Dutch and Belgians all found it difficult to work together. The French were completely taken by surprise by the attack through Belgium; the British troops were sent reeling back towards the Channel port of Dunkirk. There, the French prepared to make a stand while the British sent hundreds of boats across the Channel to take their soldiers off the beaches. The evacuation of the troops from Dunkirk was called Operation Dynamo.

SOURCE 4B

From the margin of the sea, at fairly wide intervals, three long thin black lines protruded into the water, conveying the effect of low wooden breakwaters. They were lines of men, standing in pairs behind one another far out into the water, waiting in queues 'till boats arrived to transport them, a score or so at a time, to the steamers and warships that were filling up with the last survivors. The queues stood there, fixed and almost as regular as if ruled. No bunching, no pushing.

Alan Devine, *Miracle at Dunkirk*

SOURCE 4C

The first day of the evacuation, 27th May, proved disappointing. Only 7,669 troops were brought out by a motley assortment of destroyers, passenger ferry steamers, paddle steamers, self-propelled barges and Dutch schuits . . . Later a volunteer Armada of some 400 yachts, lifeboats, launches, river tugs, cookie boats, pleasure craft, French and Belgian fishing boats, oyster dredges . . . ferried 100,000 men from the beaches on 30th May.

Stephen Webbe, *Memoirs*

? Questions

a   What problems faced those who were in charge of the evacuation?

b   Why could the bigger ships not come in close to pick up the men?

c   How did the little ships in Source 4C solve these problems?

THE BATTLE OF BRITAIN, JULY–DECEMBER 1940

Hitler had hoped that Britain would accept surrender terms. However, in early June, Churchill had made his attitude clear: 'We shall defend our island, whatever the cost may be. We shall fight on the beaches, we shall fight on the landing grounds, we shall fight in the fields and in the streets, we shall fight in the hills; we shall never surrender.' At this time Britain was the only country at war with Germany.

The next logical step for Hitler was to invade England. He prepared plans for an invasion which he called Operation Sea-Lion. However, the 30 to 40 kilometres of English Channel separating his forces from England was a difficult barrier to cross. Invasion barges waited on the French coast, ready to be loaded with men and equipment. They were slow vessels, easily attacked from the air.

SOURCE 5A Pilots 'scramble' for their planes

Before operation Sea-Lion could take place, therefore, the Luftwaffe had to be in control of the skies above the Channel. The Battle of Britain in August 1940 was a battle between the Luftwaffe and the RAF for this control of the air.

The Luftwaffe aimed to bomb airfields and shoot down fighters so that the RAF would be put out of action. The Germans had about 930 fighters in early August to Britain's 650. The RAF had so many only because their chief, Sir Hugh Dowding, had argued against stationing fighters in France. If they had been sent, many would have been left behind in the hasty retreat to Dunkirk. However, the RAF was desperately short of pilots. Throughout the battle, the Luftwaffe had more fighters and pilots than the RAF, so they could afford heavier losses.

The RAF did have two advantages, however. The Spitfire fighter was more manoeuvrable and better armed than the Messerschmitt, although by no means all the fighter squadrons had Spitfires. The RAF also had radar (<u>ra</u>dio <u>d</u>etection <u>a</u>nd <u>r</u>anging). This worked by sending out radio waves and recording the echo effect when the waves bounced back off enemy aircraft. British scientists had been developing radar since 1935. By 1940 it could supply information on aircraft 25 kilometres away. The RAF was, therefore, rarely caught on the ground.

▶ SOURCE 5B

In a few seconds, we were running for our machines. I climbed into the cockpit my plane and felt an empty feeling in my stomach. I knew that that morning I was going to kill for the first time.

We ran into them at eighteen thousand feet, twenty yellow-nosed Messerschmitts, about five hundred feet above us. Our squadron strength was eight, and as they came down, we went into line astern and turned head-on to them . . . I saw our section leader let go a burst of fire at the leading plane, saw the pilot put his machine into a half-roll and knew that he was mine. Automatically I kicked the rudder to the left to get him at right angles, turned the gun-button to 'fire' and let go a four-second burst. For a second, he seemed to hang motionless, then a jet of red flame shot upward and he spun out of sight.

Richard Hillary, *The Last Enemy*

In many ways, the Battle of Britain was an extraordinary battle. The numbers of men involved were, by Second World War standards, very few. The battlefield was the sky over England so people at work in the fields could see the dog-fights going on overhead. At the end of August, the RAF, although in a desperate position, was still able to carry on fighting.

However, the situation soon changed. On 23 August German planes, lost in the dark, accidentally dropped some bombs on London. The next night Churchill ordered the first air raid on Berlin, which killed a number of German civilians.

Hitler was furious and ordered the Luftwaffe to switch their targets from British airfields to British cities. Through the autumn of 1940, therefore, 13,000 tons of bombs were dropped on London alone and thousands more on other cities. This did not, of course, make life any easier in Britain. However, on 17 September, Hitler called off Operation Sea-Lion. Britain was at least safe from invasion. Churchill paid tribute to the pilots: 'Never in the field of human conflict was so much owed by so many to so few.'

EVENTS FROM JANUARY TO DECEMBER 1941

Invasion of Russia

Hitler now turned his attention to the invasion of the USSR. In terms of numbers of soldiers involved, numbers of dead and the effect on the outcome of the war, this was by far the most important campaign of all. Some writers have said it was Hitler's greatest mistake, but the USSR had always been Hitler's main enemy. He detested the Russians as Communists, he loathed them as Slavs, an 'inferior race'. He had said many years earlier in *Mein Kampf* that he would carve a new German empire out of the USSR.

EASTERN EUROPE
Western Europe was safely conquered, except for Britain which was so weak that it would be in no position to attack Germany for some years. Hitler now turned to eastern Europe.

Austria, most of Czechoslovakia and half of Poland had been taken into Germany in 1938 and 1939 (see Map 13-1). In the remaining states of eastern Europe he was far from unpopular: most of the rest of eastern Europe regarded the USSR as the greater menace. In 1939–1940, the USSR had seized all of Lithuania, Latvia, Estonia. half of Poland and slices of Finland and Romania.

Germany, Japan and Italy had signed a Tripartite Pact in September 1940. The remaining independent countries of eastern Europe now hurried to seek protection from the USSR by joining this pact. By early 1941, Slovakia, Hungary, Romania and Bulgaria had joined.

The whole of the mainland of Europe was now either occupied by Germany or by one of its allies, or was neutral. Hitler thus had a huge reservoir of men and industrial resources from which to launch his invasion of Russia.

ITALY ENTERS THE WAR

Italy was just as ill-prepared for war as many other countries in 1939, despite Mussolini's aggressive speeches. He did not immediately bring Italy into the war in 1939, However, by 1940 Hitler was so successful that Mussolini was afraid he would miss out on the rewards if he did not join in. He therefore declared war on Britain and France ten days before the fall of France. The Italians intended to take over British colonies in Africa while Britain itself was under attack.

The British navy retaliated by severely damaging the Italian fleet in its base at Taranto. Italian troops then invaded Egypt, where they outnumbered the British and Dominion troops by ten to one. In spite of this, the Italian invasion was halted and its troops were rapidly driven back. Italian soldiers had previously shown their bravery only against badly armed Ethiopian tribesmen. They surrendered to General Wavell, the British commander, in huge numbers. At the same time, the Italians were driven out of Ethiopia and the Emperor, Haile Selassie, was restored.

For these reasons, in the early part of 1941 Hitler had to divert troops away from the invasion of Russia in order to prop up his ally Mussolini. He came to the Italians' rescue in North Africa by sending one of his most able commanders, Erwin Rommel, with some of his best Panzer divisions. From February 1941 to August 1942, Rommel drove the British further and further back towards Egypt. He was soon within striking distance of the Suez Canal and of the Arabian oil fields beyond. These advances, however, did divert German soldiers and supplies from the Russian front and may have fatally weakened the German invasion forces.

Hitler's efforts to control other countries in eastern Europe were also nearly wrecked by Mussolini. Having taken Albania in 1939, Mussolini attacked Greece in 1941. Once again, he was defeated, this time by combined Greek and British forces. Hitler had to step in, as he feared British threats to his oil supplies in Romania. The German Blitzkrieg rapidly overran Yugoslavia and Greece. Paratroopers captured Crete for Germany. Yugoslavia was split up and puppet governments set up; Greece was occupied by Italy. In both countries, however, highly active resistance movements kept German troops busy and were a drain on German resources.

OPERATION BARBAROSSA

For the time being, however, that did not seem to matter. The German attack on Russia, Operation Barbarossa, was launched in June 1941. Hitler felt that he must succeed. Russia had been defeated in 1905 by Japan, in 1917 by Germany and nearly defeated in 1939 by Finland. The Soviet army had been weakened by Stalin's purges of 1937–1938. Many of the peoples under Soviet rule would welcome the Germans as liberators. Hitler's troops were fresh from victories all over Europe. 'We have only to kick in the door,' he said, 'and the whole rotten edifice will collapse.'

He was nearly right. The Blitzkrieg on Russia thrust forward in three directions (see Map 13-2): in the north, to Leningrad, to cut off possible aid from the Allies; in the centre, to Moscow, the centre of government and transport networks, and in the south, to the grain-growing areas, the industrial Donbas region and the Soviet oil fields beyond. Stalin had put all his hopes on buying peace through the Nazi–Soviet Pact. He refused to believe in the German invasion until it happened, despite being repeatedly warned by Allied spies and his own advisers.

At first, the Soviets could do nothing but retreat. By early autumn 1941, German troops had laid siege to Leningrad, reached the outskirts of Moscow and driven over 1,000 kilometres into southern Russia.

The war in the USSR, however, was going to be different from war in other countries.

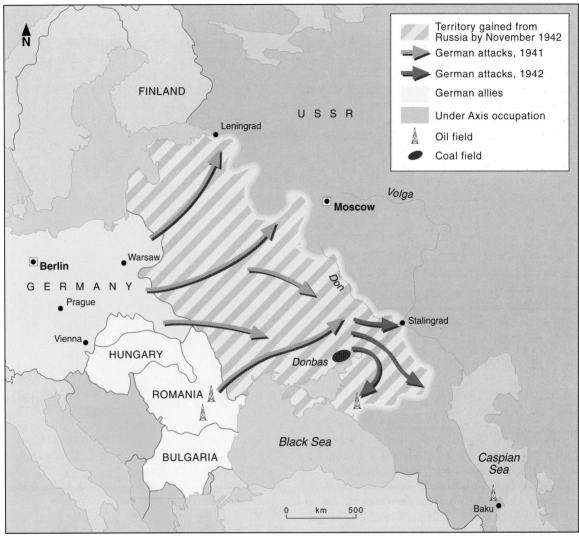

Map 13-2 The German attack on the USSR 1941–1942

▶ **SOURCE 6A**

It was appallingly difficult country for tank movement – great virgin forests, widespread swamps, terrible roads, and bridges not strong enough to bear the weight of tanks. The resistance also became stiffer, and the Russians began to cover their front with minefields; it was easier for them to block the way because there were so few roads.

The great motor highway leading from the frontier to Moscow was unfinished – the one road a Westerner would call a 'road'. We were not prepared for what we found because our maps in no way corresponded to reality. On those maps all supposed main roads were marked in red, and there seemed to be many, but they often proved to be merely sandy tracks.

Such country was bad enough for the tanks, but worse still for the transport accompanying them – carrying their fuel, their supplies and all the auxiliary troops they needed. Nearly all this transport consisted of wheeled vehicles, which could not move off the roads, nor move on it if the sand turned into mud.

General Blumentritt

▾ **SOURCE 6B**   A road into Russia

▾ **SOURCE 6C**

Great Lenin, who founded our State, used to say that the basic qualities of the Soviet men should be valour and daring: they should be fearless in battle and resolved to fight against the enemies of our country. The Red Army and Navy and all the citizens of the Soviet Union must defend every inch of the Soviet soil, fight to the last drop of their blood, defend their towns and villages, and show their daring and ingenuity – qualities that are characteristic of our people.

In the event of the retreat of the Red Army all railway rolling stock must be brought away. We must not leave a single engine to the enemy, nor a single railway coach. We must not leave a single pound of grain or a single gallon of petrol to the enemy. The collective farmers must take away all their cattle and place their corn in the care of State organisations to be transported to the rear zone. All valuable materials which cannot be taken away must be resolutely destroyed.

Joseph Stalin

? Questions

a   What problems did the size of the USSR pose for the Germans?

b   What problems can you see arising for the Germans from Sources 6A, 6B and 6C?

c   How would the situation in Source 6B add to German difficulties?

d   Taking into account the information in all of these sources, in what way was the German invasion of the USSR different from the successful German campaigns of 1939–1941?

The invasion of the USSR was different in many ways from the successful German invasion of Denmark, Belgium, Holland or France. This time, German forces had to travel hundreds of kilometres away from Germany. Keeping the front-line troops supplied became a problem. The poor road system of the USSR made this even more difficult.

The retreating Soviets were ordered by Stalin to leave nothing which the Germans could use. This was called a 'scorched-earth' policy. This time they were not marching through busy towns and villages where food, petrol or places to sleep were easily available. In Russia they were in huge open spaces, where villages had been burned, animals killed and stores carried off.

Although the Soviet soldiers were not well equipped, they fought bravely, regardless of casualties. They put up the stiffest resistance whenever possible, then removed all they could, mined the area and retreated again. Perhaps they had become used to taking orders under Stalin's dictatorship during the 1930s. Perhaps their courage came from the memory of their past defeats and a determination that their country should survive. Sometimes Soviets behind the German lines sabotaged the Germans' long supply lines; these Soviets were called partisans. The partisans killed Germans without mercy and the Germans took savage reprisals, sometimes on innocent peasants.

The German forces had almost reached their targets by November 1941, but the Soviets, with half their country in ruins, had not surrendered. Then the Russian winter set in. Transport, which had been difficult, now became impossible. Petrol froze in the tanks. The German soldiers did not have sufficient winter clothing and suffered agonies from frost-bite.

▼ **SOURCE 6D**

Those Arctic blasts . . . had scythed through out attacking troops. In a couple of days there were 100,000 casualties from frost-bite alone. 100,000 first-class experienced soldiers fell out because the cold had surprised them . . .

If only the battle for Moscow had started 14 days earlier, the city would now be in our hands . . . if - if - if. If Hitler had started Barbarossa six weeks earlier . . . if he had left Mussolini on his own in the Balkans.

H. Haape, *Moscow Tramstop*

▼ **SOURCE 6E**
German troops and a convoy of horse-drawn sledges in the USSR

SOURCE 6F

The bodies were frozen stiff. And those invaluable boots were frozen to the Russians' legs. 'Saw the legs off', ordered Kageneck. The men hacked off the dead men's legs below the knee and put the legs, with boots still attached, in the ovens. Within ten or fifteen minutes, the legs were sufficiently thawed for the soldiers to strip off the vital boots.

H. Haape, *Moscow Tramstop*

Questions

a What evidence do Sources 6D and 6F give us that Operation Barbarossa was running late?

b What reasons were there for the attack on the USSR being delayed?

c What evidence is there in all the Sources 6A–F that Germany could be defeated on the Russian Front?

Just before Christmas 1941, the Soviet Marshal Zhukov, in a temperature of -40°C, counter-attacked and drove the Germans back from Moscow. The invading forces prepared heavily armed encampments called 'hedgehogs', and dug in for the winter. It was going to be a long, bitter fight.

The war at sea

Another long, bitter fight was taking place far to the west, in the cold, grey Atlantic. This was the battle between German U-boats and British shipping. Britain had to bring in supplies by sea, including food, essential war materials such as oil, and weapons. After the early U-boat successes, the merchant ships sailed in groups, called convoys, each with a naval escort. Convoys would assemble off the coast of Canada and take a northerly route to Britain. Similar convoys were sent into the icy waters north of Norway carrying supplies to the USSR. The U-boat answer to the convoy system was to hunt in 'wolf-packs' or groups. A group would attack a convoy from all sides, making the job of the escort impossible.

SOURCE 7A

We were attacked by a German wolf-pack in the North Atlantic . . . They sank four ships the first night. There seemed to be fires and explosions everywhere and before midnight, we had been feeling sorry for . . . the men on a tanker that was burning fiercely when we passed her. Then we copped it. It must have been about the morning . . . The blast knocked me flying and she lurched and began to go down right away. We had no time to get the boats away, or get men up from below . . . then a few of us were struggling in icy water for a life-raft. In a few minutes, the ship had gone down with most of my mates and only seven of us left on this raft.

S. Champion, *A British Seaman*

SOURCE 7B

A depth-charge attack on a German U-boat
Had they spotted us? If so warships would be on our track within an hour. . . . The sea was ghastly calm, perfect for their asdic. A report came from the hydrophone operator 'Propellers at high speed. Probably destroyers.' 'Dive to seventy-five fathoms. Silent speed.'

We were all ready, with our felt shoes on and all but the most essential lighting shut off to save current . . . The enemy worked in triangular formation, with us in the middle, and I must say they worked superbly. We had never known the first charges to fall with such uncomfortable accuracy as these did . . . All the glass panels on our controls were shattered and the deck was strewn with splinters. Valve after valve was loosened and before long the water came trickling through . . .

Faces are pale and every forehead sweating. We all know what the other man's thinking . . . By the time we've had 16 hours of it we have long given up counting the depth charges . . . The steel bulkheads are buckling and may give at any moment.

'Well it's not everyone who gets such an expensive coffin,' someone remarks. 'Four million marks it cost.'

A German U-boat Commander

▼ SOURCE 7C Convoy of merchant ships escorted by the Royal Navy, April 1940

USA AND LEND-LEASE

In 1939, as we have seen, the USA hoped to stay out of the war. President Roosevelt made it clear that Britain could buy equipment, but that it would be on a strictly 'cash and carry' basis. In the presidential election campaign of 1940, he again promised Americans that they would not have to fight. After winning the election, Roosevelt took a more helpful attitude to Britain. In 1941, he organised a scheme called 'Lend-Lease', by which Britain could borrow or hire military equipment. American factories began to turn out large numbers of ships and planes which were sent to Britain. Many Americans objected to Lend-Lease, but Roosevelt said it was just like lending your garden hose to a neighbour whose house was on fire. However, in December 1941 the Japanese attacked the American base at Pearl Harbor. This ended America's reluctance to enter the war with one blow. Roosevelt immediately declared war on Germany and Japan. The USA was now whole-heartedly on Britain's side.

The Battle of the Atlantic had gone well for Germany in 1941 and early 1942. Sometimes less than half the ships in a convoy reached their British ports. When America came into the war, however, things were not so easy for Germany. Convoys could be more heavily protected. Long-range aircraft were able to take off from America to guard convoys and try to spot U-boats. Gradually, the tide turned and the U-boats began to be sunk in great numbers: 43 were sunk in May 1943 alone.

THE HOME FRONT

Was it a people's war?

▼ SOURCE 8A

This war has to be fought as a people's war. If we are to defend and protect this island, there's no way to avoid that. But the wartime way of life blasts away all that was rotten before.

From a wartime radio broadcast
by J. B. Priestley

We saw in Chapter 9 that there was a lot that was 'rotten before' in Britain in the 1930s. There were still a million unemployed when war broke out. In many areas, men had not worked for most of the time since the end of the First World War. Their families had had to make do on the dole, a pitiful sum, just enough to keep them from starving.

Unemployed young people felt these were wasted years, their lives rotting away in idleness.

Then came the war. The nation needed them and, as Priestley says in Source 8A, it had to be a 'People's War' in order to be won.

What did this mean? It went further than the First World War in involving everybody. It meant quite a different approach from wars in the past, where fighting men had gone off and everyone else just stayed at home. We have seen that this was a war of technology. Making weapons was therefore as important as using them, so factory workers were, as Prime Minister Winston Churchill said, 'in the front line'. It was a people's war because people were killed in their own homes in bombing raids: 60,000 before the war was over. It was a people's war because people's everyday lives were disrupted as never before, by evacuation, by shortages of food, by being ordered what to do by the government. Britain was second only to the USSR in being organised for 'Total War', with everyone at the command of the state to use in the war effort.

In this situation, the morale of the people was obviously important. If they had refused to join in the people's war, Britain would have been defeated. But there was a price to be paid: what Priestley calls the 'blasting away' of all that was rotten in pre-war Britain.

Evacuation

Government planners before the war calculated that there would be up to 600,000 deaths from bombing raids in the first few days of the war. (Their figures were one of the reasons for the appeasement policy of the 1930s.) Plans were therefore made to evacuate all children, pregnant mothers, mothers with young children and disabled people from cities to rural areas.

On the first weekend of the war 827,000 children, 524,000 mothers with young children, 13,000 expectant mothers, 7,000 blind and handicapped people, with 103,000 teachers and helpers were evacuated. Another two million made their own arrangements, often going to the USA or Canada. By the end of September one-third of the British people had moved home.

It didn't always go smoothly. Evacuees tell of being offered around like in a slave auction. Hosts were sometimes amazed at the bad clothing, dirt, disease and lack of toilet training of some evacuees, although this was not always true as Source 8E indicates. Most of all, it gave country dwellers some

▼ **SOURCE 8B** Evacuees and their teacher wave goodbye to their mums at Blackhorse Road Station, London, September, 1939

idea of how poverty had hit some city children in the 1930s. In this way evacuation contributed to the call for change after the war.

► SOURCE 8C

The day arrived, and early in the morning I said goodbye to my two little daughters, dressed in their little kilts and yellow jerseys and clutching their big dolls. I lay in bed and cried all day.

Evacuees' mother, in B. S. Johnson, *The Evacuees*, 1968

► SOURCE 8D

People looked us over and chose children. It was 'Who'd like to go with this nice lady?' or 'Here's a couple who are looking for a nice little girl'.

Alison Smithson, evacuee, in BBC TV film

► SOURCE 8E

I think all London teachers resented the assumption, the very wrong assumption, that tended to be made by many villagers, that every child that came from London must have come from a slum, that they'd been neglected by their parents and above all that they were dirty.

Stanley Reed, London teacher, in BBC TV film

► SOURCE 8F

It was entirely different to see rolling green hills, cows and sheep instead of the grimy bricks and mortar that was London. My son and I were never homesick, we were too happy enjoying the beautiful Dorset scenery.

London evacuee

❓ Questions

a What does Source 8B seem to tell us about how evacuees and their parents reacted to evacuation?

b The government wanted evacuation to succeed, so only cheerful pictures were published. How does that affect your opinion of the usefulness of Source 8B?

c What does Source 8C tell us about the pain of evacuation?

d What do Sources 8D and 8E tell us about the

reaction of host families in the country to evacuees?

e By the end of 1939 60% of evacuees had gone home; does that mean evacuation was a failure?

f How does Source 8F add to our understanding of evacuation?

g Write an account of evacuation based on these sources and your own knowledge. Include comment on how evacuation added to the idea of a 'people's war'.

The Blitz

When German bombing of British cities started in late August 1940 it was both better and worse than expected. Better, because there were actually fewer casualties than the planners had feared; worse, because the bombing of cities, with their tightly packed housing, meant that so many houses were destroyed. For every civilian killed, 35 were made homeless by the blitz.

SHELTERING
The government-built surface shelters were unpopular. They were cold, insanitary and not very safe. Anderson shelters, made of two curved pieces of corrugated iron embedded in the ground, were widely used. People could stay in their own garden and the shelters survived everything except a direct hit.

Many Londoners felt that the tube stations would be a good place to shelter, but they were, at first, forbidden to use them for this. This was because the government were concerned that people would, through fear, stay down there and never come up. In fact, sheer pressure of people forced London Transport to open up the stations for shelterers.

► SOURCE 8G

By 4 p.m. all the platform and passage space of the underground station is staked out, chiefly with blankets folded in long strips against the wall - for the trains are still running and the platforms in full use. On average, one woman or child guards places for six marked out in this way. When evening came the rest of the family crowded in.

Tom Harrisson, *Living through the Blitz*, 1976

SOURCE 8H
Bomb-damaged houses in
Stepney, London, 1940

SOURCE 8I
King George VI and Queen Elizabeth visit tube
shelterers, November, 1940

Rationing

Sixty per cent of the food British people ate in
peacetime came from abroad. Soon after the war
started there were shortages. Goods from Europe
were not available; items from Canada and the East
had to run through the U-boat blockade. At first
shortages meant higher prices, which only the rich
could pay. This was obviously unfair in a 'people's
war' and rationing was introduced in January 1940.
Everyone had a ration book with a certain number
of 'coupons' for essential items, like meat, cheese,
butter, eggs, milk, tea and sugar. It took a lot of
organising, usually by the women in households, to
make the system work. Meals were boring, but they
were nutritious and rationing was regarded as fair.

Pregnant mothers, nursing mothers and babies got
extra rations and every schoolchild got one third of
a pint of milk at school. Households were also
encouraged to 'Dig for Victory' by growing their
own food. Golf courses and parks were dug up for
allotments.

Women and the war

In December 1941 the government made a calculation that they needed two million more workers. To
meet this they had to enlist women. In 1941 all
unmarried women between 20 and 30 could be
called up for war work. In 1942 19 year-olds were
added. Married women were not called up but
could volunteer. By July 1943 all women up to the
age of 51 were registered for employment and by
1945 60% of the workforce in Britain were women;
eight out of ten married women and nine out of ten
single women were either working or in the forces –
the ATS (Auxiliary Territorial Service) the WAAF
(Women's Auxiliary Air Force) or the WRNS
(Women's Royal Naval Service). A powerful campaign of posters and broadcasts urged women to
volunteer.

SOURCE 8J
Today we are calling all women. To
those thousands who have not yet
come forward I would say that here
and now every one of us are needed.
We are fighting for our lives, our
freedom, and our future. We are all in
it together.

From a radio broadcast by Diana Thomas,
May 1941

SOURCE 8K
Government propaganda poster encouraging women to join the Land Army

Come and help with the

VICTORY HARVEST

SOURCE 8L
Women building a tank

SOURCE 8M
The chance of spending her days outside her own home, of making fresh contacts and seeing fresh people is something which neither strain nor fatigue can spoil.

From Mass Observation, 1944

Women were under all sorts of pressure. Women married to servicemen found it difficult to manage on the pay so looked for work, but there was very little childcare available. Employers reluctantly gave more flexible hours for women so that they could shop or look after their children. Women were paid less than men for the same work and received less compensation for injuries.

For some women, the war was an interruption, and an unpleasant one, in their lives. They longed to get back to family life at home. For others, however, a job and money of her own, a chance to learn and practise a skill, to travel and see new things, meant that many women loved these years. It was also going to be much harder, after the war, to argue that women could not do certain jobs.

? Questions

a What arguments are used in the poster (Source 8K) and the broadcast (Source 8J) to persuade women to volunteer for war work?

b What skills would the women in Source 8L need to build a tank?

c What did women like about their war work?

d Why was it difficult for many of them to take a full-time job? How aware were employers and the government of these problems?

The bombing of Germany

Allied bombing of Germany was intended to weaken the German war effort. Industrial regions like the Ruhr and cities like Hamburg and Cologne suffered heavy bombing during the years 1942–1945. The raids meant a great deal of disorganisation and chaos. This was a help to the Allies, especially when they were advancing on Germany after 1944. However, the effect on industry was much less than people thought at the time. During 1943–1944, when the Allied bombing of German factories was heaviest, industrial production actually increased. The raids which caused the most casualties were those aimed at the German cities like Hamburg. Fire bombs caused giant fire storms, whirlwinds of flame, which were impossible to control.

▼ SOURCE 9A

Trees three feet thick were broken off or uprooted, human beings were thrown to the ground or flung alive into the flames by winds which exceeded a hundred and fifty miles an hour. The panic-stricken citizens knew not where to turn. Flames drove them from the shelters, but high-explosive bombs sent them scurrying back again. Once inside, they were suffocated by carbon-monoxide poisoning and their bodies reduced to ashes as though they had been placed in a crematorium, which was indeed what each shelter proved to be. The fortunate were those who jumped into the canals and waterways and remained swimming or standing up to their necks in water for hours until the heat should die down.

A German secret report

▼ SOURCE 9B

Reports from the Rhineland indicate that in some cities people are gradually getting rather weak in the knees. That is understandable. For months the

working population has had to go into air-raid shelters night after night, and when they come out again they see part of their city going up in flames and smoke. The enervating thing about it is that we are not in a position to reply in kind to the English. Our war in the East has lost us air supremacy in essential sections of Europe and we are completely at the mercy of the English.

Dr Joseph Goebbels

? Questions

a What do you think was the purpose of the raids described in Source 9A?

b Do you think the British were right to inflict bombing like that described in Source 9A on German civilians?

c Why do you think the report in Source 9A was a secret report?

d Why, according to Dr Goebbels in Source 9B, are the Germans unable to hit back at British cities in the same way?

e How do you think Dr Goebbels would try to counter the effect of the bombing raids on German workers' morale?

TURNING POINTS 1942–1943

North Africa

In the spring of 1942 the Soviets were still bearing the full force of the German attack. They called upon the Allies to distract Germany by invading Europe and opening up a 'Second Front'. The British and Americans were not ready for this. A full-scale invasion of northern Europe would demand more forces than the Allies had available. However, Roosevelt and Churchill needed victories in order to keep their critics quiet. Churchill was particularly keen to attack in North Africa, and persuaded Roosevelt that this was a good idea. This plan was called Operation Torch. For the two years of 1942 and 1943, therefore, North Africa and the Mediterranean were the main battlefields for the Allied troops. The only direct attacks on the European mainland were the commando raid on Dieppe in 1942 and the RAF bombing raids on Germany.

THE BATTLE OF EL ALAMEIN
The North African campaign began with a two-sided attack on the German forces in North Africa

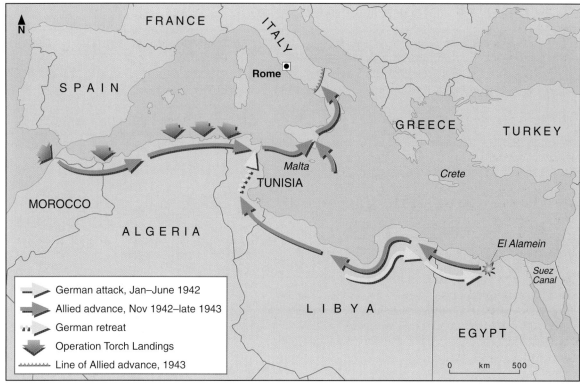

Map 13-3 The campaign in North Africa 1942–1943

(see Map 13-3). In the east, in Egypt, the British army was bringing together massive reinforcements under a new commander, General Bernard Montgomery. In October 1942, he attacked Rommel at El Alamein. This time, the British had the advantage of bigger forces.

▶ SOURCE 10A

The desert has been described as '. . . . miles and miles and bloody miles of absolutely damn all'. There was a seeming eternity of barren inhospitable nothingness . . .

All vehicles could be seen moving from afar because of the trail of dust that billowed up behind or to one side. You might wear sand goggles but your face was coated with sand that caked itself into a beige mask . . . Hands and arms, necks and knees became coated with this same sand, which penetrated under your shirt, and caught in your throat, and made your eyes smart. Your hair became matted . . . Along your limbs the trickling sweat would

cleave little rivulets through the sandy coating . . .

The tanks cut deep ruts in the sand. Half the surface of the desert might appear to be in the air at one time, and drivers would keep their windscreen wipers going in order to clear the dust and so see a few yards ahead.

Cyril Jolly, *Memoirs*

▶ SOURCE 10B

Dearest Lu,

The battle is raging. Perhaps we will still manage to be able to stick it out, in spite of all that's against us - but it may go wrong, and that would have very grave consequences for the whole course of the war. For North Africa would then fall to the British in a few days, almost without a fight. We will do all we can to pull it off. But the enemy's superiority is terrific and our resources very small.

Letter from Field Marshal Rommel to his wife

▼ **SOURCE 10C**   British tanks moving up at El Alamein

? Questions
a Use Sources 10A and 10C to describe conditions at the Battle of El Alamein.
b Why did Rommel not have sufficient troops?
c Why did Rommel also have a problem in getting supplies?

After a few days, Montgomery's forces broke through. Soon, he was chasing Rommel westwards towards Libya and Tunisia. Rommel was partly a victim of his own success. He was really too far advanced for his own supplies to reach him. Hitler showed very bad judgement as supreme commander: he would not let Rommel retreat. The Germans were also having to divert all the men and supplies they could spare to the Russian front. A shortage of oil was beginning to hold them back. Britain, in contrast, now had a rich new ally in the USA.

OPERATION TORCH

Meanwhile, in the west of North Africa, Operation Torch was launched. American and British troops invaded Morocco and Algeria. The Vichy French forces surrendered after a day, and the Allied forces advanced east towards Tunis. The actual advance on Tunis was not completed until May 1943. Thousands of Germans, whom Hitler could ill afford to lose, were taken prisoner.

ITALY INVADED

This was followed up by the Allied invasion of Sicily, then Italy. Mussolini was now ageing and ill, not the strong leader he had once been. He was dismissed by the Italian government, which made peace. In a daring German commando raid Mussolini was then captured (they called it 'rescued') and taken to north Italy. There, a puppet republic was formed with Mussolini as its head, to continue the fight. As 1943 came to an end therefore, the Allies were still well south of Rome, fighting a tough, reorganised German defence. Meanwhile the Italians themselves only wanted peace.

These two years had been successful for the Allies. Churchill said: 'It may almost be said that before El Alamein, we never had a victory; after El Alamein, we never had a defeat.' The Battle of the Atlantic was turning against Germany too, but there was still a long, long way to go and events in Africa and Italy were not as important as the great struggle in the USSR.

The Russian Front 1942–1943

The battlefront between the German-held areas of the USSR and those still in Soviet hands was nearly 1,600 kilometres long. In the north, the city of Leningrad was under siege. Here, there was no distinction between soldiers and civilians: everyone had to work to resist the German attack. Starvation faced everyone. Rats, crows, carpenters' glue and grass were all eaten. In all, one million Russians died in the siege of Leningrad.

STALINGRAD

In the centre of their front line of advance, the Germans were still 160 kilometres from Moscow. The main movement in 1942 came in the south. A two-pronged advance was planned by Hitler: one would drive south-eastwards towards Baku and the Soviet oil fields he needed so badly. The other would turn on Stalingrad and then up the Volga River into central Russia. The main Soviet resistance was at Stalingrad, where the city became the toughest battlefield of the war. The Soviets resisted street by street, house by house, room by room.

▶ SOURCE 11A

We have fought fifteen days for a single house, with mortars, grenades, machine-guns and bayonets. Already by the third day, fifty-four German corpses were lying in the cellars, on the landings and the staircases. The front is a corridor between burnt-out rooms; it is the ceiling between two floors. Help comes from neighbouring houses by fire escapes and chimneys. There is a ceaseless struggle from noon to night. Imagine Stalingrad: eighty days and eighty nights of hand to hand struggles.

A. Clark, *History of the Second World War*

▶ SOURCE 11B

I was horrified when I saw the map. We're quite alone, without any help from outside. Hitler has left us in the lurch. Whether this letter gets away depends on whether we still hold the airfield. So this is what the end looks like. When Stalingrad falls you will hear and read about it. Then you will know that I shall not return.

Anonymous letter from Stalingrad

The winter of 1942–1943 made things worse for the Germans. Then the Soviets broke through the German line to the west and south of Stalingrad. The Germans' supply line, always too long, was now cut off. German General von Paulus asked Hitler for permission to surrender to save the lives of what men he had left. He said he was running out of food, ammunition, dressings and drugs. Hitler refused: 'Surrender is forbidden. The Sixth Army will hold their position to the last man and the last round.' In February 1943, von Paulus surrendered. Of the 285,000 men in his army at Stalingrad in November 1942, he had 91,00 left.

Once again, Hitler's stubbornness made defeat worse. An organised retreat would have shortened the battlefront, shortened the supply lines and saved lives. As it was, he had lost men and weapons in large numbers.

The Soviet advance stopped in March 1943. Hitler counter-attacked with tanks at Kursk in July. Here, the biggest tank battle of the war was fought, with nearly 1,500 tanks on each side. After another fearsome battle the German attack was halted. The almost suicidal courage and endurance of the Soviet soldiers amazed the Germans.

▶ SOURCE 11C

The Russian soldier has an almost incredible ability to stand up to the heaviest artillery fire and air bombardment, while the Russian command remains unmoved by the bloodiest losses. The Russian soldier values his own life no more than those of his comrades. To step on walls of dead, composed of the bodies of his former friends and companions, makes not the slightest impression on him. He is immune to the most incredible hardships.

Panzer General Mellenthin

? Questions

a Use the text and these sources to make a list of the advantages the Soviets had over the Germans in the Battle of Stalingrad. You should think about: supplies; morale; leadership; attitude of the soldiers.
b What does General Mellenthin, Source 11C, seem to think about the Soviet soldiers' attitude to the loss of life?
c What does Source 11C tell us about Soviet commanders attitude to losses of men in battle?

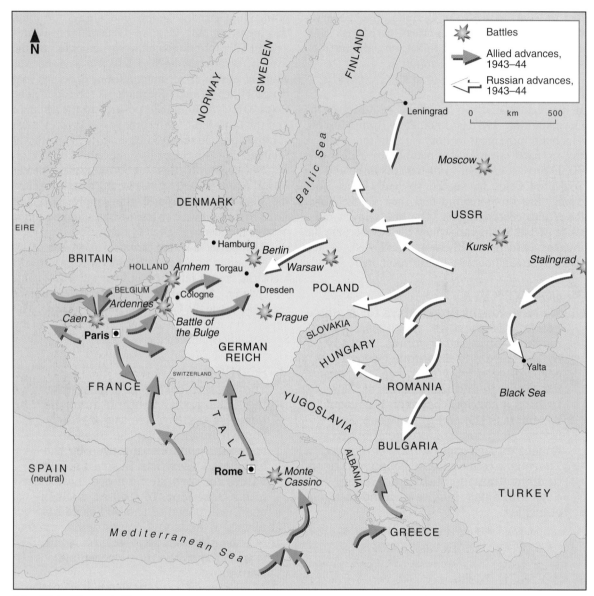

Map 13-4   Victory in Europe

From this point on the initiative passed to the Soviets. Their heavy tanks pushed westwards, followed by the masses of the Red Army, living almost without supplies.

THE TEHERAN CONFERENCE

In 1943, Stalin, Roosevelt and Churchill met in Teheran. They agreed that the western Allies would invade western Europe in 1944. Stalin promised to help the USA against Japan once Germany was defeated. The USSR was promised land at the expense of Poland; Poland was to be compensated at the expense of Germany: it was the first outline discussion of what to do when the war was over.

THE NORMANDY LANDINGS 1944

The main event of this year was the Allied invasion of France in June. Although the Germans were expecting an invasion at some time and at some place along the coast from Holland to Brittany, they could not defend the whole coastline all the time. In early June decoy invasion preparations were made along the narrow part of the Channel,

▼ SOURCE 12B   US troops landing in Normandy on D-Day

between Dover and Calais. The main invasion was then launched on the beaches of Normandy (see Map 13-4). It was a massive combined US and British operation, with the US General Eisenhower as Supreme Commander and the British General Montgomery as his second-in-command. Soldiers had been trained for months in advance, equipment prepared and assembled. A prefabricated harbour, 'Mulberry Harbour', and a cross-Channel oil pipeline, Pluto, were built.

▼ SOURCE 12B

By the spring of 1944 all southern England had become a gigantic air base workshop, storage depot and mobilisation camp. On 1st January American forces in Britain numbered three quarters of a million, and in the following five months they increased to over one and a half million. While British and Canadian troops assembled in south-eastern England, the Americans gathered in the western and south-western coastal belt. Between Dorset and Cornwall lay 'occupied England'.

B. Lidell Hart, *The Other Side of the Hill*

? Questions

a Why were the Americans so important on D-Day, the first day of the Allied invasion of Europe?
b What is meant by 'occupied England' in Source 12A?
c Can you explain why the soldiers in Source 12B are not meeting any German resistance?

The invasion was successful. By the end of the first day, 156,000 men had landed on French soil. The Allied forces pressed on inland with some hard fighting. In August 1944, the Resistance staged a rising in Paris. General de Gaulle arrived in the city with French troops, to an overwhelming reception. He became the new President of France.

An attempt to move rapidly across the Rhine and into Germany after dropping British paratroops on Arnhem was a costly failure. By September, however, the Allies had freed most of France and Belgium. Their advance began to slow down. They needed time to prepare for the final attack on Germany itself.

The main German hope at this time was pinned on their rocket-launched bombs. The V-1s, or 'doodle-bugs', were launched in June, followed in September by the supersonic V-2s each carrying a ton of explosive. Several thousand Londoners were killed and millions evacuated to the countryside. However, people did not panic as Hitler had hoped. In fact, some German commanders were now worrying about the future. In July 1944, there was a plot to assassinate Hitler. A bomb was planted in his map-room. It exploded but failed to kill him. Five thousand Germans were rounded up and executed as a result of the Bomb Plot. Not only Stauffenberg, who had placed the bomb, but also Field Marshal Rommel were arrested. Hitler gave Rommel the choice of facing trial or taking poison; Rommel chose suicide.

THE BATTLE OF THE BULGE
The lull in the Allied advance in the autumn gave the Germans a chance to counter-attack. In December 1944 they advanced in the Ardennes area, causing the Allies to retreat. This was called the Battle of the Bulge because of its effect on the Allied front line. After some severe fighting, however, the Germans' lack of supplies and the strength of Allies air support brought the advance to a halt early in 1945.

The Eastern Front

Hitler was also having to fight on two other fronts. In Italy, the Allied forces were still slogging northwards. Heavy German resistance at Monte Cassino was gradually overcome. In 1944, the Allies entered Rome and Florence.

As you can see from Map 13-4, the Soviets made huge advances in the east. In the north, the siege of Leningrad had ended. All along the line south to the Black Sea, the Germans retreated. In the centre, the Soviet advance drove the Germans out of Russia and into Poland. When the Soviets reached the outskirts of Warsaw, the Polish Resistance rose in revolt. The uprising was put down by the Germans with great savagery: 300,000 Poles were killed and their beloved capital reduced to rubble. The Soviets said they were too exhausted to

help; this may have been true, but it remains a cause of bitterness among Poles that they were left to die unaided. The Soviets have been accused of allowing the Polish Resistance to die so that they could take over Poland more easily.

In the south, too, the Soviet forces drove the Germans out of Russia. From there, the Soviet army was responsible for ending Nazi rule in most of southern and eastern Europe. Czechoslovakia, Hungary, Romania, Bulgaria and Yugoslavia were occupied by Soviet troops. In Yugoslavia the Resistance partisans, led by Tito, played a large part in defeating the Germans. The rapid events of 1944 were to have an important effect on how the map of Europe was redrawn after the war.

By the end of 1944, therefore, Germany's enemies were pressing in on all sides. For the Allies, considering the peace was now as important as calculating how to defeat Hitler.

THE END OF THE THIRD REICH

The Yalta Conference

Early in 1945, the Allied leaders met at Yalta, in southern Russia. It was the last time Roosevelt, Churchill and Stalin would meet. By the end of 1945, Roosevelt was dead and Churchill had been defeated in the British General Election. They agreed that Germany, once defeated, should be divided into four zones. Three of them would be occupied by the USSR, USA and Britain. The fourth zone should go to France. They also agreed that Berlin too should be divided into four zones. The problem of the boundaries in eastern Europe was also discussed. In later years, the western Allies were criticised for handing over eastern Europe to Stalin. However, as Map 13-4 shows, there was very little that the British and Americans could do about it, as the Red Army was already in occupation of most of eastern Europe. The best they could do was to get Stalin to promise to hold free elections in eastern Europe once the war was over.

The fall of Germany

It did not take long to end the war. Germany's resistance was weakened by the massive air-raids on its cities. The climax of these raids came in February 1945, when 3,000 bombers attacked the historic and beautiful city of Dresden. The city was crowded with thousands of refugees fleeing from

SOURCE 13A

British troops guard former SS men while they unload the bodies of their victims, killed at Belsen concentration camp

the Soviet advance. In the fire storms which followed, 100,000 people died. The city was completely flattened. Such raids did little to stop the production of war materials, but the German people realised that defeat was now unavoidable.

In the west, the Allies were held up by the Rhine, until it was crossed at Remagen, near Cologne. From there, the British and Canadians advanced into north Germany while the Americans pushed into central and southern Germany and Austria. The Soviets pressed westwards, reaching Berlin and beyond (see Map 13-4). Soviet and American soldiers met at Torgau in April 1945.

As the allies advanced, they came to the concentration camps, and the full horror of Nazi rule became clear. Photographs like the one in Source 13A soon filled the world's newspapers, bringing feelings of bitter hostility towards the Germans. Allied soldiers sometimes forced local civilians to visit the camps and see what the Nazis had been doing.

❓ Questions

a What kind of problems would the events shown in Sources 13A and 13B make for the German people in the future?

b In Source 13C, which soldiers were from which country?

c What was the mood of these soldiers?

d Why was this mood likely to change when the war ended?

SOURCE 13B

The ruins of Berlin

◤ SOURCE 13C
Soviet and American soldiers in Germany,
May 1945

ERWIN ROMMEL 1891–1944

Adolf Hitler had retired to his deep underground bunker in Berlin. At the end of April, with
the Soviets just a few kilometres away, he married
Eva Braun and then they committed suicide
together. Admiral Doenitz took over as leader of
Germany. He tried to make a separate peace with
the USA and Britain, but they refused, and the war
in Europe ended on 7 May 1945.

Fifty-five million people were killed in the
Second World War, three-quarters of them in
Europe, mostly in eastern Europe. Half of them
were civilians, a fact which clearly points to the
type of war it was. Twenty-seven million Russians,
seven million Germans and 400,000 British lost
their lives. While people were being killed in the
fighting, about 11 million were being executed in
German concentration camps. Six million of them
were Jews. The others were gypsies and other racial
groups, prisoners of war and so-called 'enemies of
state'.

Apart from the death and destruction, the
Second World War brought a completely new kind
of world into being. The victors of the war were the
USA and the USSR. All the other countries, even
those on the winning side, were pygmies compared
to these giants. The new 'Super Powers' held the
world in their hands.

Erwin Rommel came from a middle-class family
in Württemberg, south Germany. In the Kaiser's
Germany before the First World War the
German army was much admired, and Rommel
joined up in 1910. In the First World War, he
fought in France, Italy and Romania.

Rommel did not choose the easy route to
promotion, which was to join the General Staff,
but remained an infantry officer. In 1937 he
wrote a book on warfare, *Infantry Attack*. He
did not join the Nazi Party; like many Germans
from middle and upper classes, he found the
Nazis crude and vulgar.

In February 1940, he led the Seventh Panzer
Regiment in their Blitzkrieg attack on France.
As a result of his success he was made commander of German forces in North Africa in
February 1941. Up to then, the British forces
had been driving the Italians out of Libya;
Rommel's arrival meant that the British had to
retreat. His skill in using tanks in the desert
meant that the Germans advanced rapidly. By
the middle of 1942, the British were driven back

into Egypt. The whole Middle East, with its essential oil supplies, seemed to open up before the Germans. Rommel gained the nickname 'Desert Fox' for his skillful command of tanks, but he also gained the respect of his British enemies. The respect was mutual: Rommel admired his opponents, General Wavell and General Montgomery.

After the Battle of El Alamein, in 1942, Rommel led the German retreat. In March 1943 he was recalled to Germany. He saw by then that defeat was inevitable, and tried to persuade Hitler to make peace terms. He was ignored. About this time, he made contact with the anti-Hitler plotters in the Germany army. They hoped he would become leader of Germany if Hitler was removed, but he did not know about the attempts to assassinate Hitler.

In 1944, he was put in charge of Channel defences. Again he disagreed with Hitler over policy. He felt that more men and equipment were needed to prevent the Allies making a landing. After the success of D-Day, he again called on Hitler to seek peace. In July 1944, he was injured in a British air-raid, so was in hospital when the 'Bomb Plot' took place. The link between the plotters and Rommel was soon made. Rommel was arrested and persuaded to take poison. He was then given a full military hero's funeral in October 1944.

ASSESSMENT

Describe, explain and analyse

1   Choose one of the following 'turning-points' of the Second World War:

   i) The Battle of Britain, 1940.

   ii) The Battle of El Alamein, 1942.

   iii) The Battle of Stalingrad, 1942–43.

a) Describe what happened in each battle.

b) Explain who won and why.

c) Explain why it was a turning-point in the war.

2   a) In what ways was the Home Front in the Second World War a 'people's war'?

   b) How did: the Blitz, evacuation and rationing all contribute to the feeling that it was a 'people's war'?

   c) How did the idea of a 'people's war' affect people's views about the country after the war?

3   a) Choose two of the items in the following list and say how they contributed to the defeat of Hitler.

   i) US aid.

   ii) Battle of Britain.

   iii) Soviet war effort.

   iv) Italian defeats.

   v) Hitler's mistakes.

   vi) The war at sea.

   b) Choose two which you think were the most important and explain your choice, comparing them with other factors.

Evidence and interpretations

1   A real advance in the achievement of women's equality.

2   As in the First World War, women were called upon to help win the war, but they were still not treated as equals.

a   Write a paragraph in support of each of these statements.

b   Use your own knowledge and what you have read in this chapter to say which of the two statements you think is more correct.

14: The Second World War in the Far East

The Second World War moved into the Far East with the Japanese attacks on the US Pacific Fleet, lying at anchor in Pearl Harbor, Hawaii, on 7 December 1941. Why did the Japanese launch this attack?

JAPANESE SUCCESSES 1937–1942

Japan's generals had decided to solve the problems of the Depression of the 1930s in Japan by seizing an empire. They started in 1931 by invading Manchuria, part of northern China (see Map 14-1 and page 107). In 1936, Japan joined Germany and Italy in the Anti-Comintern Pact: an alliance of the three military dictatorships against Communism. However, Japan's next victim was not a Communist country: in 1937, Japan invaded China. Soon large parts of China were in Japanese hands.

The outbreak of war in Europe opened up great possibilities for the Japanese. The British, French and Dutch empires in the Far East could not be defended while their European homelands

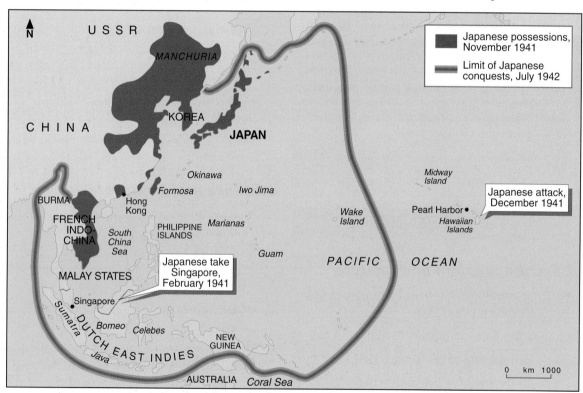

Map 14-1 Japan's conquests in the Far East

were under attack. The Japanese spoke of 'freeing' the peoples of Asia from white colonial rule. They spoke of a 'New Order' in Asia. However, what they really had their eyes on were the food and raw materials which Asia could produce to boost Japanese industry: rice, coal, rubber, tin and oil. After France was defeated, the Japanese occupied Indo-China in 1941. The whole of the Far East seemed to be open to them, and only two countries could stop them: the USSR and the USA. By June 1941, the USSR was fighting for its life against the German invaders; only the USA was left.

Pearl Harbor

In mid-1941, President Roosevelt imposed a ban on all trade with Japan in iron, steel and oil, and froze all Japanese money in the USA. His aim was to force Japan to keep the peace. The Japanese faced a clear choice of backing down or going to war. They realised that they would lose a war with the USA unless they could gain an advantage. The military leaders in Japan, therefore, planned a secret and surprise attack to knock out the US Pacific Fleet. They calculated that this would gain

▶ **SOURCE 1A**
US battleships burning at Pearl Harbor, Hawaii, 7 December, 1941

them a two-year period of supremacy at sea during which they could seize all the territory they wanted in the Far East. They would then be too strong to be dislodged by the USA.

Late in 1941, the Japanese Admiral Yamamoto led his aircraft carriers, secretly, across the Pacific until he was about 480 kilometres north of Pearl Harbor (see Map 14-1). Spies had supplied the Japanese with details of the great US naval base. The Japanese knew where the American ships were anchored, the depth of the water, details of the anti-aircraft defences and when most of the ships would be there. From Yamamoto's carriers 360 Japanese bombers took off and flew to Pearl Harbor in two waves early on the Sunday morning of 7 December. The US fleet was caught completely unprepared.

? Questions
a Why do you think the Japanese chose a Sunday morning for the attack?
b Why was it important to destroy installations, including airfields as well as ships?

Eight battleships were sunk or damaged; ten other ships were sunk; 188 aircraft destroyed; 159 aircraft damaged and 2,403 people killed. The Japanese lost only 29 aircraft. It seemed as if the attack was a complete success. The US commanders had half expected an attack, but were completely wrong over the directions from which it would come. Certainly the sailors and airmen in Hawaii were not on the alert. The close, paired ranks of the ships and planes made easy targets. Fortunately, however, part of the US fleet, including aircraft carriers, was at sea and so escaped. So did a large amount of the oil stored onshore. Most important of all, Japan had now taken on the most powerful country in the world, the USA. President Roosevelt called the attack 'a day of infamy'. American isolation ended suddenly and for good.

Japanese advances

The Japanese pressed home their advantage. They took the US bases of Guam and Wake Island in the Pacific. They captured Hong Kong from the British and moved into Malaya, then a British colony. Three days after Pearl Harbor, a similar air attack sank two warships of the Royal Navy, the *Repulse* and the *Prince of Wales,* off the Malayan coast. The Dutch East Indies and the Philippines were invaded early in 1942.

SOURCE 2A

They [*the Japanese*] wore the lightest of uniforms, a singlet, cotton shorts, rubber-soled shoes. There was no uniformity about either the colour or the form of their dress. Both dress and equipment were as light as they could be, and all our commanders agreed that their cross-country capacity was remarkable . . . Often they wore Malay sarongs . . . This . . . troubled our troops since the country through which the war was being fought was fairly thickly populated and our men were never able to distinguish between friend and foe . . . In the matter of food also the Japanese were at the advantage. Being rice-eaters, they were able to live off the country, eating the same food as the Malays and the Chinese used to eat. The British troops were dependent upon elaborate catering arrangements. The Japanese soldier would set off through the jungle carrying a bottle of water and a large ball of rice, with some preserved seaweed and a few pickles to make the rice palatable. Those were his rations for three or four days.

Nearly all the Japanese infantry were armed with tommy-guns or other light automatic weapons. They were ideal for this close-range jungle fighting . . .Their local knowledge was excellent. They had good maps with them, and their guides were mostly former Japanese residents of Malaya whose job it had been to gain a detailed knowledge of the terrain . . .

One of the most conspicuous features of the campaign was the great use which the Japanese made of bicycles . . . Bicycles . . . enabled their forward troops to progress at great speed.

Ian Morrison, *Malayan Postscript*

SOURCE 2B

Our front-line soldiers [*the British*] were at this time equipped like Christmas trees, with heavy boots, web equipment, packs, haversacks, waterbottles, blankets, groundsheets and even greatcoats, so that they could hardly walk, much less fight.

F. Spencer Chapman, *The Jungle Is Neutral*

? Questions

a   What advantages did the Japanese soldier have? Think about: clothing; rations; weapons; information; transport.
b   Why did they wear the same clothes as the local inhabitants?
c   In what ways were these particularly appropriate for fighting in the jungles of South-East Asia?
d   How did the British soldier compare with the Japanese in each of the headings above?
e   Who do you think was responsible for the differences?

The big British base at Singapore was heavily defended against sea attack. The approach by land was through jungle and swamp, so was not defended. The Japanese attacked Singapore, crossing from Malaya, and in February 1942, the British surrendered. The Japanese took 80,000 prisoners of war.

JAPAN 1942-1944

Map 14-1 shows that the Japanese empire was largely made up of islands, with thousands of miles of sea between them. Control of the sea was, therefore, vital. However, as Admiral Yamamoto had shown, battleships could easily be sunk by aircraft flying from aircraft carriers. To control the sea, it was now necessary to control the air. A naval war would now be fought from aircraft carriers, protected by other warships. Whole battles would be fought between fleets which at no time came within sight of each other, but which launched aircraft at each other. It was a lesson which the USA rapidly learned, from the experience of Pearl Harbor and the sinking of the British warships.

The Battle of the Coral Sea

In May 1942, the Japanese fleet met the US Pacific fleet in the Battle of the Coral Sea (see Map 14-2). Both sides suffered heavy damage, but the Japanese lost two carriers to America's one. Furthermore, the Japanese failed to capture the rest of New Guinea, from which they could have attacked Australia. This was their first setback.

The Battle of Midway

The next month, a Japanese attack was launched on the US-held island of Midway. By now the US had broken the Japanese radio code, so the Japanese had no surprise advantage. In fact, Yamamoto was badly misled about the size of the US force he was attacking. At the Battle of Midway in June 1942 four Japanese carriers were sunk. It was the turning point of the war in the Pacific.

Allied counter-attack

The counter-attack on the Japanese positions was three-pronged. US Admiral Nimitz led the sea-borne attack westwards across the Pacific. By mid-1944, he had retaken the important base of Guam. In the south-west Pacific, General MacArthur began to fight his way north-westwards towards the Philippines. His strategy was called 'island-hopping': he could not hope to destroy Japanese positions island by island. By leapfrogging to important bases, he cut Japanese supply lines, and Japanese positions he missed would be isolated and dealt with later. In 1942 and 1943, MacArthur moved up to the Solomon Islands after a successful landing at Guadalcanal in August 1942.

Meanwhile, the third line of attack on the Japanese was launched by the British in Burma. At first, they had little success. Apart from the Japanese, they also had to deal with the heat, the tropical diseases and the hazards of the jungle itself. Prisoners taken by the Japanese were treated badly. The Japanese believed that surrender was shameful and that it was much better to die fighting or even to commit suicide than to be taken by the enemy. The prisoners they captured were regarded with contempt, badly fed and often worked to death or allowed to die of disease.

Both MacArthur in the islands and General Slim in Burma found the Japanese fierce and fanatical fighters.

▶ SOURCE 3A

There were about thirty of us wounded soldiers left in the cave. Those who could move assisted others . . . They all shouted, 'Long live the Emperor' before leaving the world . . . I still have two hand grenades: one to destroy myself and one for the enemy. I don't know whether or not my rations will last until we are rescued. I determined to

kill myself before I lose the power to pull the grenade pin.

A Japanese soldier on Wake Island, 1944

▶ SOURCE 3B

The Japanese are the bravest people I have ever met. In our armies, any of them, nearly every Japanese would have had a Congressional Medal or a Victoria Cross. It is the fashion to dismiss their courage as fanaticism, but this only begs the question. They believed in something and they were willing to die for it . . . What else is bravery? They pressed home their attacks when no other troops in the world would have done so, when all hope of success was gone. The Japanese simply came on, using all their skill and rage, until they were stopped by death. In defence they held their ground with a furious tenacity that never faltered. They had to be killed, company by company, squad by squad, man by man, to the last. Frugal and bestial, barbarous and brave, artistic and brutal, they were the [enemy].

J. Masters, *The Road Past Mandalay*

❓ Questions

a What was the attitude of the Japanese soldiers towards death?
b From these sources, describe what particular problems there were in fighting the Japanese.
c Do you agree with the author of Source 3B that the Japanese were brave?
d How far does Source 3A support the judgement of the Japanese soldier given in Source 3B?
e Which of these sources is more useful for finding out about the Japanese, the one by a Japanese (3A) or the one by a British writer (3B)?

JAPAN 1944–1945

By 1944, American superiority was beginning to become obvious. In 1941, the Japanese had risked attacking the greatest industrial nation in the world.

Even though the major US effort went into the war in Europe, Japanese tactics had clearly failed. Table 14-1 shows how bad Japan's position was.

Table 14-1 Japan's resources, 1941–45

Japanese shipping losses:			
1942	1,150,000 tons		
1943	2,070,000 tons		
1944	4,120,000 tons		

Japanese stocks of essential materials:			
Oil	1941	43 million barrels	
	1945	4 million barrels	
Steel output	1944	7.8 million tons	
	1945	1.0 million tons	

Aircraft production:			
	1941	1942	1943	1944
USA	19,453	49,445	92,196	100,752
Japan	5,088	88,610	16,693	29,180

❓ Questions

a Explain how each of these groups of figures shows a weakness in Japan's war effort.

b Which single item do you think was the most important in contributing to Japan's defeat?

Battle of Leyte Gulf

Still the Japanese fought on with savage determination. In October 1944, MacArthur invaded the Philippines. The Japanese threw what was left of their navy into an attack on the invasion fleet, in the Battle of Leyte Gulf (see Map 14-2). The Japanese lost four more carriers and two battleships: their navy had now really ceased to exist. On land, 170,000 Japanese soldiers died trying to prevent the American advance on Manila, the capital of the Philippines.

Kamikaze pilots

At this stage, the Japanese began to send Kamikaze pilots against the American fleet. Kamikaze means

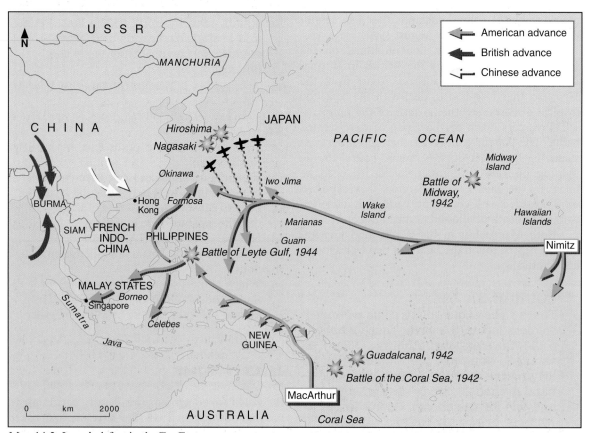

Map 14-2 Japan's defeat in the Far East

'Divine Wind', and pilots would deliberately crash their planes, loaded with explosives, on to an American battleship. To commit suicide in this way was regarded as an honourable thing to do. The pilots were treated as heroes before their last missions. Before the end of the war, Kamikaze pilots had sunk 34 US ships and damaged 288 more.

Japanese defeats

In 1944, the Japanese had invaded India. The invasion was stopped by General Slim at Imphal. From then on, the British pressed on into Burma, driving the Japanese back. Behind their lines, guerrilla soldiers called 'Chindits', led by Orde Wingate, destroyed supply lines. Soon, the 'Burma Road' was open. This was the only land route to China. Up to this time the Chinese had been supplied by air-lift over the Himalayas – a very dangerous route to fly. Now US aid could reach China by land. However, the Chinese leader, General Chiang Kai-Shek, showed little inclination to fight the Japanese. He was more interested in crushing his own enemies, the Chinese Communists (see Chapter 15). If Japan were to be finally defeated, it would have to be by the USA.

With this in view, attacks were launched

◤ SOURCE 4
US marines plant a flag on top of Iwo Jima

against two islands which could be used as bases for air-raids on Japan itself. In February 1945, Iwo Jima was taken and in April, Okinawa. In each case, the Japanese fought to the last man for every inch of ground.

Although the Japanese were prepared to sacrifice any number of lives to stave off defeat, the Americans saw things differently. In taking Iwo Jima, 4,000 Americans died, and at Okinawa, 12,000. How many Americans would have to die before Japan surrendered? This was a problem which, in a democracy like the USA, worried President Harry Truman (who had taken office after Roosevelt's death) considerably.

THE END OF THE WAR 1945

Japan was clearly on its knees. The Emperor himself wanted peace, but his generals were prepared to fight on. The Americans were now able to bomb Japanese cities at will. In March 1945, 80,000 people died in a raid on Tokyo. The US navy was by now able to prevent supplies getting through to Japan, and there was widespread hunger throughout the country.

The atomic bomb

By mid-1945, however, President Truman had at his command a way of ending the war rapidly: the atomic bomb. The work on an atomic bomb had been going on since 1942. Called the Manhattan Project, it was now nearing completion. It is important to remember that some of the leading scientists working on the Manhattan Project – for example Einstein, Fermi and Szeland – had fled to the USA to escape Nazi and Fascist dictatorship. On 16 July 1945 an atomic bomb was successfully tested at Los Alamos in the Nevada Desert. The blast was seen over 300 kilometres away.

Potsdam

At the Potsdam meeting in July 1945, Truman, Attlee (who had succeeded Churchill as Prime Minister) and Stalin agreed that the USSR would join in the war in the east within a month. The Allies also announced that the atom bomb would be dropped on Japan if it did not surrender. The Japanese either did not understand or did not believe the threat.

On 6 August, Colonel Tibbetts piloted his bomber, the 'Enola Gay', to Hiroshima, a Japanese city in the south-west of the main island, and dropped a single atomic bomb.

▼ SOURCE 5A
'Mushroom cloud' from the atom-bomb detonation

▼ SOURCE 5B

Suddenly a glaring pinkish light appeared in the sky, accompanied by an unnatural tremor which was followed almost immediately by a wave of heat and a wind which swept away everything in its path . . .

Many were killed instantly, others lay writhing on the ground screaming in agony from the intolerable pain of their burns. Everything standing upright in the way of the blast - walls, houses, factories and other buildings – was annihilated. Trams were picked up and tossed aside . . . Horses, dogs and cattle suffered the same fate as human beings . . . Even the vegetation did not escape. Trees went up in flames, the rice plants lost their green-ness, the grass burned on the ground like dry straw . . .

Up to about three miles from the centre of the explosion, lightly built houses were flattened as though they had been built of cardboard. Those who were inside were either killed or wounded. Those who managed to extricate themselves by some miracle found themselves surrounded by a ring of fire. And the few who succeeded in making their way to safety generally died some twenty or thirty days later from the delayed effects of the deadly gamma-rays . . . About half an hour after the explosion, whilst the sky all around Hiroshima was still cloudless, a fine rain began to fall on the town and went on for about five minutes . . . Then a violent wind arose and the fires extended with terrible rapidity because most Japanese houses are built only of timber and straw.

A Japanese journalist, Hiroshima

❓ Questions

a What are the stages of an atomic explosion?
b How large an area was affected?
c How did people die?

On 8 August, the USSR declared war on Japan. On 9 August, a second atomic bomb was dropped, on Nagasaki. This was the only other atomic bomb

▶ SOURCE 5C   Hiroshima after the bomb

that the USA possessed, but the Japanese did not know this and surrendered on 14 August. General MacArthur signed the Japanese surrender terms.

In Hiroshima 70,000 Japanese died, and 40,000 more in Nagasaki; thousands more have died from radiation sickness in the years since then. President Truman has been heavily criticised for his decision to drop the atom bombs. His main reason for ordering them to be dropped was that he wanted the war to be finished quickly, without further loss of American lives. It has also been suggested that a quick end to the war prevented the USSR, whom the USA was beginning to see as a rival, from taking any territory in the East.

What options did Truman have?

1. A blockade so that no supplies reached Japan at all and the country would be slowly starved into surrender.
2. A demonstration of the power of the bomb to Japanese observers who could explain to their leaders exactly what it could do to their country.
3. Demanding less than unconditional surrender from the Japanese. The British General

Montgomery argued for this: 'The removal of the obstacle of unconditional surrender would have saved lives because, I consider, Japan would then have surrendered earlier.'
4. Dropping the bomb. Winston Churchill supported Truman's decision to do this: 'To bring the war to an end, to give peace to the world.'

What do you think Truman should have done?

The war in the East was over in 1945, but its effects were long lasting. First, the attack on Pearl Harbor ended the isolationist policy of the USA forever. Since December 1941, the USA has been unable to ignore the rest of the world and go its own way. Second, the dropping of the atomic bombs gave birth to a totally different world. Humankind now has the capacity to destroy itself on an unbelievable scale. The bombs dropped on Hiroshima and Nagasaki were equivalent to several thousand ordinary bombs; nuclear bombs of today are several hundred times more powerful than those dropped on Japan.

The world has had to live with this threat of total destruction ever since 6 August 1945.

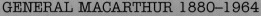

GENERAL MACARTHUR 1880–1964

General Douglas MacArthur was the key figure in the American victory in the Pacific war. His intelligence and skill as a general brought the USA success with limited forces. His toughness and courage inspired the soldiers and sailors in the savage battles they had to fight. In peacetime, his personality led him into more controversial actions.

Douglas MacArthur was born in Arkansas. He was the son of an army officer and went to West Point, the US army college. In the First World War, he gained rapid promotion, fighting on the Western Front and working for the occupying forces in Germany up to 1920.

Between the wars, the USA had a small army: US policy was isolationist, and large forces were not required. MacArthur did his best to keep up the efficiency of what forces there were. He spent some years as Superintendent of West Point. In the 1920s, he made his first contact with the East, serving two terms in the Philippines. He came to have a close understanding and respect for the Filipino people.

Much more controversial was the 1932 'Bonus army' incident: in the depths of the Depression, with 12 million unemployed, First World War veterans came to Washington to ask for their 'bonuses', payable in 1945. Many camped on the outskirts of the city. MacArthur was sent to clear them off, which he did with some ruthlessness, using cavalry and tear-gas.

MacArthur retired in 1937, but was recalled in 1941. He led the resistance to the Japanese in the Philippines, from a base in the hills of Bataan. When he was forced to leave in early 1942, he promised the Filipinos that he would be back. In March 1942, he was put in command of Allied forces in the south-west Pacific. Gradually, the tide turned. 'Island-hopping' northwards, he returned to the Philippines in autumn 1944, as he had promised. On 2 September 1945, he received the Japanese surrender.

MacArthur was put in charge of organising Japan for peace. For a while, he was virtually dictator of the country: he removed all the old militarists and demobilised the army; he reorganised the economy and the constitution; he made changes in land ownership, education and the legal position of women. Modern Japan is, in many ways, his work.

In 1950, war broke out in Korea. MacArthur was put in command of the UN forces, which were mainly American. He was largely successful but wanted to carry the attack into China to press his advantage. This led to quarrels with President Truman, and in April 1951, he was sacked.

Unlike General Eisenhower, MacArthur was not attracted into politics. He lived quietly in New York until his death in 1964.

ASSESSMENT

Describe, explain and analyse

1   **a)** What did the Japanese do at Pearl Harbor on 7 December 1941?

   b) What were they trying to achieve?

   c) Did they succeed in their aims?

2 **a)** Choose two of the items from the list below. Describe how it led to the defeat of Japan.

  i) General MacArthur.

  ii) US industrial strength.

  iii) The atom bomb.

  iv) The Burma campaign.

  v) The battle of Coral Sea.

  vi) Island-hopping.

b) Choose the item which you think was the most important factor in the defeat of Japan. Explain your choice, comparing it with other items.

Evidence and interpretations

◤ SOURCE A
The world will know that the first atomic bomb was dropped on Hiroshima - a military base. We used this in order to shorten the agony of war, in order to save the lives of thousands and thousands of young Americans.

President Truman

◤ SOURCE B
Gentlemen, can I tell you what really worries me? Russia's spreading influence in Eastern Europe. Romania, Bulgaria, Yugoslavia, Czechoslovakia, Hungary are all living under a Soviet shadow. It will be impossible to persuade Russia to remove her troops from Poland, unless she is impressed by American military might. Now our possessing and demonstrating the bomb will make Russia more manageable.

James Byrnes, adviser to President Truman

a What were Truman's motives for dropping the bomb, according to what he says in Source A?

b Use your own knowledge to explain his decision.

c What were Byrnes' reasons for dropping the bomb, according to Source B?

d Use your own knowledge to explain what he meant.

e Which of these two interpretations do you think seems more likely? Explain your answer.

15: China to 1949

China is now a powerful country which plays an important part in world affairs. It has a huge population of over 1,080 million people. Nearly one in every four human beings is Chinese. This chapter explains how in 1949 this huge land, with its ancient civilisation, became the second country to have a Communist revolution.

EARLY HISTORY

For many centuries China was cut off from the rest of the world. If you look at Map 15-1 you will see that China is surrounded by mountains, jungle, deserts or oceans. This did not matter to the Chinese because, in the valleys of the great rivers along the eastern plain, the land was fertile. The area is large, and civilisation grew up here many centuries before Christ. Except for the Japanese, rather rudely called 'the shrimp people' by the Chinese, they met no other civilised peoples. To them, China was everything; in fact, the word 'China' means 'the earth' or 'the world'.

Map 15-1   China

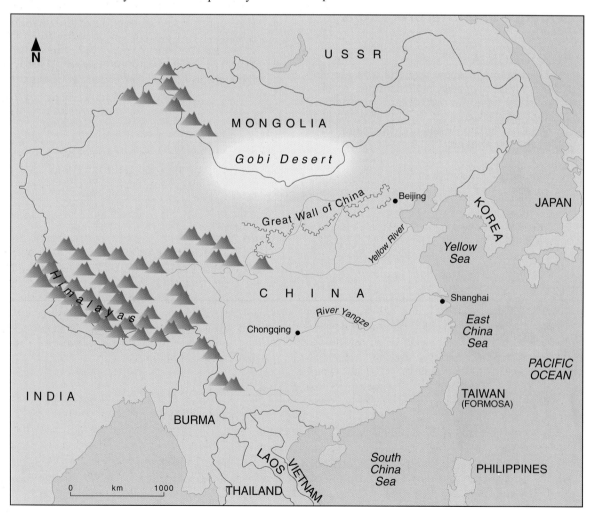

In 1793, King George III of Britain sent a mission to the Emperor of China with gifts. He received this reply:

► SOURCE 1

You, O king from afar, have yearned after the blessing of our civilisation . . . Our Celestial Empire possesses all things in abundance and lacks no product. There was therefore no need to import the manufactures of outside barbarians for our own produce . . . The Throne's principle is to treat strangers from afar with indulgence and exercise a pacifying control over barbarians the world over . . . Tremblingly obey, and show no negligence.

Quoted in F. Schurman and O. Scheel, *Imperial China*

❓ Questions

a What is the attitude of the Emperor to George III?
b What is the attitude of the Emperor to imports?
c What sort of things do you think the British would offer to trade in 1793?
d How does the Emperor regard all other nations of the world?
e What do you think would be the British reaction to this reply?

This attitude to the world outside China is deep-rooted in the Chinese people.

The people

There has been a great rise in the population of China in recent centuries. In 1700 there were 100 million Chinese, but by 1900 this had risen to 400 million. Most of these people were peasants: poor farmers struggling to keep alive on tiny plots of land. In 1930, for example, the average peasant holding was under four acres in size. The rising population made this shortage of land worse. Half, or even three-quarters, of the crops had to go to the landlord as rent. Then there were taxes to pay. Money-lenders took advantage of the peasants, charging high interest rates. If the crops failed, the peasant would not be able to meet his bills. In a really bad year, millions died.

► SOURCE 2

We have always been farmers. But we did not have our own land. We rented it. For three generations we rented the same land. The landlord's name was Wang.

Landlords did not eat as we others did. They ate meat and vegetables every day. Wang was an incredibly mean person. He made you give back the tiniest coin due to him. He was hard. If people could not pay he punished them.

People hated the landlords, but there was no way of getting round them: 'As long as we have our daily food we must be satisfied,' people said. 'We must do what our masters say. They own the land and the oxen.' Everybody owed him money. As long as you owed him money you could not get permission to leave the village in order to look for a better landlord. The landlord ate up people's work. They ate and we worked.

J. Myrdal, *Report from a Chinese Village*, published 1965

❓ Questions

a What differences were there between the lives of the peasants and those of the landlords?
b What powers did the landlords have over the peasants?

WOMEN

The peasants of China were used to this poverty and did not think of change. Custom and tradition ruled their lives. Tradition taught that women were inferior and had no rights. They had to obey their husbands or fathers completely. Wives could even be sold by their husbands. The Chinese people did not think of changing this any more than they thought of throwing out the landlords.

The government

China was ruled by an emperor, living in Beijing. Since the 17th century, the emperors had all come from the Manchu Dynasty, invaders from the north. They had conquered China and made every Chinese person wear their hair in a pigtail, Manchu-style, as a sign of conquest.

▼ **SOURCE 3**   Dowager Empress Cixi, who ruled China from 1861 to 1908

There were strict rules at court. For example, the Empress had been given a Rolls-Royce, but she never used it. This was because it was forbidden for a servant to sit beside, or with his back to, the Empress.

❓ Questions

a Notice the Empress's long fingernails and her platform shoes. These were signs of the upper classes. Why do you think peasant women did not grow their fingernails long or wear platform shoes?

b Do you think the kind of government described here would be able to deal with 20th-century problems?

Under the emperors the work of governing China was carried out by the mandarins. These were educated, upper-class Chinese. In 1900 they lived by the same laws and rules which had been in use in China for centuries. Even their religion worked against any change. They studied the writings of Confucius, who said that in the past everything was good, therefore all change is bad. The mandarins made sure that the laws were obeyed.

▸ **SOURCE 4**   A law court

? Questions

a What is the attitude of those before the court?
b On whose side do you think the mandarins would be: the landlords' or the peasants'?
c Why would the peasants hate and fear the law court?

Thus, the small group of landlords, mandarins and the Emperor (about 10% of the population), held all power and most of the land. They lived by the old traditions dating back hundreds of years. These traditions were now becoming increasingly out of date.

The foreigners

In the 19th century, China's civilisation was overtaken by European countries. These countries developed factories and produced goods which the Chinese could not match. European countries wanted to trade with Chinese, and sell them industrial goods. At first they were given the same answer that George III received. This time the Europeans fought back. First, the British in the 'opium wars' of the 1840s, then other countries, forced the Chinese to trade.

By 1900, many parts of China were really controlled by foreigners (see Map 15-2). This foreign control was established by making a number of 'unequal treaties' with the Chinese. The emperors were powerless to stop them: their old-fashioned weapons could not take on European guns and warships. The Chinese, who had thought themselves superior for so long, were angry. In one Chinese city controlled by foreigners, there was a sign at the entrance to a park: 'Chinese and dogs not admitted'. There was a rising against the foreigners in 1900, called the Boxer Rising. It was put down, and many Chinese were executed. The power of foreigners within China was another reason why some educated Chinese were ready for change.

From what has been said so far, it is clear that China was ripe for change. However, most of its people were completely uneducated: they did not think of China as a country. A peasant was worried about poverty in his own village. He did not think about China as a whole. Sun Yatsen

Map 15-2   Areas and towns under foreign control in 1900

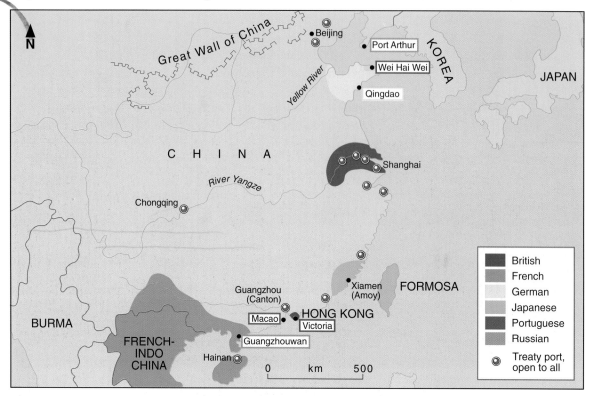

described the Chinese people as 'grains of loose sand' pushed this way and that.

SUN YATSEN AND THE 1911 REVOLUTION

Only a few people in China worked to change these conditions. They were the tiny number who had some education and knowledge of the outside world. One of these was Sun Yatsen. Trained as a doctor, he travelled outside China, to Britain, France and the USA. A small group of his followers began to prepare for a revolution. His ideas for the future of China were based on his 'Three Principles':

1. Nationalism: the Manchu emperors and the foreigners should be driven out of China.
2. Democracy: China should be ruled by a president and parliament, elected by the people.
3. Socialism: the government should take over all businesses, all transport and all farms. These should should be modernised so that everyone had a good standard of living.

When the old Empress, Cixi, died in 1908, the new Emperor was her nephew, Pu Yi, who was only three years old. This seemed a good moment to choose to plot for a revolution. Sun Yatsen's supporters were working towards this when their plans were discovered, but they decided to go ahead. On 10 October (the tenth month, hence the 'Double Tenth') 1911, the Emperor was overthrown and a republic declared. All over China, people cut off their pigtails, the hated mark of Manchu rule. Sun Yatsen was in the USA at the time. He hurried back to become the first President.

The warlords

Unfortunately, Sun was not supported by the mass of the Chinese people, who did not know what was going on. Into the gap left by the removal of the emperors came, not Sun Yatsen, but a series of warlords. These were men who had put together their own armies. With them, a warlord could rule a city, a province or even for a time the whole country. Sun was forced to resign in 1912. He became President again in the south in 1917, but the rest of China was ruled by a number

▼ **SOURCE 5** Execution during the warlord period

of selfish warlords. It was a bad time for the Chinese people.

? Questions
a How is this execution being carried out?
b Why do you think this execution is being carried out in public?
c Why are events like this a sign of bad government?

In Chapter 4, we saw that there were two revolutions in Russia in 1917; in China, there is a gap of 38 years between the two; it took from 1911 to 1949 for Sun Yatsen's 'grains of loose sand' to join together in a Communist victory. There were three reasons for the failure of Sun's Revolution of the Double Tenth, 1911:

1. The warlords were too powerful;
2. Sun's supporters were few in number, as only a few Chinese were educated;
3. Most of the Chinese people did not know what was happening to their country.

THE MAY THE FOURTH MOVEMENT
Slowly this situation began to change. At the Treaty of Versailles in 1919, the Chinese asked for all the lands that Germany had held in China to be handed back. Instead, the lands were given to Japan.

On 4 May, there were angry demonstrations in the streets of Chinese cities. This 'May the Fourth Movement' showed that the Chinese were beginning to care what happened to their country. Their resentment at being controlled by foreigners increased. It gradually brought the Chinese people to think and act together.

THE GUOMINDANG (GMD)

Meanwhile, the Russian Revolution had taken place in 1917. Sun Yatsen had been disappointed that Britain and the USA failed to support him. He admired the Russian Communists and asked them to come and give him advice. He reorganised his party, renaming it the Guomindang (Nationalist) Party – the GMD. At the same time, the Russians helped to set up a small Chinese Communist Party. Sun Yatsen was not a Communist, but he worked with them and allowed Communists to join the GMD. The Russians also trained Sun's soldiers. They set up a military academy at Whampoa. Sun realised that the warlords could only be defeated by war. In 1925, just when he seemed ready to take on the warlords, Sun Yatsen died.

CHIANG KAISHEK AND CIVIL WAR

The next leader of the GMD was Chiang Kaishek. He had been trained as a soldier in Russia but admired the European fascist dictators. His supporters were mainly in the cities: merchants, landlords and bankers. His government was corrupt and offered little to the peasants. He became increasingly hostile to the Communists.

The Northern Expedition and the Shanghai Massacres

Chiang's first task was to remove the warlords. This was done in the two-year Northern Expedition. In 1926, the Guomindang forces set out from Guangzhou (Canton) and reached as far north as Shanghai; by 1928 the rest of China was taken. The Communists helped in the Northern Expedition and worked among the people of the cities as they fell to the Guomindang. They helped workers organise trade unions; they helped the peasants throw out the landlords. This kind of activity worried Chiang and his supporters. In 1927, he turned on the Communists and ordered the Shanghai Massacres: any known Communist was rounded up and killed.

A few Communists escaped, and for the next few years were hounded by Chiang's forces. At first, with Soviet advice, the Communists worked in the cities. Karl Marx had said that only industrial workers could lead a revolution. Events in Russia in 1917 seemed to prove this. In China, however,

there were few workers; time and again the Communists' efforts in the cities failed. One man who realised this was Mao Zedong; he saw that in China it had to be the peasants who would lead a Communist rising.

▶ SOURCE 6

In a very short time . . . several hundred million peasants will rise like a hurricane . . . a force so swift and violent that no power however great will be able to hold it back . . . They will sweep all the imperialists, warlords, corrupt officials, local tyrants and evil landlords into their graves.

Mao Zedong

❓ Questions

a What does Mao say the peasant rising will be like?
b What were the grievances of the peasants?
c Why were there so few industrial workers in China?

Mao was the son of a peasant, so knew all about their problems. He had worked hard to get a university education, sometimes going without food for days. He had joined the Chinese Communist Party at its beginning in 1921. His ideas about a peasant rising were not popular in the party at first, and he was dismissed from the Chinese Communist Party Committee. He went to the province of Jiangxi and began to work among the peasants. Landlords were thrown out and land shared out among the peasants. Soon, he had a Red Army of 11,000 in Jiangxi.

The Long March

Chiang was determined to crush the Red Army. Each year, from 1931 to 1934, he surrounded and attacked Jiangxi. Finally, Mao decided to break out. He did not, at first, know where to go, but marched west towards the Laoshan Mountains. Later, he decided to take a roundabout route to another Communist-held area at Yan'an in the remote north. It was a bold idea. They were attacked by Chiang's modern army and air force most of the way. Most people in the countryside had learned to hate soldiers and would not help them. Their route (see Map 15-3) took them

Map 15-3   The Long March

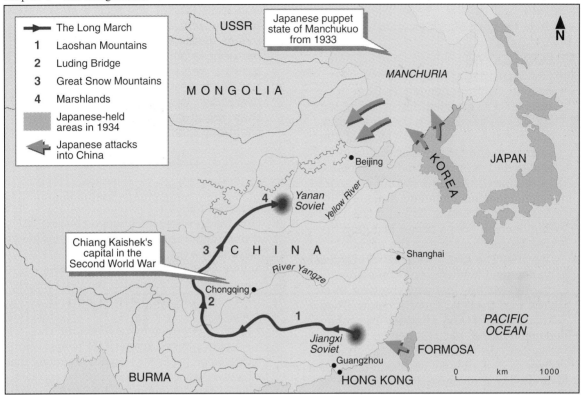

SOURCE 7A   A painting made in 1950 of the crossing of the Luding Bridge in 1935

through mountains, deserts and swamps. They eventually walked over 9,600 kilometres. Yet, incredibly, the Long March succeeded.

▼ SOURCE 7B

Crossing the Luding Bridge:
Platoon Commander Ma Ta-Chai stepped out, grasped one of the chains and began swinging, hand over hand, towards the north bank. (Most of the planks on the Communists' side of the bridge had been removed.) The platoon . . . followed. As they swung along Red Army machine-guns laid down a protecting screen of fire and the Engineering Corps began bringing up tree trunks and laying the bridge flooring. The army watched breathlessly as the men swang along the bridge chains. Ma Ta-Chai was the first to be shot into the wild torrent below. Then another man, and another. The others pushed along, but just before they reached the flooring at the north end, they saw enemy soldiers dumping cans of kerosene on the bridge, and setting them on fire. Watching the sheet of flame spread, some men hesitated, but the platoon political director sprang down onto the flooring . . . calling to the others to follow . . . They ran through the flames and threw their hand-grenades into the midst of the enemy. More and more men followed, the flames lapping at their clothing . . . The bridge became a mass of running men, with rifles ready, trampling out the flames as they ran.

Agnes Smedley, *The Great Road*,
published in 1958

▼ SOURCE 7C

The grass grew in long clusters in shallow water. Between one clump and another the water was very deep. The clusters of grass were dead and rotten, with new grass sprouting on the rotten grass. Under the dense green grass was layer upon layer of rotten grass immersed in the water, so that when you stepped on a clump your foothold was shaky and slippery. Between the clumps the soil was exceptionally soft and loose, and if you took a step you would sink down at least eighteen inches. Sometimes there were bottomless pools of mud. If you weren't careful, and took a false step, a man and his horse would sink down: the more they would struggle, the deeper they would go and if no one pulled them out that was the end of them.

Li Chang-chuan
Quoted in D. Wilson, *The Long March*

❓ Questions

a How far does Source 7B support Source 7A?
b If they support each other, does that mean they must be right?
c Source 7A is a Communist propaganda painting from 15 years after the Long March. How might that affect how we use it as evidence?
d Source 7B is written by an American who knew, and admired, many of the people who had gone on the Long March. How might that affect how we use it as evidence?
e Which of the two sources, 7A and 7B do you think is more reliable for finding out about the Long March. Explain your answer.
f What do these sources and the text tell us about the difficulties the Communists had to face on the Long March?
g What effect would the news of the Long March have on the Chinese people?
h Write an account of the Long March based on these sources and your own knowledge.

The Long March is important for several reasons:

1. The Communists survived.
2. Mao Zedong was now their leader.
3. Mao's ideas, of a Communist revolution based not on the industrial workers, as in Russia, but on peasants, prevailed.
4. The Long March was seen as a great Chinese achievement, something to be proud of. For years the Chinese had been defeated and humiliated by other nations but now some Chinese had done something heroic. Most Chinese people heard about the Long March. They therefore learned that the heroes were Communists.

War with Japan

Meanwhile, Chiang Kaishek had another problem to face. Since 1931, China had been invaded by Japan (see Chapter 11, pages 107–108 and Map 15-3). At first the Japanese invaded the northern province of Manchuria. Chiang did very little about this as he regarded the Communists as the greater enemy: 'The Japanese are a disease of the skin; it can be cured. The Communists are a disease of the soul; it affects the whole body.' The Japanese began to move south into the rest of China. The Communist Chinese in Yan'an were not near the Japanese, but declared war on them. This made the Communists appear more patriotic, fighting for China. Chiang continued to ignore the Japanese and attacked the Communists. Then, in 1937, Chiang was kidnapped by one of his own generals and made to declare war on Japan.

The war with Japan went on until 1945. At first, the Japanese did well. By 1942, most of coastal China was in their hands. Chiang retreated into the mountains of the south-west. His allies, Britain and the USA, supplied him by air and by the famous 'Burma Road'. Chiang's Nationalist forces did not do very well against the Japanese. US General 'Vinegar Joe' Stilwell was not impressed by Chiang. 'Chiang Kaishek's ignorance and fatuous complacency are appalling, the little dummy!' he wrote in his diary.

Red Army tactics

The Communists, however, learned how to defeat the Japanese. They fought with guerrilla tactics. The Japanese controlled the towns and cities and, by day, the roads. The Communists worked among the peasants and soon controlled the countryside. By night, they used the roads. The Communist guerrilla tactics were never to meet the Japanese head-on but to melt away if attacked. When the Japanese were weak, or caught unawares, they were attacked suddenly. Mao put it this way:

When the enemy advances, we retreat,
When the enemy halts, we harass,
When the enemy retires, we attack,
When the enemy retreats, we pursue.

The Red Army soldiers worked hard at overcoming the deep-rooted opposition of most Chinese to soldiers. They had eight strict rules:

1. Speak politely.
2. Pay fairly for what you buy.
3. Return anything you borrow.
4. Pay for anything you damage.
5. Don't hit or swear at the people.
6. Don't damage crops.
7. Don't take liberties with women.
8. Don't ill-treat captives.

You can see from looking at these eight rules that many soldiers, especially under the warlords, must have behaved badly.

At the same time, the Communist soldiers encouraged the peasants to throw out their landlords. Thus, Communist ideas spread with the Red Army.

SOURCE 8

Now listen closely to my song,
Workers and peasants are very poor,
Eating bitterness while landlords eat meat,
Working while the landlords play,
Ah, so hard!
First we must unite and raise the red banner,
Second, sew a badge upon your sleeve,
Third, destroy reactionaries in the village,
Fourth, capture rifles from the landlords,
Arm ourselves!
Enter Shanghang, disturb no merchants
And always protect the poor,
Capture the landlords and tiger gentry,
No compromise with them,
Bandits all!
You are poor, I am poor
Of ten men, nine are poor
If the nine poor men unite,
Where, then, are the tiger landlords?

Red Army song

Questions
a Who are the Red Army's enemies in this song?
b Who are their friends?
c How would the peasants benefit from what the song tells them to do?
d How would the Red Army benefit from what the song tells them to do?

This peasant support was vital to the Red Army guerrilla tactics. As Mao said, 'The peasants are the sea, the Red Army the fish who swim in it.' The Red Army soldiers helped the peasants reorganise the land; in return the peasants gave food, shelter, weapons and information to them. Many peasants joined the Red Army. As Mao said, 'Power grows out of the barrel of a gun'.

Civil war, 1945–1949

In 1937, the Communists held 77,000 square kilometres of China, with two million people. By 1945, when Japan surrendered, the Communists controlled 777,000 square kilometres and 95 million

▶ SOURCE 9A
Red Army soldiers

people. However, when Japan surrendered to the USA, the Americans decided to replace Chiang Kaishek as ruler over all of China. The Americans hoped that Chiang and Mao would work together, but both refused. A civil war soon broke out which continued for three more years, 1947–1949.

The Communists continued their guerrilla warfare against the Nationalists just where they had left off fighting the Japanese. Chiang had always supported the landlords, so peasants and Reds continued to work together.

THE NATIONALIST ARMY
Another factor in this last civil war between Nationalists and Communists was the behaviour of Chiang Kaishek and his soldiers. As Chiang became older, he became more and more of a dictator. His government was corrupt; inflation was high, and aid from the USA went into the pockets of Chiang, his family and friends. The GMD had become the party of the landlords. Madame Sun, Sun Yatsen's widow, said that Chiang had not put into practice any of Sun's principles. His soldiers, unlike the Red Army, treated the areas they were sent to badly. It was clear, even to the Americans, that Mao and the Communists were more popular than Chiang. The Chinese people were no longer just 'grains of loose sand'. The long years of war, the Japanese invasion, the Long March and the work of the Red Army had united the Chinese people behind Mao. Chiang's soldiers began to desert to the Reds in large numbers, taking their American weapons with them.

▶ SOURCE 9B
When the GMD fled and the Eighth Route Army [Red Army] came, the land was divided up . . . After that, life was better. Having land and not needing to pay rent to anyone, there was enough for us to eat . . .

One day I was keeping watch on the village when one of the soldiers came, quite on his own . . . We let him come right into the village. He went into a cave. We caught him there, as in a trap. He looked very anxious when we carted him off. When he got to the guerrillas he said to them: 'Don't kill me. I'm just a farm boy too . . .' The guerrillas replied: 'We shan't kill you. We

Communists don't kill our prisoners. We are going to convert you.' So then they gave him instruction, and after that he was let go, so that he could go back to his own village where he was to tell people what the [Red] army was and what our aims were and how we treated prisoners.

J. Myrdal, *Report from a Chinese Village*, published in 1965

? Questions

a Why did the man in Source 9B support the Reds?

b Compare the behaviour of the Nationalist and Red armies.

c Why do you think the Nationalist soldiers were ready to desert?

Gradually, the Red Army took over more and more of China. In Beijing, in September 1949, Mao Zedong declared the formation of the People's Republic of China. Chiang fled to the island of Formosa, and the long years of civil war in China ended with a Communist victory.

SUN YATSEN 1866–1925

Sun Yatsen was the son of a peasant family: he knew what it was like to spend long, back-breaking hours in the rice fields, trying to grow enough to eat; he knew how old-fashioned the peasants were, how difficult it would be to make a revolution among them. Yet he led the revolution which removed the emperors in 1911. He also kept alive the idea of a real revolution in China during the terrible warlord years.

The change in Sun's life was due to his brother. He had emigrated to Hawaii and had made a success of his life. He invited Sun over to join him. In Hawaii, Sun received an education from English missionaries. From them, he learned how England was governed, with a Parliament, laws and a monarch who, since the 17th century, had to accept what Parliament decided. He compared this with the emperors and mandarins in China, with their power and their cruelty. Sun also made comparisons between the modern ships, trains and engineering skills of the Europeans and the backwardness of China.

When his education was finished, he returned to China. He was very critical of the things he saw: the old gods, the old ways of farming, the power of the landlords. Soon he was asked to leave. He was pleased and went to college in Hong Kong.

He obeyed his parents enough to marry the wife they had chosen for him, a simple peasant girl. Much later, he divorced her. From 1886, he began to train as a doctor. In Hong Kong, he also saw how foreigners were making money out of his country. In a naval battle in 1885, the French warships shattered the wooden Chinese junks in a matter of minutes. Sun later said: 'From 1885, that is from the time of our defeat in the war with France, I set before myself the object of the overthrow of the Dynasty, and the establishment of a Chinese republic on its ruins.'

In 1894, he began to work as a doctor in Guangzhou (Canton), a city in southern China. However, he also worked for a revolution. Guns were smuggled into China, and his followers called themselves the 'Dare-to-Dies'. The first attempt in 1895 failed. Sun just escaped and worked from Tokyo from then on.

He worked out his Three Principles to turn China into a modern, free and democratic country. For the next 16 years he travelled all over the world, especially in the USA, raising money. He also built up support in China. His ideas, in speeches and newspapers, spread among educated Chinese. Sun even visited China many times under a false name and with a false Japanese passport. There were many attempts at a revolution until finally, in 1911, they succeeded.

Sun hurried to China, only to find that the warlords' armies were in control. From his base in Guangzhou, he kept alive the idea of a real revolution. He made the link with Russia and was on friendly terms with the Communists. He was all prepared to make a bid to take over the rest of China when he died, in 1925.

It is difficult to say what would have happened if he had lived a few more years. Would he have quarrelled with the Communists as Chiang Kaishek did? If he could have stayed on good terms with the Communists, would Mao have been so successful? Certainly his widow (his second wife) was disgusted with the Guomindang under Chiang Kaishek. Whatever might have happened, Sun Yatsen is among the great revolutionary leaders of this century.

ASSESSMENT

Describe, analyse and explain

1   **a)** Describe China at the beginning of the 20th century. Your account should include: peasants, mandarins, rulers, foreigners.

b) Why did Sun Yatsen's revolution of the 'Double Tenth' fail?

2   **a)** What were the 'Shanghai Massacres' of 1927?

b) Why did Chiang Kaishek fail to win the support of the majority of the Chinese people? In your answer you could mention:

i) Opposition from the Communists.

ii) Links with merchants, bankers and landlords.

iii) Corruption.

iv) No effort to win peasant support.

3   **a)** Describe the Long March.

b) Why did it take place?

c) What were its results for:

• The Communists?

• The peasants?

• The Guomindang?

• The landlords?

4   **a)** Describe the problems faced by Chinese peasants in the 1930s.

b) How did the Red Army help the peasants to deal with these problems?

c) How did the peasants help the Red Army?

5   **a)** From each of the two lists below, select one item and explain how it contributed to the success of the Communists in China in 1949:

Communists.	Nationalists (GMD).
Peasant support.	Corruption.
Long March.	US support.
Guerrilla warfare.	Landlords' support.

b) Choose two items from the whole table which you think were the most important causes of the Communists' success. Explain your choice by comparing them with others.

Topics for discussion

1   What did Mao mean by 'Power grows out of the barrel of a gun'?

2   In what ways was the Chinese revolution different to the Russian one? In what ways was it similar?

Suggest reasons for the differences.

16: China since 1949

CHINA IN 1949

An American writer who knew Shanghai in the old days before 1949, gave the following report in 1960.

▼ SOURCE 1A

Gone the glitter and glamour; gone the pompous wealth beside naked starvation . . . Goodbye to all that: the well-dressed Chinese in their chauffeured cars behind the bullet-proof glass; the gangsters, the kidnappers; the exclusive foreign clubs, the men in their white dinner jackets, the women beautifully gowned; the opium dens and gambling halls . . . the beggars on every block and the scabby infants urinating on the kerb while mothers scratched for lice . . . The block-long funerals . . . the tiers of paper palaces and paper money burning at the rich man's tomb; the day's toll of unwanted infants and suicides floating in the canals, the knotted rickshaws with their owners fighting each other for customers, the pedlars and their plaintive cries; the armoured white ships on the river 'protecting foreign lives and property'. . . . Gone the wickedest and most colourful city of the East.

E. Snow, *The Other Side of the River*

? Questions

a What does the difference between the conditions described in Source 1A, and those shown in Source 1B tell you about Chinese Communism?

b What do you think would happen to the rich people described in Source 1A when the Communists took over?

▼ SOURCE 1B Street in Beijing today

When Mao Zedong took over China in 1949, he took on all his country's problems: it was very poor; most of the people were peasants who could not read or write; there was hardly any industry; there had been nearly 40 years of civil war and foreign invasion. Perhaps the biggest problem of all was the attitude of the Chinese people. They mistrusted all modern ideas in farming, industry, education, medicine and women's rights.

One problem which Mao did not have to face at first was opposition. The Chinese Communists, unlike the Russian Communists in 1917, had the support of most of the people. Their opponents, the Guomindang under Chiang Kaishek, had fled to Taiwan (Formosa). This meant that Mao could move gradually at first.

However, Mao was a lifelong revolutionary. He had not led the Communists on the Long March in order to replace the mandarins and landlords with new party bosses and highly paid 'experts'. Twice before his death in 1976 he organised revolutions against this trend. He wanted to make sure that China's new rulers kept in contact with the working masses. This policy of 'continuous revolution' disrupted the country. It has also made China a very different country from the other Communist power: the USSR.

THE EARLY YEARS

Land redistribution

The main reason that the Chinese peasants supported the Communists was that they wanted their own land. In the areas held by the Communists before 1949, landlords had been thrown out and their land shared among the peasants (see Chapter 15).

This process was now extended to the whole of China by the Land Reform Law. In every village, the poor peasants were encouraged to 'speak bitter' against their landlords. All their feelings about the years of hardship, when they had never dared to complain, poured out.

◤ **SOURCE 2A**   A People's Court: the judges are seated; the girl witness says she was nearly sold to a landlord

▼ SOURCE 2B

At a meeting, Old Chang [one of the peasants] told how Ning's [the landlord's] men had beaten his son to death because they had fallen behind with the rent. A weeping girl took up the story: 'You took our plough, chains, everything, because we could not pay the rent.' The list of Ning's crimes was very long and at last he broke down: 'I'm to blame . . . wholly to blame. You can divide up my houses and land. A year later, Ning was tried for his crimes and shot.

P. Townsend, *China Phoenix*

? Questions

a Do you think Source 2A and Source 2B show a fair trial?

b Compare the scene in both Sources with the Mandarin court in Chapter 15, Source 4, page 163. Comment on the differences.

Many landlords were executed, but many more simply handed over their lands and became farmers. By 1950, land had been shared out all over China. Most peasants approved of this change: it was what they had always wanted. Mao thus gained their support. He was also careful not to attack the better off peasants, as Stalin had done.

Co-operatives

However, the peasants found that they were still poor. They did not have much land and they still used their old-fashioned farming methods, so they did not produce more crops. Mao and the government were worried too: a census in 1951 showed that China's population was 600 million and rising fast.

If famine was to be avoided, something had to be done. The next stage, therefore, was to set up co-operatives. Peasants from one or more villages were persuaded to combine their land. Together, they would buy machines and better seeds, produce more food and sell at a good price. Any profits made would be shared out among them. Communist Party workers went round the villages persuading peasants to set up co-operatives. This change went on slowly through the 1950s.

Industry

In industry, too, Mao was able to start creating his Communist state without opposition. In 1949, most industry in China belonged to foreigners or to Chiang Kaishek's supporters. Foreign businesses were squeezed out. Any businesses still in Chinese hands were heavily taxed until their owners gladly handed them over. The Chinese who knew how to run them carried on as managers. Inflation was stopped by insisting on buying and selling at low, fixed prices. The Soviets lent $3 billion, machines and experts. In 1953, with Soviet help, Mao launched his first Five-Year Plan. This was successful in developing heavy industry: new areas of China were developed, railways and roads were built.

Other changes

EDUCATION

A massive campaign was organised right from the start to teach the Chinese people to read and write. In 1949, only 20% of the people were literate; by 1980, 90% were literate. Most of those still illiterate were the elderly. Teachers were sent into the villages, teaching the children by day and the adults in the evenings. They received an education in Communism. The books they read from were the works of Marx, Lenin or Mao. They were encouraged to be hard-working, cheerful, loyal to their leaders and helpful to others. In the old days, education was the road to a safe middle-class life away from hard work in factory or field. Under Mao, no one receiving education was allowed to forget the importance of manual work. Pupils worked part-time in factories; students worked for two months a year in communes, and their professors for one month.

▼ SOURCE 3

Secondary school teaching of Communism, 1966

Form 1 – Obedience to the party, love for Chairman Mao, readiness to help one's neighbour.

Form 2 – History of man's development: primitive society and feudalism, followed by capitalism, colonialism and imperialism, which are transformed by revolution into Communism.

Forms 3 and 4 – Reading, analysing and learning the works of Mao Zedong.

Forms 5 and 6 – Introduction to the works of Marx and Lenin.

Adapted from H. Portisch,
Eye Witness in China

? Questions

a How are pupils taught about Communist thinking?

b From what you have read here, what do you think of Chinese education?

WOMEN'S RIGHTS

In the old days women were second-class members of society. Arranged marriages and child betrothals were common and women were their husband's or their father's property. The Marriage Law of 1950 banned all these practices.

This was followed by a wave of divorces, three-quarters of them brought by women. The aim of the Marriage Law was to break the traditional power of the male-dominated household. As part of their policy of changing how the Chinese people thought, the new Communist leaders wanted people to feel part of the nation and to belong to the wider community.

The Chinese Constitution (Article 53) gives women 'equal rights with men in all spheres of political, economic, social and cultural life.' Also 'equal pay for equal work.' Mao realised that women were a huge source of labour (see Sources 4A and 4B): every effort was made to provide nurseries in the communes so that women were relieved of childcare.

However, as we know in Britain, attitudes are hard to change. Women were still denied education and did the worst jobs. There was even widespread child betrothal. One visitor estimated that women did 80% of the work on the communes while men gave the orders and attended political meetings. After the failure of the 'Great Leap Forward', Deng Xiaoping's re-emphasis on the family also weakened women's position. Male heads of households became important again and women had to add housework and childcare to their other work.

HEALTH

Disease and lack of hygiene were common in the old China. Nowadays every street has a committee to tidy up rubbish and litter, arrange the supply of water and keep the area healthy. Women play a large part in working on these committees. Killer diseases such as cholera, typhoid and tuberculosis were common in China before 1949, as in Britain in the 19th century. Now they have been almost completely wiped out.

There is a shortage of doctors, especially those trained in Western medicine. For this reason and because the full training of doctors takes so long, 'barefoot doctors' have been trained. These are people trained in basic medical skills, but not given a full doctor's training. They are soon ready to go out into the villages to deal with common diseases. Serious cases are sent to the fully-trained doctors. Women, again, are playing a large part in this movement. All health care is free, and the old traditional Chinese methods, such as acupuncture, are practised alongside Western skills.

THE GOVERNMENT

Although the Communists were popular in 1949, there were, of course, many people in China who opposed them or did not support them. The 'speak bitter' campaign against the landlords removed many opponents, as did the campaign against businessmen. No one knows how many people died in the Communist take-over, but it was probably several million. In a year or two, the pattern of government became clear: it was a one-party state, run by Mao Zedong and the Communist leaders who had been with him fighting the Japanese and the GMD. This one-party state was backed by complete control of all radio, newspapers, books and cinema. The mass media were used to encourage people to follow the party line and persuade them to accept it. The growth of education also helped the spread of the government's ideas.

There has been much disagreement within the one-party state over the years. In 1957, Mao launched the 'Hundred Flowers' campaign. The full slogan was 'Let A Hundred Flowers Bloom, Let a Hundred Schools of Thought Contend'. This invited criticism from anyone. The result was such a wave of criticism that the campaign was stopped. Strong opponents, especially from the old educated classes, were sent for 're-education' to work in fields or factories. They had to learn about Communism through manual labour. It is difficult to say whether Mao really wanted criticism from the 'Hundred Flowers', or whether he used it to flush out opponents to deal with them.

THE GREAT LEAP FORWARD 1958–1965

After nearly ten years of Communism, Mao was worried that China was settling back into old ways. He saw a new middle class of 'experts' growing up, running the factories, businesses, hospitals and universities. To Mao they were too much like the old Mandarin class who ruled China under the emperors. He felt that the USSR was going the same way, especially after the death of Stalin in 1953. Mao wanted to make another revolution, based on the masses of peasants and workers. Thus he announced the 'Great Leap Forward'. The targets of the Second Five-Year Plan (1957) were abandoned. New higher targets for agriculture and industry were set up. How was China to achieve them? Mao, as a Marxist, believed that the Chinese people could achieve them if they worked together. The central idea was to be the commune.

Communes

A commune was an even bigger grouping of peasants than a co-operative. It was a unit of several villages or even small towns. As it was bigger than a co-operative, even more machines and greater improvements could be undertaken. The people in a commune were divided into brigades of workers of about 1,000 to 2,000 and then into teams of workers of 50 to 200 people. The commune then planned for all these people to work together on big schemes such as dams, reservoirs, terracing or irrigation. It was quite common to see some large construction like a dam being built by hundreds of people using only shovels and baskets. Women worked alongside the men.

SOURCE 4B

They [female engineering students] all heatedly asserted that they did everything other students did. There was a tendency to give them light work, but they did their turn at the furnaces, the same carrying work, the same risks; they wanted complete equality in work assignments. Did I know who was the first volunteer to

SOURCE 4A   Women building-workers

carry a cable across the Yellow River rapids at San Men Hsia at the start of the big dam there? A woman engineer!

E. Snow, *The Other Side of the River*, published in 1963

? Questions

a What are the women in Source 4A doing?

b Do many women in Britain become engineers?

c Why do you think equality of the sexes has been so important to the Chinese since the Revolution?

A commune also set up, built and ran its own schools and hospitals. It organised its own trade. It even started its own industry. In the Great Leap Forward, Mao asked communes to mine coal and iron and set up their own blast furnaces. Millions of people who had never done so before began to operate 'backyard' blast furnaces. In this way, Mao hoped to make use of the one thing China had above all else: people – hard-working, ingenious, willing millions of them. As Mao said, 'I have wit-

nessed the tremendous energy of the masses. On this foundation, it is possible to accomplish any task whatsoever.'

The government tried to persuade people to join communes by a tremendous propaganda campaign. It is difficult to know if many Chinese refused, but probably not many did so. By the end of 1958, all of China was organised into 26,000 communes.

◤ SOURCE 5B

Winter and summer, visitors from all over China come to Shashiyu to see the changes made, how this parched land and these once barren hills have turned into orchards and terraced fields of grain. They also come to take back with them the spirit of people who literally grew grain and fruit trees on rocks, carrying soil up slopes now terraced by walls and forested with pine and spruce.

We arrived at Yen's winter worksite where young men and women were

◤ SOURCE 5A

Students building their own university in Yan'an

burrowing a tunnel 250 metres through the hill to tap water which flowed down the other side.

J. Schumann, *China's Changing Countryside*

? Questions

a What are the good and bad points of getting students to build their own school or university, as in Source 5A?

b In what way were these peasants 'doing the impossible' in Source 5B?

c Why were these changes not carried out in the old days under the landlords?

d Why do you think the commune at Shashiyu had so many visitors?

However, Mao's trust in the masses of the Chinese people to achieve the almost impossible targets of the Great Leap Forward did not work out: the change was too sudden and the lack of expert knowledge too great. Much of the 'back-yard' iron and steel made by the communes was of low quality and could not be used. Because the peasants were busy elsewhere, crops were neglected. There were bad harvests from 1959 to 1961. Widespread famine caused the deaths of 16 million people and many more went hungry. The withdrawal of all Soviet help in 1960 (see below) made matters worse. In the face of these failures, Mao resigned as head of state in 1959.

There was a leadership split and Deng Xiaoping introduced more right-wing policies to help recovery. Family farms and small markets were encouraged.

THE CULTURAL REVOLUTION 1966–1976

By the late 1960s, Mao felt that China was once again losing contact with true, classless Communism. Once again, the experts were taking over, running everything, getting the best jobs, even getting their children into good jobs. The only things that mattered seemed to be efficiency, making things work, rather than contact with the masses.

Mao himself had not really been running China personally since his resignation in 1959. Orders were given in his name, but the real rulers were falling into the trap of ignoring Mao's view of revolution. Mao, now in his seventies, appealed to the young people to launch a 'Cultural Revolution' against all revisionists.

In June 1966 all the schools in China closed. At a rally of one million young people in Beijing, he called on them to be 'Red Guards', seeking out 'revisionists' and 'revisionism' everywhere. The Red Guards made use of the 'Little Red Book', a pocket collection of sayings from all the writings of Mao, for their ideas. Millions flocked to Beijing to see Mao. Millions more went out into the towns and the countryside, armed with Mao's 'Little Red Book'. Huge posters with the names and 'crimes' of teachers and party bosses appeared on the streets. They made their victims confess to their 'wrong' thinking. Some were beaten to death or hounded to suicide.

▶ SOURCE 6A

One teacher at Wachi Middle School made the following statement: 'I was a graduate from the old University. I am teaching Chinese language and literature. Before the Cultural Revolution I concentrated on my study. At that time my aim was to become a specialist in order to make an easier living and have a cosy family. I never said a word about "You should serve the people heart and soul". I never allowed the students to criticise me. If I made a mistake I always put on an air. I was always correct.

During the Cultural Revolution my students had a chat with me to change my thinking. I came to realise that it is not the sole purpose for students to study intellectual knowledge at school. If everybody seeks personal fame and gain, who will build our country and who will make the revolution in China and the world?'

Quoted in *The Times Educational Supplement* by G. N Brown

Some victims were harshly treated:

▶ SOURCE 6B

I saw rows of teachers, about forty or fifty in all, with black ink poured over their faces . . . Hanging on their necks were placards with such words as 'reactionary academic' or 'class enemy' . . . They all wore dunce caps.

▶ SOURCE 6C   Red Guards

. . . All were barefoot, hitting broken gongs . . . Beatings and tortures followed: electric shocks, being forced to kneel on broken glass.

Ken Ling, *Red Guard*

? Questions

a What do you think is the age of the Red Guards in Source 6C?

b Describe their uniform and weapons.

c What was the fault of the teacher in Source 6A?

d Do you think that students should criticise their teachers?

e What effect would the events described in Source 6B have on education in China?

Students refused to sit for examinations, as examinations showed up inequalities between them. All books, plays and films had to be about workers or peasants, or stories with a Communist message. Many writers and artists suffered at the hands of the Red Guards. Museums were destroyed and shop windows displaying foreign goods were smashed.

Factories were reorganised to give power to the workers in helping to run them. In the countryside, students and graduates were sent to work alongside the peasants. All this tremendous disruption of life soon caused problems. Transport ground to a halt, production of food and industrial goods went down. This threatened the life of the millions of Chinese people who lived close to poverty.

It is not certain how the Cultural Revolution ended. It seems likely that eventually the army moved in to restore order. Certainly it was not until well into the 1970s that schools, factories and farms were back to normal. Probably a million Chinese died as a result of the Cultural Revolution.

CHINA AFTER MAO

Then, in 1976, Mao died. Within a month right-wing leaders had re-taken control. Mao's widow, Jiang Qing, was arrested and put on trial. All the crimes of the Cultural Revolution were heaped on her and the 'Gang of Four' so that Mao's personal reputation remained untouched. By 1978 Deng Xiaoping was clearly in control. He was determined to follow the 'Four Modernisations': of agriculture, industry, science and defence. People were allowed more freedom to grow what they wanted on their own farms for market. Small private businesses were allowed and trade opened up with the outside world. 'Special Economic Zones' were set up for foreign investors to join with local Chinese in building factories.

To keep the rapidly growing population under control, the 'One-child' policy was introduced in 1978. Couples who only have one child are rewarded and those with more are punished. This was a

▶ SOURCE 7   Student demonstration in Tienanmen Square, Beijing, 1989

tremendous blow to old family values, which saw large families as insurance for the parents' old age.

However much economic freedom was allowed, Deng drew the line at political freedom. In 1989 students used Gorbachev's visit to Beijing for a demonstration in Tiananmen Square in front of the world's media for more freedom. After two weeks Deng ordered them to be shot or arrested.

FOREIGN AFFAIRS

Four ideas run right through Chinese foreign affairs during the whole period since 1949.

1. China has a hatred of foreigners. This dates from the time when foreigners ruled large parts of China under the emperors. The humiliation of the 'unequal treaties' was not forgotten. The Chinese Communists felt that they had had to fight foreigners such as the Japanese, as well as their own ruling class, in their revolution. Thus they feel sympathetic to colonial countries wishing to be independent.

2. China is a poor peasant country. China thus aligns itself with poorer Third World countries.

3. The Chinese Communists had won their victory in 1949 almost without help from anyone. They regarded the USSR as a friend, but an equal friend. This was not how the USSR saw it, and they soon became enemies.

4. Communist China started in 1949 with the complete opposition of the USA. The USA had supported Chiang Kaishek and regarded the Communist victory in China as yet another advance for world Communism. During the years of the Cold War, China was almost completely cut off from contact with other nations, except for a few fellow-Communists. Only since the late 1970s has the USA changed its policy and the Chinese modified theirs, so that China is now a part of the world community.

Incidents on China's borders

TAIWAN

In 1949, Chiang Kaishek fled to Taiwan (Formosa). Here, he was massively supported by the USA with aid and weapons. Throughout the 1950s the Nationalist government of Chiang Kaishek made repeated threats to invade and reconquer China. In response the Communists threatened to invade Taiwan. In the 1980s a policy of 'one country, two systems' allowed an improvement of relations between of Taiwan and China while allowing Taiwan to retain its capitalist economy.

KOREA

The Chinese played a large part in the Korean War. In 1950, the North Koreans invaded the South, who appealed to the United Nations. The USA supplied most of a UN force which then invaded North Korea. The Chinese helped the North Koreans until a ceasefire was agreed in 1953. To the USA, the Chinese were helping in the advance of Communism in Asia. To the Chinese, however, they were helping an ally on their borders following threats made to China by the US general in charge, General MacArthur (for full details, see Chapter 17).

TIBET AND INDIA

Tibet had been conquered by the Chinese in the 18th century. In 1911, when the Revolution took place, Tibet declared itself dependent. The Chinese had never accepted this and invaded Tibet in 1950. By 1951 the Chinese were in control, turning Tibet into a province of China. In 1959, the Tibetan religious leader, the Dalai Lama, objecting to the spread of Communism in Tibet, fled to India. Since then Tibet's ancient Buddhist way of life has been steadily crushed by its Chinese rulers.

The border between Tibet and India had never been settled, as it was high up in the Himalayas. The Chinese wanted to build a highway into Tibet and quarrelled with India over the border. There was some fighting in 1962 and the Chinese advanced slightly, but it did not become a full-scale war.

VIETNAM

The USA was determined to prevent the spread of Communism in South-East Asia. When civil war broke out in Vietnam, the USA supported South Vietnam against the Communist North Vietnam. China gave aid to the North and watched the situation very closely. However, Chinese troops never actually took part. Relations between Chinese and Vietnamese have never been good. China sees Vietnam as pro-Soviet, and so a threat. In 1979, Chinese troops invaded Vietnam, but were driven out.

HONG KONG

The problem of the 99-year lease of part of Hong Kong, signed with the British in 1898, was solved by the same 'one nation, two systems' deal made over Taiwan. Hong Kong returned to Chinese rule in July 1997, but Hong Kong's capitalist system is guaranteed for 50 years.

Relations with the USSR

At first, the two Communist nations were allies, and the USSR helped China's Five-Year Plan. However, a split began to develop, for several reasons. Mao did not like Khrushchev. Mao thought he was betraying Marx and Lenin in two ways: first, by suggesting that the USSR and the capitalist West should co-exist – that is, live together without hostility; and second by giving privileges to Party members and experts so that they lost contact with the people. The Soviets, Communists since 1917, regarded the Chinese as junior partners. Mao had found the Soviet advice given to him in the 1920s of no use at all. He had worked out his own form of Chinese Communism, based on the peasants (see Chapter 15). Mao regarded himself as the true successor of Marx and Lenin.

In 1960, the split became open and the Soviets left China. The two sides drew further apart over the years. In addition to the war of words and ideas, there were border clashes. The USSR tried to seize Chinese territory. In 1969, shots were fired between soldiers on each side. The USSR and China remained enemies until Gorbachev's visit to Beijing in 1989 made relations easier.

Relations with the USA

The USA was hostile to Communist China from the very beginning. To the USA, the success of Mao in China was part of the world-wide advance of Communism in the years after the Second World War. The USA and its allies kept Mao's China out of the United Nations and completely isolated. This was part of the USA's policy all over the world: to 'contain' Communism (see Chapter 17, page 191).

? Questions

a What did the USA hope to achieve at this time by putting pressure on China?

b What is meant by a 'cold war'?

To the USA, China was part of international Communism, steadily advancing. The actions of China in Korea, Vietnam and Tibet seemed to confirm this. When the Chinese exploded a test nuclear bomb in 1964, the danger seemed all the greater.

The Chinese, however, saw it differently: the Americans were helping their old enemy, Chiang Kaishek, and it seemed that the huge American forces were threatening China. The Chinese army was large, but poorly armed and not really capable of a foreign war. A nuclear attack on China by the USA seemed a possibility. To develop their own nuclear weapons seemed to be their only defence. American activity on China's borders in Korea and Vietnam seriously worried China's leaders. Threats like that of US General Le May to 'bomb the North Vietnamese back into the Stone Age' added to the tension. Mao called the atom bomb a 'paper tiger', calculating that China could afford to lose 300 million people and still emerge from a nuclear war as the leading nation left on earth. Such a calculation would also be made by the Americans, so, Mao argued, the atom bomb was not a real danger.

With US support, China's seat at the United Nations was occupied by Chiang Kaishek's Taiwan. Several times it was proposed that China should be admitted to the UN, but each time the USA and its allies voted against it. More and more countries began to feel that the UN was weakened by not having the biggest nation in the world represented there. In the end, in 1971, a majority of UN members voted for the admission of China and the expulsion of Nationalist China (Taiwan). This marked the end of China's isolation and the beginning of its move into a normal position among the nations.

Following the experience of Vietnam, the US began to change its foreign policy. It no longer seemed possible to fight Communism everywhere. President Nixon's Secretary of State, Dr Kissinger, came to realise that the world contained several brands of Communism. In 1972, Nixon visited Beijing and met Mao. The new-found friendship increased as trade began to develop between China and western countries.

Since the death of Mao in 1976, the Chinese attitude towards foreigners has become even more friendly. Special economic zones have been opened to allow foreign companies to invest in factories in China.

MAO ZEDONG 1893–1976

Mao's father was a little better off than the rest of the peasants in their village in Hunan: he was the village money-lender. He still had to work very long hours in the fields, and Mao had to help him. Although his father was close to poverty, he was still hated by the other peasants for his high rates of interest. Mao annoyed his father as a boy: when there was work to be done, Mao would be reading or lending a hand to the very poor peasants.

At eighteen, Mao moved away to Changsha to study. He supported Sun Yatsen's revolution of 1911 and cut off his pigtail. He devoted his life to study and to getting tough. He would work many hours in the library, living on one meal a day, sleeping rough and swimming in icy rivers. The next move was to Beijing, where he worked as a library assistant. He met the professors and joined in the exciting discussions about China's future. The May the Fourth Movement was at its height in Beijing in 1919.

In 1920, Mao became a Communist, and attended the first Congress of the Chinese Communist Party in 1921. There were 57 members. Mao worked for the Communist Party as an organiser and writer. He joined the Northern

Expedition of 1926 and just escaped the Shanghai Massacres. From 1928 to 1934, he worked in the countryside, in the Jiangxi soviet. Here he learned how to work with the peasants, how to help them with their problems and gain their respect. He rejected the Russian Communist theory of working only in towns, with factory workers. For this, he lost the support of the Chinese Communist Party.

When he decided to march with his supporters, from Jiangxi all the way to Yan'an, he knew it was a desperate idea. His only possessions were a sunhelmet, an umbrella, two uniforms, one sheet, two blankets, one water jug, a rice bowl and a knapsack for important papers. On the Long March, he had to leave behind his wife and children, never to see them again. By 1935, at the end of the March, he was clearly the leader of the Chinese Communists.

The rest of the story has been told in the last two chapters: how the Red Army worked with the peasants against the Japanese and the GMD, how the Communists won in the end and how the same methods were used to take over all of China. This chapter explains his determination to keep China from turning back to the 'capitalist road'. In the Cultural Revolution, his little red book, his name and his young Red Guards turned the country upside down. Posters of Mao were everywhere. Chaos ensued, as it had done after the 'Great Leap Forward' in 1958. Only his death in 1976 prevented another disgrace. Today he is remembered critically in China, for his revolutionary achievement as well as his disastrous attempts at 'permanent revolution'.

ASSESSMENT

Describe, explain and analyse

1 a) In their first few years of power after 1949, what did the Chinese Communists under Mao Zedong attempt to do about: the peasants; industry; education; the position of women; health?

b) Choose two of these items and explain the Communists motives in doing what they did.

2 a) Describe what happened in the 'Great Leap Forward'.

b) What was Mao trying to achieve by it?

c) Why did it fail?

3 a) What happened in the Cultural Revolution?

b) What was Mao trying to achieve by the Cultural Revolution?

c) Compare it with the 'Great Leap Forward'. What are the differences? What are the similarities?

Evidence and interpretations

'A great Revolutionary leader.'

'A fanatic who caused great suffering to his people.'

You will need to refer to both Chapter 15 and Chapter 16 in your answer.

a Use you own knowledge to write a paragraph in support of *each* of the judgements of Mao Zedong given above.

b Which of these two views do you agree with most? Explain your choice, drawing on what you know of the whole of his life.

Topics for discussion

1 What are the differences and similarities between Soviet and Chinese policies for agriculture? Which has been more successful? Why?

2 What would Mao think of the policies Deng has carried out in China?

17: The Cold War

When the Second World War ended, the USA and the USSR were clearly masters of the world. They were so far ahead of all other countries in power and influence that they were called the 'Super Powers'. Other countries, such as Britain, France, Germany, Japan and China had been powerful before the war. By 1945 the war had left them so crippled that even those who had been on the winning side of the war fell far behind the super-powers. Almost as soon as the war ended, relations between the USA and the USSR cooled. There was hostility between them for the next 45 years.

Why was this important? This hostility between the USA and the USSR always stopped short of actual war with each other. As both super-powers had nuclear weapons, a real war between them could have meant the total destruction of each other and everybody else on earth. A 'cold war' was a war fought by every method except actual fighting. It was a war of words, propaganda and threats. Each side stockpiled weapons and forces which it hoped it would not have to use. Several real wars were fought, but by substitutes or allies: America, or America's ally, fights the USSR's ally – for example, in Korea and Vietnam. Never did American fight Russian.

HOW DID THE COLD WAR BEGIN?

The two superpowers had never fought each other before and had been allies in the Second World War. One of the main reasons for hostility lies in the history of each country before 1945. Stalin, the ruler of the USSR, felt his country was always being threatened or attacked. Russia had been invaded by Germany in 1914. After the 1917 revolution, several countries had sent armies to help the Whites try to crush the new Communist state (see Chapter 5, pages 44–46). In the 1930s no country had joined him in opposing Hitler, and some even gave way to Hitler. Then in 1941, Germany had invaded Russia again. Two and a half million Soviet civilians and seven and a half million Soviet soldiers were killed, millions of acres of land laid waste and hundreds of towns and cities destroyed in the Second World War. Stalin was bitter that the western Allies had not helped relieve pressure on the USSR by invading western Europe before 1944. By the end of the war, therefore, Stalin's main aims were to make the USSR safe from invasion and to rebuild his shattered country. He was also very suspicious of the West and, like most of his people, had a deep hatred and fear of Germany.

Americans too tried to learn the lessons of history. They regretted their isolation in the years between the wars. They realised that they now had the power to play a large part in world affairs. The lesson of the 1930s seemed to be that dictators must be faced and stopped, by force if necessary.

COLD WAR IN EUROPE 1945–1949

The three leaders, Roosevelt, Stalin and Churchill, met at Yalta early in 1945. Their armies were closing in on Germany. Stalin spoke of his feelings about the other leaders to a fellow-Communist:

▶ SOURCE 1A
Perhaps you think that, because we are allies of the English, we have forgotten who they are and who Churchill is. They find nothing sweeter than to trick their allies. And Churchill? Churchill is the kind who, if you don't watch him, will slip a kopek out of your pocket . . . And Roosevelt? Roosevelt is not like that. He dips his hand only for bigger coins.

Joseph Stalin to Milovan Djilas

? Questions
a   What is Stalin's attitude to his allies?
b   Can you see any difference between his attitudes to Churchill and Roosevelt?
c   If this is how Stalin felt, why was he an ally of Britain and America during the war?

Roosevelt and Churchill had worked out their aims during the war in the 'Atlantic Charter'. These included a United Nations (UN) Organisation to keep peace in the world. Stalin had not taken part in these discussions. Americans believed strongly in democracy and were deeply hostile to Communism. As the war came to an end, therefore, the differences between the superpowers began to appear.

Yalta

At Yalta, the three leaders discussed the UN, which Stalin agreed to join, although without much enthusiasm. He wanted the frontiers of Poland moved so that the USSR should gain some of eastern Poland. The Poles would be compensated by some of eastern Germany. Roosevelt was not keen on this, but Churchill was ready to accept it if the USSR agreed to accept British influence in Greece. It was agreed to divide Germany temporarily into four occupation zones: Soviet, American, British and French. Churchill feared that Roosevelt was too pro-Soviet. He had therefore pressed for a French zone to be added to the other three. This would add another anti-Soviet voice to the armies of occupation. At this stage the Allies had no plans for the permanent division of Germany.

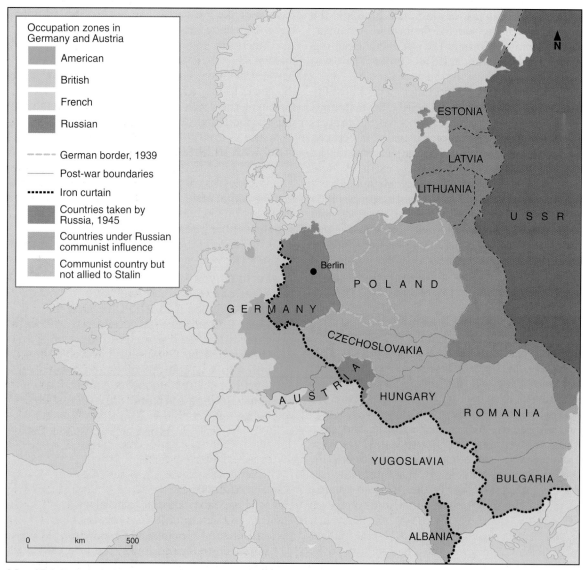

Map 17-1 Europe 1945

Potsdam

After the defeat of Germany, the Allies met again, at Potsdam, in mid-1945. By that time, Roosevelt had died and Churchill had been defeated in the British general election. Stalin, therefore, met with Truman and Attlee. Arrangements were made for the trial at Nuremberg of captured Nazis. Twenty-one leading Nazis were put on trial at Nuremberg. They included Goering and Hess, Foreign Minister Ribbentrop, Gestapo chief Kaltenbrunner, slave labour organiser Saukel, fierce anti-Semite Streicher, Generals Keitel and Jödl and Admirals Raeder and Doenitz. Some were sentenced to death, others to terms of imprisonment, although Goering committed suicide before his sentence could be carried out. Other Nazis were also punished: in the Soviet zone useful Nazis were kept on while others were shot without trial. In the western zones, four million people had to fill in a questionnaire about their activities over the previous 15 years.

Relations between the Allies continued to worsen. Stalin was told about the atom bomb, which increased his suspicions and fear of the West. At the same time, the Allies were worried about his take-over of eastern Europe. The Polish–Russian boundary had been moved westwards (see Map 17-1). The USSR also gained territory by taking land from Finland, Lithuania, Latvia, Estonia, Czechoslovakia and Romania. By this time Soviet territory had expanded 480 kilometres westwards. They had taken over 22 million people who had not been in the USSR in 1939. Later, Truman and Attlee were criticised for allowing this to happen. However, with Soviet armies all over eastern Europe, there was little they could have done to stop it.

Eastern Europe

The Soviet advance did not stop there. Over the next three years, most of eastern Europe came under Soviet control. In Bulgaria, Hungary and Romania, Communist governments took over. In Poland, Communists joined at first with other parties, but in 1947 won rigged elections and expelled their rivals. In Czechoslovakia, the Communists had won only 38% of the votes, but in 1948 the Prime Minister was forced to accept Communists into his government. Then Jan Masaryk, a Czech hero and non-Communist Foreign Minister, was found dead in suspicious circumstances. Within days Communists were in a majority in the Czech government.

Often the next stage in a Communist take-over was even more sinister: an eastern European Communist leader would be called to Moscow, where he would 'disappear'. He would then be replaced by a pro-Soviet, pro-Stalin leader.

The Communist Parties in eastern Europe were at first quite popular: Communists had often been leaders in the resistance against the Nazis. It was easy to arrange Communist take-overs. The only countries where Stalin did not get his own way were Yugoslavia and Greece. In Yugoslavia, the local Communists had thrown out the Germans without much help from the Red Army. Their leader, Tito, set up a Communist state, independent of the USSR, ruling it himself until his death in 1980. He sent supplies to the Greek Communists, who were fighting a civil war against the Royalists. The Royalists were helped by the British. Stalin stayed out of this civil war as he had agreed with Churchill.

Stalin turned the countries of eastern Europe into satellites of the USSR. This meant that they were little more than Soviet provinces. 'Cominform', set up in 1947, made sure that their Communist parties were controlled from Moscow. 'Comecon' controlled their economies for the benefit of the USSR. Poland had to send coal, Romania oil and Czechoslovakia machine tools to

◤ SOURCE 1B
Nazi war criminals on trial at Nuremberg

meet Soviet needs; their armed forces served Soviet policy. Eventually, eastern European forces were united in the Warsaw Pact of 1955.

By 1948, the USSR was in control of half of Europe. Stalin may have intended this as an enormous 'buffer' zone for defence. As commander of the victorious Red Army, he may have felt that he had the right to do as he liked in order to rebuild the USSR. To Westerners, this Soviet advance exceeded their worst fears. Churchill stated those fears most sharply in a speech in the USA as early as 1946.

SOURCE 2B A guard-tower at the Berlin zone border

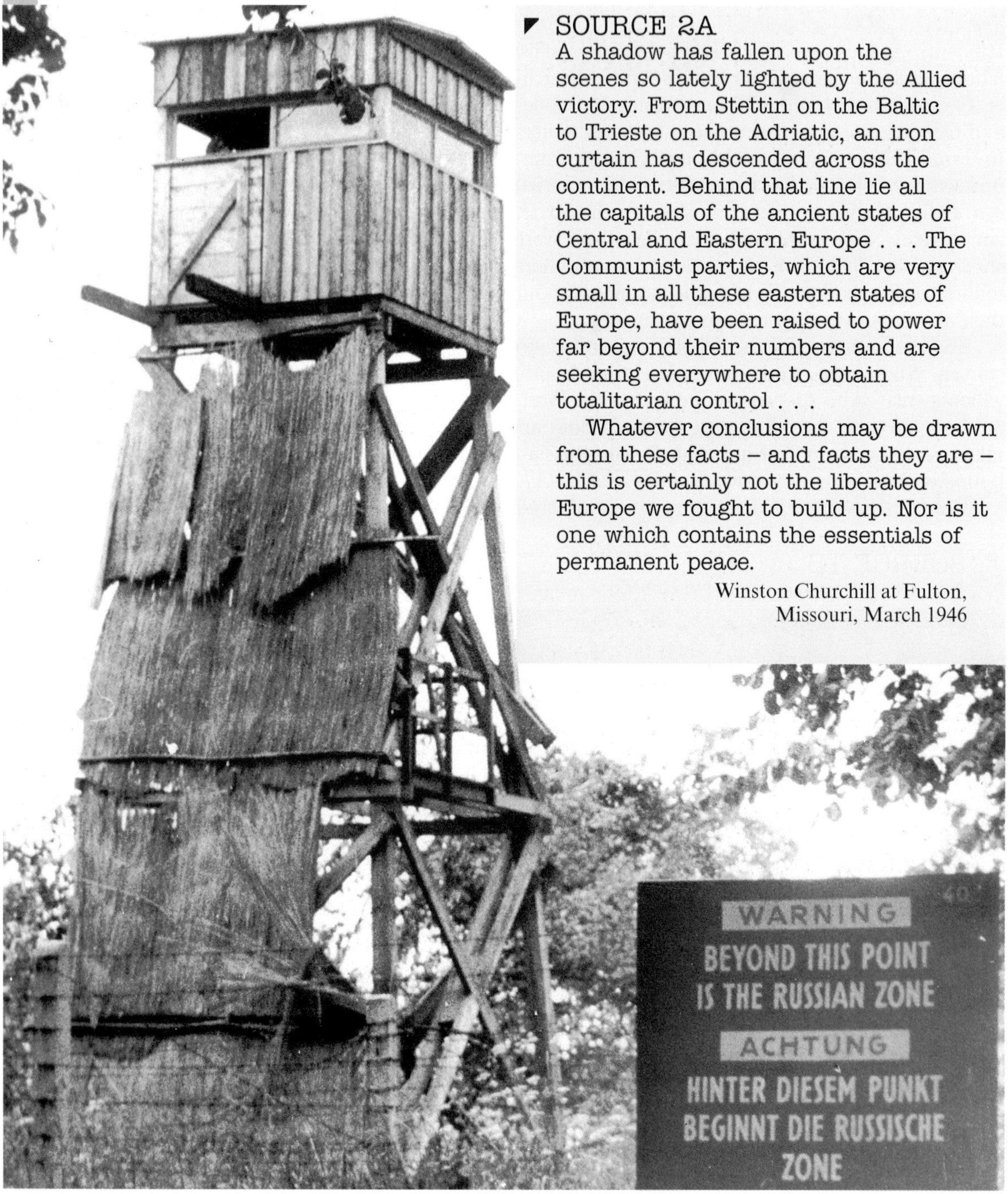
WARNING
BEYOND THIS POINT
IS THE RUSSIAN ZONE
ACHTUNG
HINTER DIESEM PUNKT
BEGINNT DIE RUSSISCHE
ZONE

SOURCE 2A

A shadow has fallen upon the scenes so lately lighted by the Allied victory. From Stettin on the Baltic to Trieste on the Adriatic, an iron curtain has descended across the continent. Behind that line lie all the capitals of the ancient states of Central and Eastern Europe . . . The Communist parties, which are very small in all these eastern states of Europe, have been raised to power far beyond their numbers and are seeking everywhere to obtain totalitarian control . . .

Whatever conclusions may be drawn from these facts – and facts they are – this is certainly not the liberated Europe we fought to build up. Nor is it one which contains the essentials of permanent peace.

Winston Churchill at Fulton, Missouri, March 1946

President Truman immediately declared his agreement with Churchill's speech. Americans had watched the collapse of eastern European governments with horror. There were strong Communist parties in Italy and France too; who knew which country would fall to Communism next? In 1947, Truman set up the National Security Council (NSC) to unite all three armed forces, together with the Central Intelligence Agency (CIA). The job of the CIA was to work secretly to support pro-Americans and undermine anti-Americans anywhere in the world.

The Truman Doctrine

In the same year, the British government said that it could no longer afford to help the anti-Communist forces in Greece. Truman stepped in with what was called the 'Truman Doctrine'.

▼ SOURCE 3

I believe that it must be the policy of the United States to support free peoples who are resisting attempted subjugation by armed minorities or by outside pressures. If Greece should fall, confusion and disorder might well spread throughout the Middle East. The free people of the world look to us for support in maintaining those freedoms. If we falter in our leadership, we may endanger the peace of the world.

The Truman Doctrine

? Questions

a Name some of the capitals and countries Churchill is referring to in Source 2A.
b What is meant by 'totalitarian control' (Source 2A)?
c Use Source 2B to describe what the 'iron curtain' actually looked like.
d What two reasons does Truman give for a country becoming Communist?
e What does Source 3 tell us about US attitudes towards Communism?
f How does it explain why the USA was becoming 'the world's policeman'?
g How would Stalin reply to Churchill's views in Source 2A and Truman's in Source 3?

The Truman Doctrine was the beginning of US policy for the Cold War. This policy was called 'containment': the USA would help any country threatened by Communism so that Communism could not advance further – it would be 'contained'. The Truman Doctrine, therefore, was intended to support democratic countries.

In fact, Americans assumed things which may have been true in Europe in 1947, but were not always true after that. They assumed that Communism could come to a country only through an armed minority take-over or outside interference – never through the choice of the people. They assumed that as soon as one country became Communist, the neighbouring one would follow – the 'Domino Theory'. They assumed that Communism would go on trying to expand unless it was stopped. It is true that at this time they had no spies at a high level in the Kremlin, so they had to guess what Stalin's real motives were. You should try and decide when these assumptions were true and when false during the years which have followed.

Most significantly, the Truman Doctrine also committed the USA to play a big part in world affairs. The USA, not the UN, would be the world's policeman.

Marshall Aid

Truman felt that Communism did well when people were poor and suffering. It could best be resisted by economic aid to build up prosperity. In 1947, his Secretary of State, General George Marshall, put forward a plan to give billions of dollars of aid to Europe. He saw that most of western Europe was still shattered from the war and would need help to recover. If it did not, the USA would be left on its own to face the USSR. Western European countries had to be made strong enough to defend themselves. The US Congress was not keen on the idea, but just as they were discussing it came the news of the brutal Communist take-over of Czechoslovakia. Congress then voted to give 4 billion dollars. Before the end of the war, an American adviser had said:

▼ SOURCE 4

In the first place, our own interest is to maintain full employment . . . and expand it sufficiently to absorb the twelve million or more men and women who will come back from the services.

> The great thing which creates purchasing power is people . . . if the people can develop their own countries, they will become an increasing market for all goods including our own.
>
> Dean Acheson, 1945

❓ Questions

a What had happened in the USA before the war which the Americans were anxious to avoid happening after the war?

b How would Marshall Aid solve the 'problem of markets'?

There are differing views about Marshall Aid, as it was called. It could appear to be a generous gesture to an ailing Europe. Indeed, so interesting was the idea that even the USSR applied for Marshall Aid, although it never received any. However, there were strings attached to the aid. Clearly, one aim was to build up strong anti-Communist countries. Another view is that it helped US industry by creating markets for US goods.

Certainly, Marshall Aid did rescue and restore prosperity in Britain, France, Italy and the rest of western Europe. It also helped US industry and gave American companies much power in western Europe.

Why did Berlin become a flashpoint?

The main problem thrown up by the bad relations between the USSR and USA was Germany. The four-power occupation set up at Yalta would work only if the four co-operated. Within a few months of peace, however, the Russians had refused to allow anyone else into their zone. In the Soviet zone, factories were being dismantled and shipped to the USSR. Soon the people in the three western zones were starving. The German population was swollen by some 16 million refugees who had moved in from eastern Europe and countries which were expelling their German minorities. Britain and France, in great difficulties themselves, were reluctant to give food and money to Germany. The only solution seemed to be to allow some economic revival in the three Allied zones. Stalin was furious: his hatred of Germany was immense. The problem of its defeated population did not move him, and he accused the West of re-erecting the Nazi state.

The flashpoint was bound to be Berlin, a four-zone island-city inside the Soviet zone (see Map 17-2). When the Allies proposed to help revive their zones by setting up a new currency, Stalin closed all access to Berlin. He hoped to force an Allied retreat, but Truman was firm: 'We are going to stay, period,' he said. The Americans thought of using

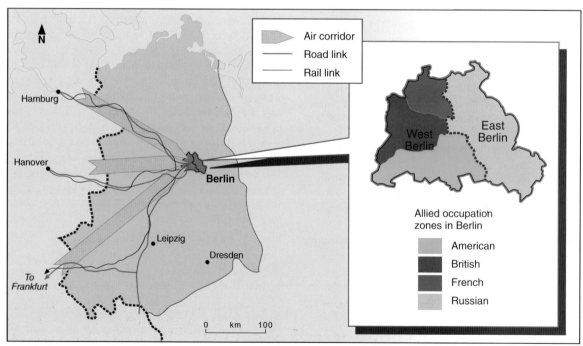

Map 17-2   Germany in 1948–1949

▼ SOURCE 5A American plane being loaded with supplies for Berlin, 1948

their army or even the atom bomb, but decided to ferry supplies into West Berlin by air. Stalin too stopped just short of violence and did not shoot down the planes.

▼ SOURCE 5B
Then the day came when the airlift started. Father didn't believe it. He rode to Tempelhof airport on his bicycle. He was away a long time. When he came home, he said 'They're actually doing it. They're flying food into Berlin. But they won't be able to bring in enough. Think of this huge city with its millions of people!'

A Berlin secretary

❓ Questions
a What sort of supplies would have to be brought in?
b What are the fears of the writer in Source 5B?
c Why was it so important to the USA to hold on to Berlin?

Despite the fears, the Berlin Airlift succeeded. Plane after plane brought in supplies – 27,000 trips.

Then, after 318 days, from June 1948 to May 1949, the Soviets backed down and opened up the route to the city.

NATO
German unity was now impossible. The Soviet zone became East Germany, under Communist rule. The three Allied zones became West Germany, which included West Berlin. In 1949, the western European countries formed the North Atlantic Treaty Organisation. This alliance was based on the USA, which always provided its Supreme Commander. By the terms of NATO, the USA took on the lion's share of defending western Europe against attack. NATO members are shown on Map 17-1.

CONTAINMENT AROUND THE GLOBE

In spite of the Berlin Airlift, Marshall Aid and NATO, the feeling in the USA in 1950 was that they were losing the Cold War. In 1949, the USSR had exploded its first atom bomb, so the US monopoly was broken. In 1949, too, China had become Communist. This was seen as another

Communist take-over by Moscow. Spies were caught in the USA and Britain, and Joseph McCarthy was leading a 'witch hunt' against suspected Communist sympathizers in the USA. In 1950, Truman received NSC 68: a paper from his National Security Council which recommended that the USA make a great effort to oppose Communism anywhere in the world. Truman had to consider this policy within a year because of events in Korea.

Why did Korea become a flashpoint?

In 1945, the Japanese in North Korea had surrendered to the USSR, those in South Korea to the USA. Elections were to be held for a united Korea, but in the meantime separate governments were set up. Both were dictatorships, Communist in the north, capitalist in the south. In 1950, North Korean troops invaded South Korea very nearly taking the whole country (see Map 17-3). It is still uncertain whether they were acting on their own or whether it was Stalin's idea. Truman acted fast: he sent troops to nearby Japan and battleships to wait off the coast. He also asked the UN to condemn the invasion. He and his advisers saw it as an exact

repeat of the Manchurian or Ethiopian incidents of the 1930s when the League of Nations had failed to stop dictators. Normally the USSR had a veto at the UN, but they had withdrawn in protest at the UN's refusal to admit Communist China. The UN was therefore able to order its forces to drive back the North Koreans.

Although the Korean war was a UN action, the USA provided 50% of the army, 86% of the navy and 93% of the air force. The American, General MacArthur, who was in charge, took orders from Truman, not the UN. MacArthur landed behind North Korean lines and soon defeated them. At this point, however, Truman could not resist the attempt to push back the Communists. North Korea was invaded. As the armies reached the Chinese border, Chinese leader Mao Zedong warned them to stop. They did not, and a large Chinese army attacked MacArthur. Truman and MacArthur now disagreed over the war. Truman did not want to get entangled in a war in Asia. He thought Europe was more important, so looked for peace in Korea. MacArthur felt the battle against Communism should be fought in Asia first. He wanted to carry on fighting, and even talked of atom-bombing China.

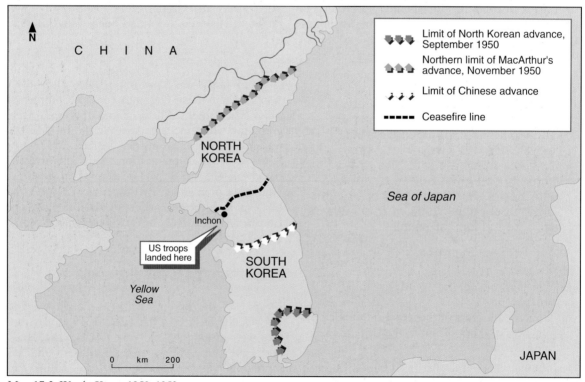

Map 17-3 War in Korea 1950–1953

SOURCE 6A

It seems strangely difficult for some to realise that here in Asia is where the Communist conspirators have elected to make their play for global conquest. That here we fight Europe's war with arms, while the diplomats fight it with words. If we lose the war to Communism in Asia, the fall of Europe is inevitable. There is no substitute for victory.

General Douglas MacArthur, 1951

As President of the USA, Truman was Supreme Commander. MacArthur was sacked in 1951 and a compromise cease-fire worked out in Korea in 1953 (see Map 17-3).

THE DULLES YEARS

From 1953 to 1959, John Foster Dulles was American Secretary of State to President Eisenhower. He was a determined Cold War fighter. He wanted to go further than just 'containing' Communism: he spoke of 'liberating' certain areas from Communism. This would be done by using propaganda to stir up rebellions in the satellites. The arms race continued. Both the USSR and the USA built up stocks of nuclear weapons and tested bigger and bigger bombs. The launching of the Russian 'sputnik', a small satellite, into orbit round the earth in 1957 shocked the Americans. They felt that if the USSR could put a satellite into space, they would soon be able to bomb US cities with nuclear missiles.

Dulles built up the ring of containment around the USSR by a series of alliances. In 1951, he had negotiated an alliance with Japan – an amazing turn-around only ten years after Pearl Harbor. An alliance was made with Australia and New Zealand. The South-East Asia Treaty Organisation (SEATO) linked the USA with Thailand, the Philippines and Pakistan in 1954. In 1955, the Baghdad Pact joined the USA with Turkey, Iran, Iraq and Pakistan. (In 1959, after Iraq left, this

SOURCE 6B

Nuclear test explosion in the Pacific, 1956. A bomb this size was 100 times more powerful than the ones dropped on Hiroshima and Nagasaki in 1945

alliance was renamed CENTO – the Central Treaty Organisation.) To Dulles, these alliances were defensive, part of containment. To the USSR, they appeared offensive, designed to hem in the Communist countries.

From 1955, the USSR was ruled by Nikita Khrushchev. He announced that he intended to live in 'peaceful co-existence' with the West and that he wanted to settle disputes through 'discussion, not through war'. In 1955, Soviet troops withdrew from their zone of Austria. Khrushchev met Western leaders personally in 'summit' meetings. Little was done at these summits, but perhaps they did lead to a slightly easier relationship.

The Berlin Wall

Khrushchev could also cause trouble, however. In 1959, he demanded that Allied soldiers leave West Berlin. At that time, the contrast between drab East Germany and prosperous West Germany was so great that some two million East Germans had crossed over to the West. This was disastrous for East Germany and, in 1961, a wall was built across the city to make escape harder.

CUBA

Khrushchev's greatest threat to peace came in 1962, in Cuba. One of the worst sides of the US Cold War policy was that they supported some corrupt right-wing governments as long as they were anti-Communist. One of these was the brutal

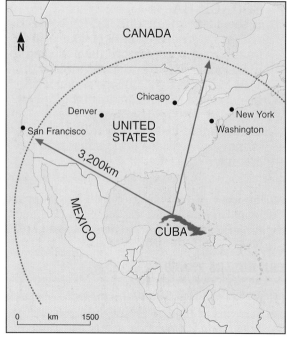

Map 17-4   Cuba and the USA

dictatorship of Batista in Cuba. In 1959 it was overthrown by Fidel Castro. Castro only wanted to be free of US control, but to the USA his only choice was to become an ally or an enemy. When pressure was put on Castro by the USA, he turned to the USSR for help. In 1961, the USA backed an attempted invasion of Cuba at the Bay of Pigs. Then in 1962, US spy planes took photographs of Russian missile bases in Cuba. Map 17-4 shows what a threat this was to the USA.

▚ SOURCE 6C   The Berlin Wall

▼ **SOURCE 7A** Photograph from a U2 spy plane, of a medium-range ballistic missile base in Cuba

Earlier that year, the USSR had tested even bigger nuclear bombs. Soviet missiles in Cuba would tip the balance of power in their favour. The new President, John Kennedy, dared not appear weak in the face of this threat. He told his armed forces to prepare for a nuclear attack on the USSR, demanded that Khrushchev withdraw his missiles and sent the US navy to stop any more missiles getting through to Cuba. As Soviet ships with missiles on board steamed towards Cuba, the world waited for the nuclear holocaust.

▼ **SOURCE 7B**

If assurances were given that the President of the United States would not participate in an attack on Cuba and the blockade were lifted, the question of the missile sites in Cuba would be an entirely different question. We and you ought not to pull on the ends of the rope in which you have tied the knot of war, because the more the two of us pull, the tighter that knot will be tied.

Letter from Khrushchev to Kennedy

❓ Questions

a What is Khrushchev's offering in Source 7B

b What does he mean by the 'knot of war'?

Kennedy agreed to Khrushchev's offer. The blockade was lifted, the missiles crated up and sent back to the USSR. It was the closest to nuclear war that the world had yet come. Out of the crisis came a closer relationship between USSR and the USA. The 'Hot Line' was set up: a direct telephone link from the White House to the Kremlin in Moscow, in 1963. In the same year, the USSR and the USA signed a Test Ban Treaty to stop further testing of nuclear weapons. Soon, however, the USA was involved in another war in Asia.

VIETNAM

In 1954 the French were driven from their former colony of Indo-China. The rebels who had driven them out were mainly Communists, led by Ho Chi Minh. Indo-China was divided into four states: Laos, Cambodia, North Vietnam and South Vietnam (see Map 17-5). It was hoped that the two

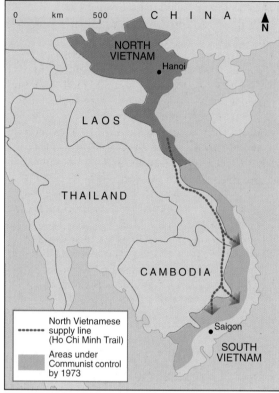

Map 17-5 The Vietnam War 1956–1975

Vietnams could later be united. Meanwhile North Vietnam became a Communist country under Ho Chi Minh. In South Vietnam power was in the hands of a small group, usually from the Roman Catholic landlord class and often corrupt. They had little support among the Buddhist peasants of South Vietnam. By the late 1950s rebellion had broken out. The rebels called themselves the Vietcong and received help from North Vietnam and other Communist countries. The USA began to help the South Vietnamese government. Before long, a major war was taking place. During Kennedy's presidency, American 'advisers' in Vietnam were increased from 500 to 10,000. By 1968, there were 500,000 Americans in Vietnam, with 300 dying per week, at a cost of 30 billion dollars a year.

The Vietnamese war showed up the over-simplification of US Cold War thinking. To put it another way, a policy formed by events in Europe in the 1940s was not necessarily the right one in Asia in the 1960s. They insisted on seeing the war as an attempt by North Vietnam, and behind them China, to take over first South Vietnam and then the rest of Asia. The 'domino' theory still held.

SOURCE 8A

For Hanoi (capital of North Vietnam) the immediate objective is the conquest of the South. For Beijing, however, Hanoi's victory would only be a first step towards eventual Chinese rule over the two Vietnams and South-East Asia and towards exploitation of the new strategy in other parts of the world.

Robert Macnamara, US Defence Secretary, 1964

SOURCE 8B

You walk down a road between the rice paddies. There are Vietnamese in every paddy bent over working. None of them looks up when you pass. Then all of a sudden a mortar shell lands right in the middle of the patrol and a couple of guys you've been buddies with are dead and a couple of others are screaming in agony.

The Vietnamese are still working in the paddies just like they were, as though nothing had happened. Did one of them lob the mortar? If so, which one? Should you kill all of them or some of them?

US journalist Richard Hammer describes the feelings of US soldiers

SOURCE 8C

Dear Editor,

Here are portions of a letter I have received from my son who is now stationed in Vietnam.

'Dear Mum and Dad, today we went on a mission and I am not very proud of myself, my friends or my country. We burned every hut in sight! (He goes on to describe how one of the soldiers with him threw a grenade into a hut). After he threw it and was running for cover we all heard a baby crying from inside the hut. There was nothing we could do. After the explosion we found the mother, two children and an almost new-born baby. The fragile bodies were almost torn apart. Well Dad, you wanted to know what it's like here...Does this give you an idea?'

Needless to say I was much disturbed to read this letter. I think the American people should understand what they mean when they advocate a continuation of our war effort in Vietnam.

A GI's Dad

Letter to a local paper in the USA, March 1967

SOURCE 8D

In sending US troops to South Vietnam, the US imperialists have met a people's war. The people's war has succeeded in gathering all the people to fight their attackers in all ways and with all kinds of weapons.

North Vietnamese General Giap, 1967

? Questions

a What does Source 8A tell us about US motives for fighting the war in Vietnam?

b Use Sources 8B and 8C to describe the difficulties US soldiers faced in fighting this war.

c What do sources 8B, 8C and 8D tell us about what the war was like: for US soldiers? for the Vietnamese people?

d How do Sources 8B and 8E help to explain the events described in Source 8C?

e What would you want to know about Source 8C in order to assess its reliability?

f How useful is Source 8C for telling us about: the way the war was fought? feelings about the war back home in the USA?

g Use Source 8B and your own knowledge to explain in your own words what General Giap, in Source 8D, meant by 'a people's war?'

h One of the aims of the US war effort was to win the 'hearts and minds' of the Vietnamese

SOURCE 8E   US soldier with Vietcong suspects

people. On the whole they failed. How far do these sources explain this failure?

i Use all the sources and your own knowledge to explain what the Vietnamese war was like.

j What other evidence would you like to see to make your account more accurate?

The Vietcong used guerrilla tactics. They had become experts in these methods in years of war against the French. By day they mingled with the peasants in the rice-fields of South Vietnam. By night they mined roads and passed on information. The jungle gave cover to their soldiers. They knew every track and ambush. They were on better terms with the South Vietnamese peasants than the Americans, who were foreigners – 'long noses'. Supplies were carried from the North on bicycles down jungle tracks, called the 'Ho Chi Minh Trail'.

The war also showed what has been called 'the arrogance of power': the Americans could not believe that they might not win. From 1965, there were massive bombing raids on North Vietnam to try to stop supplies to the South. By 1970, more bombs had been dropped on North Vietnam than were dropped during the entire Second World War. Helicopter gunships, gas and napalm were all used. The jungle was even sprayed with defoliant to destroy the vegetation which gave cover. In spite of all this the guerrilla tactics of the Vietcong and North Vietnamese worked. The 'little men in black pyjamas', as the Americans called them, gained control of more and more of South Vietnam.

By 1968, the cost of the war in deaths and money was becoming too great for the American people. Putting into practice the policies of Truman and Dulles now proved too expensive. An anti-war movement gained strength (see Chapter 18). President Nixon proposed 'Vietnamisation' – handing over the war to the South Vietnamese. A peace was negotiated in Paris in 1973. By 1975, South Vietnam had fallen to the Communists and its capital, Saigon, renamed Ho Chi Minh City. Communists also took over in Laos and Cambodia. This was mainly as a result of Nixon's decision to bomb these countries, which had turned the people there against the USA and towards the Communists.

DETENTE IN THE 1970s

Détente means an 'easing of tension', in this case between East and West. It was a climbing down from the 'eyeball-to-eyeball' confrontations of the

Dulles era. The USA built closer relations with the USSR and China. Some agreement was reached on limiting the arms race. Crises did not reach the brink of nuclear war as they seemed to in the 1950s and 1960s. There were several reasons for this. A major one was the split between the USSR and China in 1960. For the USA, it meant that they could no longer regard Communism as a single enemy. For the USSR and Chinese there was the danger of being isolated, of being the odd one out of three. Both tried to come to terms with the USA.

The Vietnam War was an important lesson for the USA. Despite their nuclear supremacy and huge wealth they lost to a small, poor country. It appeared that most Vietnamese preferred a Communist government without being bullied or forced into it. It was a huge blow to US self-confidence.

▶ SOURCE 9A

We shall pay any price, bear any burden, meet any hardship, support any friend, oppose any foe to assure the survival and success of liberty.

President J. F. Kennedy, 1961

▶ SOURCE 9B

America cannot, and will not, conceive all the plans, design all the programmes, execute all the decisions and undertake all the defence of the free nations of the world.

President Nixon, 1972

In this mood, the USA was willing to look hard at the cost of the arms race. Diverting billions of dollars to be spent on weapons weakened the US foreign aid programme. The problems of poverty at home remained unsolved. The USSR too wanted to use its resources to raise the standard of living for its people. Most important of all, of course, was the fear that nuclear war could break out, with the prospect of total destruction of most of the human race. Strategic Arms Limitation Talks (SALT) were held from 1969 between the USSR and the USA. This resulted in an agreement in 1972, SALT 1, limiting nuclear weapons. Relations between the USA and USSR were good at this point, and both leaders visited each other's countries.

Throughout the Cold War both sides recognised that each has certain areas of influence. No

US help was given to Hungary in 1956 or to Czechoslovakia in 1968 when these countries tried to throw out their Communist rulers, and were crushed by Soviet tanks (see Chapter 23), pages 256–257). The USA crushed left-wing governments in Dominican Republic in 1965 and Chile in 1973 without the USSR becoming involved.

The spirit of détente brought about the Helsinki Conference of 1975. The 35 states which attended agreed to guarantee all frontiers and respect human rights. This seems to have meant different things to different people in the next few years. To the USA it meant complaining about the suppression of the rights of individuals in the USSR. To the USSR it meant being allowed to get on with running their own country in their own way without interference. Relations began to deteriorate in the late 1970s. SALT 2, due for renewal in 1977, was not completed until 1979. Then in December 1979, Soviet troops invaded Afghanistan and the USA refused to sign the Treaty.

The 1980s saw a return to Cold War attitudes on the part of the USA, led by President Reagan. He called the USSR 'an evil Empire'. A Second Cold War began. US forces intervened in the civil wars in El Salvador, Guatemala and Nicaragua. Even more dangerous, new Cruise and Pershing missile systems were invented and deployed among the USA's NATO allies. This led the USSR to develop new SS-20 missiles. In response, Reagan developed a massively expensive and complicated nuclear defence system called 'Star Wars'.

THE END OF THE COLD WAR

Hostility between the two sides in the Cold War in the mid-1980s was as bad as ever, when along came Gorbachev. He wanted to carry out radical changes in the USSR. (These are explained fully in Chapter 23.) To do what he wanted, he had to remove the huge burden of the cost of the Cold War. Military spending was soaking up perhaps 25% of the wealth of the USSR. One of his policies for the USSR was *glasnost*, meaning trust or openness. If he was more open with the West, real disarmament could take place because he would let Americans see that the missiles really were being dismantled.

In two meetings between Gorbachev and Reagan, at Reykjavik in Iceland in 1986 and at Washington in 1987, the Cold War came to an end. Gorbachev's policy for Eastern Europe has been called the Sinatra doctrine – 'I did it my way'. This meant letting countries decide their own forms of government and place in the world. In the amazing autumn of 1989 Communist governments in East Germany, Poland, Czechoslovakia, Hungary, Romania and Bulgaria all fell. The Berlin Wall was torn down. This time, unlike in Hungary in 1956 and Czechoslovakia in 1968, no Soviet tanks rolled in to stop them.

The West was taken by surprise. Who was the enemy now? Nuclear weapons systems remained in place. NATO wondered whether to ask the USSR to join. There was talk of a 'New World Order', of

SOURCE 10

Russian nuclear bombers lying in a field after being dismantled

peace for all. There was talk of the 'Peace Dividend' – lower taxes because there was no need to have huge armed forces and expensive nuclear weapons. Having geared up for war over 45 years, however, Western countries were uncertain how to react to these rapid changes.

ASSESSMENT

Describe, explain and analyse

1 Look again at the section 'The Cold War in Europe' (pages 185–191)

a) What did the USA think the USSR was doing from 1945 to 1949?

b) What did the USSR say they were doing?

c) Which analysis of these actions do you believe?

2 a) Choose three of the items from this list and describe how each contributed to the Cold War.

   i) The 1948 takeover of Czechoslovakia.

   ii) Marshall aid.

   iii) Berlin Airlift.

   iv) Korean War.

   v) Cuban missile crisis.

   vi) Failure to ratify SALT 2.

b) 'The Cold War was based on suspicion and misunderstanding'. Is this statement true for the three items you have chosen?

3 a) Describe what the Vietnam War was like.

b) Why was the USA involved?

c) Why did they fail to win? In your answer you could mention:

   • Guerrilla tactics of the Vietcong.

   • Loss of public support at home.

   • Rising cost of the war.

   • Rising US death toll.

4 Read Sources 9A and 9B.

a) Write a summary of each of these two sources in one sentence each.

b) How do they differ?

c) Why were US presidents making such different statements about US policy only 11 years apart? What had happened to change US attitudes?

5 a) Choose three items from this list and describe how they contributed to détente.

   i) 1963 Test Ban Treaty.

   ii) SALT 1.

   iii) Helsinki Conference, 1975.

   iv) SALT 2.

   v) Nixon's visit to China, 1972.

b) None of the items on this list really made much difference to the Cold War. Why was it so difficult to bring about trust and disarmament?

c) Why did the Cold War eventually end in 1986–1987?

Evidence and interpretations

SOURCE A
US and Soviet soldiers meet in Germany in May 1945.

SOURCE B

The lessons of history were learnt in this century slowly, expensively, bloodily. Twice war swept across Europe; twice the USA was forced to intervene. After the 1918 armistice, a League of Nations was established to keep the peace. But American policies of that time kept the US out, and, lacking authority, the League could not prevent the outbreak of World War II. America was forced to give the neutrality of earlier centuries, when oceans were barriers and wars were not global.

Commentary from a US newsreel, 1945

SOURCE C

Destruction of the Russian city of Murmansk during the Second World War. All that remains of the buildings are piles of rubble.

SOURCE D

The peoples of the great Soviet state have won the right to be respected as one of the great powers in the world. The glorious Red Army, advancing on the Fascist beast, saved the world from the bloodthirsty Hitlerite regime. The German army invaded our Soviet motherland, destroying everything in its path and reaching the outskirts of Moscow in 1941. Only superhuman efforts by the Soviet people forced them to retreat. As the Red Army drove them back across Soviet soil, the horrifying tide of Nazi atrocities was discovered. The victorious, liberating Red Army, led by the genius of its great leader and commander Comrade Stalin, completely cleared the German invaders from the soil of the Soviet Union, Poland, Romania, Bulgaria, Finland and a considerable part of Czechoslovakia and Hungary.

Description of the war from
Soviet newspapers, 1945

SOURCE E

Across the vast expanse of the globe there was famine, national ruin, pestilence and moral disintegration. Without help, recovery might never be achieved. In the background was the growing struggle between two great powers to shape the post-war world. Looking towards Europe from Moscow, Soviet Russia was expansively stabbing westwards, knifing into nations left empty by war, with misery and chaos as allies.

Commentary from US newsreel, 1946

a Source A shows US and Soviet soldiers embracing; by ten months later Churchill was talking about an 'Iron curtain' (see page 189). What had happened in between?

b What were the 'lessons of history' that the USA had to learn, referred to in Source B?

c What reasons does Stalin give in Source D for Soviet actions in Eastern Europe?

d What else does this source tell us about Soviet attitudes at this time?

e What other reasons for Soviet attitudes at this time are shown in Source C?

f What does Source E tell us about US attitudes to:

    i) What the USSR was doing?

    ii) Why they were able to do it?

g Use these sources and your own knowledge to judge which interpretation of events is more accurate: the one in Source D or the one in Source E.

18: The USA since 1945

When the Second World War ended in 1945, the USA was clearly the richest, most powerful country in the world. The war itself had put American industry to work: 86,000 tanks, 6,500 ships, as well as aeroplanes and guns had been built. Industrial production in 1945 was three times what it had been in 1941. Farming, too, had prospered: helped by Roosevelt's New Deal, agricultural production was up by one-third. America itself, alone of the great powers, had suffered no war damage from bombing or fighting at home.

Most important of all, the USA possessed the atom bomb, a terrifying new weapon. Possession of the bomb and the sheer power of the USA meant that it could not avoid playing a large part in world affairs after the war. American presidents had to spend a great deal of their time on foreign policy.

In 1945, American troops were stationed in many parts of Europe and the Far East. Over the next 35 years, they were to find other battlefields: Korea, Vietnam and elsewhere (see Chapter 17). This chapter, by contrast, is about events inside the USA: how American governments tried to keep the country prosperous and dealt with problems at home.

PRESIDENT HARRY TRUMAN 1945–1952

When Roosevelt died in 1945, his Vice-President, Harry Truman, took over. Some Americans were afraid that the Depression would return when the war ended. The presidents in the 1920s had believed in letting the business world take care of its own affairs. FDR had reversed this policy and brought the US government into economic affairs in a big way.

Truman was a 'New Dealer' and continued this involvement. Government contracts continued to go out to American business in peacetime. This kept up employment. Even Eisenhower, President from 1952 to 1960 and a Republican, kept up this policy and gave out huge government contracts for road-building.

Prosperity

All through the 1950s and 1960s, prosperity increased. America's lead over the rest of the world was astonishing: with only 6% of the world's population, America made 45% of the world's steel, 74% of the world's cars and 86% of the world's nylon. The standard of living of the average American was three times that of the average Briton in 1960. Out of every ten American households, eight had a car, eight had a telephone, nine had a television and seven had a washing-machine. A boom in consumer goods, things for the ordinary American family, took place. Buying more meant more jobs and so more money to spend. It became important to keep America spending: a huge advertising business grew up to persuade people to buy more.

To keep people spending, 'obsolescence' was important: things would wear out, or go rapidly out of fashion, so you would have to buy again. To help you keep on spending, hire-purchase was arranged on a huge scale: you could buy more than you could pay cash for.

SOURCE 1A
Prosperous suburb of a US city: Beverly Hills, Los Angeles, California

SOURCE 1B
Inner-city area of a US city: Philadelphia, Pennsylvania

? Questions

a What signs of wealth can been seen in Source 1A?

b What clues are there that the area in Source 1B is not so prosperous?

After the war years, people were glad to return home and enjoy life. They felt they had earned their prosperity. However, it was also a time of complacency.

The Fair Deal

The New Deal had tried to bring a return to prosperity. It had also tried to help the less fortunate Americans: the poor, the old and the ill. Truman also had plans of this kind. He called them the 'Fair Deal'. The two main problems he wanted to tackle were poverty (by no means all Americans shared in the prosperity) and civil rights (the USA was still unfair in its treatment of the 12% of its citizens who were black). However, FDR had had the US Congress on his side during the New Deal. As a Democrat, he could count on a Democratic majority in Congress to pass the laws he wanted.

Until 1948 Truman had to deal with a Republican Congress. They blocked much of the Fair Deal. Even when Democrats regained control of Congress in 1948, Truman did not have things all his own way. A Housing Act in 1949 encouraged the building of good, cheap houses. However, Democrats from the south blocked Truman's hopes for civil rights. His only major achievement was a law to stop segregation (racial separation) in the US armed forces.

McCarthyism

Foreign affairs, especially the growing Cold War, began to have an effect on events inside the USA. By 1950, American Cold War policy had suffered setbacks: China had become Communist, the Korean War had broken out and the USSR had learned how to make atom bombs. How could this be? How could the mighty USA, world leader in 1945, be outdone?

A clue for some people was given by spy scares. A British scientist, Dr Klaus Fuchs, admitted giving atomic secrets to the Russians. Then an American, Alger Hiss, was accused of spying for USSR. Senator Joseph McCarthy began to claim that the USA was riddled with spies, Communists and their friends. As Chairman of the Un-American Activities Committee, he had the right to summon anyone before him to answer his charges. It is true that in the days of the New Deal, FDR had given jobs to people who were radicals, liberals, Socialists, or American Communists. In the 1930s, Communism had seemed to some people the only alternative to fascism. However, to say, as McCarthy did, that there were hundreds, even thousands (he changed the numbers regularly) of Communists and spies in the government was ridiculous.

Unfortunately, very few people dared to oppose Senator McCarthy. To do so made one look like a friend of America's main enemy. Even to be accused by him was enough to get people sacked from their jobs. Authors accused by him found it impossible to find publishers. Hollywood actors, producers and writers – among them Charlie Chaplin – were accused and driven out of work. It was a witch hunt.

Not one of the hundreds of people accused by McCarthy was ever actually convicted of spying, but no one dared speak out against his bullying and his lies. Politicians were careful: young Richard Nixon supported him; John Kennedy was neutral; President Eisenhower 'refused to get in the gutter with the guy'. (What do you think he meant?) Eventually, McCarthyism burned itself out. By 1955, the Korean War was over. When the proceedings of the Un-American Activities Committee were televised, people were shocked at McCarthy's rudeness and bullying. He lost the public's support. McCarthyism was, however, a nasty episode in American history.

PRESIDENT DWIGHT EISENHOWER 1952-1960

President Eisenhower was a popular president. As a successful Second World War general, he won the elections of 1952 and 1956 easily. He brought businessmen into his government. Their main aim was to keep the economy booming. They succeeded in this, and throughout the 1950s the standard of living of the average American rose. Wages kept rising, and hours of work fell. This boom was mainly due to a world trade revival, but Eisenhower received much of the credit for it. By the late 1950s he was often ill and appeared an old man. By that time, too, cracks had begun to appear in this great American prosperity.

Poverty

In 1960, many Americans, both black and white, were still poor. In rural areas, poor whites and poor blacks struggled to make a living on small farms. In some areas of the Appalachian Mountains, mining had declined, leaving unemployment and poverty.

In the richest country in the world, there were areas with bad housing and schools. In a country which produced so much food that the surplus was often burned or dumped in the sea, many people went hungry.

This was partly a matter of the American way of life. The old-fashioned American belief was that anyone could do well if they worked hard; if they were poor it was their own fault. There was therefore no health service, no dole, no social security. They thought that such 'welfare' systems just encouraged people to be lazy. There was no sickness benefit system and very little old-age pension. Unfortunately, people cannot help being hit by bad luck, illness or old age. Single-parent families, the old and the ill made up a large number of the poorest Americans.

▼ SOURCE 2
Poor white family in Mississippi

❓ Questions
a What signs of poverty are there in this picture?
b Compare this picture with Source 1A. Why is there such a contrast in the USA?

Blacks in America

Black Americans were often poor, but they suffered another difficulty as well: discrimination. Despite the statement in the US Constitution that all men are created equal, blacks were not treated equally. After the abolition of slavery in 1856, most blacks stayed in the South, where they made up nearly half the population. The whites ruled the South, however, passing laws to make separate white and black facilities legal. Thus the signs 'White Ladies' and 'Black Women' were common. Blacks had to sit at the back of buses, whites at the front. White and black seating areas were made in restaurants. Separate white and black schools were built. They were separate and unequal as well: on average, the southern states spent 45 dollars on each white child's education and 13 dollars on each black child per year. In many states there was a literacy test in order to vote. With bad education and white judges, it is not surprising that few blacks voted.

Roosevelt, Truman and Eisenhower had all tried to use Federal (Washington) power to break this inequality. The local, state governments under white control, however, had been largely successful in resisting this pressure.

During and after the Second World War, many blacks moved north to the cities and to California. There was no segregation in the North, but they still often met prejudice. They were discriminated against in jobs, forced to take cheap, bad housing in the black ghettos. As blacks moved in, richer white city residents moved out to the suburbs. Many blacks in the cities saw themselves in a trap: with poor education and poor jobs, they could not get out of the ghetto. Bad housing and family stress turned many to drugs and to crime. By 1960, the crime rate in American cities had reached enormous proportions. Add to these difficulties the problems of pollution and the motor car, and the cities' plight becomes obvious. Yet the cities do not have the money to deal with these problems, as their more prosperous citizens move out to suburbs, leaving the poor behind.

PRESIDENT JOHN F. KENNEDY 1960–1963

In 1960, John F. Kennedy, a young, vigorous Democrat won the presidential election. Many looked to him to take energetic action to deal with the problems of the USA when he took office in 1961. He brought many new men from universities to work with him. As we shall see, his actual achievements in just under three years do not amount to much, but his name and face still stand for a belief that American ideas and energy can solve any problem. He appointed the first black ambassador, the first black naval commander and the first black Federal judge. He announced plans for health care, care of the elderly and help to unions, calling these plans the 'New Frontier'. Time and time again, however, his proposals were blocked by Congress. Democrats from the South opposed change, opposed welfare and opposed racial equality, voting with Republicans against him.

Martin Luther King

Meanwhile, the battle for black civil rights in the South had been slowly gaining strength. In 1954, the Supreme Court had judged that separate black and white schools were illegal. In 1957, there were riots at Little Rock, Arkansas, when a black girl enrolled at the white high school. Eisenhower used Federal troops to enforce the integration. In 1955 in Montgomery, Alabama, Mrs Rosa Parkes, sitting at the front of a bus, had been asked to give up her seat to a white woman. She refused and was arrested as a Communist agitator. A boycott of the local bus service followed. This was led by Martin Luther King, a young black minister. The bus company depended on black customers (richer people had cars), and was forced to give way after a year. Discrimination on buses was declared illegal.

? Questions

a   What weapons are the police in Source 3A using?
b   Martin Luther King was a supporter of non-violence. Explain how he hoped to use these methods to achieve his aims. Source 3B may help you.
c   Explain why the local police opposed civil rights.
d   What could the Federal government do to help the civil rights movement?

▼ **SOURCE 3A**   Police dealing with civil rights demonstrators

▼ SOURCE 3B
Martin Luther King

In 1961, the campaign was on another front: discrimination in stations and eating areas. 'Freedom riders' went into the South to insist on their rights to equal treatment. The local people met them with violence, supported by the local police. Some civil rights workers were killed and their murderers let off by white juries.

Kennedy was able to help these campaigns through his brother, Robert Kennedy, the Attorney General. In 1962, the President sent Federal marshals to enable a black student to enrol at the all-white University of Mississippi. In 1963, he began a tour of the South to try to influence people. He had a speech to make in Dallas, Texas, with the words 'We ask that we may achieve in our time, and for all time, the vision of "peace on earth, goodwill toward men".' The speech was never made. He was assassinated that same day.

PRESIDENT LYNDON JOHNSON 1963–1968

Kennedy's successor was Lyndon B. Johnson, a rough and ready Southerner. The clever Kennedy men did not like him. He may have been crude, but he had started his career as a New Dealer. In 1964, the Appalachian Recovery Programme was passed, to deal with poverty and pollution in the Appalachian Mountains. He passed the Civil Rights Act, 1964, for integration in shops, cinemas and restaurants; the Education Act, 1965; and the Voting Rights Act, 1965. He introduced 'Medicare', a system of health care for the over-65s, and 'Medicaid', a health system for the poor. He certainly used the shock of Kennedy's assassination to push through these laws, claiming that he was doing Kennedy's work. However, his own experience as a Southern Democrat was vital. He also brought in a huge programme of government help for the cities, which he called the 'Great Society'. Unfortunately, by the later 1960s, the Vietnam War was taking more and more time and money. As American involvement in the war increased, so the chance of dealing with problems at home slipped away.

At the same time, black Americans were turning to other leaders. Bitter over the death of Kennedy, many blacks turned to the 'Black Power' movement. Some leaders were Muslim, looking for a religion which non-white people could feel was their own. One of their most famous followers was the world heavyweight boxer Cassius Clay, who changed his name to Muhammad Ali. Others tried to teach their fellow blacks to be proud of being black.

▼ SOURCE 4A
The only thing we own in this country is the colour of our skins. . . . We have to stop being ashamed of being black. A broad nose, a thick lip and nappy hair is us and we are going to call that beautiful whether they like it or not.

Stokeley Carmichael

▼ SOURCE 4B
Black Power was nothing to do with violence. Black Power is when black people respect themselves. Black Power is when black people stop . . . filling the jails while white men fill the colleges.

Hosea Williams

▼ SOURCE 4C

Some black American medal winners at the 1968 Olympics gave the Black Power salute

? Questions

a   What is Stokeley Carmichael trying to say to black people in Source 4A?
b   What contrast does Hosea Williams make between blacks and whites in Source 4B?
c   Why would the Olympics be a good moment for a Black Power demonstration (Source 4C?)

In the late 1960s, American universities and cities were centres for many protests. There were two issues: civil rights for black Americans, and opposition to the Vietnam War. Often these two issues joined together, as black leaders pointed out that 12 in 100 Americans were black, but 23 in 100 soldiers in Vietnam were black. The race issue flared into riots in Watts, California, in 1965, and in Newark, Detroit and Chicago in 1966. In 1968, Johnson announced that he would not stand again for the presidency, mainly because of opposition to the Vietnam War. There was more violence in that year, with the assassinations of both Robert Kennedy and Martin Luther King.

PRESIDENT RICHARD M. NIXON 1968–1974

The 1968 election was won by Richard M. Nixon who promised to put an end to the Vietnam War. At first, Nixon continued the war, even extending it into Cambodia. This produced further protests, in which four students were shot by National Guardsmen at Kent State University. In 1973, however, he withdrew American soldiers from Vietnam.

No major laws on civil rights were passed by Nixon but it was a calmer period. Some progress was made on the basis of the laws which Johnson had passed. All over America, even in the South, blacks made progress: more went on to college and more voted. By 1975, 120 cities had black mayors. There are still many poor blacks, however, and much bad feeling remains which occasionally explodes into violent riots.

Watergate

President Nixon's peace efforts made him popular, but he was a suspicious man. He and his advisers felt he had to win the 1972 presidential election at any cost. Some of Nixon's men broke into the Watergate building (where his Democratic opponent's headquarters were), to see what plans his opponent had. They were caught and put on trial. Nixon said he knew nothing about Watergate and won the election easily.

However, the trials of the burglars and newspaper publicity gradually led to Nixon's closest advisers, even to Nixon himself, being blamed. In 1973 Nixon's Vice-President resigned and was replaced by Gerald Ford. In 1974, Nixon was forced to reveal his tape-recorded conversations about Watergate. In August 1974 he resigned, the only American president ever to do so.

Gerald Ford, the Vice-President, took over as President until the 1976 election. He tried to restore some confidence in the presidency after the shocks of Vietnam and Watergate.

PRESIDENT JIMMY CARTER 1976–1980

The next President of America, the winner of the 1976 election, was Jimmy Carter, an unknown Democrat. He was obviously honest, and promised open, clean government. However, events in the world brought problems for which he had no solution. There was inflation and rising unemployment. Oil prices were rising so Carter proposed an Energy Bill to cut down petrol consumption. This was rejected by Congress. American diplomats in Iran were held hostage by Islamic students in 1980. Carter's rescue bid failed when US helicopters broke down. At this stage the American people were left uncertain and demoralised. Vietnam and Watergate, the assassination of several leaders and the failure of so many hopes were all blows to their self-confidence. In the 1980 presidential elections the American people turned back to more old-fashioned views. The winner was the ageing ex-Hollywood film actor and Governor of California, Ronald Reagan.

PRESIDENT RONALD REAGAN 1980–1988

Reagan promised to reduce taxes and restore pride in being American. To some extent he did both these things. He was a clever performer on television and won both the 1980 and 1984 presidential elections easily. At home, the economy picked up. In foreign affairs his forceful anti-Communist views were pursued in spectacular plans for a multi-billion dollar defence plan known as 'Star Wars'. However, he found himself dealing with Soviet leader Mikhail Gorbachev. Together they drew the Cold War to a close (see Chapter 17).

PRESIDENT GEORGE BUSH 1988–1992

George Bush had served twice as Ronald Reagan's Vice-President and appealed to Americans who wanted Reagan's policies to continue.

PRESIDENT BILL CLINTON 1992–2000

Bill Clinton was much younger than George Bush. Clinton and his wife, Hillary, a career woman in her own right, seemed to stand for new values in American politics, particularly in helping poorer Americans with the cost of health care and improving their education. However, he soon faced stiff opposition from a strongly Republican Congress.

Table 18-1 Post-war presidents of the USA

1945–1952	Harry Truman	Democrat
1952–1960	Dwight D. Eisenhower	Republican
1960–1963	John F. Kennedy	Democrat
1963–1968	Lyndon B. Johnson	Democrat
1968–1974	Richard M. Nixon	Republican
1974–1976	Gerald B. Ford	Republican
1976–1980	Jimmy Carter	Democrat
1980–1988	Ronald Reagan	Republican
1988–1992	George W. Bush	Republican
1992–2000	Bill Clinton	Democrat

JOHN FITZGERALD KENNEDY 1917–1963

John Fitzgerald Kennedy was the second of eight children. His father, Joseph Kennedy, was Irish and a millionaire by his own efforts. He encouraged his sons to be fiercely loyal to the family and fiercely competitive towards one another. John was always encouraged to compete with his older brother, Joseph. It was Joseph who was expected to go into politics.

John attended Harvard University and joined the US Navy. He was made commander of a patrol boat, PT 109. One night in 1943, his boat was rammed, cut in two and sunk. With several of his crew, he clung to the wreckage for five hours. Despite an injured back, he struggled to an island and saved his men.

The Kennedy family plans changed in 1944 when Joseph was killed in a USAF bomber over England. John went into politics to take his place. He was a Congressman in 1946, a Senator in 1952. His good looks, his energy, his money and his attractive wife Jacqueline helped his career. He was not an outstanding Senator but stood as the Democratic candidate in the 1960 election against Richard Nixon. The campaign was unusual in one way: Kennedy and Nixon held four debates on television, the first time TV had been used in this way. Kennedy just won, by only 100,000 votes out of the 68 million cast. He was the youngest President ever (43), and the first Roman Catholic President.

Like FDR, Kennedy gathered people of ideas around him. His youth, his humour and his young family brought fresh air into the White House. One real achievement was the Peace Corps: an organisation where young Americans could serve a year or more as teachers or nurses helping poorer people in Africa, Asia or South America. The lack of progress in other matters is explained in this chapter. He made it quite clear, however, that he was keen to help the poor, the old and the black people of America.

In foreign policy, he was as tough as any other president. Over Cuba, Berlin and Vietnam, he stood very firm against the USSR. In 1963, however, after the Cuban crisis, he did sign the Test Ban Treaty and improved contacts with the Soviet Union.

He would probably have won a second term of office in the 1964 election. His assassination in 1963 was a blow to millions, inside and outside the US.

ASSESSMENT

Describe, explain and analyse

1   **a**) Describe how black Americans were discriminated against in the USA in the post-war years.

    b) What kinds of protest took place against this situation?

    c) How did the federal government respond?

    d) How successful have government measures to remove discrimination been?

2   Write two paragraphs for *each* of the following Presidents.

    The first should describe their aims;

    The second should analyse their achievements.

- Truman
- Kennedy
- Johnson
- Reagan

19: Israel and the Arab World

Why has there been conflict in the Middle East?

This chapter is about the causes and results of conflicts in the Middle East this century. It also looks at why the rest of the world has often been involved in these conflicts and how attempts have been made to make peace. The problem is: who should live on this land?

Most of the land on Map 19-1 is desert and so is very poor. But near rivers or the sea, the land is fertile and good crops can be grown. One of these fertile areas is Palestine, the region between the Mediterranean Sea to the west and the River Jordan and the Dead Sea to the east. Most of this region now forms the State of Israel, but people have lived here for centuries. The most important city in this area is Jerusalem, a holy city for the followers of three great religions: Judaism, Islam and Christianity.

At the time of Jesus Christ, the Jews lived in Palestine. It had been their homeland for many centuries. At this time, it was part of the Roman empire. The Jews rebelled against their hated Roman masters and were defeated. In AD 135, therefore, the Roman Emperor declared all Jewish religious customs illegal and banned the Jews from the city of Jerusalem. Many Jews left and settled all over Europe and the Middle East. There was no one country they could call home. However, despite everything, they kept their own religious beliefs and customs. Many dreamed of having their own country again where they would be safe from persecution. Naturally their thoughts turned to Palestine and to the holy city of Jerusalem. This desire for a national Jewish homeland was called Zionism. From the 1890s, Jews began to settle in Palestine.

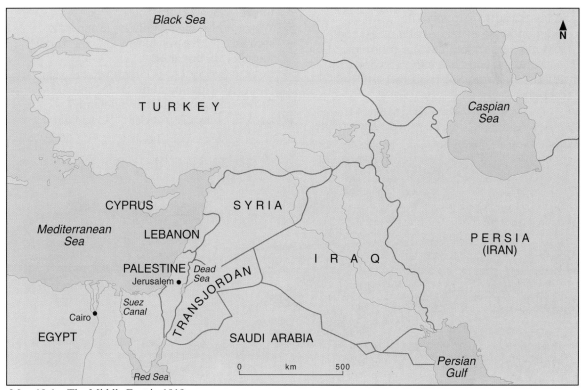

Map 19-1   The Middle East in 1919

Meanwhile, the Arabs had moved into Palestine about AD 700. By 1900, they too naturally regarded Palestine as their homeland. For the Arabs, who were Muslims, Jerusalem was also a holy city.

By 1900, all this area was ruled by the Sultan of Turkey. An Arab nationalist movement existed, made up of people who wanted independence from the Turks.

The First World War

The Ottoman or Turkish empire was on Germany's side in the First World War (see Chapter 2). The British began to support the idea of Arab independence as a way of making war on the Turks. In 1914, Lord Kitchener wrote a letter to the Sherif (ruler) of Mecca, one of the leading Arabs, offering British help. T. E. Lawrence, a British officer, was sent to help the Arabs in sabotage work against the Turks. He became known as Lawrence of Arabia.

Sherif Hussein wrote to Sir Henry Mac-Mahon, British High Commissioner in Egypt to pin the British down. MacMahon replied:

▼ SOURCE 1

Subject to modifications, Great Britain is prepared to support the independence of the Arabs in all the regions demanded. On the other hand, it is understood that such European advisers as may be required will be British.

Sir Henry MacMahon to Sherif Hussein
October, 1915

At this time, however, promises were also being made to the Jews. There were many Jews living in the USA. At first, the USA had remained neutral in the First World War. The British hoped that by supporting the Jews in their desire to return to Palestine, the Jews in America might bring that country into the war on Britain's side. This letter was written by the British Foreign Secretary, A. J. Balfour, in 1917 to a leading Zionist:

▼ SOURCE 2

His Majesty's Government view will favour the setting up in Palestine of a national home for the Jewish people. It being clearly understood that nothing shall be done which may prejudice the civil and religious rights of the existing non-Jewish community in Palestine. I should be grateful if you would bring this Declaration to the knowledge of the Zionist Federation.

Balfour Declaration, November 1917

? Questions

a   Why did the British regard the Turks as a threat to them?

b   Why was blowing up railways (Source 1B) such an effective way of wrecking the Turkish war effort in this area?

c   Look at Source 1A. Is it clear what is being promised? How might the Arabs and the British interpret this letter differently?

d   Look at Source 2. Is it clear? How might

▼ SOURCE 1B   Turkish railway trucks destroyed by Arab fighters

Zionists and the British interpret this
document differently?

e   How does Balfour, in Source 2, try to deal with
the rights of the people already living in
Palestine?

f   The British have often been blamed for the
problems of Palestine by promising different
things to different people. Is this a fair
criticism? How would you defend British
actions at this time?

THE BRITISH MANDATE

After the war, the Turkish empire was broken up
and Palestine given to Britain to look after as a
mandate (see Chapter 3). The terms of the mandate
were: to allow Jewish immigration into Palestine
and to protect the rights of the local Arab population. At the time, this seemed reasonable. Between
1920 and 1930, 100,000 Jews went to live there.

In the 1930s, these numbers increased. In 1936
alone, 60,000 Jewish settlers poured into Palestine.
The rise of Hitler in Germany, and of fascist
dictators in other parts of Europe, led many European Jews to look for a refuge. In 1918, 10% of
Palestine's people had been Jews. By 1939, the
number of Jews had risen to nearly 40%. The
Arabs were becoming very angry by now at the
numbers coming into Palestine. To try to prevent
trouble between the Arabs and Jews, the British
cut down on Jewish immigration. In 1939, they
laid down a quota of 77,000 Jewish immigrants
over the next five years.

After the Second World War, the world was
horrified at the news of the concentration camps
and at the attempts by the Nazis to eliminate the
Jews. Many people thought the Jews should be
given their own land so that they could be safe
from persecution. Jews had fought with the British
in the war; now they thought it right that the
British should let more Jews into Palestine. In 1946
240,000 Jews wanted to come into the country. The
British, still worried at Arab reactions, stuck to the
quota system and turned refugees away.

The end of the Mandate

Pictures like Source 3, coming so soon after the
news of the Holocaust, shocked the world. Many
people, especially in the USA, felt that the Jews had
won the right, because of the Holocaust, to a land
of their own where they could be safe. The question
was – where?

? Questions

a   Why were the British turning away the
refugees in Source 3?

b   What would be the reaction of people in the
rest of the world to such a scene?

▼ SOURCE 3   Refugee ship being sent back from Palestine to Cyprus by British soldiers

The Arabs in Palestine were afraid of being out-numbered in their own country. They blamed the British for letting in too many Jews; the Jews blamed the British for not letting in enough. Small bands of Jewish guerrillas, like the Stern Gang, attacked the British for restricting Jewish immigration. In 1946, the King David Hotel in Jerusalem, where the British had their military headquarters, was blown up by Jewish guerrillas. There were also outbreaks of violence between Jewish and Arab groups.

The British offered talks between Jews and Arabs, but they both refused. The problem was then taken to the United Nations in 1947. The UN suggested dividing Palestine between Jews and Arabs, as shown on Map 19-2. The Arabs refused to accept this. They thought the Jews had no claim at all on what they considered to be their own land.

Heavy fighting broke out between Jews and Arabs. The Arabs were helped by the neighbouring Arab countries of Egypt, Jordan and Syria. How-ever, in May 1948, the day before the British were due to hand over Palestine to the UN, the Jewish leaders in Palestine took control. They declared the formation of a new state of Israel. David ben Gurion was to be the first Prime Minister.

THE STATE OF ISRAEL

In the next 15 years there were four wars between Israel and its neighbours.

1. 1948–1949

As soon as the state of Israel was proclaimed, Egypt, Syria, Jordan and Iraq sent forces to help the Palestinian Arabs. However, the Israelis fought desperately and drove the Arab armies back (from the area within solid lines to the brown shaded area with dotted lines on Map 19-2). Israel survived, but was still in a very dangerous position. Jerusalem was divided, trade with Arab countries was banned. The Suez Canal was closed to Israeli shipping.

Map 19-2   Israel, after the 1948 War

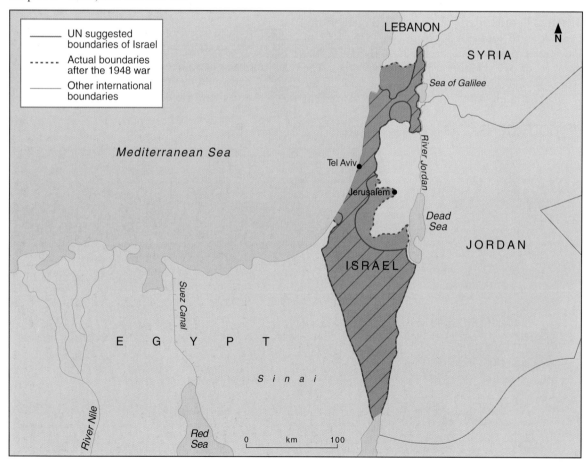

Thousands of Palestinians fled from Israeli forces and became refugees in Egypt, Jordan and Syria.

2. *THE SUEZ CRISIS, 1956*

In 1956 a war in the Middle East swept in many other countries. How did this happen? What were the motives of those who took part?

Israel. Many Palestinians turned to guerrilla warfare against Israel. Palestinian guerrilla fighters (fedayeen) attacked Israeli settlements. In 1955, 238 Israelis were killed. In return, Israeli raids on Egypt killed 63 people. The Israeli government wanted security for its people and more defensible boundaries.

Egypt. The British had controlled Egypt from 1882 to 1952. From 1954 it was ruled by Colonel Nasser. He was determined to make his country more independent. He also wanted to develop Egypt's economy. He had a plan to dam the River Nile at Aswan to provide power and water for the whole of Egypt. The USA had offered much of the $90 million he needed.

After the Israeli raid Nasser asked the USA for weapons; the USA, where more Jews live than in any other country in the world, refused. Furious, Nasser turned to the USSR, which supplied him with aeroplanes and 300 tanks. The USA did not like this and cancelled the Aswan Dam loan. Nasser, in retaliation, took over the Suez Canal. Although it runs through Egyptian territory, the Suez Canal was owned by a private company in which the British and French governments had

shares. It was also a crucial waterway for Middle Eastern oil to get to Europe.

Britain. The British Prime Minister, Sir Anthony Eden, had been one of those who had opposed the British policy of appeasement in the 1930s. He thought Nasser was another sort of Hitler and had to be resolutely opposed.

A secret deal was made between Britain, France and Israel. As Antony Nutting, a British Minister who resigned over the issue, explained:

▶ SOURCE 4B

The Israelis would take the initiative and invade Egypt. Britain and France would then intervene in order to separate the two combatants. This in turn would be such a humiliation that Nasser would be toppled from his perch.

From Antony Nutting's memoirs

Everything went as planned at first. Israeli troops invaded Egypt as far as the Canal (see Map 19-2). Britain and France ordered Israelis and Egyptians to withdraw, although this meant Egyptians withdrawing inside Egypt and left the Israelis still in Egyptian territory. Nasser blocked the Suez canal by sinking ships across it and the next day British and French paratroops landed in the Canal Zone.

The USA, however, did not support its allies Britain and France. Many people in Britain and the

▶ SOURCE 4A   The Suez Canal blocked, 1956

▶ **SOURCE 5**

Arab prisoners of Israeli forces, June 1967

rest of the world disagreed with the actions of the British Prime Minister, Anthony Eden. British and French troops were forced to pull out of the Canal Zone. The Israelis withdrew to their old boundaries. UN forces took over Sinai and the canal.

3.   THE SIX-DAY WAR, 1967

The boundaries on Map 19-2 show how small Israel was from 1948 onwards. It could easily be sliced in two by attackers. In the north, Syrian forces overlooked Israeli territory from the Golan Heights. In 1966 a new government in Syria began to threaten Israel with war. Nasser was also building up arms and in May 1967 he asked the UN to withdraw its forces on the Israeli border. Some Israelis, such as Moshe Dayan, wanted to extend their country's boundaries to feel more secure. In June 1967 they decided to attack first. In six days, the Israeli army, brilliantly led, advanced on all three fronts (see Map 19-3).

? Questions

a Compare the uniform and the equipment of the Arabs and the Israelis in Source 5.
b Describe the landscape of this fighting area. How would this affect the war?

Israel now had borders which were more defensible, but a lasting peace was no nearer. The Arabs were bitter. The newly conquered lands contained a million Arabs who were now ruled by Israel.

Obviously the cease-fire would not last for very long.

4.   YOM KIPPUR WAR, 1973

Egypt and Syria by now had excellent weapons from the USSR, especially SAMs (surface-to-air missiles). They attacked Israel on Yom Kippur, the most solemn Jewish religious day. The Egyptians gained a hold on the east side of the Suez Canal. After fierce tank battles, the Israelis drove them back and advanced a little further into Egypt and Syria.

Egypt and Syria had been supplied by the USSR. Israel had bought weapons from the USA, Britain and France. After the 1973 war, both superpowers, the USA and the USSR, began to work for peace in the region.

Why do other countries get involved?

The simple answer is that the Middle East is the source of 60% of the world's oil. In the modern world, oil and petrol are essential, especially for most forms of transport. This is another reason why other countries are closely interested in what happens in this area. Most of the oil in the Middle East is sold to Western countries.

The oil-producing Arab countries support their Arab and Palestinian neighbours with money, but at the same time do not want to hurt the Western countries too much in case they buy less oil. After the 1973 Yom Kippur War, the oil-producing countries put up their prices by 70% to those countries which had supplied Israel with weapons. This had a serious effect on the West: the price of petrol rose by 25p a gallon almost at once. By increasing the price of oil, they hoped to make the West put pressure on Israel to make a compromise with the Arab countries.

THE PALESTINIANS

At the core of the problem of finding peace is the rights of the Palestinians. When most of Palestine became the Jewish state of Israel, many Palestinians found themselves living under Jewish rule. The wars, especially the Six-Day War of 1967, increased the number of Palestinians within Israeli borders as Israel took over more land (see Map 19-3).

Some Palestinians had fled to Jordan, Egypt and Lebanon, where there are huge refugee camps.

1 Israel says that the Palestinians were free to stay. The Palestinians say that they were driven out as Jews took over their homes and farms.
2 Israel says that the Arab countries should look after the refugees; the Arabs say that they are too poor and that the UN should solve the problem because it was the UN which offered Israel independence.

THE REFUGEES
As long as the refugees remained, they reminded the world that Israel was set up on land which had been Arab. A whole generation of Palestinians grew up in the camps. Many became guerrillas: they hijacked aircraft, raided Israel, sent letter-bombs and attacked Jews. They said that they had to fight this way as they did not have a country to fight from. They did not want the world to forget them.

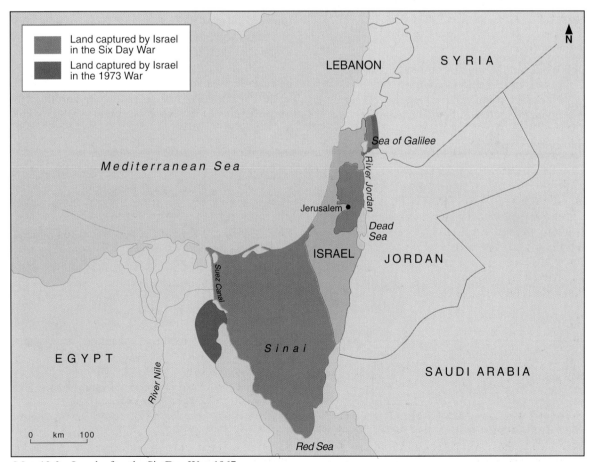

Map 19-3   Israel, after the Six Day War, 1967

SOURCE 6A

The soldiers cannot pour their lead
Into the sun as it crosses
The frontiers every day;
A stray animal may feed quietly,
Untouched by soldiers' fire,
As it trespasses the lines.
While I stand, an exile,
Separated by barbed wire
From my native land.

Poem by Palestinian refugee

SOURCE 6B

I am proud that he did not die in this camp. The press comes here and takes our pictures standing in queues to get food rations. They give the impression that we are a 'nation of beggars'. This is no life, I am already preparing my eighteen-year-old boy so he can replace my first son and fight for liberation.

Mother of a Palestinian guerrilla
killed in Israel

❓ Questions

a What can the sun and animals do, in the poem, which refugees cannot?

b Name the countries in which the refugee in the poem in Source 6A could be living.

c Why does the woman in Source 6B feel ashamed?

d What does she want her next son to do?

e What is the difference between the moods of the writer of Source 6A and the woman in Source 6B?

At first the Palestinians hoped that their Arab neighbours would rescue them by attacking and destroying Israel. In four wars this did not happen. The Palestinians then decided they had to destroy Israel themselves. Without a country of their own they resorted to terrorism. They felt the Western countries, especially the USA, were to blame for setting up and continuing to back Israel. American cities, citizens and aircraft were often targets. Among their most spectacular terrorist actions was the hijacking and blowing up of three airliners at Dawson's Field, Jordan, in 1970. In 1972 Israeli athletes at the Olympic Games at Munich were assassinated by Palestinian guerrillas.

They did not succeed in defeating Israel, but they did succeed in keeping that country in a state of unease and in forcing the rest of the world not to forget that the situation was not resolved.

In their efforts to find a base the Palestinians have made use of any situation to hand. In 1970–71 some Palestinians tried to take over Jordan, but were driven out by King Hussein. In 1975 some

SOURCE 6C   Hijacked airliners burning at Dawson's Field, September 1970

Palestinians joined left-wing Muslims in the Lebanon in an attempt to take over that country. Syria invaded Lebanon in 1976 and enforced order. Raids by Palestinians from Lebanon led to an Israeli invasion in 1978 and again in 1982. The PLO army had to leave Lebanon for Tunisia.

THE SEARCH FOR PEACE

By the 1970s both sides were in positions which made it difficult to begin to talk peace. The UN could not find a way of reconciling them

▶ SOURCE 7

1. Israel to withdraw from territories occupied during the Six-Day War.
2. . . . recognition of the sovereignty, territory and independence of every state in the area and their right to live in peace within secure and recognised boundaries.

UN Resolution 242, November, 1967

No Arab country would agree to part 2, as they did not accept Israel's right to exist. So Israel refused to comply with part 1. Since the 1973 Yom Kippur War other nations realised they had too much to lose by warfare in the Middle East and tried to put pressure on both sides for peace. President Sadat of Egypt felt he could regain Egyptian territory lost in 1967 by negotiation. At the Camp David agreement, 1978, arranged by US President Jimmy Carter, gradual Israeli withdrawal from Sinai was arranged.

PLO leader Yassir Arafat also turned to diplomacy after 1974. He was welcomed by the United Nations and announced that he wanted peace. World opinion began to recognise that the Palestinians had a case. At the same time, a more right-wing and uncompromising Israeli government was elected, led by former guerrilla fighter Menachem Begin. It allowed Jewish nationalist and religious groups to settle in the West Bank, in areas of good land left by Palestinians when they fled from the Israeli Army. The existence of these settlements made it much harder for any Israeli government to reach an agreement with the Palestinians who regard the land as theirs, stolen in war.

World opinion had been largely on Israel's side since the Second World War. Things began to change from the early 1980s, with the settlements policy and the actions of the Israelis in Lebanon.

In 1982 Israelis, or their Lebanese allies, massacred Palestinians in refugee camps at Chatilla and Sabra. An Israeli peace movement began and held massive anti-war demonstrations.

In 1993 a left-wing government was elected under Yitzhak Rabin. He reached an agreement with Yassir Arafat in which the Palestinians were to have self-rule over Gaza, Jericho and parts of the West Bank. This agreement was very difficult to achieve and keep to. Both leaders have been criticised by their own peoples. Jewish settlers have refused to give up their settlements on the West Bank. Some Palestinians are angry that the deal accepts the right of the state of Israel to exist.

ASSESSMENT

Describe, explain and analyse

1   a) Describe what happened in Palestine when the British decided to give up their mandate in 1947.

b) Why did the British decide to do this?

c) What were the attitudes of: Zionists; Palestinian Arabs; other Arab countries; world opinion to what should happen in this area at that time?

2   Look at the following list of reasons why the state of Israel was set up in 1948:

i) The Balfour Declaration.

ii) Anti-Semitism in Europe in the 1930s.

iii) The British Mandate.

iv) The Holocaust.

v) Israeli guerrilla organisations.

vi) UN Resolution on partition.

vii) Attitudes of neighbouring Arab countries.

a) Which are long-term reasons? Choose one and explain it.

b) Which are short-term reasons?

Choose two and explain how they helped to bring about the State of Israel in 1948.

3 **a)** Describe what happened in any one of the four wars that took place in the Middle East from 1948 to 1973.

b) Why was Israel successful?

c) Why has that war failed to bring lasting peace to the region?

Evidence and interpretations

▼ SOURCE A
The responsibility for the fact that Arabs became refugees must lie with those who attacked Israel. Large numbers of refugees left the country at the call of the Arab leaders, who told them to get out so that the Arab armies could get in.

> Mrs Golda Meir, later Prime Minister of Israel, speaking to the UN in 1961

▼ SOURCE B
Many Palestinians were deported by the Israelis before the war and many left before the war, being afraid due to our propaganda that when the Israelis come, they will either harm them or massacre them.

> An Israeli speaking in 1991

▼ SOURCE C
When violence and conflict erupted, many of them were not equipped to deal with it. But the main reason is that the Palestinians left as a result of being expelled by Jewish armed gangs, as a result of a series of massacres, as a result of a policy of intimidation.

> A Palestinian speaking in 1991

a What different reasons for the flight of Palestinians from their homes in 1948 are given in Sources A and C?

b Read who spoke each of Sources A and C and when. How far does that explain their interpretation of what happened?

c Does the fact that one is an Israeli and one a Palestinian mean that both are unreliable?

d Does the fact that Source C was spoken much more recently mean that it is more likely to be correct?

e Does Source B support either Source A or Source C?

f Whose views are you reading in Source B? What is the significance of this information?

g Why has it been so difficult to get at the real reasons why Palestinians fled in 1948?

20: The United Nations

ORIGINS

Quite early in the Second World War, in August 1941, Roosevelt and Churchill met on a warship in the North Atlantic. They drew up the Atlantic Charter as the basis of their war aims. They put forward the 'Four Freedoms' as their reasons for fighting: freedom from want, freedom of speech, freedom from fear, freedom of religion. The front cover of this book shows a poster illustrating these ideals, which became their foundation for a better world after the war.

Despite the failure of the League of Nations (see Chapter 11), Roosevelt and Churchill proposed setting up an international peace-keeping organisation. They felt that the idea of the League was a good one but that there had been faults. They hoped to put these faults right. The 'Four Freedoms' became the Charter of the United Nations. This was discussed at Dumbarton Oaks in 1944 and signed at San Francisco in 1945. There were 51 member countries at the beginning.

ORGANISATION AND DIFFERENCES FROM THE LEAGUE OF NATIONS

Table 20-1 shows the organisation of the UN. The headquarters is in New York. The General Assembly is where all member nations meet. Almost all countries in the world are members, unlike the League. Here, speeches are made on any issue, and each country has one vote. All other parts of the UN are responsible to the General Assembly.

The Security Council is the active part of the UN. Its members meet regularly to deal with crises as they happen and recommend action (the Council of the League only met occasionally). The USA, USSR, Britain, France and China are permanent members. Other countries, in rotation, also serve on the Security Council, but the five permanent members have a veto – that is, any one of them can stop the Security Council acting. This may seem unfair, but it was realistic to give the five major powers this power of veto as they would have to co-operate in any major action to make it work anyway. The veto was intended as an exceptional and rare necessity. The Security Council could settle disputes in three ways: by offering to help in an argument; by imposing economic sanctions, such as a boycott, on a country which was in the wrong; or, going much further than the League, by actually raising an army to give help to a country which had been unfairly attacked.

Another difference between the UN and the League is the post of Secretary-General. As we shall see, an energetic and determined Secretary-General can do a great deal for the UN. The League had no such job.

Table 20-1 Organisation of the United Nations

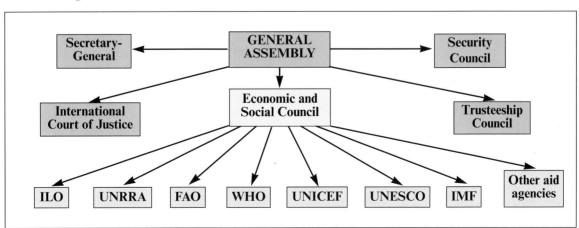

The other agencies of the UN follow on more or less where the League left off. They work for peace too, by attempting to deal with causes of war, such as poverty, exploitation and hunger.

THE UNITED NATIONS IN ACTION

Aid agencies

The aid agencies have continued to carry out important work in the needy areas of the world. UNRRA (United Nations Relief and Rehabilitation Administration) looks after the refugees who have suffered from the many wars that have taken place since 1945. In fact, from 1943, UNRRA dealt with the problems left by the Second World War. Since then, several wars in the Middle East have created the problem of Palestinian refugees, and again, UNRRA helps here. The ILO (International Labour Organisation) tries to protect workers all over the world. It also teaches people skills to enable them to support themselves. The FAO (Food and Agriculture Organisation) advises on all aspects of agriculture. Production of food is now a major problem as the world's population rises so rapidly. The WHO (World Health Organisation) trains people in fighting disease. UNICEF (United Nations International Children's Emergency Fund) works for all aspects of the health and welfare of children. The IMF (International Monetary Fund) and World Bank act as bankers to poorer countries. UNESCO (United Nations Educational, Scientific and Cultural Organisation) deals with education and attempts to bring the peoples of the world into a closer understanding of one another.

The Disarmament Commission, International Telecommunications Union and Universal Postal Union deal with their own important international issues.

Political issues in the early years

In the years since 1945 the UN has reflected changes in the world outside. The Cold War (the split between the USSR and the USA, see Chapter 17) was soon being played out in the Security Council. In the 1940s the Western powers had a majority in the UN. The USSR had not taken part in drawing up the Atlantic Charter. Now the UN seemed only an American tool. The USSR used its veto many times in the Security Council. The Russian word '*Nyet*' (No) was soon only too familiar to the world. This permanent blocking of the

► SOURCE 1

WHO clinic in Cameroon, West Africa: a medical assistant gives anti-malarial drugs

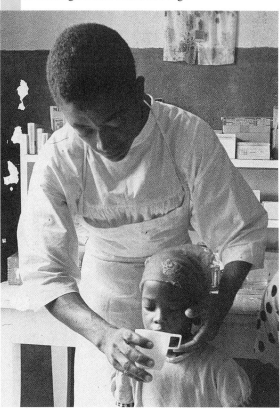

Security Council seemed to be crippling the new organisation. In 1950 a formula was produced to get round it, and was called 'Uniting for Peace'.

► SOURCE 2

If the Security Council, because of lack of unanimity amongst its permanent members, fails to exercise its primary responsibility for the maintenance of peace and security ... the General Assembly shall consider the matter immediately with a view to making appropriate recommendations to members including, in the case of a breach of the peace or an act of aggression, the use of force.

UN Resolution

? Questions

a What reason does the General Assembly give for taking over an issue?

b What powers does the General Assembly intend to use?

The 'Uniting for Peace' procedure can thus take an issue out of the hands of the great powers and deal with it in the General Assembly. This is an important shift of power inside the UN.

In 1949, Chiang Kaishek's Nationalist China was defeated by Mao Zedong's Communists. Chiang withdrew to the island of Taiwan (Formosa) but the USA would not admit China to the UN. For the next 23 years, China was excluded and Chiang's government continued to occupy a Security Council seat.

When the Korean crisis (see page 192) occurred in 1950, the invasion of South Korea by North Korea was seen as just the kind of aggressive act the UN was set up to stop. At the time, the USSR had withdrawn from the Security Council in protest over the UN's refusal to recognise Mao's China. With the Soviet veto removed, the UN could act more freely. The General Assembly condemned the North Korean invasion and the Chinese support for North Korea. A UN army was sent to support South Korea. The USA provided most of the army, but 15 other nations contributed forces. Although most of the fighting was done by Americans, it did prove that the idea of a UN army was not impossible.

The power of the Secretary-General was an issue during the 1950s and 1960s. The first Secretary-General, 1945–1952, was Trygve Lie of Norway. The USSR continually attacked him as a supporter of the Western countries. They tried to get the post replaced by a committee on which they would have a veto. Instead, the UN appointed a man from neutral Sweden, Dag Hammarskjöld, who was Secretary-General 1953–1961. Hammarskjöld wanted the UN to be a genuine servant of its members. He wanted to promote peace actively.

After the Suez invasion of 1956 (see page 215), the 'Uniting for Peace' system was used to get round the British and French veto. The General Assembly condemned the invasion of Egypt by Britain, France and Israel. Hammarskjöld organised a UN peace-keeping army to stand between Israel and Egypt. It remained in Gaza and in Sinai from 1957 to 1967.

In 1960, the Congo (now Zaire) became independent (see page 244). The ex-Belgian colony had

▼ **SOURCE 3**   Cartoon, 1950: the man is US President Truman

HISTORY DOESN'T REPEAT ITSELF

? Questions

a Explain the point of the cartoon.

b What does it tell us about US attitudes to the UN and the League of Nations?

not been prepared for independence, and soon law and order broke down completely. Hammarskjöld organised an army of 20,000 troops provided by member countries, mainly India, Ghana, Ireland, Canada and Nigeria. Their light blue uniform carried the olive branch, the UN symbol.

? Questions

a What clues are there to the reason why all these people are lining up in Source 4?

The UN army tried to restore peace and order to the Congo. Hammarskjöld also called on the other resources of the UN, especially the WHO and the FAO. Together these organisations tried to fill the gap left in the Congo by providing doctors, nurses, medicine, experts and advisers. Gradually, law and order were restored. The UN army also had to fight the province of Katanga to achieve this, as it

was trying to break away on its own. Hammarskjöld was killed in a plane crash while trying to negotiate a peace settlement in the Congo. He was replaced by his deputy, U Thant from Burma, who held the job from 1961 to 1971.

In 1964, U Thant ordered a peace-keeping force into Cyprus to keep Greeks and Turks apart. He did not, however, have Hammarskjöld's positive approach on some issues. When Nasser asked the UN to withdraw their peace-keeping forces from Gaza and Sinai, he agreed. Within weeks, the 1967 Arab–Israeli war had broken out.

Changing membership

By the 1960s, the UN had changed in another way. The original 51 members had been joined by many others, as former colonies gained their independence. There are now 184 members.

▼ **SOURCE 4**   UN armoured car, Elisabethville, Congo, 1961

In 1945 there were only four member states from Africa and 12 from Asia. Since then, new African and Asian nations have joined. This means that the 'Third World' countries have a majority in the General Assembly. If they wish, they can outvote the Russians and the Americans. The UN, set up by the great powers, has now become the voice of the weaker nations of the world. It is one of the main ways in which the poorer, undeveloped nations make their opinions heard.

Secretary-General Dag Hammarskjöld was insistent that the United Nations should continue to speak for these poorer and weaker nations.

◤ SOURCE 5

It is not the Soviet Union, nor indeed any other big power, who need the United Nations for their protection; it is the others. I shall remain at my post in the interest of all those other nations as long as they wish me to do so.

Hammarskjöld's reply to the request from Soviet leader Krushchev that he should resign, 1961

The UN: decline of an ideal?

It would be easy to list all the failures of the UN. There continue to be wars all over the world and poverty and famine are as widespread as ever. It failed to play any significant part in the Cuban crisis of 1962, the Soviet invasion of Afghanistan in 1979, or the Falklands War of 1982. In all these cases powerful countries preferred to act on their own to get the result they wanted, rather than to refer the problem to the UN. The UN sanctions imposed on Rhodesia to end Ian Smith's Unilateral Declaration of Independence in 1965 were unsuccessful. South Africa, and other countries, ignored the trade boycott. UN forces in the Middle East have failed to prevent savage wars breaking out.

There have been some successes. The agencies of the UNO have made real improvements in the health of the world's population. Killer diseases like smallpox have been eliminated. However, important issues like population control and control of environmental pollution divide the UN between rich and poor nations. So does controversy over the work of the World Bank and the IMF. These organisations have been accused of increasing the already huge wealth gap between rich and poor in the world by unsuitable developments in poor countries that do nothing for their people but only help rich investors. Sometimes charities can do more good than the UN because the UN is too large to work efficiently on the small-scale schemes poor people in poor countries need.

The UN, like the League before it, was set up with the highest ideals. As the wars which brought them into being have faded, so has the idealism. It

◤ SOURCE 6   UN soldiers in former Yugoslavia unloading food for the victims of war, 1992

is sometimes impossible to stop wars if, as in the former Yugoslavia for example, people are determined to fight each other. UN action can be hindered by countries' unwillingness to join in, to find their share of the cost, or by the strict rules it has to follow. Experience in Yugoslavia and Somalia in the 1990s has led some people to suggest that the UN should form a permanent army, trained to intervene rapidly in a conflict. Is the world willing to set up such a police force?

Secretary-Generals of the UN
Trygve Lie (Norway) 1946–1953
Dag Hammarskjöld (Sweden) 1953–1961
U Thant (Burma) 1961–1971
Kurt Waldheim (Austria) 1971–1981
Javier Pérez de Cuéllar (Peru) 1981–1991
Boutros Boutros Ghali (Egypt) 1991–

DAG HAMMARSKJÖLD 1905–1961

Dag Hammarskjöld is regarded as one of the few heroes of the brief history of the UN – a man who gave his life for the ideal. Yet he was not the usual kind of hero, a soldier or a political leader, but a quiet man of strong principles.

He came from Sweden, and for most of his life worked in university or government in his country. He was Professor of Economics at Stockholm University from 1933 to 1936, and Deputy Foreign Minister in 1951. When Trygve Lie, the first UN Secretary-General, retired in 1953, he succeeded him and was re-elected in 1957. Resolving the Suez crisis of 1956 was one of his major successes. He showed his determination that the UN should play a leading part in peace-keeping anywhere in the world. The peace-keeping force showed that the UN armed forces did have a useful job to do.

His concern to use the powers of the Secretary-General for peace was also shown in the Congo crisis. Here he came up against Russian opposition to his actions, but he was certain that this was a crisis which the UN ought to help solve. It was while visiting the area that he was killed, when his plane crashed. He was awarded the Nobel Peace Prize in 1961.

ASSESSMENT

Describe, explain and analyse

1   **a)** Describe two main differences between the UN and the League of Nations.

b) Show how these differences have worked out in practice by describing two incidents in the history of the UNO.

c) Explain whether you think the UN has been more or less successful than the League.

2   **a)** Describe how the United Nations came to be set up in 1945.

b) What problems did it have to face in its early years?

c) How has the UN changed in the last 30 years?

d) What problems does it now have to deal with?

Evidence and interpretations

There are several cartoons by David Low in this book (see pages 61, 108, 120, 223, 261, 267).

a   Choose three and explain what Low was trying to say in each.

b   Can you tell what Low's own beliefs were?

c   How useful are cartoons as evidence to historians?

21: India and Pakistan

BRITISH INDIA

In 1900 India was the most treasured part of the British empire, often called 'the jewel in the crown'. The British Raj (British rule) extended over 300 million people. The present-day countries of India, Pakistan, Burma, Bangladesh and Sri Lanka were all included within the borders of British India.

Britain had ruled India since the 18th century. The British ruled 60% of the land directly, while 40% was ruled by Indian princes under British guidance.

In 1887 Queen Victoria was made Empress of India, and British monarchs continued to hold this title up to 1947. If you look at a coin minted before 1947 you will see the letters 'IND. IMP.' on the 'heads' side around the head of the ruler: this stands for INDIAE IMPERATOR – Emperor of India. The King's or Queen's representative in India was called the Viceroy.

▼ SOURCE 1   Indian princes with British Army officers, 1907

Questions

a What does the appearance of these princes tell you about their wealth?
b Who seem to be the most important people in this picture?
c What else does this picture tell you about relations between the British rulers and Indian princes?

Little did this group in Source 1 know that 40 years later the great British Raj would come to an end.

India has one-fifth of the population of the world. Two-thirds of the people in India under the Raj were Hindus. Most of the rest were Muslim, but there were also Sikhs, Buddhists, some Christians and members of other religions. The Hindu religion divided people up into 'castes' or groups. Members of the highest caste were called Brahmins, and those who were beneath even the lowest caste were called 'untouchables'. Untouchables were not allowed to have anything to do with other Indians, even to live near them. In addition to these religious and social divisions, India had great problems of poverty and lack of education. It was a country of poor peasants using primitive farming methods. Disease and famine were common.

British rule

The British rulers tried to tackle some of these problems. Civil servants, judges and engineers worked hard in India. A railway system was built to link the country. Laws were enforced by British magistrates. Schools and hospitals were built. The English language was the only way in which some Indians, who spoke different languages, could talk to one another.

On the other hand, Britain and the British gained enormously from the Raj. British people who went out to India had a better standard of living than they could expect at home. The economy was also run to benefit Britain. Very little

industry was developed until after the First World War in case it competed with British industry. India supplied raw materials, such as cotton, and bought British-made goods. The British did not mix freely with the Indians and kept all top jobs in the army and civil service in British hands.

Some British spoke of handing the country over to the Indians 'one day'. But to most British in India that day was a very long way off.

? Questions
a Is there any way of telling that the photograph below (Source 2) was taken in India, not in England?
b What can you tell about the British way of life in India from the photo?

In 1885 a group of educated Indians formed the Congress Party in order to press for more power for Indians. The First World War helped the Congress Party's aims. Britain needed all the soldiers it could get. India was promised more self-government if Indians came to fight in Europe. Over a million Indians fought in the war.

When the Government of India Act, 1919, was

▼ SOURCE 2   British tea party in India, 1907

passed, it did not give Indians all they wanted. They were allowed a national Parliament and local parliaments which dealt with health, education and agriculture. But the decisions of these parliaments could be blocked by the Viceroy, and British kept control of finance and law.

Demonstrations were held against the Act. At Amritsar, North India, in 1919, General Dyer ordered his troops to fire on a demonstration of over 5,000 Indians. 379 Indians were killed and 1,000 wounded.

Such an incident was not typical of British rule; in fact, Dyer was dismissed soon afterwards. However, it gave a great boost to the demand for independence. Most of all, it brought to the fore-front a new and remarkable leader of the Indian people.

MOHANDAS GANDHI

Gandhi was born in 1869 and went to Britain to train as a lawyer. In 1893 he went to South Africa to work for Indians there. In South Africa he worked out his ideas of non-violent protest. In 1915 he answered a request to come to India to help the Congress Party. He refused to be leader of the Congress, but was its main force and guide for the next 33 years.

▶ **SOURCE 3A**   Gandhi

Non-violence

Gandhi was a deeply religious man, although not a strict Hindu. He was a vegetarian, abstained from sex, wore only a loin-cloth and often fasted. He believed that violence only caused more violence, that truth and right would always win in the end. His peaceful, non-violent protest was based on this belief – *satyagraha*. This means that his methods were sit-downs, strikes, marches, boycotts. Even when faced by police wielding sticks, he and his followers would not fight back.

▶ **SOURCE 3B**
My personal faith is absolutely clear. I cannot intentionally hurt anything that lives, much less fellow human beings, even though they may do the greatest wrong to me and mine. Whilst therefore I hold the British rule to be a curse I do not intend harm to any single Englishman. I know that in embarking on non-violence I shall be running what might be termed a mad risk. But victories have never been won without risks.

Gandhi, 1930

▶ **SOURCE 3C**
Let some General Dyer stand before us with his troops. Let him start firing. It is my prayer to God that if this happens I should continue to talk to you cheerfully and that you should all remain sitting calmly then, under a shower of bullets, as you are doing now.

Gandhi, 1922

❓ Questions
a Use your own words to describe how Gandhi intended to protest.
b Do you agree he was taking 'a mad risk'?
c What other protest movements described in this book used non-violence?

The Congress Party had been supported only by educated Indians. Gandhi made the movement for independence a popular one. He intended to build a new India after independence, with no divisions of religion or caste. Gandhi always worked with both Hindus and Muslims. He worked with untouchables, whom he called *Harijans* (little brothers) and adopted a Harijan child. The Indian people called him *Mahatma* (Holy One). Indians hold holy men in great respect, and his beliefs won mass support.

Under Gandhi's influence the movement for *Swaraj* (self-rule) changed into a mass movement. This was seen in the protests of 1930. The British had set up the Simon Commission to look into the Indian situation. They did not, however, ask any Indians to sit on the Commission. The Congress Party protested. Gandhi led a march – the Salt March – to the sea, where he boiled some sea-water to make salt. This was a protest against British taxes on salt, and the long march and peaceful protest gained massive support. Gandhi was invited to attend conferences in London in 1931 and 1932. He amazed the smartly-dressed British by arriving at meetings in London dressed only in his loin-cloth.

A new Government of India Act, 1935, resulted from these meetings. It gave more power to Indians at local and national levels. Then a new problem arose as Indians voted. The 92 million Muslims were out-voted by the Hindus in eight out of eleven provinces. Muslims were 24% of the population, and the Congress Party had always tried to speak for both Hindus and Muslims. Now Muslims began to demand a separate country for themselves. They formed the separate Muslim League to achieve this. However, the Second World War shelved this problem for the time being.

THE SECOND WORLD WAR

When the Second World War broke out Indian soldiers once again fought for the British. At first Congress stayed aloof from the war, but the Japanese advances of 1941 changed the situation. Some Indians even went over to the Japanese and formed Indian forces in the Japanese army. The Japanese tried to encourage this (see Source 4).

Gandhi, with his belief in non-violence, could not, of course, fight alongside the Japanese. However, he used the situation to force Britain to give way on independence. Strikes and demonstrations were organised. Churchill sent Sir Stafford Cripps to India in 1942 to offer the Indians self-government. Gandhi did not really trust Churchill,

SOURCE 4

Japanese anti-British poster. The words, in two Indian languages, say 'Set the devils right with a stick'

? Questions

a Describe and explain how the cartoonist has shown the Indian, the British officer and Churchill (in the bowler hat).
b What feelings is the poster trying to stir up?
c What, does it say, should Indians do?

who was a firm believer in the British empire. The campaign of opposition to the British was stepped up, under a new slogan, 'Quit India'. This did not have much popular appeal, however, and led to the arrest of most of the Congress leaders. They spent the rest of the war in gaol, but had high hopes of the 1945 Labour government in Britain.

INDEPENDENCE

After the war Britain could no longer afford to hold on to its empire. The new Labour Prime Minister, Clement Attlee, was pledged to offer India independence. The Muslim problem now came to a head: the Muslim League would not be part of an India ruled by the mainly Hindu Congress Party. Led by Mohammed Ali Jinnah, they wanted a country of their own. They were in a majority in the Punjab, Afghan, Kashmir, Sind and Baluchistan – and putting these names together gave them the name of the country they wanted: 'Pakistan'. Pakistan also means 'land of the pure'.

As the leaders squabbled, terrible violence broke out between Hindu and Muslim. While 5,000 Muslims were killed in Calcutta, Muslims slaughtered Hindus in Bengal. In the spring of 1946 Attlee announced that the British would leave in 1948. He appointed Earl Mountbatten as the last Viceroy. Mountbatten tried to force the politicians

to reach agreement by pulling the date of independence back to March 1947.

The lines of division were drawn on the map (see Map 21-1). Even with Pakistan in two parts, 1,600 kilometres apart, many Muslims were left in India and Hindus in Pakistan. As independence came, terrible massacres took place on both sides. Millions of refugees fled across the boundaries – six million Muslims left India, four and a half million Hindus left Pakistan. Whole coach and train loads were killed. Probably a total of 400,000 people died.

Then, at the height of the upheaval, while trying to persuade people not to be violent, Gandhi was shot dead by an extremist Hindu.

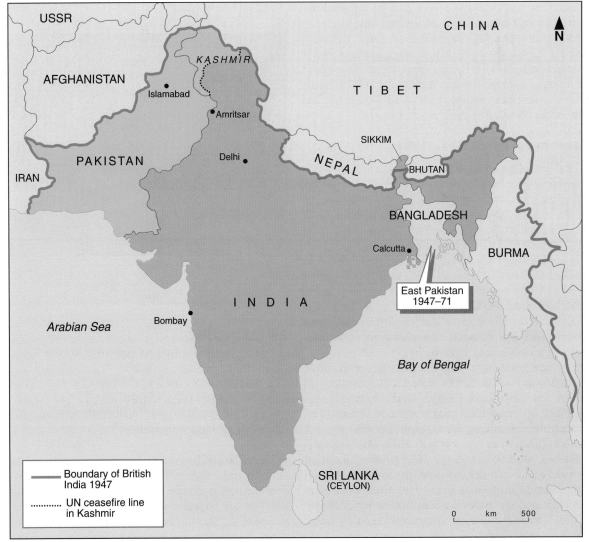

Map 21-1   India and Pakistan

This book shows that the 20th century has been a violent one. This history seems to show that violence can succeed, but it also shows, as Gandhi insisted, that violence breeds violence. His idea of non-violent protest brought his country to independence. It has also provided an example to other protestors, notably Martin Luther King of the USA.

INDIA SINCE INDEPENDENCE

In 1947 India became the largest democracy in the world. Vast divisions of caste and religion, wealth and poverty faced the new country. All adults, including women, untouchables and Muslims were allowed to vote. Despite enormous difficulties, this democracy has survived. This is in strong contrast to the many countries which started independence as democracies but have since become dictatorships. It also shows that the Congress Party had a deep admiration for British ideas, even if they spent a lifetime fighting Britain. A good deal of the credit for this smooth passage must go to the first Prime Minister, Jawaharlal Nehru.

Jawaharlal Nehru, 1947–1964

The problems that India has had to face since independence have been typical of a Third World country. The main problems are poverty, hunger and lack of education. In order to pay for food and necessary industrial goods India has had to make money. This meant selling goods for export as well as developing more industry. Gandhi had called industry 'the curse of mankind' but Nehru realised that some industrialisation was necessary. He borrowed the idea of five-year plans from the USSR. Since 1951, under a series of five-year plans steelworks, hydroelectric power stations and factories of all kinds have been built.

Nehru did not, however, treat the problem of agriculture in the Soviet way. Each peasant still kept his own farm. Some land, however, was divided up among the poor so that no one had too much. In some areas, for example, no one can own more than 16 acres, by law. Rich farmers, and princes, were heavily taxed. The government tried to persuade peasants to join up to buy and sell their produce together, in co-operatives. They were encouraged to use new seeds and new fertilisers. This 'Green Revolution' improved yields by up to 50% in some crops.

These changes resulted in the growth of India's economy by 42% in the 1950s. However, this was almost completely set back by the huge and continuing population rise: 439 million by 1962, 590 million by 1974, 751 million by 1990. This great burden of extra mouths to feed kept the country still very poor.

Indira Gandhi

Nehru was succeeded by Lal Shastri, from 1964 to 1966, and then by his own daughter, Mrs Indira Gandhi. A drought and famine, from 1966 to 1967 led Mrs Gandhi to adopt more socialist measures. Her forceful birth control campaign also gained her many enemies.

▶ SOURCE 5

Poster advertising India's birth control campaign

❓ Questions

a Why do Indian parents still want to have big families?

b What effect would large families have on Indian standards of living?

c Why do you think the birth-control campaign is resisted by many Indians?

In the 1970s inflation made India's situation worse still. By this time older, more conservative Congress leaders had split from Mrs Gandhi. They did not like her socialist policies, especially when she nationalised the banks. In 1975 she was taken to court. She therefore declared a state of emergency:

the laws were suspended, censorship of the press was introduced and opponents arrested. She ruled as a dictator. She called an election in 1977, expecting to win. The people of India voted against her, and calmly elected her opponents. However, the opposition to Mrs Gandhi did not hold together, and she was re-elected in 1980. In 1984 she was assassinated. She was succeeded by her son, Rajiv Gandhi, who was Prime Minister until 1989 when he too was killed in a suicide bomb attack.

Except for five years, India was ruled from 1947 to 1989 by the members of one family. Under their rule, India has managed to develop modern industry and still have peasant farming. The tension between the old and the new, however, is always strong, with religion playing an increasing part in politics in recent years.

Foreign policy

Nehru's main aim was to remain at peace and to carry out a 'non-aligned' policy in the world. This means that he did not wish to be dragged into alliances with either the Americans or the Soviets. In this he was joined by several countries who had also gained their independence. This group came together at the Bandung Conference in 1955. Along with China, Egypt, Indonesia and many other countries from Africa and Asia, India tried to steer a path between the two superpowers.

TIBET
Nehru's friendship with China meant that India raised no protest when China invaded Tibet in 1951. However the Tibetan–Indian border, in the high Himalayas, is not well-mapped. In the days of the British Raj advantage had been taken of China's weakness to extend India's boundaries in disputed areas. In the 1950s it was clear that Chinese soldiers were working in areas which had been regarded as Indian. In 1962 these border arguments led to war. India lost, but the Chinese did not advance far into India. They merely took the land they felt was theirs and which they needed to build their road network. The war did, however, lead Nehru to think about defence. He started work on an Indian atom bomb, a scheme that would have saddened Gandhi.

PAKISTAN
India was also involved in wars with Pakistan. The hurriedly drawn borders of 1947 left several areas in dispute. Control of the upper waters of the River Indus, for example, vital for irrigation, was not settled until 1959.

Most conflicts, however, have taken place over Kashmir. This province had a Muslim population but a Hindu ruler, who wanted it to join India. Fighting broke out in 1947. The problem was eventually settled by the UN, who divided the state into two. Even so, Kashmir still remains a source of conflict between the two countries. India also helped Bangladesh in the war against Pakistan in 1971.

India's foreign policy is an interesting study of how far non-violence can be taken in politics. On the world scale Nehru and Mrs Gandhi successfully worked for peace. On their own borders, it was more difficult. Besides Kashmir and China, Nehru had to use force to persuade some princes to join India, and in 1961 to expel the Portuguese from the city of Goa. India has also developed nuclear power.

PAKISTAN AND BANGLADESH

The divided country of Pakistan was difficult to rule from the start. In 1948, its founder, Mohammed Jinnah, died. Pakistan's government became more corrupt until the army stepped in and took over in 1958. General Ayub Khan introduced some industrialisation under a series of five-year plans. He built a new capital at Islamabad. He did not follow Nehru's non-aligned policy, but joined the Western Alliance group. Pakistan became a member of CENTO and of SEATO. In 1969 he was succeeded by another general, Yahya Khan. He called the first free elections in 1970.

Bangladesh

East Pakistan, 1,600 kilometres away from West Pakistan and more industrialised, had always resented being ruled from the West. When elections were held in 1970 conflict arose between the two parts. Nearly all the seats in East Pakistan were won by Sheikh Mujib ur-Rahman's Awami League. In the West a left-wing government led by Zulfikar Ali Bhutto was set up. The Awami League wanted self-government for the East, and the situation rapidly grew worse. In 1971 civil war broke out between the Pakistani army and Mujib's 'Mukti Bahini' fighters. Soon millions of refugees were flooding into India, and Mrs Gandhi sent troops from India to help defeat the Pakistani army.

Several of Mujib's colleagues who had fled to India declared themselves the government-in-exile of the new state of Bangladesh. Mujib became the first Prime Minister of Bangladesh in 1972. India and Pakistan patched up their differences at the Simla Conference in 1972, attended by Mrs Gandhi and Bhutto.

In Pakistan Bhutto ruled as Prime Minister 1973 until the army took over again in 1978. Bhutto's party was banned and he was executed in 1979. General Zia ul-Haq became President, enforcing strict Islamic laws. On his death in 1988 in an air crash, Zulfikar Bhutto's daughter, Benazir, became Prime Minister.

Bangladesh faced huge problems in 1972. Industry and communications had been destroyed in the war, there were millions of refugees, and great poverty. Sheikh Mujib, the founding father of Bangladesh, was attacked and killed by army officers in 1975. General Zia ur-Rahman took over, but was himself killed in 1981, without democracy being set up. Military rule eventually ended in 1990, and elections the following year were won by a group of parties led by General Zia's widow, Begum Khalida Zia, who became Prime Minister.

JAWAHARLAL NEHRU 1889–1964

Jawaharlal Nehru (on the left) with Mohammed Ali Jinnah in 1946

Nehru's father was a rich, well-educated lawyer. He wanted his son to have a good education, and he admired the British. Jawarhalal was therefore sent to Harrow, an English public school. He did well and went to Cambridge University. He was interested in the history of Italy, a country which had thrown out its foreign rulers in the 19th century, and began to feel that his own country should do the same. At that time his father was a leading member of the Congress Party. In the early years most Congress members were rich Indians who only wanted to share with the British in running India. Nehru annoyed his father by his talk of driving the British out of India completely. Then, in 1916 he met Gandhi.

Gandhi changed young Nehru's life. Not only did he agree with Gandhi about complete self-rule for India, but also he learned more about his own country. His family was high-caste Brahmin, and his work with Gandhi brought him into contact with the really poor people of India for the first time. He met fellow-Indians who lived on the streets of Bombay and Calcutta. He met women miners. He met poor villagers, living on the edge of starvation. He learned to speak to them and to understand their problems.

Of course Nehru accepted Gandhi's belief in non-violence. This did not stop him getting into trouble with British police for his speeches and demonstrations. He was first arrested in 1921, and spent a total of 14 of the years between the wars in prison. Prison gave him time to read and to think. He read how the Russian people had been poor before the Revolution, but were building the country up in Five-Year Plans. He became a socialist, but rejected the dictatorship which Stalin had created in Russia. In 1929 he became President of the Congress Party.

When independence came in 1947 Nehru was the obvious choice for Prime Minister. We have seen how, through democratic methods, he set about building up his country. He became a respected world leader, refusing to belong to East or West in the power struggle. His strength and wisdom helped his country through the first 17 difficult years and kept it stable and united.

ASSESSMENT

Evidence and interpretations

▼ SOURCE A

When war broke out in 1914 between England and Germany, I raised a volunteer ambulance force .... I was motivated by the belief that it was possible by such services to gain the status of full equality in the Empire for my countrymen.

> Gandhi, speaking about his actions in the First World War

▼ SOURCE B

The British government today represents Satanism. When a government takes up arms against its unarmed subjects, then it has forfeited the right to govern.

> Gandhi, after the 1919 Government of India Act and the Amritsar massacre

▼ SOURCE C

Spinning his own cotton, which he did for half an hour every day, was for Gandhi a form of protest: he was refusing to buy British-made cotton goods, he was identifying with Indian peasants who span their own cotton and also protesting against industrialisation.

▼ SOURCE D

They marched steadily with heads up, without cheering or any possibility that they might escape serious injury or death. The police rushed out and methodically beat them down. There was no fight, no struggle; the marchers simply walked forward until struck down. Not one of the marchers even raised an arm to fend off the blows.

> A description by an American journalist of the end of the Salt March in 1930

▼ SOURCE E

He gave us a scare! His programme filled our jails. You can't go on arresting people for ever you know, not when there are 319 million of them. And if they'd taken the next step and refused to pay taxes! ... but he couldn't control men's passions. They became violent and he called it off.

> Lord Lloyd, British Governor of Bombay

▼ SOURCE F

It is not the British people who rule India but modern civilisation rules India through its railways, telegraph, telephone, etc ... India's salvation lies in unlearning what she has learnt in the last 50 years. The railways, telegraphs, hospitals, lawyers, doctors, will have to go.

> Gandhi, writing in 1909

a Why did Gandhi raise a volunteer ambulance force for the British in the First World War?

b Use Source B to explain his change of feelings in 1919.

c What did the marchers described in Source D gain by behaving in this way, as opposed to violent attacks?

d Use Sources C, D and E to describe Gandhi's methods of protest and why they were successful.

e Would the suggestions in Source F benefit the people of India?

f Use these sources and your own knowledge to write your own judgement of Gandhi.

22: The USSR and Eastern Europe since 1945

In Chapter 17 we saw how, very soon after the war, Europe was divided into two. This chapter deals with the eastern half of Europe. In the east, the USSR controlled satellite countries: Poland, East Germany, Czechoslovakia, Hungary, Romania and Bulgaria. The countries of Western Europe were independent, but close ties of trade and military alliance linked them with one another and with the USA. Between the two was the barrier of wire, watch towers, searchlights and guns which Churchill called the Iron Curtain. This situation lasted for 45 years, until the dramatic changes of 1989–1991.

THE USSR

THE SOVIET UNION AFTER 1945

In 1945 large parts of western USSR were completely devastated. Cities, schools, farms and industry in the areas fought over in the war were destroyed. Iron production was down to 25%, and steel down to 50% of the 1938 figures. All the achievements of the pre-war Five-Year Plans (see Chapter 8) were gone. Stalin had to re-build his weakened country.

In 1946 a new Five-Year Plan was launched. Once again the Russian people toiled to meet their production targets. Once again people's efforts had to be concentrated on building up heavy industry. Once again food, clothes and consumer goods took second place.

The USSR was now a world superpower and work went ahead on producing nuclear weapons in order to challenge the USA. This was very expensive. Many men had been killed (there were some 52 million women and 31 million men in Russia in 1945), so women worked at heavy jobs like road-mending. Rebuilding the country was a long process. Even in the 1950s there were not enough houses and the number of livestock was actually less than it had been in 1913.

JOSEPH STALIN

Stalin's own personal dictatorship continued. The secret police, the KGB under the control of Beria, continued its work. During the war conditions had been relaxed, but now the heavy hand of dictatorship returned. Soviet soldiers who had invaded Europe had seen a better standard of living there. The KGB clamped down on the dangerous idea that Communism might not be the best form of government. The KGB moved into the satellites of eastern Europe, too. Independent points of view were crushed. The labour camps began to fill up again. Ethnic groups within the USSR who had welcomed the German invasion of 1941 suffered; Tartars, Kalmucks and others were moved thousands of kilometres from their homelands to the east of Siberia.

The worship of Stalin himself continued. All his rivals were now dead and only flatterers were left. The old dictator remained in the Kremlin, never venturing out. He relied on films and reports to keep him informed. Even in 1953 he was talking of new purges, and there was another wave of arrests. Before the trials could take place, however, Stalin died. He had ruled the USSR, in war and peace, for 26 years.

Nikita Khrushchev 1955–1964

There was no obvious successor to Stalin. For a time there was 'collective leadership' – shared leadership. Beria, the secret police boss, was removed and executed. There was a struggle for power which Nikita Khrushchev eventually won in 1955. Khrushchev was the son of a peasant, and often seemed earthy and ill-mannered. However, he must have been clever enough to survive under Stalin. He had been in charge of building the Moscow Underground and was the tough boss of the Ukraine region. He had his own ideas: in foreign policy he spoke of 'peaceful co-existence' with the West, of competition in trade and ideas, not weapons. This would certainly suit the USSR, which could not afford massive arms spending at the same time as improving living standards. Khrushchev was keen to improve the standard of living.

▼ SOURCE 1A

We must help people eat well, dress well and live well. You cannot put theory in your soup or Marxism in your clothes. If after forty years of Communism a person cannot have a glass of milk or a pair of shoes, he will not believe Communism is a good thing, whatever you tell him.

Khrushchev, quoted in Paul Richardson, *Britain, Europe and the Modern World*

? Questions

a In what way do Khrushchev's words in Source 1A contrast with Stalin's aims (see Chapter 8)

b Why were housing (Source 1B) and holidays (Source 1C) so important to Soviet workers in the 1950s?

▼ SOURCE 1B Workers' housing in Moscow

▼ SOURCE 1C Russian holidaymakers by the Black Sea

Khrushchev's plans for improving material things were called 'goulash communism'. He hoped to be able to give the people the prosperity promised by Communism while still retaining the Communist system. He boasted to the Americans that Soviet production would overtake theirs.

1. Agriculture He proposed to increase grain production by one-third by opening up the millions of acres of 'Virgin Lands' (land never before cultivated) in Central and Southern USSR. New collective farms were set up. Grain production rose by 50% from 1953 to 1958.

2. Industry He believed that Stalin's centralised planning system for industry was inefficient. He transferred more power to local planning councils, 'sovnarkhozy'.

3. The space race In 1957 Khrushchev shocked the West by announcing that the USSR had put a satellite, a 'sputnik', in space. This was followed up in 1961 when Yuri Gagarin became the first man to be sent into space. Khrushchev made the most of these propaganda successes.

When Khrushchev had talked of peaceful rivalry with the West, this was the kind of thing he meant. But it led to the space race with the USA; in which both sides tried to outdo each other in space exploration. There was a military side to this, too, as the rockets could be used to launch missiles as well as satellites.

▼ **SOURCE 1D** Khrushchev in the USA, 1959

Khrushchev also changed policy in another direction. At the Twentieth Communist Party Congress in 1956 he made a three-hour speech about Stalin. He accused Stalin of encouraging a 'cult of his own personality', and of killing his rivals in the purges. Examples were given of all the horrors of Stalinism. Inside Russia this was followed by some relaxation of censorship and the release of many prisoners from the labour camps.

This relaxation was not to be taken too far, however, for fear of loosening Soviet control too much. In East Berlin there had been riots soon after Stalin's death. Khrushchev's speech attacking Stalin now led to riots in Poland. Gomulka, a popular Polish Communist removed by Stalin, was brought to power.

HUNGARY 1956

There was also unrest in Hungary. The Communist takeover of Hungary was fairly gradual but by 1948 the country was safely in the hands of Rakosi, a dictator and slavish follower of Stalin. Agriculture was neglected in favour of industry, usually to the benefit of the USSR. Farms were collectivised. The Hungarian standard of living fell by 5% from 1949 to 1955. It was also the worst police state in Eastern Europe. There were 100,000 in the Secret Police, the hated AVOs.

Khrushchev's speech attacking Stalin brought demonstrations in Hungary. Secret policemen were attacked. A government was formed, led by the popular Prime Minister Imre Nagy, which included some non-Communists. They even talked of leaving the Warsaw Pact

This was too much for Khrushchev, and Soviet tanks were sent in to crush the Hungarians. In the fighting 30,000 died and 200,000 fled. Nagy was arrested and executed in 1958. Soviet control was reimposed.

❓ Questions

a Why do you think the Hungarian rebels were so keen to destroy the statue in Source 2 ?

b What evidence is there in this picture of fighting having taken place?

THE FALL OF KHRUSHCHEV

By the early 1960s things were going wrong for Khrushchev. Soil erosion in the 'Virgin Lands' led to crop failures. The sovnarkhozy were no more efficient than central planning. He was blamed for the split with China in 1960. He was blamed for the near-nuclear war over Cuba in 1962. In 1964 he was dismissed. It was a sign of the changes he had made that he was allowed to live quietly in retirement: under Stalin he would have been executed.

The Brezhnev years 1964–1982

After Khrushchev's attempts to reform the system, the USSR now returned to 20 years of no change. Brezhnev was an old Stalinist who wanted to keep things the way they were.

CZECHOSLOVAKIA 1968

The next country to try to reform Communism to make it work better was Czechoslovakia. In 1967 the old Stalinist leader was replaced as party First Secretary by a new man, Alexander Dubcek. Dubcek began to introduce changes. He wanted less censorship, less control by the secret police and more open discussion. He was still a Communist,

and tried to reassure the USSR that he did not intend going as far as Hungary had in 1956. These ideas caused great excitement in the 'Prague Spring' of 1968. Dubcek called it 'socialism with a human face'. The USSR preferred its own faceless control. In August they sent in tanks to remove Dubcek. Despite the passive resistance of the Czechs, Soviet rule was reimposed. The 'Prague Spring' soon ended.

POLAND

There was a different kind of protest movement in Poland. A demand for a free trade union started among the shipyard workers at Gdansk in 1980 and spread to all other workers. It was eventually allowed, and called itself 'Solidarity'.

Solidarity soon became the focus of all opposition to the government, helped by the strength and independence of the Roman Catholic Church in Poland. It was a great embarrassment to them because a Communist government is supposed to

▼ **SOURCE 2** Huge statue of Stalin being pulled down, Budapest, 1956

rule in the name of the workers. In 1981 the Polish army took over the country. This was slightly preferable to the Poles than a Soviet Army invasion and the uneasy situation remained through the 1980s until 1989.

MIKHAIL GORBACHEV

When Brezhnev died in 1982 he was followed by two more old men, Yuri Andropov and Konstantin Chernenko. But in 1985 Mikhail Gorbachev took over the USSR. Compared to the boring old men who had been ruling the USSR for decades, he was very different: he was only 54, intelligent, charming, smiling, with an equally intelligent and well-educated wife, Raisa. He was deeply critical of the corruption and what he called the stagnation of the Brezhnev years. He wanted to reform the USSR and in doing so he changed world history.

Why did the USSR need reform?

LOW STANDARD OF LIVING
The USSR had still failed to give its people the better standard of living they wanted and which Khrushchev had promised back in 1955 (see Source 1A). The economy was still centrally planned and run and was very inefficient. The USSR had plentiful supplies of raw materials and huge amounts of fertile land. Yet there were still shortages of all kinds of goods and food. Most citizens had to spend hours queueing for basic items in the shops.

LACK OF FREEDOM
This affected all aspects of life. Managers were not expected to make their factories more efficient; they were not expected to find out what customers wanted and make it, but just to make what Moscow told them. Prices were fixed by the government at artificially low levels, so managers had no idea whether they were making a profit or not.

Many people were corrupt and took bribes. Party officials, called the 'nomenklatura', had special privileges: their own country houses, 'dachas', their own cars, holidays, special shops where Western goods were on sale, travel abroad, servants, etc.

There was no freedom to point all this out. Some writers wrote stories and accounts of what was happening and passed them to their friends. These 'dissidents' would then make their own copies themselves, by 'samizdat', or self-publishing. An example of this lack of free speech was that when the serious nuclear accident happened at power station at Chernobyl in 1986 news was suppressed at first. Soviet citizens also had very little idea of what was really happening in the war in Afghanistan.

▼ SOURCE 3　Industrial pollution at Norilsk in Siberia, one of the most polluted cities in the world

MILITARY SPENDING

The cost of the war in Afghanistan and, especially, the Cold War, was crippling the Soviet economy. Maybe 25% of the Soviet budget was being spent on war, compared to 7% of the budget of the USA.

ECOLOGICAL DISASTER

In fact Chernobyl was only one of a horrendous series of ecological disasters which had happened in the USSR. Many of the rivers, and Lake Baikal had become impossibly polluted. The Aral Sea had almost disappeared. Industrial effluent was poisoning children and adults in many cities.

Gorbachev's reforms

Gorbachev was a life-long Communist and believed that the system could be made to work. He wanted to reform it through two great changes:
• *glasnost* (openness) 1986. This meant more democracy, more freedom of speech.
• *perestroika* (restructuring) 1987. This meant changing the Soviet economy so that goods were made which people wanted, at a price which reflected what they cost to make, not what the government said the price should be. In other words, a free market.

WHAT WERE THE RESULTS?

1. The Cold War Gorbachev ended the war in Afghanistan which had cost 15,000 Soviet lives. He successfully ended the Cold War in meetings with US President Reagan in Reykjavik, in 1986, and in Washington, in 1987.

2. Eastern Europe. Gorbachev believed people should be allowed to choose their own form of government, the so-called Sinatra Doctrine: 'I did it my way'. He made it clear to Communist leaders in Eastern Europe that he would no longer support them with Soviet tanks. In an amazing few months from August to the end of 1989 communist governments fell in East Germany, Poland, Hungary, Czechoslovakia, Bulgaria and Romania. All these collapses were peaceful, except in Romania. No one stopped the people of East and West Berlin when they pulled down the Wall which had divided their city since 1961. In 1991 the two parts of Germany were united again. The Warsaw Pact was dissolved.

All these events made Gorbachev a popular figure outside the USSR.

3. The USSR It was a different story inside the USSR. Gorbachev's problem was how to move from a completely controlled economy to a free one. It was different in eastern Europe: Communism had only been established since the late 1940s, but how do you change people who had known nothing else since 1917?

In fact glasnost undermined perestroika. That is, free elections and openness took power away from the people who had been running the system. But these were the only people who could arrange the restructuring. By 1990 the USSR had free speech and free elections but also enormous price rises, crime, speculation, a black market and a catastrophic fall in most people's standard of living.

The most powerful force which Gorbachev's reforms let loose was nationalism. The USSR had taken over and continued to rule the Tsar's empire of different peoples and regions. The 15 republics which went to make up the Union of Soviet Socialist Republics now wanted to rule themselves. During 1990 and 1991, Lithuania, Latvia, Estonia, then Armenia, Azerbaijan, Belorus, Georgia,

▼ **SOURCE 4** The Berlin Wall comes down

Kazakhstan, Kirghizistan, Moldova, Tadjikistan, Turkmenistan, Ukraine and Uzbekistan all became self-governing states. The ruler of Russia was Boris Yeltsin, Gorbachev's old rival. He was now more powerful than Gorbachev, President of a collapsed USSR.

In 1991 the old Communists tried to take over the government in a coup. Gorbachev was isolated away from Moscow. The coup failed, however, when Yeltsin defied them. Soon after his return, Gorbachev resigned. Yeltsin took reform a stage further: he did not try to reform Communism, he abandoned it. The Communist Party was banned and vigorous efforts were made to go over to a market economy.

▼ SOURCE 5A

Our country has not been lucky . . . It was decided to carry out this Marxist experiment on us. We have proved that there is no place for this idea.

Boris Yeltsin, 1990

▼ SOURCE 5B

The changes of the last decade have far exceeded our boldest hopes. But the price is beyond our worst fears.

Otto Lacis, journalist on the newspaper *Izvestia*

and President in 1990 but events were passing him by. The collapse of the USSR and the 1991 coup led to his resignation.

Two judgements on Gorbachev:

(i) from the Mayor of St Petersburg in 1991: 'Gorbachev's mistake was to try to reform what was unreformable.'

(ii) From historian Eric Hobsbawm in 1994: 'Gorbachev was a tragic figure who destroyed what he wanted to reform, and was himself destroyed in the process.'

MIKHAIL GORBACHEV 1931–

Gorbachev is the son of an agricultural engineer and was educated at Moscow University where he studied law. He met and married Raisa, a philosophy student, and joined the Communist Party in 1952.

He went back to his home to work as a manager in agriculture. His ability and his desire to reform brought him to the notice of the government in Moscow in 1978. He was appointed General Secretary of the Communist Party in 1985 on the death of Chernenko and began his radical reform programme.

His ending of the Cold War and the freeing of the states of eastern Europe made him popular in the west, but his reforms failed inside the USSR. He was elected head of state in 1988

ASSESSMENT

Describe, explain and analyse

1 a) Describe the uprisings in *either* Hungary in 1956 *or* Czechoslovakia in 1968.

   b) Why did the uprising take place?

   c) Why did the Soviet government decide to crush it?

2 a) Describe what it was like to live in the USSR at the time Gorbachev came to power.

   b) What were the aims of glasnost and perestroika?

c) How successful were they?

d) Why did Gorbachev resign in 1991?

Evidence and interpretations

Look at the two quotations at the end of the brief biography of Gorbachev opposite.

1   Explain in your own words what each one is saying.

2   Do they agree with each other?

3   Use the information in this chapter to explain how far you agree with these two interpretations.

Czechoslovakia, 1968

▾ SOURCE A

There is an enormous difference in the whole atmosphere. People are looking happy, they smile and there is a much higher level of conversation in cafés and restaurants. You can see people talking excitedly to each other at every street corner. The papers are simply snatched away from the newsmen as soon as they appear. All this is quite unusual in the Communist world.

> Ian McDougall, BBC Correspondent in Prague,
> the capital of Czechoslovakia, March 1968

▾ SOURCE B

The aim is to end the leadership of the Communist Party, to undermine socialism and turn Czechoslovakia against other Socialist countries. Thus the security of our countries is threatened.

> Soviet leader Brezhnev, May 1968

▾ SOURCE C

Socialism is for us the only possibility. We lived under another system 25 years ago and it wasn't a happy time for Czechoslovakia. We want to stay with other Communist countries. The main change is just to bring back a human face to Socialism, to find a more honest, more human way to fulfil the aims we have in mind.

> Czech leader Igor Kratochvil
> on BBC radio, May 1968

▾ SOURCE D

Cartoon from a Swedish newspaper. The man is Czech reform leader Dubcek; the hammer and sickle is the Soviet symbol.

▾ SOURCE E

Party and government leaders of Czechoslovakia have asked Russia for help, including armed forces. This request was brought about by the threat to the Socialist system in Czechoslovakia. Nobody will ever be able to seize a single link from the community of Socialist states.

> From the Soviet statement of 20 August 1968
> when 40,000 troops invaded Czechoslovakia

▾ SOURCE F

Young people were talking to the soldiers around the tanks. The conversation usually went: 'How can you shoot our children who are unarmed?' The Russian soldiers, who were hardly more than boys replied: 'We didn't shoot them.' A girl asked: 'But you would shoot if you were given orders to?' And the boy was embarrassed and tried to shrug it off.

> BBC Report, August 1968

▼ **SOURCE G**
Students argue with Russian soldiers in Wenceslas Square, Prague

▼ **SOURCE H**
Twice in this century the Russians have had to face an onslaught from the centre of Europe. Only they know the full extent of their losses in the last war and the country is still governed by men who fought in it. The Russians have no intention of dismantling their defences to the West.

Czech historian Z. A. B. Zeman

a What can you tell about life in Czechoslovakia before 1968 from reading Source A?

b Why was it necessary to give more freedom to the people in order to bring change to the economy?

c What are Brezhnev's fears in Source B?

d How does Kratochvil, in Source C, try to reassure him?

e What is the cartoon, Source D, saying about the Czech situation?

f The Czechs complained that: 'We are being criticised for what we do not say, blamed for what we do not think.'

Use Sources B, C and E to explain what they meant.

g Which of Sources F and G do you find more useful for finding out what it was like when the Russian tanks were in Prague? Explain your choice.

h What further reason does Source H give for the Soviet invasion?

i Use these sources and your own knowledge to analyse why the USSR invaded Czechoslovakia in 1968.

23: Britain and Western Europe since 1945

During the war years, Britain had been the partner of the USSR and USA in the victory over Hitler. Churchill had sat with Stalin and Roosevelt in the great meetings of the Allies at Teheran and Yalta. But the truth was that Britain was not the equal of the new superpowers. The power and might of Britain, based on its industry and its empire, as described in Chapter 1, had received a terrible blow from the First World War. The decline had continued in the years between the wars, with British industry in serious trouble for most of that time (see Chapter 9).

The strains of the Second World War weakened Britain even further. In the years since 1945, the British people have tried to come to grips with the results of this decline. The British empire has gone; industry and commerce have had to adjust to new situations in the world. The picture is not all gloomy: there have been some great achievements and a general rise in prosperity. However, the question of how the British people are going to live with the results of these changes still remains. The country is far from agreed in its answers.

WHY DID LABOUR WIN THE 1945 ELECTION?

In July 1945, soon after the defeat of Germany and while the war against Japan was still going on, an election was called. It was the first since 1935, because there were no elections in wartime. Most people, including the Labour leaders, expected the Conservatives to win, because Winston Churchill, the great war hero and Prime Minister since 1940, was the Conservatives' leader. However, there was a new feeling in the country once the war was over. The voters looked back with disgust to the bad times of the 1930s, with so much unemployment and hardship. They remembered that the Conservatives had been in power for most of that time.

During the war, the Beveridge Report had proposed a scheme of 'national insurance'. The author of the report, William Beveridge, a civil servant, intended to defeat what he called 'the five giants on the road to social progress'. These giants were want, disease, ignorance, squalor and idleness. His plan was to extend the insurance scheme started by the Liberals in 1911 to cover everyone in Britain, men and women.

▶ SOURCE 1A
Cartoon about the Beveridge Report

RIGHT TURN

❓ Questions
a   Where is the bus going and who is the driver?
b   What is the attitude of the cartoonist to the Report?
c   How does he make this clear?

The Beveridge Report fired people's imaginations. They wanted to build a better world after the war. The Labour Party caught this mood. In their manifesto, 'Let Us Face the Future', they said:

▼ SOURCE 1B

The Labour Party is a Socialist Party – its ultimate purpose at home is a Socialist Commonwealth – free, democratic, efficient, progressive, public-spirited – its material resources organised in the service of the people.

Labour Party Manifesto, 1945

Although Churchill had been wartime Prime Minister, the Labour leaders were not unknown to the people, as there had been a coalition government. Attlee had been Deputy Prime Minister, Morrison Home Secretary and Bevin Minister of Labour. For once, Churchill misread the mood of the nation and tried to frighten people by comparing life under Labour with life under the Gestapo. Labour won with a majority of 146, the first ever Labour government with a working majority.

THE LABOUR GOVERNMENTS 1945–1951

There were huge problems to be faced: five million homes had been bombed; half the merchant shipping fleet had been sunk; industry had been organised for war and had to return to peacetime conditions: there were soldiers to be demobilised. Most of all, the war had been paid for by selling off British assets abroad. The result was that the country owed £1,000 million more than it owned. Nevertheless, the Labour government, led by Clement Attlee as Prime Minister, set about fulfiling its promises.

NATIONAL INSURANCE, 1946

In 1946, the National Insurance Act was passed. Every working person paid a small amount each week for a stamp which was put on a card. Employers and the government added money to this. In return, everyone could claim benefits: sickness pay during illness, unemployment benefit, old age pensions, widows' pensions, grants for maternity and for funerals. Men were entitled to a state pension at 65 and women at 60 years. All these benefits were paid 'as of right' and were not means-tested (see page 85).

NATIONAL ASSISTANCE, 1948

This system still left some people in need. For them, the National Assistance Board was set up in 1948. Anyone who was in difficulty could apply for National Assistance (the name was changed to Social Security in 1974). Money was given weekly, with grants for special items such as clothing. It was intended that everyone should be kept to a minimum standard of living.

NATIONAL HEALTH SERVICE, 1948

Another of Beveridge's 'giants' – disease – was attacked by the National Health Service Act, 1946. This came into effect in July 1948. The National Health Service (NHS) gave medical attention to everyone. Doctors, medicine, hospitals, dentists and opticians would be free of charge. The scheme was opposed by the doctors, who did not want to come under state control. The Minister of Health, Aneurin Bevan, was determined to set up the system and bought them off by allowing private patients as well.

▼ SOURCE 2

A person ought not to be deterred from seeking medical assistance at the earliest possible stage by the financial anxiety of doctors' bills . . . Our hospital organisation has grown up with no plan; it is unevenly distributed over the country and very often the best hospital facilities are available where they are least needed. In the older industrial districts of Great Britain hospital facilities are inadequate.

Aneurin Bevan, House of Commons, 1946

❓ Questions

a Why had many people not gone to a doctor if they were ill before the Act?
b What other problem did Bevan plan to put right?

Bevan, a miner's son, had seen the problems that working people had in finding money to pay for medical care when he was a young man in Wales. When the NHS started in 1948, people rushed to receive free treatment. Not only doctors, but opticians and dentists suddenly had hundreds of customers. Nine months' supply of spectacles went in six weeks. Most women were found to have half or more of their teeth decayed. Years of neglect were shown up and the job of putting things right began.

All these measures – National Insurance, National Assistance and National Health – added up to a huge increase in the Welfare State. The government had taken on the task of looking after the well-being of the people 'from the cradle to the grave'.

Housing

During the Second World War nearly half a million homes were destroyed or made uninhabitable. As a result, there was a housing crisis in 1945. Returning servicemen wanted to set up their own homes and there was a boom in marriages and babies. In desperation, 46,000 people moved illegally into disused army camps as squatters.

Bevan was also the minister in charge of housing in the new Labour government. He wanted to ensure that good-quality council housing had a high priority. Private house building was restricted. In the five years after the war, Britain built more houses than any other European country. Most of it was council housing. Bevan intended council housing to be for all citizens, not just for the working classes. It was certainly true that the need for decent housing was most acute among the working classes. However, many people still wanted to buy a house, and not enough private housing to sell was being built. This complaint was heard a good deal when the next election became due in 1950.

Another achievement of the Labour government was the New Towns Act of 1946. The idea was to build new towns away from the old cities, making a completely fresh start. All the latest ideas could be used: housing and industry were separated; houses were grouped in areas, each with their own shops, pubs and other facilities; public transport was good, and cars and pedestrians were separated. New Towns were built at Harlow, Crawley, Stevenage, Basildon, Hemel Hempstead and Skelmersdale, and there were 12 more by 1962.

? Question

a Look at Source 3. What different types of housing are being built here?

Economic policy

The British people had made tremendous sacrifices during the Second World War. Now they wanted to get on with building a better life. But it was not going to be easy.

In the words of Clement Attlee, the country was in a mess. Factories and houses were in ruins. Industry, which had been geared up to the war

▼ SOURCE 3   Harlow New Town being built

effort, now had to adjust to peacetime production. The costs of the war had left Britain with debts of £3,300. Britain had lost some of its trading links as a result of the First World War and the long inter-war depression left British industry run down, old-fashioned and uncompetitive. As if these short-term and long-term problems were not enough, the new Labour government was committed to spending large sums of money on building the Welfare State (see pages 246–247).

▼ SOURCE 4A

There were a lot of post-war problems to clear up, of course, but I thought that we must push ahead. . . . It wasn't just nationalisation for nationalisation's sake, but the policy in which we believed: that fundamental things – banking, transport, fuel and power – must be taken over by the nation as a basis on which the rest of the reorganisation of the country would depend. We had to work fast. We had to re-build the export trade. There had to be control of masses of things that were forbidden to our own people at home. Shops would have lovely china, for export only. Very frustrating but you couldn't avoid it.

*Labour Prime Minister, Clement Attlee,
speaking in 1961 about the problems
facing him in 1945*

However, the legacy of the war years was not all bad. Wartime controls in industry had been necessary and an important cause of eventual victory. Labour was now prepared to direct the economy to deal with the problems. There were also new technologies developed in wartime, such as electronics, which could be applied to peacetime production. How did Labour tackle these economic problems?

EXPORTS

Controls were put on industry, requiring goods to be made for export only (Sources 4A and 4B). With much of Europe and Japan in ruins, it was not hard to sell exports. By 1951 British exports were up 77 per cent on the 1939 figure.

NATIONALISATION

The Labour government was also determined to nationalise several key industries. This meant that they would be taken over by the government. In this way, the Labour leaders said, industry could be run on behalf of the people, for the country as a whole. In 1945, the Bank of England was nationalised. In 1947, the coal industry was nationalised and the National Coal Board was set up. The railways were nationalised in 1947, as well as other aspects of transport such as buses and road haulage. The intention was to plan transport in Britain as one complete system. Electricity, gas, airlines, and cable and wireless were also nationalised in these years. In 1949, the iron and steel industries were nationalised. This last was bitterly opposed by

▼ SOURCE 4B

Cars and tractors ready for export at the Standard factory in Coventry, 1948. Britain was the world's largest exporter of cars and lorries after the Second World War

► SOURCE 5A   Queuing for bread, 1946

the Conservatives, as was the road haulage side of transport nationalisation. They promised to de-nationalise both as soon as they came to power. However, most of the nationalisation was not unpopular at the time. Industry had been controlled by the government in the war. Controlling industry in the interests of the public, not the shareholders, was not unpopular.

Austerity

All this tremendous programme of welfare and nationalisation was carried out against a background of great economic difficulties. In 1945, J. M. Keynes had raised a huge loan from the USA and Canada just to keep the country going. Britain had to sell goods abroad in order to buy essential supplies of food and raw materials. There were shortages in the shops, and items rationed included bread, potatoes, sugar, tea, bacon, meat and butter. There was no petrol and no foreign exchange for private individuals. Most ex-soldiers soon found jobs successfully, but wages were restricted. The Chancellor of the Exchequer, Sir Stafford Cripps, kept taxes high, and the period became known as 'austerity'. Then came the bad weather of 1946–1947. With temperatures low and transport blocked, coal supplies ran short. This affected gas and electricity, which was often cut off for several hours a day.

► SOURCE 5B

The streets of London were almost blacked out. It was depressing to walk along the main thoroughfares of London, with their glimmering lights, and to see the luxury shops showing their wares by candle-light. The price of candles soared.

Greyhound-racing, mid-week horse-racing and matinee performances were banned. Gales, fog and snow delayed ships, trains and road transport. Colliers carrying precious coal were stormbound in the Tyne.

For the country in general it was a major disaster, for each individual a moment of sacrifice and, in many cases, real suffering.

H. and N. Matthews, *The Britain We Saw*

? Questions

a Why do you think the people in Source 5A would feel differently about shortages in 1946, compared with those they had experienced in the war years?

b Who would they probably blame?

c Why would the situation described in Source 5B cause sacrifice and suffering?

THE 1950 GENERAL ELECTION

By 1950 there was considerable dissatisfaction with the Labour government. Some people objected to the high taxes which were necessary to pay for the Welfare State. Others felt that the government was playing too great a part in people's lives, mollycoddling them and stifling initiative. Emigration to Australia, New Zealand, Rhodesia and South Africa increased in these years. After the 1950 general election, the Labour majority in Parliament was reduced to just six.

THE 1951 GENERAL ELECTION

Attlee carried on, clinging to his narrow majority. Two leading ministers, Cripps and Ernest Bevin, had resigned through illness. When the Korean War broke out, Attlee felt Britain, as a great power, ought to take part. He put up government spending on the armed services, and introduced charges in the NHS. Bevan bitterly opposed this, as it went against his principle of a completely free health service and resigned. Attlee called another general election late in 1951. This time, although Labour received more votes than any other party in history, the Conservatives won more seats and ruled for the next 13 years.

Table 24-1 British governments 1951–1992

Election	Party	Prime Minister
1951	Conservative	Winston Churchill
1955	Conservative	Anthony Eden (Harold Macmillan from 1957)
1959	Conservative	Harold Macmillan (Sir Alec Douglas-Home from 1963)
1964	Labour	Harold Wilson
1966	Labour	Harold Wilson
1970	Conservative	Edward Heath
1974	Labour	Harold Wilson
1974	Labour	Harold Wilson
1979	Conservative	Margaret Thatcher
1983	Conservative	Margaret Thatcher
1987	Conservative	Margaret Thatcher (John Major from 1990)
1992	Conservative	John Major

'You've never had it so good'

The main feature of the 1950s and early 1960s was the recovery of the British economy. It would be difficult to say that the Conservatives caused this recovery, but they certainly took the credit for it. In the 1959 election, Macmillan's remark 'You've never had it so good' was very true. The prosperity was spread through nearly all of society. The upper and middle classes did well, but so did most of the working classes. Average wages rose from £6.40 per week in 1950 to £11.12½ in 1959.

There were plenty of things to spend the money on: car ownership doubled, ownership of television sets went up by thirty times. Cheap air travel brought continental holidays within reach of many more families. Chain stores brought fashionable clothes within the price range of most people. Washing machines, refrigerators and vacuum cleaners became part of every household. Advertising helped to show people new things to spend their money on: ITV was started in 1955. Many more women went out to work, which helped the family income even more. Hire purchase was frowned upon by most people before the war, but became very common in the 1950s.

▶ SOURCE 6
Magazine advertisement for an electric cooker, 1955

ECONOMIC PROBLEMS: 'THE BRITISH DISEASE'

The post-war boom was heavily dependent on oil for heating, transport and power. One third of the world's oil supplies came from the Arab countries of the Middle East. When the Arab attack on Israel in 1973 failed – the Yom Kippur War – Arab oil producers decided to cut back supplies to countries which supported Israel. There was an immediate energy crisis and inflation went up to 30 per cent in 1973 to 1974. Since then, energy has never been cheap, and world trade has become much more competitive.

Britain has found it hard to compete in this stringent economic climate. Take the example of a key industry, car manufacture. In 1965 95 per cent of cars on British roads were British made; by 1980 the figure had fallen to 43 per cent. Productivity in the British car industry was low. In 1976 each British car worker made five cars, compared with eight cars for every worker in Germany and 28 in the highly automated US car industry. Many people were aware of the problem of low productivity but it was not tackled.

▶ **SOURCE 7B**
[*British car exports to the USA:*]
After the war, the British were first off the mark and had the imported car market to themselves. The Japanese were still riding bicycles, nobody had heard of the Volvo and the ugly little Volkswagen was reputed to made out of old gas ovens. English tweeds were riding high, not to mention Scotch whisky, so why not do business with

▶ **SOURCE 7A**
Cartoon from 1946 pointing out some of the problems of the British economy

"I'LL ATTEND TO THE FOUNDATIONS LATER"

your friends?
[*Then Volkswagen, Opel, Datsun, Volvo, Toyota, Renault and Fiat stepped in:*]
Poor workmanship and inefficient after-sales service have hit the British most. Typical quotes include 'Look at the rusty gutter on that MG and the neat one on the Toyota.' 'The glue's bad, rubber's bad, varnish bad' and 'I waited five months for a turning signal part'.

American writer in the *Daily Telegraph*, 1967

Why was this lack of competitiveness not challenged? High prices, unreliable delivery and poor after sales service has been called the 'British disease'. But who was to blame for the poor health of British industry? Inevitably, everyone blamed everyone else.

Employers blamed the trade unions. They said unions were more interested in holding on to jobs and pushing up wages than modernising industry by introducing new technology.

► SOURCE 8A

It was the trade unions. Their attitudes towards progress were lamentable. Simple things: a portable hand-welding machine where one man could easily work four machines and in Sweden they did, ditto in Germany, ditto in France. In Britain, one man to one machine.

Sir Leonard Redshaw, head of Vickers shipyards

The unions blamed their employers. In the old industries like shipbuilding, relations between employers and employees were bad and unions were tough. The speaker in Source 8B thought the boom years could have been used to improve relations, but the old divisions remained. For example, at the British Aerospace factory there were four canteens, one for each grade of employee.

► SOURCE 8B

If the men had been given better job security, sick pay, pensions, better working conditions, and that was possible in the 1960s with the vast profits they made, then in my opinion they could have won the co-operation of the workers. But they felt they had a

divine right to rule and if the management attitude is of that nature then workers react in a not very positive manner.

A Clydeside trade unionist

The government was blamed by everyone. Governments were not sure what their aims were. Policies of encouraging factories to move to areas of high unemployment tended to make industries less competitive. For example, in 1948 the government persuaded Ford to move to Liverpool and ICI to set up a plant in Pontypool. Both firms would have preferred to build factories in the Midlands. When the Conservatives de-nationalised the steel industry in 1953, they still influenced the location of two new plants at Llanwern in South Wales and Ravenscraig in Scotland where unemployment was very high.

Governments had to make a difficult choice: did they want industry to be more competitive or to provide a social service? It was the nationalised industries like coal and the railways that suffered the most from these confused aims. Should coal be cheap to help industries which used coal as fuel? Or should it be more expensive to generate more money to invest in the mines and make them more competitive?

Governments faced a similar dilemma on the railways: should they be run to make a profit or to provide a service for the public, if necessary out of taxpayers' money? The Beeching Report in 1963 proposed that 14,500 kilometres (about 40 per cent) of the country's rail network should be closed as it was not profitable. However there was huge opposition to the report, especially from people who relied on the threatened lines. The result was, as usual, a fudge: some lines were saved, and only 9,600 kilometres closed. But was the government prepared to pay for the losses on the lines which remained open?

❓ Questions

a Look at Source 7A. What is the cartoonist saying about the economy?
b When did the problems become serious?
c Read Source 7B. Who do you think was to blame for the problems described?
d Use your own words to describe 'the British disease'.
e Was it the job of governments to put things right? What should have been done?

THE WELFARE STATE AFTER 1951

The first success of the Welfare State was to win the support of most people in Britain. Furthermore, although the Welfare State was established under a Labour government, it was supported by the Conservatives from early on, as Source 9A explains. This was known as 'Butskellism' after the Conservative, R. A. Butler and the Labour Party leader from 1953 to 1963, Hugh Gaitskell. The Conservatives were in power from 1951 to 1964 and from 1970 to 1974, yet they made no attempt to dismantle the Welfare State.

► SOURCE 9A

I think we should take pride that the British race has been able, shortly after the terrible period through which we have all passed together, to show the whole world that we are able to produce a social insurance scheme of this character.

R. A. Butler speaking for the Conservative Party in Parliament in 1946

As wages increased during the 1950s and 1960s, an unforeseen problem emerged: many working people earned far more than the levels of benefit paid by National Insurance. So people out of work from illness, temporarily unemployed or retired could see their incomes drop dramatically. Graduated pensions were introduced in 1961 so that people on higher incomes paid higher contributions for a larger pension. Other benefits became earnings-related in 1966 (although these were withdrawn in 1982). More and more people took out private insurance for health and old age.

The persistence of poverty

By the 1970s it seemed as if economic prosperity and the Welfare State had almost eliminated poverty. Then surveys were undertaken which showed that old age pensioners, single parents and large families living on a low wage were still in real difficulties. Four out of ten widows and pensioners were getting Supplementary Benefit (which replaced National Assistance in 1968) to bring their income up to a decent level. The number of people on Supplementary Benefit rose from 1.1 million in 1951 to 3.3 million in 1980. Another million people were probably eligible but didn't claim.

In 1968 health and welfare were put under the control of the Department of Health and Social Security (DHSS). Three years later, the Family Income Supplement (now called Income Support) was introduced to direct benefits to the most needy.

► SOURCE 9B

Cartoon from *Punch*. John Bull (the British people) is being treated like a child by his old-fashioned nanny (the Welfare State)

The cost of health

Expectations for higher standards of health care and the growing proportion of elderly people in our population have put a greater burden on the NHS. In 1974 the NHS was reorganised, putting hospitals, their staff and General Practitioners all under the supervision of local health authorities. In the 1990s the Conservative government reorganised the NHS again, so that hospitals and General Practice surgeries would be run more like businesses, in an attempt to cut costs.

The all-party agreement over the Welfare State was broken in the 1980s. Some right-wing politicians began to criticise the whole idea of the Welfare State. They said it was ruinously expensive and that the high taxes needed to pay for free health and welfare were reducing people's incentive to show initiative and earn higher salaries. They also maintained that people dependent on the Welfare State never learned to stand on their own feet, they called it the 'nanny state'. Some even argued that people who have not had to take responsibility for their own welfare may lose their sense of responsibility within the community and turn to crime or violence. Conservatives who shared these attitudes believed that the Welfare State was a terrible blight on Britain

In 1973 the Child Poverty Action Group claimed that three million children were living in poverty and that poverty was increasing. The gap between rich and poor widened in the 1980s. Today, the Child Poverty Action Group has evidence that children born into poverty are ill more often, less well-educated, more frequently unemployed and have a shorter life expectancy. They have less privileged lives with fewer holidays or opportunities for leisure activities. Cutting benefits and making claiming procedures more difficult may make people take more control of their own lives, as the right-wing thinkers had hoped. But is it fair that in families where benefits have been cut,

the children have had to endure hardships? Should we care about the people in Sources 10A and 10B?

▶ SOURCE 10B

'I just get the kids together and say, well, I'm afraid there'll be no dinner this week.'
'How would you feel, having to rout around in a second-hand shop for three hours to find shoes for the children?'

Poor people describe their lives, 1993

MRS THATCHER'S GOVERNMENTS 1979–1991

Mrs Thatcher's Conservative Party won the 1979 election committed to weakening the trade unions and helping private enterprise. These were popular policies, but she was also committed to an economic theory called monetarism. This claimed to keep inflation down and drive inefficiency out of businesses. Unfortunately one result of monetarism was higher unemployment, which reached three million people by 1982. This brought her great unpopularity and she would not have won a second term as Prime Minister but for the 'Falklands Factor'.

▶ SOURCE 10A

A girl living in bad housing as a result of poverty, 1992

SOURCE 11
Mrs Thatcher

THE FALKLANDS WAR

In April 1982, the Argentine government landed troops on the Falkland Islands. This group of remote islands in the South Atlantic, with a population of 1,800 people, had been claimed by Britain in 1765. However, Argentina also claimed the islands, which they called the Malvinas. The UN immediately passed resolutions against Argentina, and applied sanctions. Mrs Thatcher, though, chose to use military force to remove the Argentine troops. A task force of naval vessels was sent to the South Atlantic, and the Falklands Islands were recaptured after six weeks of fighting. There were quite heavy losses of men, ships and planes on both sides.

Her aggressive handling of the war won her widespread support, and she increased her majority in the 1983 election. She was also helped by splits in the opposition. In 1981 the Social Democratic party was founded by former Labour MPs who felt the Labour Party was too left-wing.

THATCHER'S POLICIES

Mrs Thatcher despised the 'Butskellite' consensus of the previous 30 years. She felt it was to blame for Britain's industrial problems and uncompetitiveness. Her solutions were:

1. To weaken trade unions. Through a series of Industrial Relations Acts, strikes were made harder and union membership fell. She took on the National Union of Mineworkers and its leader, Arthur Scargill, and defeated them in a long and violent strike in 1984–1985.

2. Privatisation. Selling off ('privatising') nationalised industries, such as oil, British Telecom, water and gas to private investors. This produced millions of pounds for the government, which was able to reduce taxes, especially for the better-off. This was to encourage people to be more enterprising.

3. Welfare changes. She believed that the Welfare State made people lazy and dependent, unable to stand on their own two feet. Cuts were made. Council houses were sold off and local authorities were not allowed to build any more.

The Thatcher years brought a huge upheaval. Some people got rich; others were made much poorer. Her successor from 1991, John Major, tried to continue her policies, particularly introducing competition to the Health Service and privatising British Rail. His government was, however, dogged by scandals and the opposition of its own supporters to the European Community (see page 274).

Northern Ireland

When Ireland became independent in 1921, the six north-eastern counties of Ulster remained part of the United Kingdom. The population of Northern Ireland is made up of two-thirds Protestants and one-third Roman Catholics. From 1921, the Protestant majority ruled Northern Ireland with their own parliament at Stormont. They did not treat their Catholic minority well: in housing and jobs. Protestants were favoured. Elections were organised so that Catholics were kept out of power. An extra police force, the 'B Specials', made up of Protestants, helped suppress the Catholics.

In 1967, there were civil rights marches by Catholics wanting fairer treatment in jobs and housing. They were attacked by Protestants with much violence. 'B Specials' raided Catholic areas. The Provisional IRA arose as a Catholic counter-attack, and soon law and order had broken down. British troops were sent in to keep order in 1969. At first, they were welcomed by the Catholics, but then they moved against the IRA. This brought violence between the army and Catholics, notably on 'Bloody Sunday', 1972, when 13 people were killed by soldiers.

The Provisional IRA, the 'Provos', stepped up their campaign for a united Ireland. They attacked army posts and murdered policemen. They claimed to be at war, and IRA members in prison went on hunger strike, even to death, to be treated as political prisoners. The most famous of these was Bobby Sands, who died in 1981. IRA violence made life dangerous, as well as inconvenient, for the ordinary people.

The British Government tried to find a solution. They abolished the Stormont Parliament in 1973 and tried to set up a power-sharing system. This was blocked by a Protestant General Strike.

A solution seemed as far away as ever, with Protestant Unionists, Catholic Nationalists and the British government and army locked in a struggle which no one could win. Then in 1994 John Hume of the SDLP negotiated terms for discussions between the British and Gerry Adams of Sinn Fein (the political wing of the IRA). Peace came to Northern Ireland for the first time in 27 years.

Multi-cultural Britain

In the 1950s, there was a shortage of workers in Britain as the economy grew. To meet this, workers from the West Indies, India and Pakistan came to Britain. They were allowed to do this as members of the Commonwealth and were therefore British citizens. In some areas, British factory owners advertised for workers in newspapers in Jamaica and Pakistan.

These new immigrants settled in Britain and hoped to stay here. However, they soon began to feel the results of racial discrimination. In housing and jobs, black people were frequently treated unfairly. There was also tension between blacks and whites in the poorer parts of many British cities.

The reaction of British governments was to cut immigration and attack racial discrimination. Unfortunately the aim of the second was made harder by the first. The Commonwealth Immigration Act, 1962, only allowed in immigrants who had a job to come to or a close relative to join. It caused some bitterness among those already in Britain, as well as those wanting to come in.

The Commonwealth Immigration Act, 1968, put restrictions on British passport-holders of Asian origin who were living in Africa where they were being persecuted. Further restrictions were introduced by the Immigration Act of 1971.

The Race Relations Act of 1965 made it illegal to practise racial discrimination or to incite racial hatred. It also set up the Race Relations Board to monitor the situation. The Board's powers were increased by the Race Relations Act of 1968. The 1976 Race Relations Act set up the Commission for Racial Equality.

However, black Britons are mainly concentrated in the poorer areas of British cities. When the economy is in decline, as in the late 1980s, unemployment hits people in these areas hardest. Neglect of housing, schools and other services in inner-city areas is not just a problem for blacks, but larger numbers of black people are involved. Riots broke out in several areas, notably Bristol, Toxteth (Liverpool), Brixton (London), Birmingham and Bradford. In this issue, as in foreign policy, Northern Ireland, the economy and most of the problems mentioned in this chapter, it is a question of British people learning to live with one another in new, and sometimes difficult, circumstances.

Defence

One aspect of British policy which governments have clung to is the 'independent nuclear deterrent'. This means that Britain should have its own atom bomb, independent of American control. This feeling was increased by the lack of American support over Suez. Enormous amounts of money have been spent on this. In 1952, Britain tested its own atom bomb, which could be dropped on an enemy by a bomber aircraft. By the late 1950s, missiles with nuclear warheads were being developed. In 1957, Britain began to work on its own missile, called Blue Streak. It was cancelled in 1960, but not before £100 million had been spent. Instead Macmillan made an agreement in 1962 to buy Polaris missiles from the USA and fit them with British warheads. They could then be launched from British submarines. The independent nuclear deterrent was therefore preserved. Many British people opposed this, and in the 1960s the Campaign for Nuclear Disarmament (CND) held large protest meetings and marches.

After a decline in the 1970s CND revived dramatically in the 1980s. US intentions to base cruise missiles on British soil, and British proposals to develop a new missile system, Trident, worried many people. Women who were particularly concerned set up a 'peace-camp' at Greenham Common, one of the cruise missile bases. The collapse of the Cold War took the heat out of the arguments, but the Trident programme was not cancelled.

EUROPEAN UNITY

In 1914 Europe had been the centre of world affairs; by 1945 the great European powers were in ruins and exhausted. World leadership had passed to the superpowers, the USA and USSR. In this situation several people in Europe put forward the idea of uniting the whole continent.

▶ ## SOURCE 12A

If Europe is to be saved from infinite misery, and indeed from final doom, there must be an act of faith in the European family.... What is the sovereign remedy? It is to recreate the European family, or as much of it as we can and provide it with a structure under which it can dwell in peace, safety and freedom. We must build a kind of United States of Europe.

Winston Churchill, Zurich, Switzerland, 1946

? Questions

a What does Churchill call Europe in this speech?
b What does he propose for Europe?

There were good reasons for uniting Europe. It seemed ridiculous in the 20th century to have so many small countries in such a small area. They had so much in common from their history; they had a common problem to be faced in rebuilding after the war.

On the other hand, there were obstacles. Even as Churchill spoke, the USSR had split Europe in two and removed the eastern half to become Soviet satellites. Also, the history of western Europe had left many suspicions and resentments. Many countries looked warily at Germany; France had its national pride; so did Britain, with its close links across the world to the Commonwealth. Unity was not going to be easy.

THE OECD
Economic links came first. Marshall Aid was given by the USA to help rebuild Europe. The OEEC

(Organisation for European Economic Co-operation) was set up to run the Marshall Aid programme. Sixteen western European countries joined. Later, the organisation became the OECD (Organisation for Economic Co-operation and Development). It helped the gradual economic recovery of Europe. However, political and military unity was still a long way off.

The Council of Europe was set up in 1949. It was intended to be a European Parliament, and several Europeans strongly wanted it to work: Monnet of France, Spaak of Belgium, Adenauer of Germany, de Gasperi of Italy. Some countries, however, notably Britain, were unwilling to go too far. An attempt was made to unite the armies of Europe in the EDC (European Defence Community). Again, Britain was unwilling to join. France was suspicious of Germany having an army again, and the idea collapsed.

THE SCHUMAN PLAN
Then the French Foreign Minister, Robert Schuman, suggested linking the coal and steel industries of Europe. Economic co-operation was always easier: if these two industries could combine then it would be impossible for any country to build up an army without others knowing. Thus the plan would allow German revival without the French being suspicious.

In 1952 the European Coal and Steel Community (ECSC) was formed. Its members were France, Germany, Italy, Belgium, the Netherlands and Luxembourg. It was an outstanding success. With Monnet as Chairman it organised co-operation between the coal and steel industries of Europe; it helped areas where the coal industry was declining. In its first ten years trade between its members increased by 170%.

The European Community

One lesson of the ECSC was that economic unity was easier than political unity. In 1957 two more plans were put forward: first, co-operation in the growing nuclear power industry, Euratom. Again Britain refused to join as its own nuclear industry was well advanced. Second was a proposal for a united trading and business area. This would be called the European Economic Community (EEC). The six members joined by signing the Treaty of Rome, 1957. They were the same six who had joined the ECSC. It was always intended that the economic unity it produced would lead eventually to a political unity, a United States of Europe.

▶ SOURCE 12B

British cartoon commenting on the Schuman plan

❓ Questions

a What do the two workers in this cartoon stand for?

b What will be the result of the Plan, does the cartoonist say?

Britain had stayed out of these organisations. The British people did not feel as close to their European neighbours as those who lived on the mainland of Europe. The British economy would be difficult to combine with Europe's. There was the sterling area: an international group of trading nations based on London. Several Commonwealth countries, notably New Zealand, had close trading links with Britain. British agriculture was very

different from the rest of the EEC countries. In 1959 Britain joined with Sweden, Norway, Denmark, Switzerland, Austria and Portugal in a free trading area: European Free Trade Area (EFTA). There were seven countries, but the population of EFTA amounted to only a quarter of that of the EEC.

Gradually, however, conditions changed. The Commonwealth became less important: from 1958 to 1964 trade between Britain and the Commonwealth increased 2%, between Britain and the EEC 98%. The EEC was successful, but Britain was having economic problems. In 1961 Britain applied to join. Some Europeans were keen to have Britain, feeling that Europe was not complete without it. Some, however, still had doubts. They felt that Britain was a half-hearted European and would drag its feet in the move to unity.

One of these was Charles de Gaulle, President of France 1958–1969. He felt that Britain was still too isolated, too closely linked to the USA and anyway would threaten his leadership of Europe. To de Gaulle Europe was a third force in the world, between the USA and USSR, with himself as a leading figure. He vetoed the application and did the same in 1967 when Britain applied again.

❓ Question

a Explain the point of each of the cartoons on page 275 (Sources 13A and 13B).

In 1969, de Gaulle fell from power and Britain joined the Common Market in 1972, followed by Denmark and Ireland. Greece joined in 1981, Spain and Portugal in 1986 and Austria, Sweden and Finland in 1995.

In many people's view, British membership has not been outstandingly successful. The CAP (Common Agricultural Policy) has meant higher food prices and problems for the highly efficient British agricultural industry. Many British people are still doubtful about how united they want to be with Europe. Proposals for a common currency and a common foreign policy do not meet with much approval. In the elections to the first European Parliament, 1979, the turn-out of voters in Britain was lower than anywhere in Europe. Mrs Thatcher was a reluctant European and negotiated Britain's exemption from social and political aspects of growing European unity. Under John Major, Conservative 'Euro-sceptics' have opposed him, arguing against further integration into Europe.

SOURCE 13A

British cartoon, 1962: De Gaulle and Adenauer are the ugly sisters; British Prime Minister Harold Macmillan is Cinderella

SOURCE 13B

British cartoon, 1967: De Gaulle is the policeman, British Prime Minister Harold Wilson is in the car

"I suspect you of driving under the influence of **America**."

HAROLD MACMILLAN 1894–1986

Harold Macmillan often appeared to be the typical upper-class Tory. However, behind his aristocratic ways he had a sharp, and caring, intelligence.

He came from a well-off family, and was the grandson of the founder of Macmillan Publishers. He was sent to Eton and Oxford, and fought in the Guards in the First World War. Like so many who were in the trenches, the war made a deep impression on him. Not only was he seriously wounded, but he also learned to respect the ordinary men under his command.

This was shown when he went into politics after the war. He considered joining the Labour Party, but decided against it. However, he chose Stockton-on-Tees as his constituency – a declining ship-building town facing great difficulties and hardship, and was their MP from 1924 to 1945.

He felt that the government should have done much more to help depressed areas such as Stockton. He was not afraid to speak out against his own party – the Conservatives – on this. He also opposed appeasement. This kept him out of power until Churchill formed his government in 1940. He carried out a successful job for Churchill in Africa, working with Eisenhower and the French. He showed skill in getting people to work together. After the war he became MP for Bromley and Minister of Housing from 1951 to 1954.

Sir Anthony Eden took over as Prime Minister in 1955 and was expected to carry on for some years. After the Suez incident in 1956 he resigned in 1957, and Macmillan became Prime Minister. He found the reputation of his country and his Party were very low on all sides.

As Prime Minister, from 1957 to 1963, he earned the description 'unflappable'. Whatever crisis was happening he seemed to have it under control. He saw Britain grow in prosperity during these years. The increase in the standard of living of working people pleased him a great deal. Most of his energy was put into foreign affairs. He visited the Soviet leader, Nikita Khrushchev, in 1959. He mended relations with the USA, badly hit during the Suez crisis. Eisenhower and Kennedy both liked him – in fact, during the Cuban missile crisis of 1962 Kennedy was in contact with Macmillan throughout. The main hope Macmillan had for peace was the 1960 'Summit' conference, though this failed through no fault of his. The 1963 Test Ban Treaty did come out of his efforts. He was also courageous enough to warn the South Africans of the 'wind of change' in Africa, in 1960.

Illness forced him to resign the premiership in 1963. He retired from Parliament in 1964.

ASSESSMENT

Describe, explain and analyse

1   a) Why did people vote for a Labour government in 1945?

   b) What were the successes and failures of this government?

   c) Does the fact that people chose a Conservative government in 1951 mean that it was a failure?

2   Choose *three* of the items from this list:

   • Housing.

   • Health.

   • Social security.

   • Industry.

   a) How did the Labour government of 1945–1950 attempt to deal with the items you have chosen?

   b) What were their aims in each case?

   c) How successful were they?

3   a) What is 'Butskellism'?

   b) Why did Mrs Thatcher dislike it so much?

   c) In what ways did she try to break down Butskellism?

   d) Did she succeed?

Evidence and interpretations

1   The Welfare State means high taxation and protects people too much so that they do not think of doing things for themselves.

2   The Welfare State, caring for people 'from the cradle to the grave' gives them security and peace of mind.

a   Which government in the period 1945 to the present day would agree with view 1?

b   Which government would agree with view 2?

c   There were 1.1 million people on Supplementary Benefit in 1951 and 3.3 million in 1981. Do these figures support view 1 or view 2?

d   How far does British history from 1950 to 1990 support each of these views?

Topics for discussion

1   Compare the Welfare State built up in Britain in the years after the Second World War with the welfare situation in the USA described in Chapters 10 and 18.

   What are the advantages and disadvantages of each?

   Which would you prefer to live under?

2   Beveridge's 'Five Giants' of want, disease, ignorance, squalor and idleness have only partially been dealt with. In what ways do these problems remain? Can they be solved?

Special Depth Study: Britain 1906–1919

THE LIBERAL REFORMS

Britain in 1906: Rich and Poor

Britain in 1906 was the richest country in the world. Income from land, industry and trade across the enormous British Empire brought some people huge wealth. The 'Upper Ten Thousand' (the 10,000 people with an income over £100,000 a year) owned several houses and could afford to entertain on a lavish scale.

▶ SOURCE 1B

On a lawn of brilliant green, one could see the sprinkled figures of the guests, some sitting under the trees, some strolling about. Round the garden spread the park: a herd of deer stood flicking their short tails in the shade of the beech trees.

[For tea] one just had scones and egg sandwiches, and paté sandwiches and cucumber sandwiches and chocolate cake and walnut cake and coffee cake. There were little plates

▶ SOURCE 1A   Tea on the lawn at Knole House, Sevenoaks, Kent, in 1899.

▼ SOURCE 1C Distribution of wealth in Britain in 1900

Class	Income	Percentage of population	Percentage of national wealth
Upper	At least £100,000 a year	1	55
Upper-middle	At least £400 a year	2	25
Lower-middle	At least £150 a year	8	11
Skilled-working	At least £80 a year	56	8
Casual workers and farm labourers	Less than £53 a year	33	1

with china handles to match from which people ate jam and toast ...
The butler, the groom of the chambers, the under-butler and the footmen would move about offering food.

Vita Sackville-West, the little girl sitting on the grass, described a tea party at Knole.

Below the very rich were the middle classes, living comfortably on about £400 – £600 a year. Even lower-middle class families, people like teachers, police sergeants, clerks and shopkeepers could live in a well-furnished house and hire a servant on an income of £150 a year.

But most people earned far less than this. In fact, large numbers of people lived in poverty (see Source 1C).

❓ QUESTIONS

a What can you learn from Sources 1A and 1B about the number of servants rich families employed?

b Compare Sources 1A and 1D and list all the differences between them.

c Which of these four sources, 1A to 1D, is most useful for finding out about people's lives in Britain in the early 20th century?

Why were the Liberal Reforms passed?

The Liberal government of 1906–1914 passed a whole series of laws to deal with different aspects of poverty. Why did they do this?

1 Information

In the first few years of the 20th century there was a great deal of interest in poverty. Many could not believe that poverty still existed in Britain. The

▼ SOURCE 1D Poor family in London

Victorians had passed laws to provide better housing, education and health and to help trade unions – all intended to remove poverty. Could there still be people in prosperous Britain who were poor? If so, there couldn't be many of them and it must be their own fault.

A number of surveys were published which provided accurate information about poverty; they also caused some surprises.

(i) **Charles Booth** was a wealthy shipowner who could not believe there were as many people in poverty as some people claimed. He began a huge survey of London's poor, published from 1889 to 1903. Far from the number being exaggerated, he found that as much as 38% of London's population lived on wages that were only just enough to live on or less.

(ii) **Seebohm Rowntree** carried out a big survey of working-class people in York, published in 1901. He realised it was important to decide what level of income was just enough to live on. Anyone below that could be defined as living in poverty. He calculated that a family of two parents and three children needed £1.08½ pence a week to live on. By his very strict definition (see Source 2A), 10% of the population were in poverty all the time, and another 18% were below it for some part of their lives. He described a life cycle in which working people hovered just above or below the poverty line all their lives. A young unmarried person could live on the low wages, but marrying and having children pushed people below the poverty line. When the children began to earn and left home, the worker passed above the poverty line, but could easily fall below it if illness or unemployment struck. Finally, old age brought poverty through loss of work or lower earnings.

◢ SOURCE 2A

A family living upon the scale allowed for must never spend one penny on a railway fare, or a busfare. They must never go out into the country unless they walk. They must never buy a halfpenny newspaper, or go to a concert. They must write no letters to absent children because they cannot afford the postage. The children must have no pocket money for dolls, marbles or sweets. The father must smoke no tobacco and drink no beer. The mother must never buy herself pretty clothes. Finally, the wage-earner must never be absent from his work for a single day.

Rowntree describes life on his poverty line

▣ QUESTIONS

a Why did Rowntree make such a precise definition of poverty?

b Why did he draw it so strictly?

c Look at the five causes of poverty shown in Source 2B. Explain why each situation led to poverty.

◢ SOURCE 2B
Causes of poverty, according to Rowntree

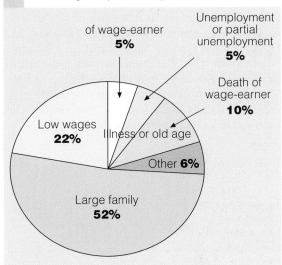

2 Defence

Government and army leaders were worried about the physical health of the British people. They were shocked to find, when they were recruiting for the Boer War (1899–1902), that so many young men were too small, too under-nourished or too ill to be taken into the army. How was Britain going to fight its wars in future?

3 The Labour Party

The Liberal Party had always tried to speak for working men (women did not have the vote at all). There were several working-class MPs by 1906, who were in the Liberal Party and called themselves 'Lib-Labs'. But in 1900 some Socialists and some trade unions set up a new party to represent working people. It took the name 'The Labour Party' and won 29 seats in the 1906 election. They were keen to point out that the other parties had failed to deal with poverty and called for higher wages and stiffer taxes on the rich to help the poor. They were a small group in 1906, but the Liberals were worried that they would lose working-class votes to them. They had to show that they cared about poverty too.

4 Other countries

Other countries, for example Germany, had set up schemes to help people in poverty and workers on low wages a few years earlier.

The Reforms

Many Liberals believed people had to choose to look after themselves, and not rely on the government to help them. But younger Liberals, like David Lloyd George and Winston Churchill, pointed out that the poor people revealed by Booth and Rowntree had no freedom to choose. The government should intervene to provide basic security in their lives. Later in the century this idea was known as the **welfare state**.

Children
1906 School Meals started
1907 School Medicals introduced, to check on the health of all children.
1908 Children's Act: children in trouble with the law to be treated differently from adults.

Old people
1909 Old Age Pensions introduced for people over 70: 25 pence a week for a single person, 37.5 pence for a married couple, if their income was less than 60 pence a week.

Working people
1908 Compulsory 8-hour day for miners
1909 Trade Boards Act controlled working hours for 'sweated labour'

Labour Exchanges
1911 Shop Act guaranteed half a day a week off for shop workers.

Illness and unemployment:
The National Insurance Act, 1911
This major piece of law-making was put forward by David Lloyd George, Chancellor of the Exchequer in the Liberal government.

- *Part One: Illness.*
  Every worker earning under £160 a year (about £3 a week) paid 4 pence (2 pence) into an insurance scheme. The employer added 3 pence (1.5 pence) and the government 2 pence (1 pence). The worker thus got 9 pence worth of insurance for his 4 pence.
  If he was too ill to work, he could claim 50 pence a week for up to 26 weeks.

- *Part Two: Unemployment.*
  This scheme covered 2 million workers in seven trades. The worker, the employer and the government each paid 2 pence (1 pence) a week. If he became unemployed the worker could claim 35 pence a week for up to 15 weeks.

▶ SOURCE 3A

Cartoon of 1909. The 'giant' is Lloyd George. A 'plutocrat', like the man hiding under the table, is someone who is very rich.

▶ SOURCE 3B

Labour Party poster, 1908. Keir Hardie, the man on the right, was leader of the Labour Party.

CAUSE AND EFFECT.

Keir Hardie: 'Look at that list, Mr. Bull not one of them would have been passed if it hadn't been for our Labour Party!'

(Note that although this amounts to a huge move to help poor working people, it is an **insurance** scheme – a Liberal idea – not a handout to the poor, which Socialists favoured).

? QUESTIONS

a How reliable is Source 3A for finding out about Lloyd George?

b How reliable is Source 3A for finding out about attitudes to Lloyd George?

c What does Source 3B tell you about the Labour Party's attitude to these Liberal reforms?

How successful were the Liberal Reforms?

1. The amounts paid to workers in times of illness or unemployment were small, and were not enough to live on. The system was intended only as a 'lifebelt', or a 'net over the abyss', as Liberals described it at the time.

2. The payments lasted only for 26 weeks or 15 weeks. It would only help someone over a temporary crisis. But after the First World War, especially in the 1930s, economic depression hit British industry. Some men were out of work for years on end and the system the Liberals set up was no help to them.

3. The system was based on the stereotype of a working man being the breadwinner for his family. This was indeed the norm at the time, but became less suitable as the 20th century went on.

4. There was no health coverage for other members of the family, who were often in dire need of better health care, especially women.

5. However, having made the four criticisms above, it was a start. The government was now involved to help the poor and further improvements took place later in the century, notably in the 1940s.

Passing the National Insurance Act

The schemes outlined above would obviously cost a lot of money. In 1909 Lloyd George prepared what he called a 'war budget' to wage war on poverty. The rich would have to pay more tax. The House of Lords threw out the budget, so the Liberals called an election, which they won. The new king, George V, threatened to create lots more new Liberal peers if the House of Lords threw out the budget again. This time they backed down and the budget was agreed. The National Insurance Act was eventually passed in 1911.

The Liberals passed a Parliament Act in 1911 so that this long crisis could not happen again, it stated that:

- The House of Lords could not reject a money bill, such as the budget.

- The House of Lords could only delay a bill for two years, not reject it completely.

- MPs should be paid a salary, so ordinary people could afford to enter Parliament.

? QUESTION

a In what ways did the Parliament Act of 1911 make Britain more democratic?

WOMEN AND THE VOTE

Women in Victorian Britain

There was great inequality of the sexes in 19th century Britain. Men were held to be superior in all things. It was widely believed that women were too weak to study and incapable of making decisions. Women did not vote or receive more than a basic education. They were not expected to work, and many jobs were completely closed to them. All of a woman's own property and possessions became her husband's on marriage. The ideal Victorian woman stayed at home and raised the children. This was not possible for working-class women who often had to work, but in worse jobs than working-class men and for less pay.

▶ SOURCE 1

Mother would teach, by action and words, that girls and women should submit to husbands and brothers. Their duty was to feed them well, run their errands and bear all burdens except physical ones.

Joseph Ashby describes how he was brought up in the 19th century.

By the late 19th century things were changing. Some women were getting educated and qualifying for important jobs, Elizabeth Garrett Anderson, for example, became the first woman doctor in Britain in 1865. There were women teachers (although they were paid less – £127 a year for a man, £92 a year for a woman). New inventions, like the telephone and the typewriter, also brought new job opportunities. Women gained the right to vote in local elections. But the big decision, the right to vote in Parliamentary elections, was still closed to them.

▼ **SOURCE 2A**
Millicent Fawcett, leading suffragist, speaking at a rally in Hyde Park, London.

▼ **SOURCE 2B**
Suffragist propaganda postcard

Suffragists and Suffragettes

Women had been campaigning for the right to vote (suffrage) from the 1860s. They could see that all their other concerns (fair divorce laws, better health care for women, fair education, etc.) depended on having a say in the place where big decisions were made – Parliament. This meant trying to persuade the all-male Parliament to change, which was not an easy task.

In 1897 the National Union of Women's Suffrage Societies (NUWSS) was set up, led by Millicent Fawcett, Elizabeth Garrett Anderson's sister. They were called *suffragists* and campaigned peacefully, writing letters, holding meetings and lobbying MPs. Members were mainly middle class, except in Lancashire where female cotton-mill workers had a long tradition of independence. There were over 500 branches of the NUWSS all over the country, but still women did not have the vote.

? QUESTIONS
a Why were most of the NUWSS groups made up of middle-class women?
b What can you learn from Source 2B about their campaign?

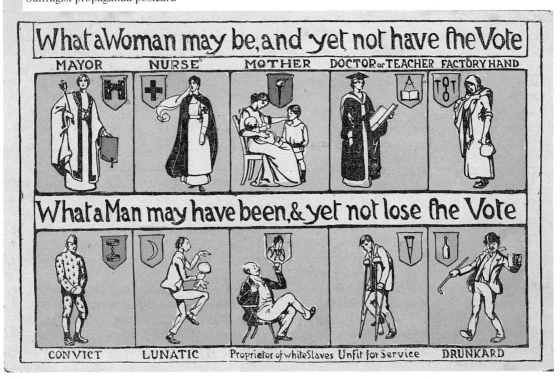

Frustrated with the lack of success of the NUWSS, Mrs Emmeline Pankhurst and her daughters Christabel and Sylvia formed the Women's Social and Political Union (WSPU) in 1903. They were soon called *suffragettes*. They thought the NUWSS was too polite. It was being ignored so they decided to step up the campaign using more forceful tactics, including breaking the law.

► SOURCE 3A

Bad laws made without due authority ought not to be obeyed, but ought to be resisted by every honest man and woman. It is such laws that militant suffragettes have broken.

Christabel Pankhurst

Suffragettes deliberately tried to get arrested and attract publicity. They interrupted political meetings shouting 'Votes for women!', they smashed shop windows, set light to letter boxes and dug up (all-male) golf courses. One suffragette, Emily Wilding Davison, tried to grab the King's horse at the Derby in 1913 and was killed.

When they were arrested Suffragettes went on hunger strike. Prison officials fed them by force, a very painful and disgusting experience, so in 1913 the government passed the 'Cat and Mouse' Act. This allowed them to release Suffragettes who were ill and then re-arrest them when they had recovered.

► SOURCE 3B

Mrs Pankhurst being arrested after chaining herself to the railings outside Buckingham Palace.

► SOURCE 3C Death of Emily Wilding Davison

SOURCE 3D

Suffragette poster about the Cat and Mouse Act

But it is important to remember that only about 60% of men had the vote at this time. The rest did not, usually because they were too poor. The Labour Party and many Liberals wanted *all* men as well as *all* women to have the right to vote. However, the person who really mattered in this decision was Asquith, the leader of the party in power, the Liberals. He was unwilling to give the vote to women on the same restricted basis as men because he feared, probably rightly, that wealthier women would be likely to vote for the Conservatives. Nor was he prepared to consider votes for all men and all women. He was also unwilling to be seen to give in to violence.

So, as war broke out in August 1914, women still did not have the vote.

THE FIRST WORLD WAR AND THE BRITISH PEOPLE

Recruiting

If you have read Chapter 2 you will know how young men rushed to join the army when war began on August 3, 1914. They all believed it would be a short, exciting war, which would be over by Christmas and they wanted to get some glory while they could. You will also know that it was certainly not over by Christmas 1914 but had become a massive struggle between the two sides which was to go on for over four years.

The British had always assumed that any war would be short, so had only a small professional army in 1914. Only a few weeks into the war, Lord Kitchener, the Secretary for War, realised it was a new kind of war. Britain would have to build up a new, large army of at least a million men. Most people in the early part of the war were against *conscription* (the automatic call-up of all men of military age). This new British army would have to be built up from volunteers.

Kitchener led a massive propaganda campaign to persuade young men to volunteer. Leaflets and posters were designed. The three posters on page 18 show the three main themes of the campaign:

1. Patriotism (see Source 7A, p.18)
This poster, perhaps one of the most famous posters ever, shows Kitchener himself. He was a great British war hero, famous for his exploits for British glory all over the world, and here he was calling on you to join up on behalf of Britain. Other patriotic posters showed St. George.

? QUESTIONS

a In what ways do Sources 3B and 3C put Christabel Pankhurst's ideas in Source 3A into practice?

b What do you think would be the effect of the Suffragettes campaign?

c Many Suffgragists were angry with the Suffragettes. Why?

Opposition to votes for women

The Suffragettes received lots more publicity than the Suffragists, but still women did not get the vote. Why?

Some men still held the old 19th century attitude that women were not fit to vote. Some were also angered, rather than won over, by the Suffragettes' violence.

2. Shame (see Source 7C, p.18)

The purpose of these posters was to make British men who had not joined up feel ashamed in front of their mothers, wives, sisters or girlfriends. Girls were encouraged not to go out with young men who had not joined up, and to hand white feathers (the symbol of cowardice) to young men in civilian clothes (see also Source 1A).

3. Hatred of Germany (see Source 7B, p.18)

Horror stories about the Germans, like the one shown here, were distributed. Other stories described German soldiers bayonetting Belgian babies (see also Source 1B).

The poster campaign was very successful. By the end of 1915 2.5 million men had joined up.

▶ SOURCE 1A

Poster: 'Daddy, what did you do in the Great War?'

? QUESTIONS

a In what different ways do Sources 1A and 1B try to persuade young men to volunteer for the army?

b How useful are these two sources for finding out about Britain during the First World War?

▶ SOURCE 1B

Poster: 'Remember Scarborough!' (The Yorkshire coastal town of Scarborough was shelled by German gunboats in December 1914. Several civilians were killed.)

Total war

This new kind of war needed even more from Britain than millions of young volunteers. It was clear that victory would not go to the country with the bravest army, but to the country which could organise its industry to keep the biggest, best-equipped army at war for longest (see Source 2). It was *total war*. Everyone in the country was totally involved with the war from soldiers on the Front Line to the factory-workers who supplied them with guns and ammunition.

In January 1916 *conscription* was introduced. Every unmarried male aged between 18 and 41 had to join the army, or do 'work of national importance'. From now on the state could take over your life.

▼ **SOURCE 2**   British army requirements, 1914 and 1918 compared

	No. of men	Lorries	Cars	Motorbikes	Field guns	Aircraft
1914	120,000	334	133	166	300	63
1918	2,500,000	31,770	7,964	14,464	6,437	1,782

Defence of the Realm Act (DORA), 1914

This Act was passed very early in the war. It gave the government powers to control people's lives in some entirely new ways and these powers increased as the war went on. By the end of the war DORA regulated:

- Pub licensing hours
- Weaker beer
- Wages in many industries
- British Summer Time
- Taking over land to grow food
- Censorship of letters, newspapers etc.
- Talking about military matters
- Wasting food
- Ringing church bells (the signal that an invasion had taken place)

There was a widespread obsession with German spies, and people believed they were everywhere. DORA regulations included controls on:

- Buying binoculars
- Lighting bonfires
- Using invisible ink
- Flying kites

? QUESTION

a What was the point of each of the items listed here?

Food rationing

Britain does not grow enough food to feed all of its population. It imports what it cannot grow from overseas. With deadlock on the Western Front, Germany began using submarines (U-boats) to sink supply ships coming to Britain. The government responded by trying to grow more food. Many parks and games pitches were taken over for food production.

However, by 1917 the food situation was desperate. U-boats were sinking one in four merchant ships on their way to Britain. The result was a shortage of food, and rising prices (food prices had doubled since the war began, while wages had stood still). This meant that richer people bought up food and poorer people went hungry. Many food shops closed at lunchtime as they had nothing left to sell. There were strikes in some areas over the high cost of food.

The government knew that they depended on the willingness of workers to contribute to the war effort. Everyone was supposed to be in this war

▼ **SOURCE 3**
Voluntary bread rationing poster

together. So the government agreed to some wage rises. They also brought in voluntary rationing, which involved trying to persuade people to use less flour (see Source 3).

However, this situation did not work and was felt to be unfair, so early in 1918 *rationing* was introduced. Everyone, regardless of wealth, got a ration book, which entitled them to a limited amount of butter, sugar and meat and no more. This was popular, although it came rather late in the war. In the Second World War this system of rationing was introduced only 5 months into the war.

Did the war change women's lives?

Women were, of course, swept up in the wave of wartime propaganda just as much as men. As soon as war broke out the Suffragettes stopped their campaign for the vote and campaigned instead for men to join the army. Women collected and sent 'comforts' to the troops (232 million cigarettes, 16 million books and 4 million pairs of socks had been sent by 1915). Women demanded to be able to serve their country in more active ways. Volunteers could join the Women's Auxiliary Army Corps (WAAC), which provided cooks, secretaries and cleaners to the army in France. More glamorous was the Voluntary Aid Detachment (VAD), which carried out Front Line nursing.

But these were hardly new roles for women. The crisis came in 1915, the army needed still more men and industry needed still more workers. The government calculated that Britain was over a million workers short and a campaign was launched to attract women into jobs which had always been closed to them (see Source 9, page 20). Trade unions relaxed their bans on women doing men's jobs and employers changed their attitudes.

The most famous industry to take on women in a big way was the munitions industry. The army generals were convinced that if they had enough guns and shells they could win the war. As Table 2–1 on page 20 shows, the number of women working in munitions increased from 212,000 to 947,000. It was hard and dangerous work and they often worked 12-hour shifts. There was permanent danger from explosions, and the poisonous chemicals in the explosives turned them yellow and caused permanent injuries. They were known as 'the girls with yellow hands'.

◤ SOURCE 4A
Women making shells

▶ SOURCE 4B

The first time you go round you think, what an interesting place. Then the evil smell became more noticeable. The particles of acid land on your face and drive you nearly mad with a feeling like pins and needles. We all went bright yellow – all our front hair and all our faces ... This doctor, he was looking at us girls one day and he said, 'half you girls will never have babies and the other half are too sick. God help you.'

A woman worker at Woolwich Arsenal
described her experiences

▶ SOURCE 4C

Woman bus conductor

Apart from munitions, other new jobs tackled by women were bus driving and bus conducting, road-mending, farming and all other kinds of manual work. Altogether over 1.3 million more women were working in 1918 than in 1914, as Table 2–1 on page 20 shows.

❓ QUESTIONS

a What can you learn from Source 4A about women's jobs in a munitions factory?

b How reliable is Source 4B for finding out about women's work in munitions?

c Do Sources 4A, 4B and 4C prove that the war changed women's lives in Britain?

d Use Sources 4A, 4B, 4C and Table 2–1 on page 20 to make an argument for giving all women the right to vote.

But did the war lead to a permanent change in women's lives? Some women gained the respect of their male workmates and employers, but many were resented. Other workers felt threatened by women coming in and taking the jobs they had spent many years learning how to do. When the war ended the female workers were rapidly fired to make way for returning soldiers. By 1921 only 31% of all women were working, in 1911 it had been 32%.

▶ SOURCE 5

There is no reason to feel sorry for the young woman who has been earning pocket money while the men have been fighting. Women who left domestic service to enter a factory are now required to return to their pots and pans.   The *Southampton Times*

What were the attitudes of the British people after the war?

1. Hostility to Germany.

Wartime hostility towards Germany and the Germans could not be switched off overnight on November 11, 1918. This attitude, encouraged by four years of government propaganda, continued in the 1918 election. Lloyd George promised to 'make Germany pay', and 'to squeeze Germany until the pips squeak'. The results of this can be seen in the cartoon in Source 1, and in the British contribution to the Treaty of Versailles (see Chapter Three). The punitive terms (the destruction of the German fleet, the 'War Guilt' Clause, the massive reparations) were all seen in Britain as no less than Germany deserved. It was these terms on which Hitler was soon to play so successfully to win power in Germany (see Chapter Six).

SOURCE 1
Detail of an anti-German poster from 1919

2. Changes in the suffrage

Everybody could see that in this 'total war' every man and woman had taken part. It was no longer fair that some could vote for the government that had called on them to sacrifice their lives and some could not. The Representation of the People Act, 1918, gave the vote to:

(i)   all men over 21, except peers, criminals, mentally ill and Conscientious Objectors;

(ii) women over 30 who were eligible to vote in local elections or were married to a man who could vote in these elections. This was about two-thirds of all women.

Note that:

(i)   Conscientious Objectors lost the right to vote for six years, until 1924.

(ii) In 1928 women gained the right to vote on the same basis as men.

SOURCE 2
My opposition to women's right to vote is well-known. However, for three years now the Suffragettes have not restarted that horrible campaign of violence. Not only that, but they have contributed to every service during this war except that of fighting. I therefore believe some measure of women's suffrage should be given.

> An extract from a speech by Herbert Asquith in the House of Commons in 1917 (by this time he was no longer leader of the Liberals).

❓ QUESTIONS
a 'The First World War had no permanent effect on the position of Women in Britain'. Use all the Sources here and Table 2–1 on page 20, along with your own knowledge, to comment on the accuracy of this statement.

b 'It was their war service, not their peacetime campaigning, which gained women the vote'. Use all the Sources here and your own knowledge to comment on the accuracy of this statement.

How effective was British wartime propaganda?

This is not an easy question to answer. How would you measure its effectiveness? One way would be to look at its aims. These were:

- to persuade the British people that they were fighting a just and worthwhile war;

- to persuade the British people that their enemy was wicked;

- to persuade millions of young men to volunteer for the army;

- to persuade women to take jobs they had not been allowed to do before;

- to persuade the British people not to waste or hoard food.

❓ QUESTION
a Taking each of these five points in turn, use this chapter to investigate whether the wartime propaganda achieved its aims in each case.

Glossary

abdicate: to give up the position of ruler.

aggressor: the one who makes the first attack in a war.

Anschluss: German word for the takeover of a country.

anti-Semitic: a prejudiced attitude against the Jews.

apartheid: the Afrikaans word for 'separateness' or 'separate development'.

appeasement: the policy of giving someone what they want in the hope that their demands will stop

armistice: truce, cease-fire.

Aryan: a person of German or Scandinavian origin – usually fair-haired, blue-eyed.

assassin: someone who murders for political reasons.

Axis: a form of alliance.

biased: one-sided, giving or holding one point of view.

bivouac: camp, usually for soldiers, in the open air.

Blighty: army slang for 'England'.

Blitzkrieg: German word meaning 'lightning war'.

Bolshevik: Russian word for 'majority', given to the more extreme members of the Russian Social Democratic Party, led by Lenin. It was this party which seized power in Russia in October 1917 and became the Communist party.

boycott: combining together to refuse to trade or do business with a person or country.

capitalism: the system of running business whereby private individuals invest their money in companies in return for interest.

censorship: cutting out of books, plays, films or newspapers etc. anything which the government does not want to have expressed.

Cheka: the Russian Secret Police, set up by the Communists in 1918. They have been called by many other names since (OGPU, MVD, NKVD), and are now known as the KGB.

Civil Service: the departments of government which run the country.

coalition: when two or more parties combine to run the country together.

collaborate: to work with the enemy forces occupying your country.

collective farm: a farm made up of all the land of several farmers and farmed as one unit under government control (compare **commune** and **co-operative**).

collective security: a way of avoiding war by which a number of countries agree to protect one another if any one country is attacked.

colonise: the takeover of a less developed country by a more developed one which settles its people there and uses its resources.

colon: the French word for 'colonist': someone from the mother country who lives in a colony.

Comintern: short for 'Communist International': the international organisation based in Russia, formed to assist the growth of communism all over the world.

commune: a system set up in China in 1956 under which all economic activity is collectively organised and people work in labour teams as directed.

co-operative: a system where people agree to pool their efforts or their funds to work together.

democracy: a system of governing a country, either directly by the people or by holding regular elections to some form of parliament or assembly which makes the law.

Democratic: one of the two main parties in the American political system (the other one is Republican). The Democratic Party is usually a little more radical than the Republican.

depression: a decline in the economic life of a country, leading to unemployment and lower living standards.

dictator: a ruler with complete power over a country.

disarmament: cutting down, or removing a country's armed forces and weapons.

discrimination: unfair, unequal treatment of a person or group (as in racial discrimination, on grounds of colour).

dividend: payment from the profits of a company to those who have put money into it (see also **capitalism**).

division: part of an army, usually 10,000 to 15,000 men.

Dominion: self governing members of the British Commonwealth: Canada, Australia, New Zealand and until 1961, South Africa.

dynasty: a ruling family or group.

election: the process of choosing who will form a government or council by means of a vote among the people for one or more candidates.

empire: a group of countries all belonging to one ruler.

entente: the French word for 'agreement' – between countries to settle their differences and try to work together. An entente is not as strong as an alliance.

Falange: Spanish Fascist Party.

Fascist: a member of the political party founded by Mussolini in Italy in 1919. Often used to describe any extremist nationalist and anti-Communist group.

Gestapo: German secret state police during the Nazi regime.

ghetto: the poorer, rundown parts of cities, originally occupied by Jews in Europe, now occupied by various racial minorities, particularly black people in the USA.

GMD: Guomindang. Chinese word meaning 'National People's Party', founded by Sun Yatsen in 1912, later led by Chiang Kaishek.

gold standard: currency which is supported by reserves of gold.

guerrilla warfare: making war with armed bands of soldiers, using irregular methods. For example, guerrilla soldiers probably do not wear a uniform; they may hide in the countryside or among the people, launch sudden attacks and then return into hiding again.

holocaust: a terrible slaughter. Usually used to describe the murder of millions of Jews by the Nazis in Germany during the Second World War.

independent: not controlled by anyone else.

industrialise: to start industries in a country.

industrial output: goods produced by factories.

inflation: rising prices.

infant mortality: the number of children who die before the age of five.

interest rate: interest is money paid by a borrower of money to the person who lends it. The interest rate is the percentage of the amount borrowed which has to be paid as interest.

isolationism: US foreign policy between the two world wars of avoiding any involvement with other countries.

Kaiser: title of the rulers of Germany from 1871 to 1918.

Kamikaze: Japanese word meaning 'divine wind'. It refers to a group of volunteer pilots during the Second World War who flew their planes loaded with explosives, straight at their target, committing suicide in the process.

kolkhoz: Russian word meaning 'collective farm'.

kulak: Russian word for a rich peasant.

lebensraum: German word meaning 'living space'.

liberal: attitude of more freedom and tolerance in a country.

Manchu: tribe from Central Asia who conquered China in the 17th century and so supplied the ruling family of the emperors of China up to their overthrow in 1911.

Mandarin: Chinese government official under the emperors, usually drawn from the upper classes.

mandate: power given by the League of Nations to one country to look after another, usually a colony formerly belonging to one of the defeated countries, in the First World War.

Marxists: followers of the ideas of Karl Marx.

Means Test: the test given to the unemployed in Britain to see whether they had any income of their own. If they did, their dole money was cut.

media: newspapers, radio, books, television (as in mass media).

Mensheviks: members of the Social Democratic party in Russia opposed to the Bolsheviks, being more politically moderate.

mission: group of people sent into a country mainly to spread religion but also to do useful jobs such as teaching medicine or farming.

mixed economy: some industries nationalised, some run by private companies, e.g. Britain.

mobilise: to get a country ready for war.

monetarism: a theory taken up by Mrs Thatcher and the Conservative party that prices can be kept unchanged if the amount of money in circulation is controlled.

napalm: an inflammable sticky jelly used in bombs in order to set fire to buildings and people.

nationalism: strong feeling for one's country.

nationalisation: the government takeover of a business or industry from private ownership in order to operate it for the benefit of the people.

Nazi: German nickname for National Socialist German Workers' Party, founded by Adolf Hitler in 1920, as an extreme nationalist and racialist party.

nihilism: opposition to all forms of government of any sort.

pacifist: someone totally opposed to war and fighting.

parliament: an elected body which, wholly or partly, makes the laws and policy of a democratic country.

Panzer: the German word for a tank regiment.

peaceful co-existence: policy of Russian leader Khrushchev (1955–1964) towards the rest of the world; living alongside one another in peace.

peasant: a farmer who works on, and mainly lives off, a small piece of land.

plebiscite: a vote of the people on a certain question.

prefabricated: a building made up of sections which have been already made so that it only has to be assembled on site.

primary evidence: a type of historical evidence which is a first-hand account, one where the author was present or directly involved with the events described (see **secondary evidence**).

productivity: the amount of goods produced by each worker in a factory.

prohibition: the banning of the making or sale of alcoholic drinks, in force in the USA from 1920 to 1933

proletariat: the working classes, especially manual workers who have only their wages and little or no property.

propaganda: false or misleading information given out to spread certain points of view.

protectionism: the policy of helping industry at home by putting import duties on the foreign-made items so as to raise their prices (see **tariff**).

purge: to get rid of many opponents by arrest, imprisonment or execution.

Putsch: German word meaning an attempt to seize the government by force.

radical: seeking thorough and drastic change.

raj: Indian word meaning 'state'.

re-armament: building up a country's weapons and armed forces again.

recession: decline in trade and industry, usually leading to unemployment.

Red Guards: armed members of the Communist party, trained like soldiers.

Reich: German word meaning 'state'.

Reichstag: German name for parliament.

reparations: money paid by Germany after the First World War to the victorious countries as compensation for war damage.

Republican: one of the two parties in the US political system (the other is the Democratic Party).

Resistance: the organisation of people in Occupied Europe who worked secretly against German rule during the Second World War.

revisionists: the word used by one group of Communists to describe another group who want to make basic changes in the principles of Communism.

revolution: overthrow of the government by force.

sabotage: deliberate damage to machines or transport (particularly carried out by the Resistance) in order to hinder an enemy.

saboteur: someone who carries out sabotage.

samizdat: Russian word meaning 'self-printing', used to describe books which are duplicated by hand because the government refuses to print them.

sanctions: ways of enforcing a decision – for example, by means of a trade boycott.

satellite: a country which depends on a larger one (usually used to describe eastern European countries under Soviet control).

secondary evidence: type of historical evidence which is not a first-hand account, one where the author was not present or directly involved in the events described.

segregation: the separation of a number of people from the main group, usually because of race or religion (the opposite of **integration**).

self-determination: the right of people to decide for themselves which country they belong to or what sort of government to have.

Socialism: the theory that economic activity (factories, farms, transport, banking, etc) should be owned and run by the government for the benefit of everyone, and that wealth should be divided equally.

Socialist: someone who believes in Socialism.

soviet: Russian word for an elected council.

Stakhanovism: Russian system of offering cash, holidays and medals as bonuses for workers to produce more. Named after Stakhanov, a coal miner.

swastika: the hooked cross symbol adopted by the Nazi Party as their emblem.

Tammany Hall: the Democratic Party headquarters in New York. As the Democrats ran New York it was from here that the jobs in the City government were handed out. Because of the widespread use of bribery by New York party bosses, it has become a term for corrupt politics.

tariff: duties paid on imports and exports.

Third World: the poorer countries of the world, so called after the First World (Capitalist) and the Second World (Communist) – both richer groups of countries.

totalitarianism: the running of a country by a dictator or one party group, suppressing all opposition and totally controlling the life of every person in the country.

trusteeship: one country looking after another (see **mandate**).

Tsar: ruler of Russia before the revolution of March 1917 (sometimes 'Czar').

ultimatum: demand made by one country to another, with the threat of war if the other does not agree.

Unilateral Declaration of Independence (UDI): In 1965 the British colony of Rhodesia declared itself independent of Britain. This declaration was one-sided (unilateral) because Britain did not agree to it. It was therefore a Unilateral Declaration of Independence.

untouchable: the lowest group in Indian society. Members do not belong to the caste system, which grades all the classes, so strict Hindus must not even touch them. Untouchables have to live separately and do the worst jobs.

veto: the power to cancel or postpone decisions.

viceroy: someone who rules a country as the representative of the monarch.

Vichy: part of southern France, run as a German-controlled puppet state after the fall of France in 1940. The government was based in the town of Vichy.

warlord: someone who rules all or part of a country because he has an army with which to back his rule.

Welfare State: a system by which the government looks after the well-being of the nation, particularly those who cannot help themselves, like the old, children, the sick, the unemployed, disabled and so on.

Zionism: the movement to set up a independent state of Israel.

ACKNOWLEDGEMENTS

The author and publishers are grateful to the following for permission to reproduce photographs:

Bridgeman Art Library/National Museum of American Art, Smithsonian Institute 92;
British Museum 73;
Camera Press 232;
Conservative Central Office 88;
Format/Ulrike Preuss 254;
John Frost Historical Newspapers 250;
Robert Harding Picture Library 203 (both);
Hulton Archive Picture Collection Ltd 4, 22 (top), 27, 34, 41, 48, 62 (top),79, 80, 82, 83, 85, 87, 91 (top), 94, 101, 115, 118, 138 (both), 139 (bottom), 165, 188, 195, 203, 208 (right), 210, 216, 227, 229, 235, 247, 249, 259, 262, 264, 267 (top), 267 (bottom), 272;
Imperial War Museum © Crown 6, 13, 14 (both), 15, 16, 18, 20, 22 (bottom), 25, 31, 55, 76, 119, 127, 128, 133, 136, 139 (top), 142, 145, 147 (bottom), 148 (left), 200, 212, 213, 215, 230, 269 (both), 270, 271, 273 detail;
David King Collection 49 (both);
Magnum Photos/Burt Glinn 238, /Josef Koudelka 244;
Mansell Collection 228;
Mary Evans Picture Library 266 (bottom);
Museum of London 268;
Novosti 35, 36, 37, 39, 40 (both), 43, 71;

Popperfoto iv, 2, 19, 53, 60, 62, 64, 65, 66, 75, 86, 91 (bottom), 97, 105, 106, 110, 111, 126, 138 (top), 148 (right), 155, 156, 157, 158, 162, 163, 171, 174, 180, 183, 187, 191, 197, 201, 206, 208 (left), 209 (both), 218, 224, 225, 226, 234, 239, 241, 255;
Punch Ltd 15, 81, 253, 258, 259, 264;
Range/Bettman/UPI 65, 194:
The Royal Archive © 2001, HM Queen Elizabeth II 261;
Topham Picturepoint 68, 95, 99, 135, 147 (top), 170, 177, /Associated Press 181, 193, 205, 237, 242, 248 Trip/A. Tjagny-Rjadno 74, /D. Saunders 173, /A. Kuznetsov 240;
Ullstein Bilderdienst 58, 66, 122, 124, 132;
Weiner Library 63, 68;
Xinhua News Agency 167, 178.

Cover photograph

'Four freedoms' poster by Norman Rockwell, reproduced by permission of the Imperial War Museum © Crown.

Every effort has been made to trace holders of copyright material, but if any have been overlooked, the publishers will be glad to make the appropriate arrangements at the first opportunity.

Published by Collins Education
An imprint of HarperCollins*Publishers* Ltd
77–85 Fulham Palace Road, London W6 8JB

www.**Collins**Education.com
On-line Support for Schools and Colleges

© Christopher Culpin 1996, 2001
This edition first published 2001

First edition published 1984, revised 1986, 1996

10 9 8 7

ISBN 0 00 327006 8

Christopher Culpin asserts the moral right to be identified as the author of this work

British Library Cataloguing in Publication Data.
A catalogue record for this book is available from the British Library.

Edited by Lorimer Poultney
Cover design by Derek Lee
Picture research by Suzanne Williams
Maps and artwork by Jillian Luff
Production by Susan Cashin
Printed and bound in Hong Kong by Printing Express

You might also like to visit
www.**fire**and**water**.co.uk
The book lover's website

Index